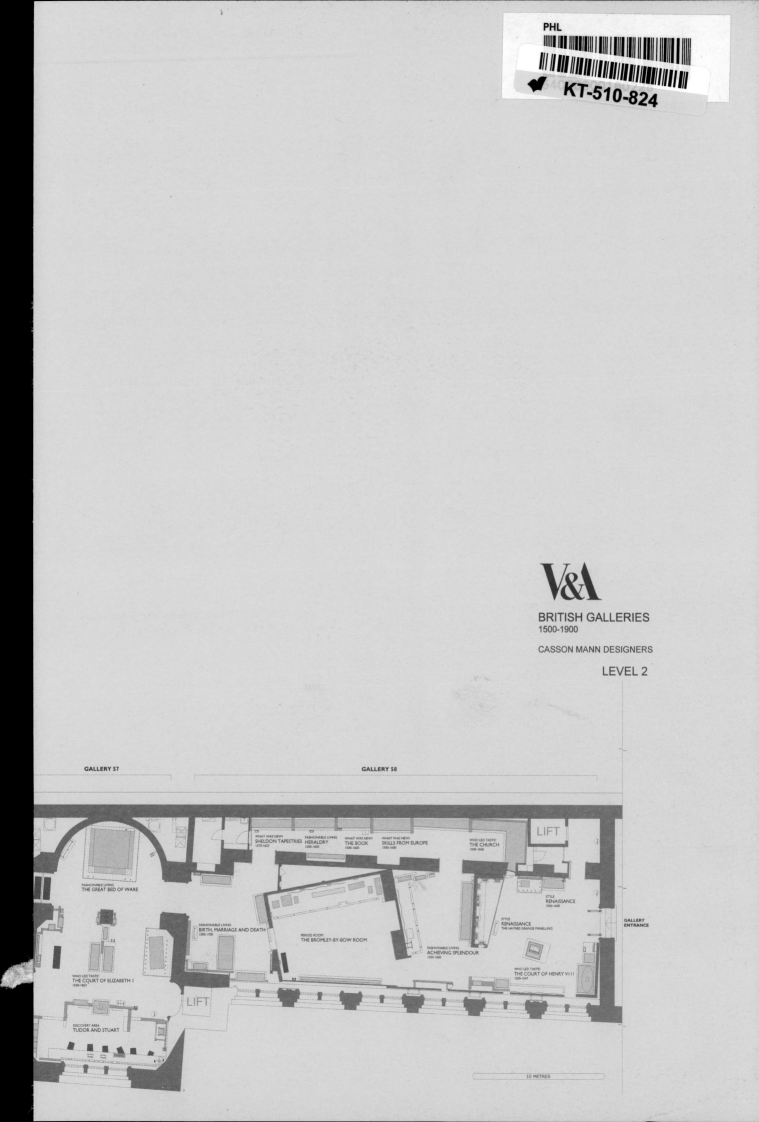

V&A

BRITISH GALLERIES
1500-1900

CASSON MANN DESIGNERS

LEVEL 2

GALLERY 57

GALLERY 58

WHAT WAS NEW!
SHELDON TAPESTRIES
1370-1625

FASHIONABLE LIVING
HERALDRY
1500-1600

WHAT WAS NEW!
THE BOOK
1500-1600

WHAT WAS NEW!
SKILLS FROM EUROPE
1500-1600

WHO LED TASTE!
THE CHURCH
1500-1660

LIFT

FASHIONABLE LIVING
THE GREAT BED OF WARE

STYLE
RENAISSANCE
1500-1600

FASHIONABLE LIVING
BIRTH, MARRIAGE AND DEATH
1300-1700

PERIOD ROOM
THE BROMLEY-BY-BOW ROOM

STYLE
RENAISSANCE
THE HAYNES GRANGE PANELLING

GALLERY
ENTRANCE

FASHIONABLE LIVING
ACHIEVING SPLENDOUR
1500-1600

WHO LED TASTE!
THE COURT OF ELIZABETH I
1558-1603

WHO LED TASTE!
THE COURT OF HENRY VIII
1509-1547

LIFT

DISCOVERY AREA
TUDOR AND STUART

10 METRES

Annali del
Laboratorio museotecnico
IV

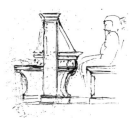

Creating the British Galleries at the V&A

A study in museology

Edited by
Christopher Wilk and Nick Humphrey

V&A Publications

LABORATORIO MUSEOTECNICO GOPPION

Creating the British Galleries at the Victoria and Albert Museum
A Study in Museology

Edited by CHRISTOPHER WILK and NICK HUMPHREY

V&A Publications in association with Laboratorio museotecnico Goppion

Copyright © 2004
First published by V&A Publications and Goppion S.p.A. 2004

V&A Publications
160 Brompton Road
London SW3 1HW

ISBN 1-85177-451-3

North American ISBN 0-8109-6624-7 (Harry N. Abrams, Inc.)
Italian ISBN 88-88714-04-9
A catalogue record for this book is available from the British Library.

V&A Publications
160 Brompton Road
London SW3 1HW
www.vam.ac.uk

Distributed in North America by Harry N. Abrams, Inc., New York
Library of Congress Control Number 2004109698

Picture credits

V&A photography by the V&A Photographic Studio

Illustrations have been provided by the following individuals and institutions. Colour plate numbers are preceded by the letters pl. or pls. Black-and-white figure numbers are preceded by the letters fig. or figs.
Birmingham Museum and Art Gallery: figs 89, 90
British Architectural Library, RIBA: fig. 86
Casson Mann: Front endpapers, Back endpapers; pls 38 (photo by Dennis Gilbert/View), 47, 49, 51, 52, 53, 55, 56, 57, 58, 59; figs 21, 22, 23, 24, 27, 47, 57, 58, 61, 63
Martin Charles: fig. 59
Country Life Picture Library: pls 69, 73; fig. 84
Nick Humphrey: figs 50, 51, 53, 64
Laboratorio museotecnico Goppion: figs 35, 36, 37, 38, 39, 40, 41
National Monuments Record: figs 80, 82, 87
Rose Innes Associates: figs 28, 77, 81, 83, 91. Photos by Dennis Gilbert/View: figs 29, 30, 31, 33, 34
Towneley Hall Art Gallery, Burnley: pl. 71

To the memory of John Cornforth

Contents

Acknowledgements

One of the greatest pleasures of working on the British Galleries at the Victoria and Albert Museum was the enthusiasm and commitment of all those involved, Museum staff as well as outside consultants and contractors. Few were more enthusiastic or more committed than Sandro Goppion of Laboratorio museotecnico Goppion. Though engaged as the supplier of cases for the galleries, Sandro became a good friend of the Museum, more likely to engage in debate about museological issues or those of world culture than discussing his own business interests. We are exceedingly grateful to Laboratorio museotecnico Goppion, not only for making possible the publication of a book with a necessarily limited readership but also for helping us to solve the problem of how we could answer the many requests for information on the project.

Working on this book allowed us to renew regular contact with former collaborators and to revisit some of the shared experiences of working on the galleries. To all the contributors listed in the table of contents we owe warmest thanks. All have managed to take on the work of recollection and of writing with good humour. Among them, we are especially grateful to Sarah Medlam, who, as in most aspects of our work, retains a grasp both of the larger picture and the smallest detail, and whom we always rely upon for her keen eye. From outside the Museum, we are particularly indebted to Dinah Casson for taking on the task of writing on the very large subject of designing the galleries, which required co-ordinating submissions from numerous consultants and committing a large amount of time from her busy schedule. Thanks are also due to our former colleague Nick Brod for his comments on chapter 9.

While we cannot revisit here the many necessary acknowledgements for the work on the galleries themselves, we would be remiss in not taking this opportunity to thank Alan Borg, CBE, FSA, former Director of the V&A, whose idea it was to undertake the project on the scale that was ultimately realised. He was fortunate in being able to rely on Gwyn Miles, Director of Projects and Estates, who worked tirelessly behind the scenes to ensure that this idea became reality: that the curatorial vision of the galleries stayed intact, that the project was properly funded, appropriately designed and built, and delivered on time and on budget.

For their work in realising this publication, we owe thanks to Isa Ferioli of Goppion; to Ken Jackson and Peter Kelleher of the V&A Photographic Studio, who produced numerous additional photographs to a tight schedule; to Charlotte Benton, for research on press coverage of the galleries; to Kristine von Oehsen, who helped prepare the bibliography; to Geoff Barlow and Mary Butler of V&A Publications; to Michael Bird, the book's copy editor; John Noble, indexer; Dario Accanti, designer; and Carlo Bertoncello, who printed the book to such a high standard.

This book is dedicated to the memory of John Cornforth who acted as consultant on the British Galleries project and who unexpectedly died as this book was going to press. John worked with us, week in, week out, over a period of years and was more than generous in the time he devoted to the project. We benefited enormously from his unrivalled knowledge and experience, his expert eye and, not least, his judgement in matters of taste. Awarded a Honorary Research Fellowship at the V&A in 2001, he continued his active interest in the galleries and other aspects of the Museum's work. Like all who study and interpret British houses and their contents, we owe him countless debts of gratitude.

C.W. and N.H.

Notes on Contributors

Anthony Burton worked for many years at the V&A and is the author of (among other publications) *Vision and Accident: The Story of the Victoria & Albert Museum* (London, 1999).

Dinah Casson is a partner at Casson Mann. She led the Casson Mann design team for the British Galleries.

Gail Durbin is Deputy Director of Learning and Interpretation and Head of V&A Online. From 1996 to 2001 she was a member of the British Galleries Concept Team.

Morna Hinton is Head of Learning Services at the V&A. From 1996 to 2002 she was the British Galleries Hanoverian Team Educator.

Nick Humphrey is Curator, Furniture, Textiles and Fashion Department at the V&A. From 1996 to 2002 he was the British Galleries Tudor and Stuart Gallery Team Co-ordinator.

David Judd is Education Officer for Families and Young People at the V&A. From 1997 to 2002 he was the British Galleries Victorian Team Educator.

Frances Lloyd-Baynes is Documentation Manager and Head of Records at the V&A. From 2000 to 2001 she was Content Manager of British Galleries Online.

Sarah Medlam is a Senior Curator, Furniture, Textiles and Fashion Department at the V&A. From 1996 to 2002 she was a member of the British Galleries Concept Team and served as Deputy Curator of the project.

Gwyn Miles is Director of Projects and Estates at the V&A. From 1996 to 2002 she was Director of Major Projects.

Giovanni Pinna is former Director of the Natural History Museum of Milan and a member of the Executive Council of ICOM.

John Styles is Head of Postgraduate Studies at the V&A. From 1996 to 2001 he was historical adviser to the British Galleries Project.

Nick Umney is Director of Collections Services at the V&A. From 1996 to 2001 he was the Museum Project Manager for the British Galleries Project.

Christopher Wilk is Keeper, Furniture, Textiles and Fashion Department at the V&A. From 1996 to 2002 he was Curator of the British Galleries Project and a member of the Concept Team.

Introduction

Christopher Wilk

The British Galleries 1500–1900 was the largest project undertaken by the Victoria and Albert Museum since the complete reinstallation of the Museum between 1947 and 1952 following the Second World War. The project was driven by a fervent desire to redisplay a supremely important part of the national collections and to do so in ways that would be meaningful and engaging to our visitors. The scale of the undertaking – 3400 square metres of gallery space displaying some 3000 objects, thus larger than many museums – was undeniably spurred on by the possibility of unprecedented partnership funding from the National Lottery, specifically the Heritage Lottery Fund, established in 1994.

The V&A's collections of high-style British design and decorative art are unrivalled, in terms not only of size but also of breadth and depth. Virtually every major name is represented, including designers from Grinling Gibbons to Charles Rennie Mackintosh, Thomas Chippendale to William Morris, as well as workshops and manufacturers such as the Mortlake tapestry works, the Spitalfields silk weavers, Axminster, Wedgwood, Doulton and Liberty's. The Museum's collection of sculpture is the finest in the nation and includes works made for British patrons by Gianlorenzo Bernini, Louis-François Roubiliac and Antonio Canova. Its paintings collection, though understandably less comprehensive (owing to the existence of the National Gallery and, later, the Tate Gallery), includes iconic works, such as miniatures by Hans Holbein and Nicholas Hilliard, and oil paintings by John Constable and J.M.W. Turner. Finally, the collections include sometimes anonymous objects of singular beauty or importance to the history of design or to national history. Among these are the Great Bed of Ware, mentioned in Shakespeare's *Twelfth Night*, and James II's wedding suit.

Even by the 1980s, it was widely recognised that the galleries displaying some of these objects were sorely in need of major renovation. The galleries were worn and tired, and many fragile objects – including virtually all textiles – had been taken off view owing to the pollution seeping through the gallery windows. The English Primary Galleries, as they were formerly known, had originally been installed between 1947 and 1952; Victorian galleries were added between 1964 and 1966. Although sections were lovingly reinstalled from time to time, and always on small budgets, no complete reworking of the galleries had ever taken place.

Though the V&A had successfully developed individual new galleries during the late 1980s and into the 1990s, this was a new period in terms of undertaking such projects. Starting in the 1980s, when the V&A went from being part of a government department to trustee museum status, it had to find sponsorship for new galleries rather than having these funded through its government grant. By the 1990s, it was felt strongly that a substantial proportion of the funds for the British Galleries ought to be found within Britain itself. Many of the Museum's then most recent galleries – the Toshiba Gallery of Japanese Art (1988), the Nehru Gallery of Indian Art (1990), the T.T. Tsui Gallery of Chinese Art (1991), the Samsung Gallery of Korean Art (1992) and the Frank Lloyd Wright Gallery (1993) – had been substantially, if not entirely, funded by money from abroad, while others, including the Glass Gallery (1994), relied on support from British trusts or individuals who supported smaller scale projects. The huge scale of the existing British Art and Design galleries (so renamed in 1987), constituting 10% of the Museum's gallery space, discouraged the idea that all the galleries could be renovated in one single project. However, the very success of the V&A in opening a series of new galleries between 1988 and 1994 increased the feeling, both inside and outside the Museum, that a solution had to be found to renew the galleries devoted to national design and art. The appearance of the National Lottery at precisely this moment provided the unique opportunity for tackling what was (and remains) by far the largest set of galleries devoted to a single country or period in the Museum.

From a museological point of view, the V&A found itself at a crossroads in the 1990s. Thinking about objects in the Museum had by this time broadened considerably beyond traditional considerations of connoisseurship and style, but, while publications by Museum curators incorporated a variety of new approaches, the galleries generally continued to reflect older ways of thinking.[1] Curators, educators and administrators at the V&A vigorously debated the nature of their own museum, its roles in the wider world and its responsibilities to its audiences.[2] The intellectual assumptions which had hitherto governed thinking in the Museum were also actively questioned, reflecting broader intellectual and cultural trends as well as an engagement with historical studies, and especially with design history as an academic discipline, fostered, not least, through the presence at the Museum of the V&A/Royal College of Art course in the History of Design.[3] The Museum's own history was investigated, as part of a general antiquarian interest in the history of museums and collections, but also because the early history of Henry Cole's educationally-driven museum seemed to offer, at least in part, an inspiring model for the present day.[4] This, along with a generational change in the leadership of the V&A's curatorial departments, and the growing professionalisation of the V&A's Education Department, meant that the V&A was an institution ripe for new forms of engagement with its visitors.[5]

The range of views within the museum regarding the nature of displays was, however, predictably variable. It ranged from those who felt we should stick to addressing a 'traditional' audience of specialists who valued, above all, the Museum's object-based expertise and who wanted objects to be displayed so as to allow them 'to speak for themselves', to those who wanted a fundamental redirection of the relationship between museum and audience, aimed at making the collections more intelligible and more meaningful to a wider range of visitors through new means of communication and interpretation.

This was the institutional context as the British Galleries Project began in 1996. There were, however, wider cultural issues which fundamentally informed the ideas underpinning the project. The early 1990s was a period when representations of national identity in Britain and the very question of what it meant to be British were hotly debated in academic and political circles, as well as in the media.[6] During the course of the project a national assembly was founded in Wales, a parliament in Scotland, a peace process was underway in Northern Ireland and, in response, there were stirrings of a new English nationalism. Such debates also raised the question of how those Britons who had emigrated from other parts of the world – especially the Indian subcontinent and the Caribbean – or their British-born children perceived themselves in terms of national identity. During the gallery planning stages, the team was acutely aware that anything we offered would necessarily be seen as a comment on or reaction to these important issues.

Equally relevant to the approach taken in the galleries were the debates regarding Britain's relationship to Europe, a question with keen historical resonance. Conservative Prime Minister Margaret Thatcher fell from power in 1990, owing to deep divisions over Europe, and the subsequent government of John Major nearly imploded over the same issue, whipped up by virulent, anti-European sections of the press. It was during the Major government that the principles of the British Galleries were agreed, and the atmosphere of the moment – with anti-European and anti-immigration voices dominating headlines – certainly led us to remind our public that British design (in so far as there was such a thing) was not a self-inventing concept but one crucially dependent upon ideas, publications, imports and émigrés from other countries.

When the British Galleries 1500–1900 opened in November 2001, my colleagues and I were taken aback but delighted by the strength of the positive reception to the galleries, in the notoriously critical British, as well as in the international, media. Though we felt confident, before the opening, that we would achieve much of what we had set out to and that visitors would find much to enjoy in the galleries, critical reception is always harder to predict. Such public responses are, however, important, when favourable, both for attracting visitors and for contributing to the Museum's public reputation. We were also especially heartened by the reception within the international museum community, and we have been particularly pleased by the ways in which the British Galleries seem to have affected museum practice in different parts of the world. Above all, we were pleased to be awarded the prize for European Museum of the Year for 2003, specifically for the British Galleries, as well as the Design History Society award for excellence in scholarship in 2002, as these reflect the judgement of others who understand both the difficulties and pitfalls of what we had attempted.[7]

Since the opening of the galleries, the V&A has been regularly approached by colleagues from museums from all over the world, wishing to learn more about the details of the project. The galleries have become a teaching resource, not only about design and art in Britain but also about museum display. Even before the opening and the accompanying press coverage, word of the project and its ambitions seemed to circulate, generating an unexpectedly large amount of interest. Although the queries were varied, there was particular interest in the principles underpinning the project, the manner of its internal organization, and the educational and interpretive philosophy. Having attempted to answer the questions put to us on these and other subjects in an *ad hoc* manner during and after work on the project – usually by putting together key internal documents with articles written or talks given by team members, as well as through teaching sessions and seminars – we decided to formalize these into the present publication.

The chapters of this book aim to cover the subjects which those who have contacted us have wanted to know most about. Mindful of the fact that some readers may be interested in the content of certain chapters only, we have allowed for some repetition of essential facts. In the case of the period rooms, to which we devoted a considerable amount of work, we have necessarily taken the opportunity to document the history of these historic interiors, their redecoration and interpretation. To the subjects we have been asked most about we have added some contextualisation, namely an essay on the display of British design and art at the V&A before the British Galleries, written by Anthony Burton, expert on the history of the V&A, and a reaction to the galleries by a museum professional from outside Britain, Giovanni Pinna, ICOM Executive Council Member. Some of the information in these pages inevitably concerns the internal culture of the V&A. Though this may not be of universal interest, it is impossible to understand the nature of the project without it.

The essays in this book, then, are aimed at a professional and student audience interested in the British Galleries Project itself and the ways in which a large national museum undertook a major gallery initiative. Many of the details of this book are not the sorts of things normally published by museums or their consultants. The expert-driven nature of museums means that admitting uncertainty or hesitation is not the rule, nor is transparency about goals or ambitions. We hope that this book might be seen as an exercise in transparency and as another dimension of the project. Its aim is to document the history of the project, the thinking behind it and the process we went through, while reflecting on the successes and failures of the galleries. It is not intended as an exercise in self-congratulation but as a book for use.

Notes   1. Exceptions to this included the Late Gothic and Northern Renaissance Gallery (1985) and the European Ornament Gallery (1992). Among important and innovative books published by V&A curators were Peter Thornton, *Seventeenth-century Interior Decoration in England, France and Holland* (London, 1978), his *Authentic Décor: The Domestic Interior 1620–1920* (London, 1984), Susan Lambert, *The Image Multiplied: Five Centuries of Printed Reproductions of Paintings and Drawings* (London, 1987) and Philippa Glanville's, *Silver in Tudor and Early Stuart England* (London, 1990).
2. Staff joining the Museum in the late 1980s were struck by the intensity of discussions at informal seminars organised by curators, which explored issues such as the influence of historical and contemporary thinkers on museum display and new approaches within the Museum to collecting, to galleries and to audiences.
3. Anthony Burton, *Vision and Accident: The Story of the Victoria and Albert Museum* (London, 1999) (hereafter cited as Burton), pp. 232–33, on the challenges posed by the new modes of art history and by the burgeoning field of design history. See also chapter 3 for a retrospective view and Charles Saumarez Smith's, 'Museums, Artefacts and Meanings' in Peter Vergo, *The New Museology* (London, 1989) for a contemporary one.
4. See Malcolm Baker and Brenda Richardson (eds), *A Grand Design: The Art of the Victoria and Albert Museum*, exhibition catalogue (New York and Baltimore, 1998) with essays written by a number of V&A curators.
5. See Burton, pp. 233–38 on changes at the Museum around 1989. David Anderson was appointed Head of Education in 1990. His work on a report on education in museums commissioned by the Conservative government and later published as *A Common Wealth: Museums in the Learning Age* (London, 1997) had a considerable impact on thinking in the Museum.
6. The publication of and discussions engendered by Linda Colley's *Britons* (London, 1992), focusing on the origins of a modern sense of Britishness, were particularly important for the gallery team.
7. See Jane Morris, 'Euro visions', *Museum Practice*, issue 23 (Summer 2003), pp.12–13.

Chapter 1   British Decorative and Fine Art at the V&A before the British Galleries

Anthony Burton

Current events change our perception of the past. The great success of the British Galleries may have led many to suppose that making a show of British art and design has always been at the heart of the V&A's concerns. Not so. At the start, the Museum was, in effect, a vote of no confidence in British art and design.

The museum at Marlborough House, 1852–1857

The museum which became the Victoria and Albert Museum first opened its doors to the public on 19 May 1852.[1] It was housed in five rooms in Marlborough House, a royal residence (then unoccupied by royalty) just up The Mall from Buckingham Palace. It was linked with the Government School of Design, which had also recently moved into Marlborough House. Both school and museum were part of the Department of Practical Art (renamed, after a year, the Department of Science and Art), a newly founded government department under the management of Henry Cole, a young civil servant who had made a name for himself as a dynamic force in the organisation of the Great Exhibition of 1851.

The museum, at the time known both as the 'Museum of Manufactures' and the 'Museum of Ornamental Art', was an institution with a mission. Though it did not have a founding charter, it was plain from policy statements at the time that its mission was to exercise a beneficial influence on the design of British consumer goods, in the hope that these would sell better abroad and bring economic benefit to Britain.

Because the museum had its origin in a sense of disappointment with British design, it did not choose, at first, to acquire examples of this despised category. When it opened, it consisted of objects that the School of Design had already bought to form a private museum for its students, plus 244 objects bought as examples of good design from the Great Exhibition, with a government grant of £5000. These good examples were a mixture of traditional oriental objects and approved modern objects, mostly French:

gorgeous scarfs and shawls from Cashmere and Lahore – glittering swords, yatagans and pistols from Tunis and Constantinople – the famous 'La Gloire' vase from the Sèvres manufacture – Marrel Frères' hunting-knife of St Hubert – Changarnier's sword, from the workshop of Froment Meurice – Vecte's [sic] splendid shield – a fac-simile of the celebrated Cellini cup: – and other Art-illustrations of the highest order …[2]

Visitors would have found hardly any English objects in displays chiefly devoted to contemporary design. It did not take long, however, for the museum to develop an interest in history. Can a museum avoid concerning itself with history? And could anyone in the Victorian period, even when promoting reform in the present, resist looking to history for helpful precedents? After a few years, contemporary objects were outweighed in the galleries of Marlborough House by specimens of medieval and Renaissance decorative art, which was at that time the latest fashion among collectors. This can easily be seen from early catalogues of the museum and from a series of watercolour views of the galleries.

What can also be seen from early catalogues is that the museum's collections were primarily classified by material, rather than by period. The first catalogue separated exhibits into six divisions: 'Woven Fabrics', 'Metal Work', 'Pottery', 'Glass', 'Furniture' and 'Various'.[3] The museum aimed to influence manufacturers and craftsmen, so this stress on materials made good sense, since it reflected the interests of makers of things (rather than of consumers, or historians, or aesthetes). But the museum prospectus warned: 'As many of the articles exhibited in the Museum are lent only for limited periods, the arrangement of the Museum is liable to constant changes'; and its descriptions of the rooms reveal that display according to material divisions was carried through only to a limited extent.[4] A new catalogue was begun in 1855. Here the curator of the museum, J.C. Robinson, separated the collections into seventeen divisions. These now included 'Glyptic and Numismatic Art', 'Arms, Armour and Accoutrements', and 'Watch and Clock Work'. Division I was allotted to 'Sculpture', Robinson's main interest.[5] But the emphasis was still mainly on materials, and the museum's approach to design history remained based on materials and techniques until well into the twentieth century. It did not come naturally to the curators to think of 'British art and design' as a significant category.[6]

The reorganisation of 1857

In 1857 the museum moved to form part of an enlarged museum on the site of the present V&A in South Kensington. As well as the collections of 'ornamental art' and 'manufactures' (or indeed 'ornamental manufactures', a phrase also used), other collections now entered the museum: machinery, food, animal products, educational equipment, building materials and architectural plaster casts; with fish-breeding and shipbuilding to follow. The collections of decorative art gradually fought their way to the top of this conglomeration, especially after the original temporary iron buildings were expanded, first with brick ranges, and then with two huge, glass-roofed halls, the North and South Courts. It was in these courts that the decorative arts clustered, and a contemporary plan shows that the serried ranks of showcases were mostly devoted to such categories as ivory, alabaster, silver, bronze, majolica, porcelain and terracotta. To one side was an 'Oriental Court', and the North Court contained a concentration of Italian material. But few showcases had a national designation. There were six cases of modern design, two each of French, German and English; and in the ceramics area there were two cases of English ceramics, plus one devoted entirely to Wedgwood. So it was still difficult to get any sense of the British tradition in design.

The principle of display in the Museum was sheer accumulation. Objects were crammed into showcases, and the showcases were regimented in long, close rows. There was no attempt to make displays that were easy on the eye. The visitor had to make an effort of visual concentration and selection, like someone consulting the small print of a dictionary. There was one respect, however, in which the Museum authorities sought to create a sympathetic context for exhibits, and that was in the decoration of the rooms and galleries that contained the exhibits. It is usually expected nowadays that museum galleries will provide a discreet, neutral setting that will defer to the objects, allowing them to exude their own auras. In the Victorian period, however, the preference was for settings which mimicked the decoration of exhibits, and which provided insights complementary to the objects through iconographic programmes. In the South Kensington Museum, the North Court was fairly neutral, but the South Court was highly decorated. (For many years it has been covered up, but eventual restoration is envisaged.) The colour and texture of the ironwork was intended to be a work of art in itself. And there was a prominent iconographic programme, depicting idealized craftsmen and women engaged in making, and a frieze with tablets listing the object types collected by the Museum.

All this reflected the Museum's classification system, already described. There was an even more conspicuous iconographic programme in a series of 'full length portraits, in mosaic, of the most eminent painters, sculptors, architects, &c., of all ages and countries', high up on the walls. These thirty-five heroic portraits (known as 'the Kensington Valhalla') included artists ranging from Phidias to Velázquez, and, as might be expected, starred Raphael, Michelangelo and other Italian Old Masters. Eight British heroes were admitted: William Torel (goldsmith), William of Wykeham (as a patron of architecture), Inigo Jones, Grinling Gibbons, Sir Christopher Wren, William Hogarth, Sir Joshua Reynolds and William Mulready (a Victorian painter who died in 1863 and was a great favourite of the South Kensington authorities).[7] Here, then, a view of British art and design was hinted at.[8]

Iconographic schemes were to be found in other galleries, notably the Architectural Courts (opened 1873), where plaster casts were displayed,[9] and the Ceramics Gallery (opened 1868).[10] Prominent here were the names of towns important in the history of art. Some British towns were included, but not many.

British fine art collections before 1909

Finding the British, or English, contribution to decorative art and design, whether among the exhibits, or in the didactic decorative schemes, was never, in the nineteenth century, an easy task. By contrast, it was very easy to find at South Kensington what were called the 'British Fine Art Collections'. There was no logical reason why a museum devoted to decorative art should include 'fine art'. Surely the National Gallery (founded 1824) existed to look after this? In fact, some of the fine art at South Kensington belonged to the National Gallery. When Henry Cole's department moved into Marlborough House, they were not its first artistic tenants. Already the ground floor rooms were in use as an annexe to the National Gallery, holding Mr Robert Vernon's gift to the National Gallery (1847) of modern British paintings; and soon paintings from the Turner Bequest were shown there too.

When Marlborough House was vacated in 1856, the Vernon and Turner paintings had to go somewhere. Since there was no room for them in the National Gallery's Trafalgar Square building, they moved down to South Kensington. Here new galleries were built for them, extending from a gallery built to house another collection of modern British art, assembled by the merchant John Sheepshanks, and given by him to South Kensington in 1856. Sheepshanks gave his pictures to the Museum chiefly because he was persuaded to do so by Richard Redgrave, who was Henry Cole's right-hand man. Redgrave was in charge of the art teaching system controlled by the Department and was not officially part of the Museum's administration. He was nonetheless often consulted about Museum matters and he acted as curator of the paintings.

The National Gallery reclaimed its paintings in 1876, but the Sheepshanks Collection remained and henceforth enjoyed the title of 'The National Gallery of British Art at South Kensington'. Even after Sir Henry Tate's new gallery opened on Millbank in 1896 and tried to assume the name of 'National Gallery of British Art', the Sheepshanks Collection clung on to the title for another twelve years. Throughout the nineteenth century, the main National Gallery in Trafalgar Square sought above all to acquire Old Master paintings, and British art was not high on its list of priorities, so it was content to leave modern British painting in the hands of South Kensington. Cole's museum did not, however, continue to acquire by purchase in this field, so its collection of Victorian painting, though good, is limited, and is now overshadowed by the holdings of Tate Britain.[11] It seems that this section of the Museum was the most popular with visitors.[12] They might well have been confused by the oddly miscellaneous collections of machines, animal products, building materials and plaster casts that filled most of the Museum, but they obviously felt comfortable with paintings.

British decorative art before 1909

During the nineteenth century, some British decorative art (more often described as English than as British) crept into the Museum. Ceramics collectors usually admitted English work alongside their Sèvres and Meissen, so English ceramics arrived in the Museum right at the start with the acquisition of James Bandinel's ceramic collection in 1853.[13] English productions also formed a large section of Lady Charlotte Schreiber's collection, given in 1884.[14] A catalogue of the 'English porcelain, earthenware, enamels, etc' in the Schreiber collection appeared in 1885, happily coinciding with two books by A.H. Church on *English Earthenware* (1884) and *English Porcelain* (1885), published in a series of cheap handbooks issued by the Museum under Henry Cole's successor, Philip Cunliffe-Owen.[15]

English silver was not favoured by the first curator of the Museum, J.C. Robinson, because it was too plain to count as art, but from the 1870s it fared better, when Wilfred Cripps acted as an adviser on metalwork purchases.[16] Cripps's book (again in the handbook series) on *College and Corporation Plate* opened up a new subject. Although such plate remained the property of the historic bodies which still preserved and used it, it was visible in the Museum in the shape of electrotype reproductions. At this period the Museum was happy to exhibit reproductions if it did not possess originals (a practice not acceptable today). In the various catalogues of the textiles collections (*Textile Fabrics* by Dr Daniel Rock in 1870, *Lace and Embroidery* by Mrs Bury Paliser in 1871, *Tapestry and Embroidery* by Alan S. Cole in 1884), English textiles found their place but were subordinated to the cataloguers' attempts to take the largest possible view, historically and geographically, of textile production. English textiles entered the limelight only in a loan exhibition in 1873 of 'decorative art needlework made before 1800', which dug out the English heritage in embroidery from among the heirlooms of many old families.

As to furniture, there was little to be had from the Middle Ages, but Renaissance *sgabelli* and *cassoni* flowed in, and so did French seventeenth- and eighteenth-century furniture, which has rarely failed to be in fashion. But English eighteenth-century furniture gradually earned respect. A review of the South Kensington furniture collection in 1874 urged the Museum to acquire it:

> We should be glad to see the undoubted merits of this style recognised, if only to lead to a little reaction against what may be termed the ostentatious clumsiness and inelegance of a good deal of work which is put forward in so confident a manner as 'Gothic'.[17]

English furniture had its epiphany in an exhibition at South Kensington's branch museum at Bethnal Green in 1896. Some of the galleries there had been filled with a loan exhibition of National Portraits, which had already been shown in South Kensington between 1866 and 1868. (This, the haul from a trawl through the country houses of England, was itself a sign of a rising interest in English art.) The Bethnal Green Museum had a mission, never very assiduously pursued, to be useful to local people, so, when the National Portraits disappeared, it was decided to make an exhibition of English furniture, since furniture-making was a staple trade in east London. It was thought that the country houses of England would again yield a good catch, but this proved not to be the case, since 'inheritors of old houses have refurnished them according to fashions of their own day naturally enough, and have relegated to the attics as old or shabby objects much furniture that we should now deem precious.' It was time for the South Kensington Museum to wake up, for 'rich buyers have learned to appreciate the work of our 18th century furniture makers':

Not only so, but the Continental critics and connoisseurs have found out the merits of these examples of the cabinet-maker's art ... Museums in foreign countries are purchasing fine examples of Chippendale and his contemporaries ... It may be flattering to our patriotic sentiment that neighbouring nations should compete with us in trying to acquire them, but, however valuable that compliment, England is the home of these productions, and the best of them should be retained in this country and be accessible ... to the student and the manufacturer.[18]

That such an appeal to patriotism could now be made was in large part owing to the enthusiasm aroused by the English Arts and Crafts revival.[19] The appeal shows South Kensington reversing the ideological position it had held in 1852. Then, English had been bad, foreign good. By 1900 it was dramatically illustrated that things had changed. At the Paris International Exhibition that year, George Donaldson, an English dealer serving on the jury of the furniture section, bought a selection of continental Art Nouveau furniture – the latest thing in design – with the aim of presenting it to the V&A. It was accepted but caused a furore, because sterling English art teachers thought it set a bad example to English students. It was reluctantly exhibited, with a sign informing the world that it was in 'a style which is not consistent with the teaching at Art Schools in the United Kingdom', and instructing students to be guided by their tutors as to the 'merits and obvious faults' of this furniture. So: English good, foreign bad.

Even though British design was present in the collections (confined, however, to its humble slots in the wide European coverage), and although changing taste had brought it a new respectability, it was still, as the nineteenth century ended, not easily visible in the Museum. This was partly because of space problems. Under Sir Henry Cole, the Museum had an energetic building policy. Every time a little more money became available, Cole would run up a new gallery. He and his architects trusted that the resulting sprawl would one day be drawn together into a noble unity, and produced numerous plans for this. After Cole, impetus was lost, and the Museum remained unfinished, 'a mass of huge, shapeless sheds turn[ing] their bare backs on the public'. Inside, half a century's acquisitions were 'so tightly packed together that it was almost impossible to see them'; and they seemed bafflingly unclassified.[20] Even when the Museum got a major collection at one fell swoop, as with the Jones bequest of French eighteenth-century art, it could not arrange it clearly:

As usual at South Kensington, the things are arranged with no reference whatever to the order of the numbers on them, or to the way in which they are referred to in the handbook; so that the [sic] finding anything which is specially mentioned in the handbook, unless it be a large and prominent object, is a mere matter of chance.[21]

The reorganisation of the Museum in 1909

The unprepossessing exterior of the Museum eventually shamed the government into taking action.[22] In 1890 a limited competition was held among eight architects for a new building to encase the old sheds, and give the Museum a dignified façade. The winner was Aston Webb, who then had to wait until 1899 before work started, when the aged Queen laid the foundation stone of what was now to be known as the Victoria and Albert Museum. As the new building approached completion in 1908, the Permanent Secretary of the Board of Education, which now controlled the Museum, asked the director for his proposals for the redisplay of the collections in the spacious new premises. Unimpressed by the tentative evasions that he received in reply, he thrust the director aside and appointed six outsiders as a 'Committee of Re-arrangement'.

They could, perhaps, have transformed the Museum. Certainly, change was in the air. Since the 1850s, some forty decorative art museums had been founded in Europe, usually modelling themselves on South Kensington, and following its method of classification and arrangement by material. In recent years, however, many had come to distrust this method, thinking that it led designers to be derivative and uninspired, and that it had little appeal to the general public. They now preferred to arrange works of art chronologically, mingling objects of diverse materials so as to give an impression of the common features of the material culture of an age – of the Middle Ages, say, or the Renaissance. While this new approach was known to the committee who were charged to rearrange the V&A, they were given a strict brief by the permanent secretary. In best civil service style, he had looked for precedents to follow. He found that the Museum had at first been arranged by material in order to serve artisans and manufacturers, and this system was now reimposed at South Kensington.

At last, with plenty of space, the segregation could be determinedly carried through. Consequently, long stretches of the new galleries, which opened in 1909, were entirely devoted to textiles or metalwork. The whole top floor contained a sequence of uninterrupted ceramics 300 metres long. Furniture was ranged in long lines as in a warehouse. The effect was impressive in its orderly amplitude, but dispiriting in its monotony (fig. 1).

Tastes in display styles had changed. The interiors were now deliberately discreet. They had a muted classical trim, in such features as cornices or door frames, but the walls, where objects were to be exhibited, were, as Aston Webb insisted, 'kept perfectly plain and free from architectural features of any kind', and were painted white. Architectural critics had difficulty in settling exactly which styles the eclectic Webb had used on the exterior, but they could not miss the array of sculpture, representing British artists. Along the Cromwell Road frontage were ten painters, six architects and six sculptors. Oddly, decorative artists, ten in number, were relegated to the subsidiary frontage on Exhibition Road. If there were a message to be read from this parade of British worthies, it would seem to be that the building which they graced was concerned with British art in all its forms, and only with British art. This was not the case, but the sculpture must reflect some sort of change in the level of esteem accorded to British art.

Inside, British design could still not clearly be identified, since it turned up in widely dispersed slots within the material categories. If one sought wrought-iron work, one went to Room 22, where it was 'arranged in the following order of nationality – English, French, Italian, German, Spanish'. If one sought medieval wood-carving, one went to Room 7, and found 'ranged in order the Swiss, German, Netherlandish, French and English groups'.[23] There was, however, one place that was distinctly English: Rooms 51–57, which contained, as the Museum plan stated, English furniture from 1500 to 1800. (These galleries today form part of the British Galleries.) This made a commanding impact largely through the presence of five complete panelled rooms which the museum had acquired since 1891.

Many regarded the new arrangement of 1909 as a mistake: boring and retrograde in museological terms. It also failed to answer the growing expectation that a major British museum should foreground British art. In 1901, G. Baldwin Brown, Professor of Art History at Edinburgh, had urged the Museums Association to recognise the importance of showing 'local collections' – 'a great and serious work before the managers of museums'. He went on: 'To the central museum at South Kensington we should naturally turn for a proper representation of the industrial and decorative arts of England generally. It is here, however, that we meet with the greatest disappointment that the museums of the country generally have to inflict.'[24] Eight years later, when he contemplated the newly opened galleries of the V&A, he would not have found anything to assuage his disappointment.

Attitudes to display 1909–1945 Regrets were covertly expressed in the V&A. A confidential memorandum of 5 November 1912 on 'The Purposes and Functions of the Museum', while deferring to the V&A's original mission to reform English taste, suggested that a new approach was needed:

Not only does the increased interest in English art make it incumbent to show prominently on English soil a representative and full illustration of the best work of English craft for the instruction of Colonial students and of the large number of foreigners who come to London for the purpose, but also on purely aesthetic grounds it may be held that the national element in the collections must be fully recognised as of great importance.

The Museum staff, however, had just rearranged 145 galleries, and it was not realistic to expect them to start all over again. Many of them, however, did devote themselves with zeal and urgency to the study and acquisition of British decorative art. It was in the inter-war period that such iconic objects as the Walpole Cabinet and the Great Bed of Ware entered the Museum.

While the collection of British art thus improved, the fact that it was inadequately displayed continued to provoke criticism. When a Royal Commission on Museums and Galleries was set up in 1927, one of the many matters it considered was the V&A's treatment of British art. In its report of 1930 it pronounced:

Nowhere in London is it at present possible to see any ordered sequence or illustration of the English arts and crafts. In accordance with the 'classification by material' arrangement of the Victoria and Albert Museum, English work will be found scattered among a large number of different departments … Carefully chosen examples of English work from the different departments would form, we believe, a most instructive and beautiful display.

Now, however, a new director, Eric Maclagan, was taking this matter seriously.[25] After staging an important loan exhibition of 'Mediaeval English Art' in 1930, he found his first opportunity to change the permanent displays in 1933, when the Woodwork Department, running out of gallery space, put in a successful bid to take over the vast Octagon Court (fig. 2). Maclagan urged them to set up displays of four periods of English art, such as Elizabethan, Stuart and Georgian. But they balked at this, since it would have meant reshuffling their other galleries, and it was agreed that mixed-media displays would be created of eighteenth-century material only. Box-like constructions were set up in the court to contain furniture disposed in a more or less domestic way, along with 'kindred objects from other Departments'.[26] The displays were well received, and were said to 'point the way to a better museum'. Then the Second World War occurred.

This (from the point of view of the V&A) proved to be a blessing in disguise. Everything movable was shifted out of the Museum to remote bomb-proof stores. Maclagan prepared a plan for a complete rearrangement when the objects returned. He retired in March 1945, but a successor had already been groomed in Leigh Ashton, and he proceeded to implement Maclagan's plans, signalling what was to come with a special exhibition of 'Masterpieces of English Craftsmanship' (1945). In the galleries, Ashton instituted a two-fold display method.[27] There was so much stuff in the V&A that some of it had to remain in study galleries, still arranged by material. But the cream of it was reorganised in a historical narrative, in 'Primary Galleries'. From the early Middle Ages up to about 1500, all European art was mixed together. From then on, there was a British sequence and a foreign sequence. At last, British art and design, from the Tudors and Stuarts up to the 1820s, could be seen in one impressive chronological sweep, occupying sixteen rooms in the perimeter galleries of the Webb building. In these side-lit rooms, large objects were ranged along the inner walls, and showcases on the window side contained smaller objects (fig. 3).

Ashton's display aesthetic had advanced a good way down the road towards the favoured modernist ideal of what we now call the 'white cube'. He believed that objects should have room to speak for themselves. His favourite wall-colour was 'the loveliest light grey, a dawn-mist tone', and, in order to provide 'restful backgrounds', he had no compunction about hiding 'the Edwardian architecture, with its too numerous mouldings and fussy "features"' behind distempered screens. Ashton received great credit as an innovator, since, after two world wars, everyone had forgotten that the rest of Europe's decorative art museums had carried through similar rearrangements in 1900 or so.

The English Primary Galleries 1948–1998

These displays remained in place, with some additions and enhancements, for 50 years. The main change was to extend the coverage beyond 1820. Rooms 118–20, left empty and closed off at first, were reopened in stages between 1964 and 1966 to disclose a display of British decorative art from 1820 to 1900. The expertise necessary to acquire and document objects from the previously despised Victorian period had been nurtured in the Museum's Circulation Department and had made its trial flight in the memorable 1952 exhibition of 'Victorian and Edwardian Decorative Arts'. The new Victorian Primary Galleries were installed by curator Barbara Morris in 1964–66, following Ashton's method of display. In 1983 the sequence was extended again, proceeding round the corner into Room 74, where a display of British decorative art 1900–60 appeared. By this time, display technique had moved on, and the installation here, with huge plate-glass 'shop-windows', was by a professional designer, Christopher Firmstone.

Ashton's displays, chronological and mixed-media, told a story of British decorative art, but it was a resolutely art-historical story of evolving styles – indeed, of styles evolving apparently without human agency. 'Exuberant fancy and fertile invention gradually succumbing to a classical discipline more and more rigidly applied' was the sort of phrase deployed in the new guidebook (1957). Political or social history was not conveyed, though the objects on display were permitted to have (as the guidebook said of the Elizabethan gallery) 'the associative value of mirroring the greatest period of our history. Such a glove as shown here was given by Queen Elizabeth to her favourite buccaneer, George Clifford, third Earl of Cumberland; in such clothing and amid such furniture moved the Dark Lady of the Sonnets.' When the Victorian galleries opened, it was stressed (rather superciliously) that they were not meant to evoke Victorian daily life, like 'the Victorian rooms that are now becoming a regular feature of our local museums', but to chart documented high design in the Victorian period.

When Roy Strong became director of the V&A in 1974, some expected this to change. As Director of the National Portrait Gallery, Strong had won acclaim by a new style of gallery display in which the gallery's old faces were mingled with furniture, weapons, machines and other paraphernalia, so as to produce 'a panorama of British history'[28] – an effect entirely concordant with the Portrait Gallery's official mission. Would he try this at the V&A? At first, there was so much else to do that little changed in the permanent galleries. Strong soon came to accept that they should continue to focus on high design, perhaps with the exhibits thinned out so as to show 'only objects of the finest quality'. He also thought that British and European design should be reunited in a single sequence.[29] Portions of the British sequence were refreshed from time to time: Tudor in 1982 (where a carapace of contemporary cladding sheathed the original fabric), late Victorian in 1988, and Stuart in 1989 (a cut-price job architecturally but including some ingenious displays of textiles). The overall approach to display was retained.

In 1983, however, Strong drew breath and decided that the time had come for a radical overhaul of the permanent displays. A committee was set up and in 1985 produced a report, *Towards 2000*. Though this grappled with up-to-date ideas, it came to a fairly conservative conclusion: that Ashton's two-fold display method should remain, though Primary Galleries would now be called 'Art and Design Galleries' and study galleries would be called 'Material and Techniques Galleries'. Inherent in this idea was a sense that it was no longer quite decent to offer 'First Class' and 'Second Class' galleries. The two display methods were now to have equal validity.

Perhaps the committee underestimated the cultural shift that was occurring. Since the beginning of the 'museum age' around 1800, museums had enjoyed authority. Of course, some were trivial, demonstrating only the human propensity to hoard rubbish. But most succeeded in commanding respect, even when taciturn or secretive about their purposes and possessions. In the late twentieth century, respect for authority was no longer at a premium. After the dissolution of that most authoritative ideology, the Modern Movement, there ensued a post-modern climate of pluralism and polyvalency. At the very least, it was intellectually fashionable to question all assumptions. For many in the clerisy, 'complexity and contradiction' proved far more attractive than the sort of neatly sliced certainties that were offered by tabloid newspapers and television. And teasing out complexities and contradictions, especially with the aid of jargon furnished by literary theory and co-opted by the new art history, provided the clerisy with a discourse from which ordinary people could be excluded, thus offering highbrows some shelter in a demotic age.

Museums, no less than other institutions, were now seen as 'sites of contention', where conflicting power-groups struggled for supremacy, and where divergent interpretations jostled together. The respectable position for museum curators came to lie in an agreement that museum objects could have many meanings imputed to them, and that all meanings were probably equal. (It consequently became impossible to sustain the old ordinance, 'The V&A is *not* a museum of social history', because most of the objects in it had had a social use, which could not now be ignored in favour of their stylistic qualities alone.) How to convey to museum visitors the new multiplicity of meanings except through a multiplication of verbiage was a problem.

The problem was intensified by a conviction among museum educators that museums should forswear elitist mystification (an occupational hazard among curators) and offer, without being patronising, simple and direct explanations suited to the little-informed or novice enquirer. Explanations of complexity and contradiction were often tendered by intellectuals in a benign attempt to break down barriers, deconstruct canons or level hierarchies. But they could be heavy going for the average museum visitor. Better, perhaps, to find non-verbal methods both of interpretation and of exposition; but this was not easy either. It was in this intellectual ambience that planning for the new British Galleries began in the 1990s.

Notes   1. For background to this essay, see Burton, Anthony, *Vision and Accident: The Story of the Victoria and Albert Museum* (London, 1999), hereafter: Burton (1999), and Physick, John, *The Victoria and Albert Museum: The History of Its Building* (London, 1982), hereafter: Physick (1982).

2. *Athenaeum*, 22 May 1852, p. 525.

3. *Department of Practical Art: A Catalogue of the Articles of Ornamental Art in the Museum*, 3rd edn (London, 1852).

4. *First Report of the Department of Practical Art* (London, 1853), p. 386.

5. J.C. Robinson, *A Catalogue of the Museum of Ornamental Art, at Marlborough House, Pall Mall (Part I)* (London, 1855).

6. This attitude is paralleled in the reluctance of the British Museum to concern itself with 'national antiquities' – though it woke up to its duty more quickly than the South Kensington Museum. See Arthur MacGregor, 'Antiquity Inventoried: Museums and "National Antiquities" in the Mid-Nineteenth Century', in Brand, Vanessa (ed.), *The Study of the Past in the Victorian Age* (Oxford, 1998), pp. 125–37.

7. *Decorations of the South Kensington Museum, 1862 to 1874* [unique printed document, held in the V&A Library], pp. 4–8.

8. It is hard to read in it more than a hint. And the artistic Valhalla was, one feels, somewhat subverted by another series of (smaller) portraits of the British government ministers who had been the political overlords in charge of the Museum. It would be mischievous to suggest that the Museum was deliberately proposing an equivalence between, say, Donatello and Richard Plantagenet Campbell Temple-Nugent-Brydges-Chandos-Grenville, 3rd Duke of Buckingham, Lord President of the Council, 1866–67. But in an essay on what was British in the South Kensington Museum, it would be wrong not to mention this fragment of political history embedded in the fabric.

9. *Building News*, 25 April 1873, p. 469.

10. *Decorations of the South Kensington Museum*, pp. 19–25.

11. See Kathryn Moore Heleniak, 'Victorian Collections and British Nationalism: Vernon, Sheepshanks and the National Gallery of British Art', *Journal of the History of Collections*, vol.12 (2000), pp. 91–107. Note that the Museum also fostered the National Collection of British Watercolours, which, founded on the Ellison gift and bequest (1860, 1873) and the Constable gift (1888), was consolidated by regular purchases; and houses the largest and most comprehensive collection of British portrait miniatures.

12. Burton (1999), p. 53.

13. *First Report of the Department of Science and Art* (London, 1854), pp. 267–82.

14. Ann Eatwell, 'Private Pleasure, Public Beneficence: Lady Charlotte Schreiber and Ceramic Collecting' in Orr, Clarissa Campbell (ed.), *Women in the Victorian World* (Manchester, 1995), pp. 125–45.

15. References to the Museum's publications can be verified in Elizabeth James's exhaustive *The Victoria and Albert Museum: A Bibliography and Exhibition Chronology, 1852–1996* (London, 1998).

16. Oman, Charles, 'A Hundred Years of English Silver, 1: The Victorian Period', *V&A Bulletin*, vol. 1, no. 2 (April 1965), pp. 19–28.

17. 'The Furniture at South Kensington', *Furniture Gazette*, 24 October 1874, p. 1165.

18. Pollen, J. H., 'Introduction', in *Bethnal Green Branch Museum: Catalogue of a Special Loan Collection of English Furniture and Figured Silks* (London, 1896), pp. 25–26.

19. See Wilk, Christopher, 'Furniture Collecting at the Victoria and Albert Museum – a Summary History', in Wilk, C. (ed.), *Western Furniture 1350 to the Present Day in the Victoria and Albert Museum* (London, 1996), pp. 14–16; Saumarez Smith, Charles, 'National Consciousness, National Heritage and the Idea of Englishness', in Baker, Malcolm, and Richardson, Brenda (eds), *A Grand Design: The Art of the Victoria and Albert Museum*, exhib. cat. (New York, 1997), pp. 275–83.

20. Burton (1999), pp. 118, 155–57.

21. 'The Jones Collection at the South Kensington Museum', *Builder* (23 December 1882), p. 800.

22. For a full analysis of what is described in this section, see Burton (1999), ch.10, 'Rearrangement', and Physick (1982), ch. 13, 'The New Building Achieved'.

23. *General Guide to the Collections* (1913), pp. 57, 68.

24. Baldwin Brown, G., 'Industrial Museums in Their Relation to Art', *Museums Journal*, vol.1 (1901–2), pp. 96–97.

25. See Burton (1999), pp. 190–94.

26. *The Victoria and Albert Museum: A Short Illustrated Guide* (London, 1935), p. 12.

27. See Burton (1999), pp. 196–99.

28. Strong, Roy, 'Faces Past and Faces Present', *Art and Artists* (January 1970), p. 27.

29. Strong, Roy, 'The Victoria and Albert Museum – 1978', *Burlington Magazine*, vol. 120 (1978), p. 276.

1. Gallery 56 in 1911 showing display of 18th-century English furniture.

2. The Octagon Court (gallery 40) with a display of 18th-century furniture and decorative art in 1936.

*3. Gallery 125 in 1951 as shown
in Ashton's rearrangement of the
Museum.*

Chapter 2   The Concept of the New British Galleries

Christopher Wilk

Before the project

The British Galleries Project arose because of the widely recognised and urgent need to renovate the Museum's main galleries covering design and art in Britain from the Tudor to the Victorian periods. These galleries were filled with objects recognised as national treasures but, owing to a combination of the changing expectations of Museum visitors, the passage of time and the lack of reinstallation or redecoration, they looked worn and sorely in need of attention even by the 1980s (colour plate 43 and fig. 60). Over time, fragile object types, especially textiles, had gradually disappeared from the galleries as a reaction not only to the high levels of pollution on the busy Cromwell Road outside but, more accurately, to the self-imposed and increasingly stringent conservation requirements arising from greater monitoring of the Museum's environment and knowledge of its effect on objects. Dress and works on paper had never been shown in these galleries. As a result, although some areas displayed paintings and cases of metalwork and ceramics, furniture overwhelmingly dominated the spaces, and many visitors referred to the rooms, understandably, as 'the furniture galleries'. They certainly did not reflect the breadth of the V&A's collections.

During the 1980s, under director Roy Strong, there was regular talk of the need to refurbish these galleries, which, from 1952 until 1987, were known as the English Primary Galleries (though displaying objects made or consumed in Scotland, Wales and even Ireland) and, from 1987 until their closure in 1998, the British Art and Design Galleries.[1] There were various attempts to spruce up parts of the galleries using in-house designers before and after Strong's retirement in 1988. But it was not until 1991, during the directorship of his successor Elisabeth Esteve-Coll, that a project was initiated to reinstall three of those rooms, covering the period 1675–1760, and to apply to the National Lottery for funding. Unfortunately, that project foundered, but the work of the team that developed it left two important legacies: the unprecedented inclusion on the initial Gallery Team of a historian (John Styles, then course tutor on the V&A/Royal College of Art course in the History of Design), and his proposal that a series of three themes underpin the display of objects (see chapter 3).

When Alan Borg took over as Director in 1995, he immediately saw lottery funding as a heaven-sent but possibly short-lived opportunity to pursue the Museum's largest projects. He announced – somewhat to the amazement of his staff – that *all* the British Art and Design galleries should be tackled in a single project that would, it was hoped, be funded in part by the lottery.[2] He charged the Museum's Head of Major Projects, Gwyn Miles, with responsibility for organising the project within the context of the Museum's other gallery and building plans. The present writer (then Chief Curator of Furniture and Woodwork) was asked to head the content side of the project, responsible for what would be displayed, how it would be organised and interpreted, and what it would look like. Miles and Wilk worked together to establish the organisation and staffing of the project, and worked with Borg to agree its schedule in early 1996.[3]

It was readily agreed that the galleries would occupy the old British Art and Design galleries, on two separate floors, constituting approximately 10% of the Museum's display space (figs 5 and 6). If funds were available, storerooms adjacent to the galleries would also be used, thereby increasing the available space by 25%. It was also agreed, almost without the need for discussion, that a key aim was to display the full range of object types from the V&A's collections. Never again, we hoped, would visitors refer to these spaces as 'the furniture galleries'. The V&A is the single institution in Britain that could create such a wide-ranging display from its own collections, and yet this mixture of objects had never been accomplished before in a V&A gallery covering Europe – though it had in our Nehru Gallery of Indian art.

We especially hoped to include textiles and dress, to show the relationship of those often neglected forms of design to other object types in the Museum (for example by showing a dress next to a chair of the same period). Textiles are central to the history of material culture. Before the Victorian period they were extremely expensive, and historical records show how widely they were used at all levels of society to create fashionable and luxurious interiors. The difficulty of showing historical textiles safely often means that they are omitted from displays or ghettoised in separate (dark) rooms. We were determined to create conditions in which both textiles and dress could take their proper place in an exploration of the history of British design. We also hoped to integrate paintings into the stories we would tell, rather than merely using them as wall decoration. And we aimed to include fragile works on paper (including miniatures, watercolours, design drawings and photographs), without which the story we told would be incomplete, and the full glory of the Museum's collections could not be made available to visitors. If we could display this range of objects, in a beautifully designed suite of galleries where visitors would be able to look closely at and enjoy the collections, an important part of our mission would have been accomplished.

Organising the concept stage

From the very start, the British Galleries 1500–1900 was conceived to be different from any previous V&A gallery in terms of what visitors would see and the experience of visiting the gallery. To do this, we had to change radically the method of gallery project organisation and administration in the Museum. Until that time, it was normal practice to assemble a Gallery Team for an Art and Design Gallery by appointing a senior curator from the department that had day-to-day curatorial responsibility for the existing gallery spaces as head. Other members would include a representative of each of the Museum's nine curatorial and conservation departments, a representative from Education, as well as members from the Museum's administrative departments (including Buildings, Design, Finance, Development, Marketing and Press, as well as others). The team could, therefore, total at least twenty-six, which was clearly too large a number to work flexibly, efficiently and speedily, while maintaining close control of all the work. The representative function of many on the team also meant that, with the best will in the world, commitment levels were variable.

Instead, Borg agreed to a request to let the project be directed by a small team of three: a project curator to lead the project (the present writer), a deputy curator expert in the periods and object types being covered (Sarah Medlam) and, for the first time in a V&A project, an educator (Gail Durbin) to serve as the audience advocate, who would be involved from the very beginning, rather than coming along after the principles or even the design of a new gallery had been agreed. Having an educator on the team from the very start – rather than later in the process – was a crucial step if we were to be sincere in our effort to take new approaches to developing the galleries and, in particular, to addressing the needs of our visitors. Designated as the Concept Team, this group would have complete editorial control of the project. Having such authority rest within a project team, rather than with one of the curatorial departments, represented a new departure for the Museum. This team worked closely with a historical adviser, John Styles.

Beginning work   The first task of the Concept Team was to develop a conceptual framework for the galleries which would serve as a statement of principles and secure Borg's approval, and subsequently that of the Museum's trustees, to proceed. In order to achieve this, however, it became necessary for the three team members to establish understanding and trust between themselves, and to find effective ways of working together for what would be a long period of time (five years). A key element in developing this were the many visits we made to other museums, both in the UK and abroad, an experience which drew us together and enabled us to think of ourselves and work together as a team. We learnt, anecdotally, about how we each approached museum visiting and looking at objects, and we gradually analysed in more formal terms our responses. This knowledge was crucial in informing our reactions to ideas later in the process, and in making fundamental decisions about the galleries. It also facilitated the process of developing the key concept document for the project.

We intended the conceptual document to be one to which we could return during the project, as a means of checking progress and the direction of our work. It would also serve as the basis for the designer's brief. A paper summarising the aims and ambitions of the project was, accordingly, submitted and agreed in May 1996 ('Development of the British Galleries', see appendix 1). The motto 'blandness is not an option' was placed at its top. The term 'variety' became a watchword, signalling our desire to enliven the experience of visiting the galleries through varying interpretation and design over the large number of spaces which made up the galleries.

The Development document spoke of qualities that no one would have argued against – the need for elegant and careful design, for visual excitement, even glamour – but it also highlighted an audience-based approach that was new to the Museum. The document listed the target audiences for the galleries and attempted to explain the key principle of addressing the differing needs of different audiences at different times through the run of galleries. It also stated that research into audience and interpretive matters would form part of the project.

The view of interpretation we offered was broad: it included the design of the galleries, the intellectual organisation of the objects, visitor facilities and affected even the choice of objects. Our aim was that our approach would be transparent to visitors. Central to that approach was that all interpretation would be integrated into the gallery. We would not have separate rooms where interpretive devices would be relegated, as if they represented some sort of threat to the sanctity of the object. Instead, our aim was to use these devices – low and hi-tech – to get our visitors to look closely at the objects on view and to allow them to use the devices to illuminate their understanding of objects in new and exciting ways.

We wanted as many objects to be on open display as was safely possible. This aimed to remove an important visual and emotional barrier for all types of visitors, and we were convinced that it would lead to more direct engagement with the exhibits.[4] We wanted labels always to be easy to find, and we agreed early on that every object and label would be numbered, rather than relying on the elegant design relationships between label and object that are so clear to curators and designers but are usually not perceived by visitors. Above all, we wanted to change the experience that many museum visitors round the world have, whereby the reasons for gathering together a group of objects in a gallery are often obscure, unless explained by a guide or docent. We wanted to be explicit, as clear and as transparent as possible about our choices.

This approach took exception to the notion common among some in art museums and galleries that the experience of looking at objects should only be an unmediated one, whereby the installation of objects allowed the object to 'speak for itself'. Our view was that objects spoke to those who understood particular languages. While some of us possess the visual sensitivity, historical knowledge or imaginative skills that would make standing in front of a museum object free of interpretive support a pleasurable and meaningful experience, many museum visitors desire some form of guidance in learning how to approach museum objects. They want to know more but don't necessarily have the tools to go about this. This does not mean they do not enjoy the experience of looking or wish to be spoken down to. Though museum visitors are often highly educated they are, more often than not, not specialists in the objects or subjects in the galleries, and so they do not possess the specialist language and training that many curators implicitly assume.[5] Our challenge was to create displays which both non-specialists and specialists would find engaging, educational and meaningful.

It has to be said this approach proved controversial both within and outside the Museum. Some in the Museum even found this approach threatening.[6] It questioned the expert-driven nature of the Museum and many of the key assumptions that curators, especially, had built their working lives around (see chapter 4, p. 38). It required abandoning the belief that most visitors would understand and follow the physical or intellectual arrangement of a gallery, that they would read the labels or even look at objects for more than a few seconds. It required an openness to alternative approaches and possibilities, and the relinquishing of the authority that comes with specialist knowledge. For those who accepted these fundamental changes of direction, the project itself became an education in which modesty about one's ability to shape the visitor experience was essential. And it required an understanding that the results of even this approach could not be predicted, only aspired to.

Even the matter of having designated target audiences provoked dissent. How was it possible, some asked, to write labels for eight different types of visitor? The answer, of course, was that we could not; that the provision for certain audiences did not lie in labels. These, naturally, were written to be understood by most visitors, but we accepted that not all visitors would bother reading anything other than what was to them the most important identifier in the label (such as the object title, date or name of designer or artist). Some curators were firmly convinced that we should address those we had always addressed, our 'traditional' audience of specialists. To anyone used to engaging with visitors in the Museum's galleries, where one obtains a clear idea of the variety and often the very basic nature of visitors' questions and interests, this characterisation of our audience seemed highly inaccurate. The Museum has many audiences; specialists are a valued one, and their needs are addressed throughout the galleries, but they are not the majority. Such neglect of the diversity of our audiences was not acceptable to those within the Museum who yearned to make more meaningful the experience of visiting and of looking at our collections, and it could not be justified in an institution funded by taxpayers.[7]

Embedded in the project from the beginning was the notion that the galleries should tell a story, or series of stories, about design and art in Britain from 1500 to 1900, that went beyond a series of displays about the history of aesthetic style. It would be indefensible if we were not able to answer, in a coherent and synoptic form, based on a broad understanding of British cultural history, the question, 'what are the British galleries about?' The answer to that question was eventually spelled out in 'The Story of the British Galleries' (see appendix 3).

The issue of how the new British Galleries should be organised was discussed extensively. The Concept Team were told they had complete freedom in terms of coming up with suggestions, including ones that used a series of themes rather than a chronological arrangement. We discussed such an arrangement at an early stage. However, it seemed perverse to abandon chronology as an ordering principle, for several reasons. First, the Museum is visited by a large number of foreign tourists (at the time some 45% of our visitors). They want to learn about the history of British culture and, although they may not carry with them a neat chronology of British history, nonetheless the tradition of a chronological approach to history is universal. Secondly, chronology enables the Museum to act as a strong resource for the teaching of British history, a core curriculum subject in British schools. Finally, the V&A is unique in holding such strong collections that we could offer a comprehensive view – or one such view – of high-style design in Britain between the late fifteenth century and the early twentieth century.

The issue of the date span of the galleries was determined by practical considerations. The British collections are sufficiently broad to support our intended breath of display only from the Tudor period (starting in 1485 with the accession of Henry VII). While the galleries might have concluded with the end of the twentieth century, several factors militated against that approach. In close proximity to the British Galleries is the Museum's main twentieth-century gallery, which continued the chronological story (albeit through a different narrative). To dismantle that gallery would have meant, in practical terms, that the Museum would have been required to engage in a separate, new gallery (and fundraising) project. Finally, to include the twentieth century in the new British Galleries would have meant cutting down the pre-Edwardian content of those galleries by about one quarter. We took the decision to end the gallery with objects up to 1914, a natural stopping point for British history.

This led, inevitably, to the question of a title for the galleries. Issues around titling inevitably consume enormous amounts of time in public museums. First, it was said that 1485–1914 was insufficiently user-friendly and that it would be useful it we would agree to simplifying the gallery dates to 1500–1900, which was done. As to the title, while the team favoured 'Design in Britain 1500–1900', in recognition of the many non-British objects we hoped to display, it was felt that this sort of title did not fit in well with the Museum's internal signage and external marketing. 'Britain 1500–1900' would have been consistent with existing gallery titles throughout the Museum. However, it was felt that we needed a form of words that suggested what visitors were coming to see, a title which could be put on a poster. Simplicity won out in the end, and 'British Galleries 1500–1900' was chosen.

Once the chronological structure was agreed with Borg and a wide group of Museum staff (before the Development document was written), the three themes originally conceived for the 1675–1760 gallery project were revived (see chapter 3, pp. 31–5). More than a year later, reflecting concern that the theme of 'Taste and the Consumer' was too broad, they were transformed into four themes. Subsequently, as we approached the need to make final choices for the language to be used in the gallery, we grappled with the question of the theme titles in an attempt to make them more engaging by changing as many as possible into questions and then renaming all except one to make them more accessible in the galleries (fig. 4).

Figure 4.
Themes for the British Galleries.

Original titles 1996	Revised titles 1997
Style	Style
Taste and the Consumer	Who Led Taste?
Design and Product Innovation	Fashionable Living
	What Was New?

The concept for the themes was that, in addition to providing the historical framework, they would intellectually underpin the titled displays and that this would be represented explicitly in the galleries on text panels. Visitors who were interested might notice the repetition of themes from room to room, and some might even follow a theme throughout the run of galleries. At least, they would provide the context for the titled display. Like other interpretive elements of the gallery, it was not envisaged that the thematic structure would be used by all visitors. We expected that students in further and higher education and those who found it useful to have a firm structural or intellectual framework to their visit would value the themes most.[8]

We were vitally concerned that the design of the gallery should act both as a beautiful and provocative context for the displays and as part of the interpretive agenda of the galleries. The Development document spelled out our hopes and desires and provided the starting point for our collaboration with the designers. Once Casson Mann were hired as designers, the Concept Team worked directly with Dinah Casson over a period of months to establish an overall layout as well as to establish a working relationship (on the design process see chapters 6 and 8). In particular, we repeated with Casson some of the visits we had made earlier, thus including her in the process of the exchange of values with the Concept Team and, later, members of the wider team. We also began our work with David Mlinaric and the Historic Decoration Consultants (John Cornforth, Christopher Gibbs and John Harris). Because they had particular historical expertise but little experience of audience concerns, we sought to find common ground from which to proceed.

Creating a wider team All of the principles for the galleries were then established in the first few months of the project. Once the designers were hired and the basis of the design agreed, we moved to the next stage of the project by forming the period-based teams (Tudor and Stuart, Hanoverian, and Victorian) that would undertake the detail of selecting objects and interpretation, as well as working with the designers. These teams began work in October 1996, and consisted of curators, educators and researchers. (The make-up of the Gallery Teams and the process of working on the content of the galleries in this next stage of the project is described in detail, and through a case study, in chapter 8. The move into the implementation stages of the project is detailed in chapter 5.)

Part of the process of working on the British Galleries project was the education of the team itself. Formal monthly meetings often took the form of seminars or workshops on various topics to which we invited experts from within, as well as from outside, the Museum. While most of those dealt with educational aspects, including, for example, the theory of learning styles, audience evaluation, intepretive practice at other institutions, we also, over a period of years, conducted numerous workshops on topics including the needs of disabled visitors and writing text for galleries. Seminars conducted for a wider, invited external audience included those on the Britishness of the British Galleries, one on the needs of ethnic minority audiences, a study day on the use of inventories in research, and a series of four research colloquia for an academic and professional audience. In 1997 we organised a two-day international conference on the topic of period rooms in museums as a means of clarifying our own thoughts on those historic interiors and airing, in public, our tentative ideas. Another area of learning was provided by the decision to open a gallery of highlights of the British collections ('Best of British') during the projected period of gallery closure (1998–2001). As well as an opportunity to test installation ideas, colours and methods of object display informally, it provided the venue for the formal evaluation of design and interpretive ideas (see chapter 11).

A wider team of Museum operations staff and outside consultants joined in 1997, and especially from 1998. The galleries themselves were closed to enable work to begin in August 1998, at which point work began on removing 6000 objects from the galleries and adjacent stores. This work, all behind the scenes yet crucial to the undertaking of the project, is described in chapter 5.

What was accomplished by the teams working full-time on the British Galleries project was, of course, only possible because of the high degree of collaboration with colleagues from all over the Museum, in particular from conservators, who spent years investigating objects and preparing them for display. Museum scientists, technicians, photographers and computer specialists, as well as those from the Buildings and Estate Department, fundraisers, press and marketing staff, all devoted considerable time and energy to the project, which dominated life in the Museum for several years. The trawl through the V&A collections of objects made or consumed in Britain between 1500 and 1900 was a lengthy process that depended heavily upon the specialist knowledge and guidance of V&A curators. Many of these curators made substantial and key contributions to the new galleries. This extended review of objects in galleries and in stores, involving Gallery Team members, consultants and other V&A curators and conservators continued over the course of more than three years and is likely to have been one of the most comprehensive ever undertaken within the Museum. It is one of the reasons why the new British Galleries, while having the same number of objects as the old galleries (3000), have a completely different character: two-thirds of the objects selected came from store or from other Museum galleries, and many had not been on display in living memory.

The British Galleries Team was unusual in that most of the team had actively sought, through competitive application, to work on the project, and virtually all worked full-time on the project. They were highly motivated, far more so than on projects in which individuals are assigned to be part of a Gallery Team to assume a representative function. The motivation of those working on the project was one of its greatest assets and accounts for much of its success. It certainly explains the pleasure of working on it.

Though the work on the details of the galleries was challenging, even onerous at times, the fact that we had made the decisions of principle at the start, that we made every effort to stick to them, and that the Concept Team maintained control of the gallery content throughout the project, meant that an unusually large percentage of our original goals had been achieved. Although there were certainly compromises, regrets or outright failures along the way (these are considered within discussions of specific aspects of the project in chapters 4–6, 8–11 and in the Conclusion), nonetheless, planning such a large scheme in a new way was the successful foundation of the entire project.

Notes

1. This change in title resulted from the *Towards 2000* report (issued 1985). Its authors were Charles Saumarez Smith, Malcolm Baker and Garth Hall on behalf of a committee that also included Gwyn Miles, Joe Earle and Michael Darby. This provided the strategy for gallery presentation which was further developed by the Museum's master-plan architects, Michael Hopkins and Partners. See Anthony Burton, *Vision and Accident: The Story of the Victoria and Albert Museum* (London, 1999), pp. 227, 230 and 233.

2. Borg noted that the V&A lagged behind other national museums in making an application and correctly predicted that the size of grants to the London-based national museums would gradually diminish.

3. Based on a review of previous gallery projects, their square metreage and number of objects, Borg was told that the British Galleries would hypothetically take 15 years to complete. When told that, with new ways of working, the galleries could be completed in seven years, he insisted that it be done more quickly and, eventually, it was agreed that the project should open within six years (though work began the following year, in 1996). An opening date of the end of 2001 was chosen and kept to.

4. Although we were naturally disappointed that the National Heritage Lottery Fund (as it was then known) turned down the Museum's 1995 application to renovate the British Art and Design Galleries 1675–1760, it proved useful that their disquiet regarding the design was at least partially based on the strategy of creating micro-climates in cases, as a means of protecting objects. Instead, they suggested we think about air conditioning all the rooms, a necessary prelude to open display. They also raised the issue of our completing all the galleries in a single project. A first lottery application was submitted in September 1996, and a development grant of just over £1 million was awarded in July 1997. A further, more detailed application with the designs at Architectural Stage D was submitted in December 1997, and in July 1998 a grant of £15 million was awarded towards a total cost of £31 million.

5. These expectations were borne out not only in day-to-day interaction with our visitors but in our audience research. See Creative Research (1997i), *Audience Research for the British Galleries: Quantitative Research Findings*, vol.1, p. 32, and Creative Research (2002ii), *Summative Evaluation of the British Galleries: Report of Research Findings*, pp. 20–21

6. John Whitley, 'The V&A Team', *Daily Telegraph*, Magazine (17 May 1998), p. 53, referred to V&A scholars 'not so happy about the arrival of new technology' and quoted an anonymous keeper: 'The point of these objects is that they are so fine that they enrich our experience and our understanding just by themselves.'

7. Lest the mention of the taxpayer suggest political pressure or interference, it is worth stating that all of the guiding principles established at the beginning of this project were devised by the project team alone, with pressure neither from government nor from the most senior Museum staff or trustees. National museum life in Britain is both heavily politicised – owing to the subservient relationship to the government department funding the museum – and less politicised than the media often suggest (direct intervention in the content of a museum is rare). Ironically, suggestions made before the galleries opened that the use of visitor evaluation represented a 'New Labour' approach neatly omitted the fact that work had begun, and all the principles were agreed, in 1996 during the tenure of a Conservative government.

8. One direct result of the thematic structure was that we decided early on that all labels, within each display, would address the central subject of the display; in other words, if the display centred on style, then all the labels would address that question, rather than some dealing with questions of provenance, others with making and yet others with social context. This naturally led to the idea that a single person would be responsible for each display, rather than the Museum's former method of having each department write labels for 'their' objects.

5. Plan of the Museum showing the extent of the British Galleries, 10% of the display space of the entire museum.

6. 3D diagram of the British Galleries for Stage C design, May 1998, showing new, large lift at each end of the galleries, to supplement the existing lift.

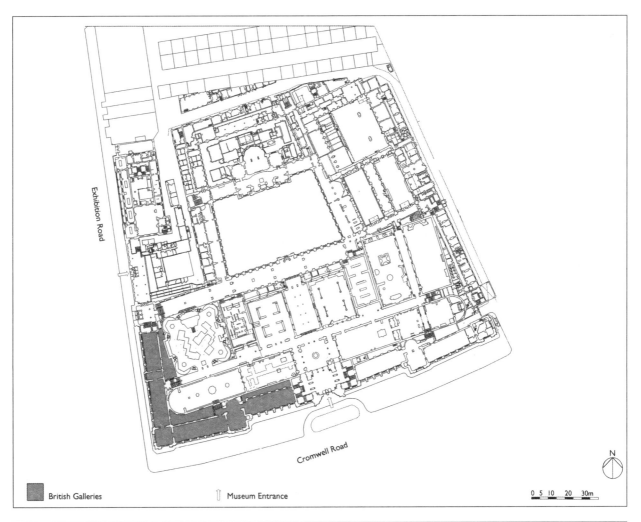

British Galleries

Museum Entrance

0 5 10   20   30m

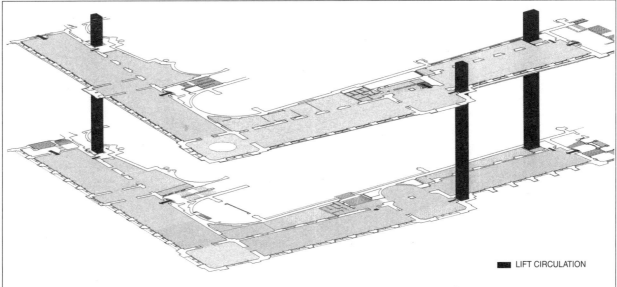

LIFT CIRCULATION

Creating the British Galleries at the V&A

Chapter 3   History in the Galleries: Developing Historical Themes for the New British Galleries

John Styles

The new British Galleries at the V&A embody many innovations. Fundamental is a change in the way the galleries engage with history. As Anthony Burton makes clear in chapter 1, the V&A has long had an uneasy relationship with history in general, and British history in particular. Organised primarily in terms of materials during its formative years in the second half of the nineteenth century, the Museum made no attempt to engage systematically with the history of British decorative art, either in its collecting or its displays. In the early twentieth century, it resisted the international trend towards displays telling the story of national taste that had come to prevail elsewhere. Only with the establishment of the English Primary Galleries in the late 1940s did the V&A start to display British objects made from different materials in a grand chronological narrative. The organising principles adopted in the 1940s were stylistic and aesthetic. The English Primary Galleries constructed a history of English style through a sequence of what were deemed to be the best objects from the V&A's collection.

By the 1980s the English Primary Galleries were beginning to lose their coherence, both intellectually and physically. Intellectually, the distinction between Primary galleries displaying the 'best' objects in a narrative sequence and Study galleries housing the others, material by material, began to look distinctly old-fashioned. In the 1940s this hierarchical divide between the best and the rest had served as an intellectual justification for the encroachment of the new, historical displays on the Museum's traditional, materials-based scheme. In the 1980s the V&A's curators remained, by and large, confident in their ability to pick the best objects. Nevertheless, their capacity to provide an intellectual defence of their choices proved vulnerable to the general attack on aesthetic hierarchies mounted by university art historians from the 1970s.

The Museum's response, in the mid-1980s, was to rethink its hierarchical division into Primary and Study galleries. The Primary Galleries were redesignated Art and Design galleries, with the aim of focusing on issues of taste and consumption. The Study galleries became Materials and Techniques galleries and were intended to emphasise processes and products. This challenge to aesthetic hierarchies was, in the case of the English Primary Galleries, accompanied by an assault on national hierarchies. In the 1940s, when the phrase 'The English Primary Galleries' was coined, it was common to use the term English in a remarkably unreflective way to refer to the whole of the United Kingdom. The Englishness of English art, including decorative art, was a key preoccupation. By the 1980s this had become unthinkable. With the V&A now priding itself on being the national museum of art and design, the English Primary Galleries became the British Art and Design Galleries.

In the short term, not much changed in practice. The new categories were simply applied to existing displays in what amounted to little more than renaming. Nevertheless, the exercise represented a fundamental redefinition of the Museum's display policy, with important implications for its relationship with history. Underpinning the reconceptualisation of the permanent displays was a distinction between two ways of looking at objects – one from the point of view of consumption, the other from the point of view of production. Approaching objects from these two points of view required curators to focus less on issues of aesthetic quality and style, and more on issues of historical context – how objects were made, how they were acquired, how they were used, how they were evaluated. Similarly, the need to establish what was British for a post-colonial era required curators to think less in terms of how a unique and authentic national style had developed, and instead to confront broader issues of authority and identity, exchange and hybridity, both within the British Isles and beyond. All this had momentous implications for future thinking about the permanent displays.

Physically, too, the English Primary Galleries were showing their age by the 1980s. Their most embarrassing feature for most of the 1980s was a huge chronological gap covering roughly the period from 1675 to 1730, the result of necessary maintenance and planned refurbishment which got as far as dismantling the previous displays but never proceeded, due to lack of money (colour plate 43). The Museum's mounting embarrassment about this gap was a crucial catalyst. It initiated the rethinking that underpinned the way the new British Galleries would engage with history.

In 1991 a team began to draw up plans to reinstall the British displays 1675–1760.[1] The essential point of departure was to consider what an Art and Design gallery of the new kind should be in practice. The broad brief for all the Art and Design galleries required that they should offer a historical narrative, incorporate objects in a variety of materials, and concern themselves with how objects were consumed. An initial decision was therefore made by the Gallery Team that, with the general visitor in mind, the new displays should interpret the period within a broad narrative incorporating a limited number of general themes. In part, this broad narrative was defined in terms of what it should not be. It should be constructed out of a multiple themes and not concern itself exclusively with style. It should deal with an intellectually coherent range of objects and not simply be a 'greatest hits' sequence based on conventional canons of artistic quality. It should incorporate new scholarship in the field, but not degenerate into presenting a series of abstruse new research findings, accessible only to the *cognoscenti*. This wish list immediately raised two crucial problems: first, what to do about questions of aesthetic value, and, second, which themes to choose.

Although it was anxious to escape from the canonical principals of the old Primary galleries, the team was acutely conscious that the V&A was not, and really could not be, a museum of general material culture or popular social history. Its collections represent objects which a variety of people in the past – consumers, collectors, curators – have considered to be the best in their field. Over the past century and a half, the Museum has collected Spitalfields silk gowns, not homespun linen aprons; marquetry cabinets, not plain cottage tables; silver tea services, not wooden plates. It was therefore decided to historicise the issue of aesthetic value – to explore for the visitor what was considered best at the time and why. In other words, the focus of the display would remain high design and the decorative arts in the period, reflecting the V&A's collecting policy over most of its 150 years, but an effort would be made to explain how particular objects came to be considered aesthetically outstanding.

Non-specialists today, whatever their own aesthetic response to museum objects, do not necessarily understand why objects were considered beautiful (or otherwise) in periods before the twentieth century. The team was acutely aware that the assumptions behind past cultures were very different from our own and require exploration and explanation. The presumption, which underpinned the old English Primary Galleries, of a culturally coherent audience could no longer be taken for granted. Non-élite objects could play an important role here in helping to explain the notion of 'the best' at work in the period. Earthenware could be juxtaposed with porcelain to demonstrate the qualities of decoration and finish that served to endow some artifacts with high status and others with low. But non-élite objects could not be the focus of the display, given the character of the Museum's holdings.

Using the analogy of the way textbooks and general histories are put together, it was decided to select three main themes for the galleries. These would be the elements from which the narrative would be woven. It was considered imperative that the themes should be strictly limited in number, in order to retain legibility. At the same time, they had to be general enough to incorporate the diversity of objects that characterised the period; they had to reflect recent interpretive scholarship in the field; and they had to enable the galleries to engage with the 'big' empirical questions that national narrative histories inevitably throw up. What distinguished high material culture in this period from what came before and after? What changed and what remained the same? What might usefully be characterised as British?

It was in considering these themes that a difficult issue had to be confronted: the relationship between art history and the Victoria and Albert Museum, which differs from the major art galleries in London, in that it is primarily a museum of design and the decorative arts. Art history poses a problem for the V&A because, for all the debate in the 1980s and 1990s among art historians about embracing a broad 'visual culture', their practice still suggested an overwhelming focus on flat art and a marked lack of interest in design and the decorative arts. Many art historians still seemed in the early 1990s to have acute difficulty in dealing with non-representational artifacts.

As far as design and the decorative arts in the period 1675 to 1760 were concerned, the team thought that much of the most fruitful new thinking had come not from art history but from design historians (not least those involved in the V&A/Royal College of Art MA course in the history of design, established in 1982 by the V&A in partnership with RCA), cultural historians and American work in the material culture tradition, as practised at the Winterthur Museum and at Colonial Williamsburg.[2] But the team was also aware that art historians working on late seventeenth- and eighteenth-century painting, such as John Barrell and David Solkin, had been centrally concerned with issues of intellectual history, patronage and consumption which bore directly on British design and the decorative arts in the period 1675–1760.[3] These historians of painting highlighted the issue of taste and cultural authority, which was important for the study not just of fine art but also of decorative art, design and demotic material culture.

It was in this issue of taste and cultural authority that the 1675–1760 team identified its first broad theme – one which was a central concern in new work on the period in a whole range of histories, which addressed important questions about the consumption of high design objects and its meanings, and which helped to historicise questions of aesthetic value and cultural hierarchy. For the period 1675–1760, the team decided to treat this theme as a story of transition from Court to Commerce, drawing on the interpretation subsequently offered in John Brewer's influential *Pleasures of the Imagination*.[4]

The Court was a key source of aesthetic and cultural leadership in the late seventeenth century, particularly under Charles II and William III, but its role declined under the Hanoverian dynasty after 1714. In the absence of state institutions on the French model for policing taste and design, the early eighteenth century witnessed the rise in importance of alternative sources of cultural authority, such as the wealthy private patron, and the commercial supplier of high design goods or polite commercial entertainment. This was a story that could be developed through certain groups of objects – the state beds commissioned by courtiers in the 1690s, which reflected the taste of prominent court designers like the Huguenot Daniel Marot; the furniture of William Kent, whose work was so closely linked with Lord Burlington and his advocacy of neo-Palladian architecture; the group of objects held by the Museum associated with Vauxhall Gardens, the key site for the development of polite commercial entertainment from the 1730s.

But the theme of taste and cultural authority also touched on a wider history of élite manners and behaviour. In the 1970s and 1980s historians from a variety of backgrounds had explored the progressive refinement of domestic life and material culture in seventeenth- and eighteenth-century England, often informed by the concept of the 'civilizing process' developed by the sociologist Norbert Elias.[5] Historians of consumption, most notably Lorna Weatherill, had analysed the spread of new domestic artifacts which implied new ways of living.[6] Mark Girouard had famously reinterpreted changes in the layout of the English country house in terms of changing notions of access and privacy.[7] And at the V&A, Peter Thornton had identified the origins of domestic comfort in the furnishing of Parisian interiors in the 1620s and had traced its spread to England and the Netherlands.[8] This aspect of the history of taste in the period 1675–1760 – the rise of polite gentility and the forms of cultural sociability and material culture associated with it – was a story that brought together many of the most striking new objects of the period, from silver coffee pots and mahogany tea tables to silk gowns and chintz curtains.

The history of élite material culture from 1675 to 1760 was, however, not just a matter of how taste was regulated and reordered. It was also a story of dramatic expansion in the range and character of the goods consumed. Consequently, the Gallery Team decided that the second of the three gallery themes should deal with product and design innovation. The principal concern here was to use objects to think about some of the main processes by which new artifacts and new designs came to be available to the élite consumer in Britain in the period. Innovation took many forms. There were British inventions, like the pocket microscope or transfer prints on ceramics. Imports were, perhaps, an even more important source of innovation, like the Indian chintzes and Chinese teapots which were quickly copied by British manufacturers. Sometimes immigrant craftspeople were the key agents of innovation, like the French Huguenots, who developed the silk industries of Spitalfields and Canterbury. A great advantage of product and design innovation as a theme, apart from the fact that it so obviously addressed the 'big' questions about what changed and what was or was not British, was that it lent itself to displays that juxtaposed objects to show borrowings, appropriations and parallels.

Here again, the team was able to benefit from outstanding research undertaken by the V&A's curators, such as Natalie Rothstein's work on Spitalfields silks.[9] It was also able to draw on a lively debate among economic historians about the nature of innovation before the Industrial Revolution of the late eighteenth century, a debate fuelled by growing doubts about the impact of the Industrial Revolution on economic growth. Particularly influential was a research project undertaken in the early 1990s by the Centre for Metropolitan History at the University of London, 'The Growth of a Skilled Workforce in London, 1500–1700', which involved collaboration with the Museum of London, the V&A and other London museums.[10] The team was keen to include here the impersonal techniques for distributing information about products and designs which achieved a new prominence in the later seventeenth century, in particular printed sheets and books of designs that could be translated by craftspeople from two dimensions into three dimensions. The number and scope of printed design sources in circulation grew enormously between 1660 and 1760, culminating in sophisticated and famous works like Thomas Chippendale's *The Gentleman and Cabinet Maker's Director* of 1754. This was again a field where the V&A's curators had made an outstanding contribution to new knowledge since the 1950s.[11]

As its third theme, the 1675–1760 Gallery Team chose the issue of style. Despite its dissatisfaction with the way stylistic concerns had dominated the pre-existing Primary galleries, the team remained convinced that addressing style should be central to the Museum's activities.[12] This was partly because questions of style continued to be so important in the historiography of the decorative arts, and partly because attention to style could counteract the centrifugal tendencies inherent in a museum where the curatorial units were based on materials, not chronological periods. However, the team was acutely aware of the need to move beyond simple period labels. What was needed was a treatment of style that was at the same time intellectually challenging and accessible to the visitor. The team was especially anxious to escape the kind of debased formalism that presents the stylistic history of British decorative art of the period 1675–1760 in terms of a rigid sequence of Baroque, Palladian, Rococo and Neo-Classical.

An alternative point of departure was to think about the period in terms of the problems that arose from the dominance of an international style – classicism, broadly defined – in an age of intense mercantilist rivalries among the European states and aggressive European commercial and colonial expansion into the extra-European world. This suggested a tripartite approach which was only loosely chronological. First, classicism would be considered as the hegemonic European style of the period 1660–1760, with French, Dutch and Italian variants of classicism as continental models competing for British attention. Second, the neo-Palladian reaction against continental influences would be presented as a search for a distinctively British classical style. Third, and finally, classicism's exotic counterpoints would be explored – in particular, Rococo, Chinoiserie and the revived Gothic.

By 1995, then, the team working on the British Art and Design Galleries, 1675–1760 had established three themes to articulate the reinstallation – style, innovation, and taste and the consumer. They were themes which moved the galleries beyond their previously predominant focus on style, they reflected recent scholarship (especially that undertaken at the V&A), and together they could sustain a broad narrative incorporating the whole range of objects from the Museum's collection.[13]

In 1995 the Museum applied to the National Heritage Lottery Fund (as it was then known) to fund the gallery project. The application was rejected with the suggestion that a broader project covering all the historic British Galleries be considered and that a new approach to the design be taken. Initially this decision sidelined the work of the team that had developed themes for the period 1675 to 1760. A new British Galleries Team began their work by subjecting the whole approach to display represented by the existing galleries – including the very idea of a chronological narrative – to radical reappraisal. But it was a reappraisal conducted within the framework established by the Museum in the 1980s for all its art and design galleries. The members of the new British Galleries Team decided at an early stage to retain a broadly chronological approach. That decision meant they had to grapple with the same problem of constructing a historical narrative around issues of taste and consumption that had already been addressed on a smaller scale for the period 1675–1760. At this point, the new British Galleries Team returned to the themes that had been developed for 1675–1760 to ask if they could be applied to a much longer time period. It was decided that they could. There were a number of reasons.

First was the fact that the new British Galleries covered the historical period from 1500 to 1900. The story of British design and the decorative arts across these four centuries lent itself to a narrative of transformation from periphery to core, from a minor role in European cultural affairs at the start of the sixteenth century to the imperial, economic and cultural power of the Victorian years. The period 1675–1760 marked a central phase in this transformation, and the themes developed to serve it could equally be applied to other phases. This would not have been the case had the new galleries had to deal with the Anglo-French cultural milieu of the high Middle Ages, or the international marginalisation of British design and decorative art in the twentieth century. Second, the brief for the V&A's art and design galleries demanded the kind of focus on issues of taste and consumption that was embodied in the existing themes. Third, the existing themes had been worked out in dialogue with recent scholarship outside the Museum. Although the later seventeenth and eighteenth centuries had been an especially lively field in cultural and art history in the 1980s and 1990s, intellectual currents are not restricted to any particular period. Many of the same issues had exercised scholars of both Tudor and Victorian Britain. Fourth, the existing themes had been developed with close attention to the nature of the V&A's British holdings, to the problems of displaying a wide range of materials and to the best recent scholarship in the Museum, as manifested in both publications and exhibitions. In other words, they were tailored to the V&A's collections and to its intellectual preoccupations.

Having decided to use the existing themes – style, innovation, and taste and cultural authority – there followed a process of extending and refining them, which was conducted principally by the present writer as historical adviser to the new British Galleries Team, in conjunction with the members of the teams that were now set up to work on the different sections of the gallerie (see appendices 2 and 3). This process went hand-in-hand with the task of using the themes to develop a broadly chronological sequence of displays, each incorporating a group of objects that articulated a particular topic (see appendix 4). As the process of refining the themes proceeded, two new issues arose. The first concerned the content of the taste and cultural authority theme. The second concerned nomenclature.

The theme of taste and cultural authority had always been made up of two linked elements. On the one hand, it dealt with the changing people and institutions that had the greatest influence on which objects were regarded as beautiful and desirable at different periods – the people referred to in the correspondence of the eighteenth-century potter Josiah Wedgwood as 'the legislators of taste'. On the other, it dealt with the ways in which objects were implicated in changing lifestyles – the way, for instance, that tea wares and tea tables were essential to the new kind of genteel, formal house visiting taken up by wealthy eighteenth-century ladies. These two elements were, of course, connected, because new ways of using objects were often promoted by the legislators of taste. In practice, however, it proved difficult for the teams putting together the new British Galleries to make those connections work in terms of display. It was still considered essential to keep the number of themes to a minimum to ensure that the galleries would offer the visitor an accessible and well-articulated narrative.

Nevertheless, it was decided for clarity's sake to divide this theme into two separate themes, one that dealt with cultural authority and the other with objects and lifestyle.

Up to this point, the names by which the themes were known were simply a matter of convenience for the curators involved. However, it was pointed out that, if the themes were to be understood by the public, more thought should be given to what they were called. The result was a new set of four names (fig. 4), designed to be understood by the widest possible range of visitors. The new names also indicated how the themes were grounded in a consistent set of historical questions about the objects in the galleries. The first theme remained 'Style', addressing the question of how things looked. The second became 'Who led taste?' It asked who decided what was considered beautiful, fashionable and desirable. The third became 'Fashionable living', examining how fashionable objects shaped the way people lived. The fourth became 'What was new?' It dealt with new designs and new products.

In the end, this new nomenclature begged an important question: who were the themes for? Were they primarily for the curators, to organise their thinking about history in the galleries and to ensure that the galleries offered a balanced, modulated historical narrative, with sufficient intellectual light and shade to sustain the visitor's interest? Or were they for the public directly, a prominent part of the way displays were to be labelled, offering a formal historical grid for understanding and moving through the galleries? The themes certainly performed the first of these two functions, but it is less certain that they have performed the second, even though they are incorporated into the gallery labelling and orientation panels. Nevertheless, whether visitors are aware of the thematic structure of the galleries or not, the themes remain crucial to the galleries' capacity to offer a coherent historical narrative that holds the public's interest and sustains their enjoyment.

Notes

1. Its two leading members were Tessa Murdoch from the Furniture Department and the present writer from the V&A/Royal College of Art MA course in the history of design. Significantly, both of them were recent recruits to the V&A. They were later joined by designer Robert Letts.

2. For examples of the new and exciting ways in which American scholars used artifacts to reinterpret the cultural and social history of the United States, see St George, R. B. (ed.), *Material Life in America, 1600–1860* (Boston, 1987) and Bushman, R., *The Refinement of America: Persons, Houses, Cities* (New York, 1992).

3. See Barrell, J. (ed.), *Painting and the Politics of Culture: New Essays on British Art, 1700–1850* (Oxford, 1992) and Solkin, D., *Painting for Money* (London, 1993). Also Lippincot, L., *Selling Art in Georgian London* (London, 1983) and Pears, I., *The Discovery of Painting* (London, 1988).

4. Brewer, J., *The Pleasures of the Imagination: English Culture in the Eighteenth Century* (London, 1997).

5. Elias, N., *The History of Manners*, vol.1 of *The Civilizing Process* (Oxford, 1982) and *State Formation and Civilization*, vol.2 of *The Civilizing Process* (Oxford, 1978).

6. Weatherill, L., *Consumer Behaviour and Material Culture in Britain, 1660–1760* (London, 1988).

7. Girouard, M., *Life in the English Country House: A Social and Architectural History* (London, 1978).

8. Thornton, P.K., *Seventeenth-century Interior Decoration in England, France and Holland* (London, 1978).

9. See Rothstein, N., *Silk Designs of the Eighteenth Century* (London, 1990).

10. See Mitchell, D., *Goldsmiths, Silversmiths and Bankers: Innovation and the Transfer of Skill, 1550 to 1750* (Gloucester, 1995).

11. See Lambert, S. (ed.), *Pattern and Design: Designs for the Decorative Arts, 1480–1980* (London, 1983).

12. The V&A's European Ornament Gallery (opened 1992), curated by Michael Snodin and Maurice Howard, approached style in an innovative way. See Snodin, M. and Howard, M., *Ornament: A Social History since 1450* (New Haven and London, 1996).

13. See Styles, J., 'A New Gallery at the Victoria and Albert Museum', *History Workshop Journal*, 40 (1995), pp. 239–43. To publicise developments and encourage dialogue with historians and art historians outside the Museum, a session was organised at the 1995 Association of Art Historians conference entitled 'Nationalism, Politeness and Commerce: English Art and Design, 1660–1760', showcasing the themes for the reinstallation.

Chapter 4   The Educational Basis for the Galleries

Gail Durbin

Museum practice in the United Kingdom has become significantly more visitor-focused over the last decade. The election of New Labour to government in 1997 was one decisive factor in this change; that additional capital and revenue funding is now substantially dependent upon demonstrating commitment to education, access and social inclusion has undoubtedly focused minds in the museum sector on these issues. The new direction has been cautiously welcomed, particularly by local authority museums, because it has enabled them to contribute to efforts by councils to make their services more relevant and accessible to their communities. But the rush to produce learning strategies and social inclusion plans has not been matched by a radical shift in the balance of spending of core funding. Investment in learning, and the visitor research that enables it to be most effective, remains a relatively low priority in most institutions unless financed by the lottery, trusts, foundations, sponsors or the government itself. The deep integration of learning that is characteristic of the British Galleries is not typical of the sector.

One of the features of the V&A which distinguishes it from other national museums in the UK is that it owes its creation to the success of the Great Exhibition of 1851, and the great experiments in public education in the arts and sciences that followed it. In his inaugural lecture as director of the then South Kensington Museum in 1857, Henry Cole declared that, 'This museum will be like a book with its pages open and not shut.' A lot of water has flowed under the bridge since then, but throughout the last 160 years the V&A has retained its tradition of intellectual challenge and its commitment to working with colleges of art and design. In this, significantly, it has more in common with some major museums in the United States and Europe than it does with, say, the British Museum or the National Gallery.[1] The Museum did not begin as a gentlemen's club, and never became one.

Opportunities for staff exchanges and lecturing, as well as the fall in real terms of the cost of air travel, have made it possible for growing numbers of staff in museums, especially those working in national museums, to travel to Europe and North America to see alternative models of professional practice. Many leading museums in the United States, above all science and children's museums (rarely art museums) have invested heavily in visitor research and evaluation over the last quarter of a century. At institutions such as the Exploratorium in San Francisco, the Indianapolis Children's Museum and Colonial Williamsburg, provision for visitors achieved professional standards of research and practice which few museums, if any, in the UK can match. Bonnie Pitman's wise and accessible report *Excellence and Equity*, published in 1992 by the American Association of Museums, succinctly summarised the implications of this work. It remains a manual for change for tens of thousands of practitioners in the United States, and has influenced many more in this country.[2]

Environmental factors have also played a part. In the 1980s and 1990s, as a result of competition from the burgeoning leisure market and the opportunities for participation offered by digital communications media, our audiences have discovered that they can have experiences at home or in commercial leisure facilities that are participative, personally relevant and tailored to their needs. Evaluation of the old and new British Galleries suggests they want to enjoy similar, if not better, experiences at publicly-funded museums.[3]

In the UK, the move to design exhibits which engage visitors more actively began in science museums and science centres. The Natural History Museum and the Science Museum, the V&A's neighbours on Exhibition

Road, were among the first to employ exhibit evaluators and develop sophisticated methodologies for visitor research, inspired in part by American models. R.S. Miles's book *The Design of Educational Exhibits* provided UK museums with their first manual of development of interactive exhibits, albeit one that was based on theories of learning and communication that are now largely disregarded.[4] The National Maritime Museum in London and the National Museum of Scotland in Edinburgh both experimented with hands-on discovery rooms in the late 1980s and early 1990s, and shortly afterwards the National Gallery created a visual computer reference centre in the Micro Gallery which was, however, firmly set apart from the galleries.[5] These were exceptions. Other national art and cultural history museums stood firm in resisting the integration of visitor participation and interactive exhibits within their permanent galleries, and for the most part still do. It is this taboo that the V&A – one of the great art and cultural history institutions of the world – has now broken.

The British Galleries Project led to a fundamental rethinking of the way the V&A offers interpretation in its galleries. The Museum moved from a position where the focus of gallery redevelopments was overwhelmingly, if not exclusively, the selection and display of objects, to one where the needs of visitors became central to every aspect of the project, including object selection and design as well as interpretation.

Fundamental to this strategy was an attempt to question the assumption that shaping the visitor experience at the V&A should be almost exclusively expert-directed. This expert-direction, common at most large national museums, is reflected in displays where labels seldom allow that there may be several points of view, and it is supported by the architecture, which can be intimidating for people unfamiliar with such institutions. Some people respond well to the idea of an institution being expert-directed and they attend tours and lectures and possibly absorb the information they are given. For others, however, the experience is paralysing. It gives them the impression that unless they share that expertise they will be unable to understand or enjoy the objects on display. This fear accounts for the fact that teachers and lecturers are often reluctant to teach their students in open galleries in case they are heard giving the 'wrong' information. Recent research by the V&A, in partnership with the Institute of Education, has demonstrated how deep-rooted these anxieties can be, even for specialist art and design teachers working with a museum of art and design.[6]

Museums can do two things about this. First, they can find better ways to share their expertise, especially the skills of looking at objects. If they can teach techniques of visual analysis, rather than simply the outcomes of it, then they will be giving people a very valuable tool to help them look at any display. Second, museums can do more to recognise the personal expertise and knowledge that visitors have developed over a lifetime and find ways of unlocking and sharing that. We set out to do just those things in the British Galleries.

It is true that we started with the idea of telling a particular story. But, for the first time, Museum staff then analysed the content of the story from the perspectives of those for whom we were telling it, taking account of how they would perceive it. Were there ways to make the story more engaging or to tie it in with the needs of the visitor? Would participation create a greater sense of involvement? Could we introduce interpretive devices into the galleries to help people of all ages to look more closely at the objects or find a use in their own lives for information and ideas embodied in our displays?

We worked hard to develop these educational dimensions of the galleries. The project team was structured to create a firm educational foundation. The use of educational theory and audience research for developing and auditing our interpretation ensured that we created galleries with a variety of approaches to the collections and maximum accessibility. Extensive travel to look at examples of good practice elsewhere played an important role, and the principles that were established for the development of the galleries were strongly underpinned by educational research.

The team set up to create the galleries was different in its structure and organisation from previous teams. First, the Concept Team was just three people and, secondly, it included an educator.[7] It is not unusual in gallery developments in big scholarly museums for the team to be large and strongly weighted with curatorial and conservation professionals (an earlier attempt to redisplay the British Galleries had a team of about 26). The small size of the British Galleries Team made real debate possible and, because one member was an educator, audience and learning issues were constantly raised. Credit should also be given to Christopher Wilk as the lead curator, perhaps influenced by his North American perspective, for being open to new approaches to audiences. He was committed from the first to including a senior educator at the heart of the project, as a member of the Concept Team – a radical move for a national museum in the UK. Traditionally one of the questions a gallery team asks is 'What do we want to say?' or 'What do we want to display?', whereas on this team there were also the questions 'Who are we saying it to?' and 'What do they need from the galleries?'.[8]

Three period-based gallery teams were formed to develop the content of the galleries. Each of these teams also included an educator.[9] Some of the Museum's most experienced education staff were selected for this important project, and in consequence the schools service of the Education Department had almost to be closed, leaving only one member of staff in charge of training for teachers. Nonetheless, the Museum believed such a channelling of resources was worthwhile. The team role was a tough one for the educators, as this level of educational involvement represented a radical departure for the Museum.

The educators needed to be able to hold their own on the gallery teams, act as audience advocates, devise and argue for specific interpretation, and try to make this as relevant as possible to the theme or subject under discussion as well as to the needs of target audiences. This was intellectually challenging work – just as challenging as that required of curators on the project – which demanded skills that were different from those required for running museum education programmes. What is undoubtedly also true is that educators think differently from curators; their training and previous experience teaches them to have an audience perspective. They are more aware, because of their previous employment in education, of the huge intellectual range of the Museum's potential visitors, and they tend to be as interested in the process as the outcome.

Everyone working on the Gallery Teams put great energy into devising ways of making the ideas of the displays clear to different visitors, and some of the best interpretive ideas were the result of close collaboration between object specialist and visitor specialist. But, ultimately, it was the responsibility of the educators to focus on the interests of the visitor as well as on the objects. From the outset we were determined to identify who our audiences were and what they needed. We used the concepts of audience type and learning style to check that what we were offering was appropriate and sufficiently wide-ranging.

When the British Galleries Project started, the Museum had no specified target audiences, and there is no agreed classification of audiences in the cultural sector, so the project developed them. We drew up a list of groups who would want to use the displays. Our final list was:

- independent learners[10]
- families
- school groups
- Further and Higher Education groups[11]
- the local audience
- ethnic minority groups
- overseas visitors
- specialists, amateur and professional.

Initial quantitative research showed the percentages of people in the old British Galleries who identified themselves as belonging to one or more of our target groups (the categories were not exclusive):[12]

- specialists 23%
- independent learners 62%
- families 31%
- overseas visitors 44%

The numbers in the four other groups were too low to be significant. The fact that some of the groups were small in number was not in itself a reason to ignore them. Rather, it confirmed that the Museum needed to do more to reach them. By this time, the watchword of the project had become *variety* and we aimed to address the differing needs even of minority interests.

Eight different audiences is a very high number to target, but we did this because the galleries cover such a large area of the Museum. If we had been dealing with a single gallery, then it might have been appropriate to have a single primary audience, but with galleries that cover 10% of the Museum's vast display space, we felt that we had to be inclusive. In reality, these audiences overlap. It is possible to be a specialist in ceramics, for example, but to come to a museum with children as part of a family visit, so that one person may fit into several groups. It is also likely that, in this example, the presence of children will mean that the needs and behaviour of the adult in the group on this visit will have more in common with other family visitors than with specialists. The people in each group do not necessarily have common learning needs: specialists may want to see many similar objects close together, whereas for families convenient public transport or parking, accessible lavatories, a reasonable café and clarity of organisation are all essential preliminaries for a successful visit. By analysing the needs of each group, we could draw up lists of their requirements and then check to ensure our gallery plans catered for the needs of all our target groups.

The choice of groups was not without controversy. With little experience of basing gallery development on the needs of audiences, some staff in the Museum feared that we would alienate our 'traditional audiences' through the introduction of low- and high-tech interpretation. Some people even imagined that one consequence would be eight different sets of labels. Our research in the galleries shows that visitors generally appreciate a choice in interpretive approaches; if they are not interested, they simply ignore them.[13] Careful design also proved vital to the successful integration of interpretation into all the galleries.

With hindsight, we would not have selected ethnic minority groups as a separate target group. The educational needs of a well-established immigrant community may be very different from one that is newly arrived. We would have achieved more by choosing to tackle such access issues as language or cultural difference across all audiences. It is also true that the project addressed some audience groups better than others. The local audience, for example, was not well served. The café and the changing displays that would have provided for their needs (especially as repeat visitors) were written out of the project at a very early stage because of a fundamental decision that the British Galleries could not unilaterally address Museum-wide questions, such as the shortage of catering facilities or lack of spaces for small exhibitions.

Side by side with drawing up our list of target audiences, we conducted research into the characteristics and learning needs of each of the nominated audiences.[14] We then thought about the implications of the results for gallery design and drew up a chart showing each target group and their needs. The characteristics of independent learners, taken from that chart, provide an illustration of the process we undertook (fig. 7). The chart is reproduced in full in appendix 5.

Figure 7.

Characteristics of independent learners:[15]

- manage their own learning (they are not driven by a formal curriculum);

- motivated by internal incentives and curiosity;

- draw on their own experiences, cultural background and interests;

- problem-centred (may, for example, wish to know how to dress the set for an amateur dramatic society production);

- not restricted by conventional subject boundaries (so that the Museum's curatorial divisions, such as Textiles and Fashion or Ceramics and Glass, have little importance to an independent learner interested in gardening or bee-keeping);

- see themselves as part of a larger learning community linked by word of mouth as well as more formal networks.

Implications on gallery design for independent learners. Museums should:

- concentrate on providing varied methods of interpretation and a choice of routes through the interpretation, rather than worry too much about details of content since, by definition, it is not possible to predict the subject matter that will interest an independent learner;

- review museum practice. There is a conflict between the needs of independent learners and normal museum practice. The latter is expert-directed and creates dependence on the expert. It takes no account of differences in prior knowledge and experience, and designs displays that take no account of interest that is for a practical purpose;

- include in the galleries connections with ideas and information elsewhere, both inside and outside the museum;

- make museum decision-making more transparent;

- give visitors the opportunity to take on the role of expert within the galleries;

- find ways for visitors to exchange information;

- provide study areas.

It will be apparent from this list that the British Galleries could not comprehensively address all of these needs and characteristics (for example, we can have little influence over visitors' existing internal incentives and curiosity), but we managed to meet many of them.

After reviewing research, we decided to use ideas about learning style as another way to think about communicating with our audiences.[16] We worked with four learning styles: analytical, common sense or problem-solving, experiential or dynamic, and imaginative. Within each of these groups, people learn in different ways. Some people prefer to learn from museums through a practical, hands-on approach, while others are more interested in starting from a theory and applying it. In her book *Exhibit Labels*, building on work by others over the previous 30 years, Beverley Serrell gives the following descriptions:[17]

- Analytical learners learn by thinking and watching, prefer interpretation that provides facts and sequential ideas, want sound logical theories to consider and look for intellectual comprehension. This is a group for whom traditional art and design museums with lots of objects and information on labels cater well.
- Common-sense learners learn by thinking and doing, prefer to try out theories and test them for themselves and look for solutions to problems.
- Experiential learners learn by feeling and doing, enjoy imaginative trial and error, prefer hands-on experience and look for hidden meaning.
- Imaginative learners learn by feeling and watching and by listening and sharing ideas, prefer interpretation that encourages social interaction, like to be given opportunities to observe and to gather a wide range of information and to look for personal meaning.

Traditionally the V&A, like many other major art museums, has catered very well for analytical learning, and presents some stimuli for common-sense learning, but has done little for experiential and imaginative learning. We planned the galleries so that visitors in any of the audience categories, or those who favoured a particular learning style, could come to the galleries and find material that appealed to them. So, for example, families or people with a preference for experiential learning could assemble a replica eighteenth-century chair from components stored in racks in the discovery areas – hands-on interactive areas aimed at families but heavily used by adult visitors – and learn about its construction. Alternatively, analytical learners could use the British Galleries Online database to study, for example, glass or costume of a particular period. Imaginative learners could choose to contribute a story about a painting on display to a file of other examples, typed up and maintained in the galleries. Schools, on the other hand, might opt to watch a video about the Great Exhibition, in a film room large enough to seat a whole class. Study of the Great Exhibition is part of the national curriculum, and the video helps pull together the many objects from the displays and look at the historical evidence that they provide.

Analysis of learning style offers an extremely practical criterion for auditing the interpretive devices in a museum gallery. Ideally, all interpretive approaches would stimulate the full range of human learning behaviour, but in practice this is very difficult. Some objects and ideas will always tie in better with certain learning styles. To check that we had covered the full range, we looked at all our interpretive ideas to see which learning styles they served well. Our aim was to ensure that anyone from one of our target groups, or any visitor with a preferred learning style, could go round the galleries and find enough that met their needs and appealed to their learning style. Throughout the project, we used our lists of audience groups and learning styles to audit our ideas and help create the appropriate balance.

Since these approaches to galleries and audiences were new for most of the project team we set up a training programme with a combination of visiting speakers and visits. This gave us the opportunity to share experiences with staff from other museums. We also decided on a different role for gallery staff within the British Galleries during opening hours – as Gallery Assistants rather than Warders – and ran a three-week training course to introduce them to the Museum, their role and the educational concepts behind the galleries.

The importance of visiting galleries at other institutions as an element in establishing the educational focus of the British Galleries cannot be overemphasised. At the start of the project, the Concept Team did not know each other very well, and we certainly approached the project from different professional perspectives. In the course of the first 18 months, the three of us visited new or recent displays where much thought had gone into how ideas would be presented to visitors. We made an eight-day trip to museums on the east coast of the United States and in Canada. We made another trip to selected cities in the West and Midwest of the USA. Once Dinah Casson had been appointed as designer, we repeated some of the journeys to share the experience with her. Further visits to Paris and Stockholm were made, once the wider gallery teams were established.

We found no single museum that reflected our aspirations for the galleries, but we saw many individual ideas that we wanted to adapt for our galleries. Some of the strongest influences came from the Art Gallery of Ontario, where the work of educator Douglas Worts showed how the visitor experience of a museum or gallery occurs at the point where the museum's agenda meets the visitor's agenda. Invitations to respond to the displays in writing and through drawing gave glimmers of what was going through visitors' minds as they looked at the works of art. Many people were experiencing strong emotional reactions, but few of these could be anticipated. They were responding less to museum interest in a painting's colour and composition, for example, than to the way in which what they saw resonated with their current personal concerns.[18] Additionally, the AGO showed how interpretive devices could be built into the galleries without spoiling the atmosphere. Pieces of specially designed furniture, which did not look odd or out of place in an art gallery, held audio equipment in the arms or provided working surfaces behind seats. Later, as part of our training course, we invited Worts and a colleague to spend a day in London with the whole project team, discussing the AGO approach.

The Museum of the American Indian in New York demonstrated that there can be no definitive view of an object, by providing alternative labels and in certain displays having every label signed by its author. Information stated whether the writer was a member of a particular Native American tribe, anthropologist, curator or craftsperson, leaving the visitor to judge the influence this may have had on what they wrote.[19] The Denver Art Museum impressed us by being permeated with a concern for learning. Every floor had a small library or video collection or audio point, short bibliographies were left round the galleries, seats were placed very close to displays, additional labelling was available for those who wanted it, and games and handling material were available. At the most basic level, visitors could help themselves to portable stools. Within the UK, the new Museum of Scotland in Edinburgh (then also at the development stage) had decided to incorporate digital interactive exhibits next to historical artifacts (something cultural and visual arts museums had hitherto resisted). This example reinforced the decision we had made to do the same

Travel also worked at a more fundamental level. It enabled the Concept Team to get to know each other. We found out about each other's prejudices and aspirations. We could discuss, on neutral territory, what worked for each of us and what didn't. We could discuss our own reactions to labels or videos or display techniques. We could observe together visitor behaviour we would have to deal with or encourage. But above all we shared the experience of being the visitor and looking at huge and unfamiliar displays with sore feet. We observed how little time we, who had a professional interest, actually spent reading panels and how quickly our attention to gallery videos flagged. We found we had different approaches to the interpretation. Christopher Wilk would look with intensity for very short periods but seldom try a practical activity himself, whereas I would generally want to have a go. Sarah Medlam was very selective in what she engaged with and was strongly averse to certain screen-based types of activity. We were the embodiment of different learning styles.

We took photographs and slides as reminders, we bought postcards and made notes. If I were to do this again, I personally would pay more attention to recording the experience in whatever ways were available to keep the experience vivid in my mind – perhaps a scrapbook or something more like an illustrated journal that included personal reflection and records of the names and contact details of all whom we met. I would try to fix everything in this single place. Travel of this sort is a wonderful experience but it is also very hard work and tiring, and museums start to merge in the memory. It is important to preserve the detail.

These visits were drawn on subsequently in all sorts of circumstances. We built up material for some very useful slide lectures on interpretation, we talked to our Gallery Teams, we showed material to the educators. However, its most significant legacy lay with the Concept Team. It changed our relationship. We now had joint prejudices and in-jokes. Travelling, looking and experiencing other museums had provided a common experience that was often referred to throughout the project. We could draw on the same images and the intensity of the experience; eating together, struggling with luggage and waiting for planes together created a closeness that helped three diverse people survive a five-year project.

A significant function of the Concept Team was to establish the principles for the development of the galleries. These included other educational principles. A significant one was that any interpretive device would, where possible, be placed next to the object being interpreted.

One of the aims in redisplaying the British Galleries was to make the objects and ideas they contain more interesting and accessible to the full range of potential visitors. This has been achieved in part by displaying the objects to their best advantage and, we hope, through clarity in gallery text. But it has also been achieved by introducing into the galleries a wide range of interpretive devices integrated within the displays to help make some points more obvious and to cater for the wide range of learning styles. The purpose of these interventions is to help visitors to use their eyes, look more closely at the objects on display and to understand or enjoy them in a manner that fits their needs. The devices range from videos and audio programmes, where more information is given, through computer interactives where visitors can influence outcomes, to activities like writing a mini-saga based on a painting where the content is generated entirely by the visitor.

Some art museums are nervous about interpretive devices, fearing that they will interfere with the 'pure' experience of relating to the object, and so, if they have them at all, they set up separate interpretive spaces. We were keen to avoid this. Interpretation is needed at the point curiosity arises. It is unreasonable to expect, in places as packed with interesting visual diversions as the V&A, that the point of query and the intensity of need will be retained if visitors have to walk some distance to satisfy it.

A conflict often arose between interpretation and aesthetics, especially once the project had prospered to the point where individual interpretive devices were being designed. Having decided to have costume that people could dress up in, we had to accept that some visitors would leave it untidy. In these circumstances discovery areas within the galleries seemed to be necessary. Once you go down the route of discovery areas, you need to put things in them. Initially the activities will be potentially messy ones, but you soon start to put other items there to follow a theme or to create balance. We were determined to include display cases within these areas so that related objects were always immediately available near by and to avoid interpretation becoming isolated from the displays.

Once we had settled on the general principles for interpretation in the galleries, it was my task to write an interpretive plan (see appendix 6).[20] This outlined the different series of interpretive devices we planned for the galleries. Some of these were high-tech, including the computer programs, videos and audio programmes.[21] 'How was it made' seemed an obvious subject for a series of videos, since so many visitors are captivated by this question. 'Object in focus' videos came from long years of working with functional objects and the non-specialist public. It is surprising how many clues about the history of an object go unnoticed by people not used to using their eyes. The audio series 'Talking about Art and Design' was originally intended to be restricted to historical comment about our objects from texts that were contemporary with the period of their making. As we were able to identify fewer such accounts than hoped, many of the programmes in this series consist of the comments of a single well-known designer (or poet, or garden historian). The series benefited from this change. Other series did not require digital technology: dressing up, construction activities and handling collections are a few examples (colour plates 60–62).

It was the job of the Gallery Teams to come up with interpretive ideas that would fall within the series outlined in the interpretive plan or to suggest new ideas that would work better. They were guided in thinking about what was relevant and what was not by the Purpose Statement for each subject recorded in the Framework Document. We asked the gallery teams to write these for each display, and the texts turned out to be enormously helpful. They helped keep the intellectual focus of the galleries by providing criteria for the selection of objects. The Gallery Teams could not propose objects simply because they liked them; the objects had to support the subject of the display. Similarly, any interpretive device had also to support the purpose of the display or it was judged irrelevant.

Once the teams had drawn up their final list of interpretive devices, these were considered at a single session by the Concept Team, who rejected some as inappropriate or ugly or impossible to squeeze in, but most were accepted. A project manager was employed to liaise with the exhibition designer and with the graphic designers to plan the design of the devices, to ensure that they would fit, and to work with manufacturers to ensure their production was of appropriate quality and their delivery was timely. The production of some interpretive devices required less of this liaison and did not need to be designed in a 'house style'. These should have been begun earlier, avoiding last-minute uncertainty.

It may be a little early to say what impact the project has had on V&A working practices. This will become clear only over time. For the moment we can say three things. There is now an expectation that all new galleries will include interpretive devices. The selection will depend upon available resources, aim of the gallery, target audience(s) and gallery design. Observation of new projects underway at the V&A shows an enthusiasm for videos and databases, which are about telling visitors things, but suggests that it may be more difficult to get agreement for the more hands-on activities, which are about visitors making their own discoveries. This is partially because low-tech devices need more regular and varied types of maintenance, but it is also to do with differing views about the appropriateness of especially hands-on interpretation within gallery spaces. For some curatorial colleagues, activities within proximity of museum objects remain an objectionable idea.

It is noteworthy that after the British Galleries, more junior staff are being included in new projects and, with the exception of very large or well-funded projects, they are tending to have only a single educator as part of the team (the British Galleries had four). You need to be a very strong person to sustain an advocacy role alone, and seniority helps. In addition, it is unlikely that in future new galleries and devices at the V&A will be planned without audience research or testing and evaluation. The value of this has been learnt by the organisation; it is simple and easy, does not need huge resources, and can improve devices and help avoid expensive mistakes. Third, a lesson to be drawn from the British Galleries is that we need to continue to train our staff in audience issues if we want to create more audience-focused galleries. The only way to keep interpretation lively and dynamic is for staff to be personally engaged in current audience research and to be aware of current developments in the field of interpretation.

The British Galleries have been well received because they contain stunning objects, are intellectually coherent and look beautiful, but they are also liked because there is something for everyone. We used an analysis of different learning styles and the needs of different visitor types to audit our interpretive ideas and develop galleries that appeal to many at different levels. People are not excluded because their learning style differs from the institutional norm or because their needs are different from those of the mythical 'average visitor'.

The British Galleries have proved one point beyond doubt, which can be observed any day of the week without extensive research. Interpretive devices are not just for children. Those involved with education know this, but for others a brief walk through the galleries will show adults trying on costume, using building bricks, testing their knowledge of style on a computer or having a go at tapestry weaving. Our task is now to find out, in greater depth, what they are learning.

Notes I am grateful to David Anderson and Christopher Wilk for their contributions to this essay.
1. Burton, Anthony, *Vision and Accident: The Story of the Victoria and Albert Museum* (London, 1999).
2. Pitman, Bonnie (ed.), *Excellence and Equity* (Washington, 1992).
3. Evaluation by the V&A of the British Art and Design Galleries (1998, not published) and evaluation of the new galleries, Creative Research (2002), *Summative Evaluation of the British Galleries: Report of Research Findings* (appendix 9).
4. Miles, R.S., *et al.*, *The Design of Educational Exhibits* (London, 1988).
5. Anderson, David, 'Learning History in Museums', in *International Journal of Museum Management and Curatorship*, vol.8, no.4 (December 1989), pp. 357–68.
6. Robins, Claire, and Woollard, Vicky, *Creative Connections: Working with Teachers to Use Museums and Galleries as a Learning Resource* (London, 2003).
7. The Concept Team consisted of Christopher Wilk, Sarah Medlam and Gail Durbin. John Styles served as historical adviser to the project.
8. It should be emphasised that this is the perspective of a large national museum. Colleagues

in regional and local museums tend to have a much longer and stronger tradition of audience focus.

9. The Educators were Morna Hinton, David Judd, Colin Mulberg (until July 2001) and Celia Franklin (from July 2001).

10. Independent learners were defined by this project as those who learn from museums but are not governed by a formal curriculum. They are difficult to define precisely and could, on the most liberal definition, be any adult not part of a formal educational group who sets foot in a museum. For the purposes of this specific survey, they were defined as anyone who said they had done any one of the following: planned to visit the British Galleries; belonged to a related club or society; expressed a professional or amateur interest; could specify something they had learnt from the galleries.

11. Further Education is generally vocational in character and available to students of 16-plus. Higher Education is generally academic in character and available to students of 18-plus.

12. In total, 252 people were interviewed. Of the 1012 people approached, 330 refused, 129 were rejected because they were either under 12 years of age or V&A staff, and 301 were excluded because there was no common language. Creative Research (1997i) Audience Research for the British Galleries: quantitative research findings, volume 1, p. 7.

13. 64% of visitors stopped and used an interpretive device but only 1% (i.e. a tiny minority of those who did not engage with the interactives) felt that the interpretation detracted from their appreciation of the objects (Creative Research, *Summative Evaluation of the British Galleries: Report of Research Findings* [2002], pp. 53–54).

14. Some of the principal sources were:

Anderson, D., *A Report on Museum Education in the United Kingdom*, for the Department of National Heritage, in association with the DfEE, the Scottish Office, the Welsh Office and the Northern Ireland Office, 1st draft (1996), unpublished. Later published with revisions as Anderson, D., *A Common Wealth: Museums in the Learning Age* (London, 1999).

Eckstein, J., and Feist, A. (eds), *Cultural Trends*, 3/12 (1991), pp. 70–79.

Eckstein, J., and Feist, A. (eds), *Cultural Trends*, 4/14 (1992), pp. 1–7.

Falk, J.H., and Dierking, L.D., *The Museum Experience* (Washington, DC (1992).

Hooper-Greenhill, E., *Museums and their Visitors* (London, 1994).

15. Brookfield, S., *Understanding and Facilitating Adult Learning* (San Francisco, 1986).

16. McCarthy, B.N.D., and Pitman-Gelles, B., 'The 4MAT System: Teaching to Learning Styles with Right/Left Mode Technique', in *The Sourcebook 1998* (American Association of Museums, 1998).

17. Serrell, B., *Exhibit Labels: An Interpretive Approach* (London, 1996), p. 51.

18. Worts, Douglas, 'Extending the Frame: Forging a New Partnership with the Public', in Pearce, S. (ed.), *Art in Museums* (Athlone Press, 1995), pp. 165–91.

19. While we did not include signed labels (although the possibility was discussed), this visit highlighted our awareness of the need to be as transparent as possible to visitors about the choices we made in the galleries.

20. Durbin, G., *Interactive Learning in the British Galleries* (2002). http://www.vam.ac.uk/bg-interactive_learning (consulted 26 August 2003).

21. Brod, N., *Diving in at the Deep End: The British Galleries at the V&A* (2002). http://www.archimuse.com/mw2002/papers/brod/brod.html (consulted 26 August 2003).

Chapter 5   The Organisation of the Project

Gwyn Miles and Nick Umney

Introduction

The British Galleries Project was undoubtedly a major undertaking for the V&A. The focus for building work at South Kensington over the ten years 1985–95 had been to get the Museum to function efficiently. This entailed overhauling the roofs, drainage and wiring, the provision of a functional fire alarm system, and a major redevelopment of a large wing at the north of the site to provide good working spaces for conservators and curators. This activity did not preclude redisplay of the collections: new galleries were opened for the arts of India, China, Japan and Korea, the Medieval Treasury and the Glass Gallery. Work was underway for a complete redisplay of the Silver Galleries. Therefore, by 1995, we had recent experience of running a variety of building and redisplay projects. The difference with the British Galleries was that we were tackling a very large area of the building (10% of display space of the entire Museum) and aiming to complete the work within five years, a much shorter time-span than the Museum usually followed for comparable redisplays (fig. 5).

The advent of lottery funding meant that we could be ambitious and tackle such a large area of display at one time. It allowed us to include building infrastructure within the project – the provision of a ramp at the main entrance, two lifts to give direct access into the galleries, toilets and climate control. However, the application procedure for lottery grants at that time was arduous. We were working to a master-plan developed for the V&A in the 1980s, but we also had to prepare a conservation plan and a business plan, which meant we had to justify the expenditure by predicting a rise in visitor numbers and demonstrating good value for money. We had to give evidence that the project would conform to conservation and documentation standards. The provision of a variety of methods of interpretation in the galleries, including computer interactives, was something new for the V&A and the arts museum sector in general. This meant that the justification for this approach had to be robust and well-argued. Another important feature of lottery funding was that we had to map out (with a broad brush) the entire project in advance and show ourselves to be capable of delivering it within time and budget. Although providing a coherent case for redevelopment is obviously a prerequisite for any major development, the lottery procedures in the mid-1990s felt like an additional layer of bureaucracy added to the already familiar government rules to which the V&A was subject as a national museum funded directly by the Department of National Heritage.

Project team selection and set-up

From the beginning, we were determined to use this project as a model for future work, not only in terms of the quality of the displays themselves but also in the method of achieving them. The organisation of the project team was of great importance. The V&A as a whole operates as a machine bureaucracy with very clearly defined line management responsibilities.[1] Some types of matrix management had been attempted in the past, but with variable rates of success. We decided that to deliver this project efficiently we would need a dedicated project team with its own clear line management responsibilities working to a project director. However, it was also clear from the outset that the work of the project team would need to be supplemented by staff with particular skills, such as curators, conservators, photographers, technicians, etc., who were working within the normal departmental structure.

The first group, the Concept Team, was established in March 1996. This comprised two curators (Christopher Wilk and Sarah Medlam) and an educator (Gail Durbin). They were advised by a historian (John Styles). This small group forged the aims and narrative structure of the galleries (see chapter 2), the essential first step before deciding what had to be done and by whom.

Next, over the summer of 1996, we selected the Design Team. This group were independent consultants rather than V&A staff, and this required us to select the firms through advertisement in the *Official Journal of the European Community*. In addition to the obvious architectural and design services, we needed a project manager, a structural engineer, and a mechanical and electrical engineer, a quantity surveyor to keep track of the finances and a planning supervisor (see appendix 12). We selected an architect (Alistair Gourlay) to provide us with the structure for the gallery (shell and core) and exhibition designers (Casson Mann) to work within this structure to provide the displays. We also hired a team of Historic Decoration Consultants, headed by David Mlinaric, to advise on period details. A critical factor in the success of the project would be the co-ordination of the work of this complex Design Team.

Once we had a functioning Design Team, it became apparent that, in addition to the Concept Team working on the content of the galleries, we needed an Operations Team to project manage the dismantling of the galleries, the conservation and photography of the objects, label-writing, mount-making, interpretive device construction and the reinstallation of the galleries.[2] The V&A staff who carried out this work were used to working on discrete projects, such as exhibitions, loans and small redisplays. The scale of this project required better programming and monitoring. The Operations Team, formed in early 1997 and headed by Nick Umney, had to sort out the detailed programme for all the Museum operations and then monitor progress, highlighting any areas where work was falling behind schedule. Once established, the work of the three teams (Concept, Design and Operations) was co-ordinated through weekly meetings of the team leaders with the Project Director, Gwyn Miles. These four individuals understood and respected the different contributions made by each of the teams, and this made for a good working relationship. The three-team structure functioned well because roles were clear: the Concept Team was responsible for the ideas and intellectual development of the gallery; the Design Team developed the expression of those ideas in the physical form which would be experienced by visitors; and the Operations Team arranged the nuts and bolts of emptying the galleries, preparing the objects and other deliverables and completing the reinstallation.

To prepare and deliver the content of the displays required (what we called) gallery teams, working to the Concept Team. Because we were working across a wide chronology, we decided that there should be three gallery teams working in parallel, dealing with the consecutive historical periods – Tudors and Stuart, Hanoverian and Victorian (see chapter 8). Again, we felt it was important for these teams to be multi-disciplinary – curators, working with educators and historians. This was a new departure for the V&A, as was the decision to appoint relatively junior members of curatorial staff to lead these teams, with more senior subject specialists in an advisory role. This mixture of skills worked well as we hammered out the content, working with the exhibition designers to shape evocative and informative displays.

The integration of so many interpretive devices in the galleries was new for the V&A. It necessitated new, dedicated staff to project manage both the design and development of the interactives. One individual was responsible for all digital media; another person worked on the hands-on, 'low-tech' material.[3] We hired consultants to develop both the video programmes and the computer interactives, working to the multimedia project manager. Once the programmes had been developed and tested, we assigned individuals, some from within the gallery teams and others from across the Museum, to prepare the content.

Thus in setting up the project team we developed a complex structure, both for the work carried out by V&A staff and for the external consultants (fig. 8). As many of the individuals in the teams had little or no experience of working on large projects, we ran several project-management training sessions, facilitated by an external consultant, Francis Hallam. This was a useful mechanism initially for setting out what we needed to achieve and subsequently helped the group to learn to work together amicably. With hindsight, the most important factor in setting up the team was the selection of highly motivated people.

Systems and communications

The key tool in delivering the project was a coherent programme which would be communicated to all members of the team. The purpose of the programme was to set out what would be delivered in the new galleries and the activities, roles and responsibilities to achieve it on time. The project was broken down into manageable tasks, which were identified with the people who would carry them out. The trick of a good programme was then to reintegrate the separated tasks to give the desired overall result.

The model adopted for programme organisation and responsibilities is shown in fig. 9. This was both integrated and hierarchical. Level 3 contains individual programmes for conservation, photography, cataloguing, decant, etc. These were developed by the individuals named in the boxes in level 3, usually a member of the project team ('consumer') working in partnership with a service provider and co-ordinated by the Assistant Project Manager responsible for documentation and information management. Information in these programmes was 'rolled up' to produce level 2 programmes to enable us to identify objectives, resource needs and schedule compatibility between design, construction and Museum operations. A further integrating step was taken to produce an overall master programme that provided a reality check on the more detailed views and supported the funding bid and Steering Group needs.[4] To align the separate, parallel views of the project to a common objective required good communication. We had to share information unsparingly, but we also had to understand one another's views of the project (which were very different), so that we could see what was important for each of us to achieve success. The ability to share information effectively and efficiently was a major requirement but one which the Museum was not able to meet at the beginning of the project.

The Museum's central inventory and cataloguing database (the Collections Information System or CIS) had been developed some years previously and did not at this time allow project-specific information to be recorded. The needs of the curatorial team early in the project to record such additional information resulted in the development of a relatively simple, stand-alone database. Further stand-alone systems already existed or were developed to support conservation and the planning of large-scale gallery decants. Up to the beginning of 1998 at least four different independent electronic tools were in use to record important information about objects in the project. The need to enable these systems to come together was readily apparent. However, it required some evolution in the Museum's technology and sustained effort over nearly a year to complete the development and implementation of an integrated system, to get everything

8. British Galleries Project Structure.

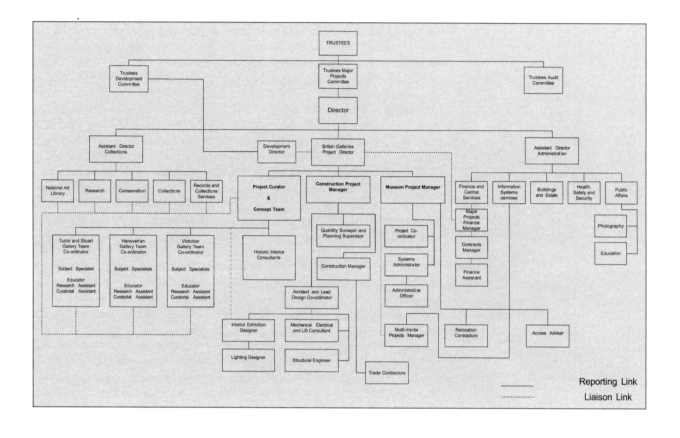

*9. Programme Organisation,
February 1998.*

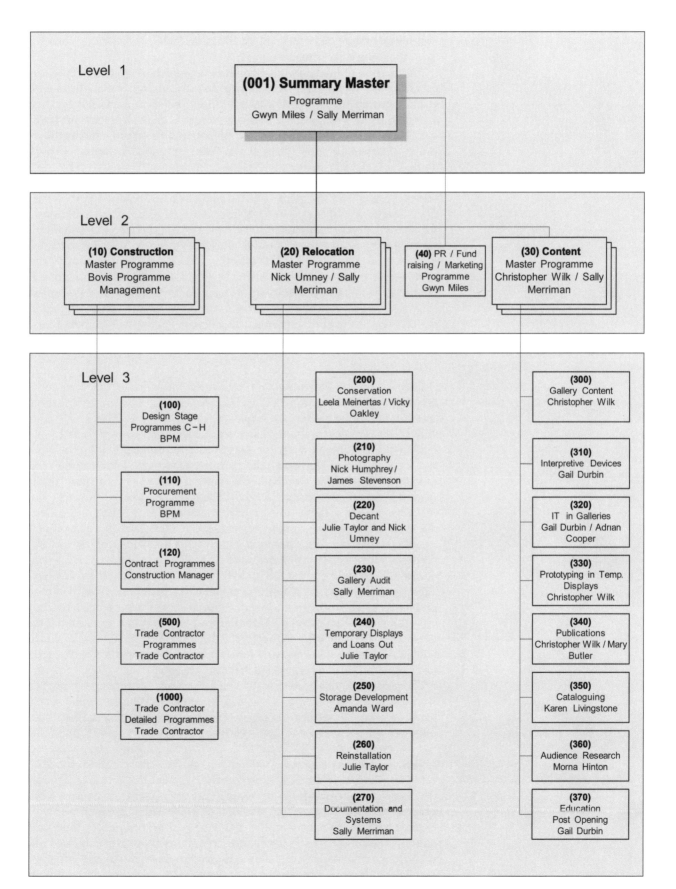

Level 1

(001) Summary Master
Programme
Gwyn Miles / Sally Merriman

Level 2

(10) Construction
Master Programme
Bovis Programme
Management

(20) Relocation
Master Programme
Nick Umney / Sally
Merriman

(40) PR / Fund
raising / Marketing
Programme
Gwyn Miles

(30) Content
Master Programme
Christopher Wilk / Sally
Merriman

Level 3

(100)
Design Stage
Programmes C – H
BPM

(110)
Procurement
Programme
BPM

(120)
Contract Programmes
Construction Manager

(500)
Trade Contractor
Programmes
Trade Contractor

(1000)
Trade Contractor
Detailed Programmes
Trade Contractor

(200)
Conservation
Leela Meinertas / Vicky
Oakley

(210)
Photography
Nick Humphrey /
James Stevenson

(220)
Decant
Julie Taylor and Nick
Umney

(230)
Gallery Audit
Sally Merriman

(240)
Temporary Displays
and Loans Out
Julie Taylor

(250)
Storage Development
Amanda Ward

(260)
Reinstallation
Julie Taylor

(270)
Documentation and
Systems
Sally Merriman

(300)
Gallery Content
Christopher Wilk

(310)
Interpretive Devices
Gail Durbin

(320)
IT in Galleries
Gail Durbin / Adrian
Cooper

(330)
Prototyping in Temp.
Displays
Christopher Wilk

(340)
Publications
Christopher Wilk / Mary
Butler

(350)
Cataloguing
Karen Livingstone

(360)
Audience Research
Morna Hinton

(370)
Education
Post Opening
Gail Durbin

transferred on to it and everybody able to use it while maintaining continuity in provision of information.

The creation of a database enabling the functional integration of information from several different sources provided all Museum stakeholders with an authoritative list of objects selected for the project and accurate location information. This in turn gave us the key ability to plan all object operations and, crucially, allowed analysis of the information about progress in conservation, photography, etc. Users of the system eventually numbered hundreds across the Museum.

A structured paper filing system was set up, and machine-readable files were organised in directories corresponding to the categories in the paper filing system. Email became a very important communication tool during the life of the project, and considerable effort was expended to try to develop document management through the email package in use at the time. However, after twelve months' effort and considerable expenditure this could not be made reliable and had to be abandoned. A project intranet was created in 1999 and became more widely available across the Museum in 2000. This was very well designed and carried much key information, but the take-up of this then-unfamiliar technology was slow. Attempts to use an intranet-based approach to collate detailed tasks for the project team had to be abandoned at prototype stage as the technology was not then sufficiently robust.

The measures described worked well within the Museum but were not as effective in promoting the vital flow of information between the Museum and the various consultants we employed. In particular, we could have done with better facilities for sharing electronic information on objects, and especially images of objects, with our designers. The Museum's data protection and security system (firewall) made this extremely difficult. Hosting projects on the worldwide web will be a future option. As it was, most information between the Museum and consultants passed in paper form.

Meetings were a simple and effective method of distributing and collecting project information among project stakeholders as well as for understanding and reconciling different perceptions and for working towards decisions. However, the communications loop was often broken, and informal decisions made without the full knowledge of all the stakeholders involved. This sometimes led to conflicting approaches being taken to common problems. In addition, contractors' representatives were changed at some crucial points in the project. Constant effort was required to reinforce the need for each group of stakeholders to be represented by a single named individual who could determine future actions. A report of progress, risks and targets was printed and circulated every month.

The point of all this effort was to ensure that tasks, schedules and progress were understood and communicated. The initial effort of developing a programme led to an attempt to describe the entire project in detail from four different perspectives – the task, the timeline, the resources required and the location of the work. Eventually, over 33,000 separate tasks were described in a series of linked gant charts in an attempt to control the project at a high level of detail. It soon became apparent that trying to describe or control the project in this level of detail was absurd for two very important reasons. First, while the use of project-management software worked well for the programmer, many people on the project found the method of display hard to understand. Even more importantly, the idea that everything is mapped out and then actioned is fundamentally flawed. In the real world things do not happen in that way. Thus planning them in huge detail only increases the probability that things will not go according to plan.

When people understood what had to be delivered and when it was required, giving them the freedom to incorporate knowledge of local conditions to determine how targets should be met, the likelihood increased that things would be done on time. As the project progressed, the programming effort continued the trend towards simplification and integration of the various detailed programmes into a smaller number of authoritative statements of project deliverables. In all areas, the monitoring of progress against programme was achieved through regular meetings with nominated individuals having delegated responsibility for programme progress. Numerical methods such as those illustrated in figs 10 and 11 proved the most effective means of monitoring these activities.

Good access to information was vital to the successful completion of the British Galleries Project, but it took some time to get the proper tools together to do it. As a result of the experience of the British Galleries Project, a project support package has been developed that provides shared access for all stakeholders to information required to support core processes.

Decant   Before any building work could take place, the existing galleries and associated stores had to be closed and their contents, some 6000 objects and twelve period room sets, relocated into a variety of destinations. A few went to existing galleries, some to a temporary gallery, 'Best of British', created for teaching and prototyping purposes (colour plates 74–77), but the majority went into redeveloped storage at an existing offsite location. Our task was to complete the relocation without loss, damage or theft of objects or injury to personnel or the building. Good planning of the object decant was vital to ensure that construction would begin on time.

Before the decant began, an audit was undertaken which ensured that all objects were fully documented, photographed and marked with their correct, unique Museum identification. A conservation condition survey using standard condition codes (1–4) and damage categories enabled us to assess objects that might be at risk during the move, to carry out remedial work and to develop method statements for packing and moving.[5] It also provided good information on dimensions needed to assess the space requirements of the move and assess the potential workload for reinstallation.

Museum technicians were assisted by specialist art movers and conservation contractors, who removed the period rooms and objects that were taken off-site. Their contract allowed us to work out costs and timings well in advance of a final object list and date being available, and provided an incentive to get the job done within a fixed term from the start. Generic method statements for packing, moving, transport and unpacking, developed for standard object types were used to work out schedules of rates for materials and labour. Specific method statements were developed for large and difficult objects. Good method statements and documentation were vital to manage risk.

Object-by-object packing into sealed consignments was recorded and signed off by both the contracted movers and the Operations Team to verify adherence to agreed methods and to check that all objects were sound and intact, both on despatch and arrival. Each consignment was monitored throughout its journey, and a separate independent list of arrivals was checked against departures to ensure that everything was accounted for.[6]

The substantial planning time available and careful rehearsal of this operation paid dividends in securing the desired result within time and budget allowances. The Museum was able to hand over the site on schedule to the construction managers on 21 May 1999.

Mitigation of construction impact

All affected areas of the Museum were surveyed to determine likely risks to collections and to identify any risks to the normal operation of the Museum arising from construction. After fire, probably the most serious damage could have arisen from (massive) insecure loads falling from height while being craned into position over the Museum's ceramics galleries. However, far more likely was that someone would drop a scaffolding pole through a roof light while building the crash deck designed to protect against such an unlikely event.

We aimed to put in place measures to protect the Museum and its collections while allowing construction to proceed without unnecessary disruption or delay. To protect against fire, breaches of security, noise and dust, the site was isolated with fire-retardant partitions from the rest of the Museum, and access was strictly controlled.[7] Authorised personnel were required to enter and leave via a single control point where they were checked for safety boots, hats and high visibility vests, issued with a badge and logged into the computerised access control system. Use of water and other hazardous materials on site was very strictly controlled.

Standard guidelines for contractors were issued by the Museum. Meetings were held with the construction managers and Museum representatives in each area that might be affected by construction work to enable everyone to understand each other's needs and fears before work started. Subsequently, demonstrations by contractors of proposed methods of work were arranged for curators and conservators to assess the potential impact on collections of each of the proposed construction techniques. Monitoring of dust and vibration in potentially sensitive and at-risk areas demonstrated the effectiveness of the control measures adopted. A regular monthly forum of stakeholder representatives was instigated to track progress and to deal with matters arising as the programme progressed. Project managers met weekly, building a level of trust that helped to curtail undesirable activities at source and develop more effective controls without bringing work to a standstill.

Handover

Having passed through the difficult first stage of heavy construction and fit-out without major incident, we then began a period of phased handover of gallery spaces from the construction manager to the Museum. This second stage in the programme was allocated to the Museum as a time for installation of objects. A third stage was allowed for the completion of fit-out work by contractors on items such as barrier rails, graphics and security systems and for snagging, which could only take place following object installation. Well in advance, we agreed organisation of work on site once object installation was underway. We instigated a series of inspections, beginning four weeks before handover, to try to reduce to a minimum the level of snagging that would be required after objects had been installed. Environmental conditions were monitored independently by the Museum in the run-up to and after the installation of sensitive material and while air-handling plant was being commissioned and tested. As a result, it was found necessary to introduce additional temporary measures for object protection, including dehumidification and the creation of temporary screens and partitions using wood and polythene.

The sequence and timing of gallery handover was carefully planned to ensure that appropriate access and security controls remained in force. Access control was achieved using full-height partitions between adjacent areas of work, and Museum security staff operating a signing-in and out system within the handed-over spaces. Cleanliness in Museum areas was aided by the partitions, dust mats and overshoes. Once an area had been handed over to the Museum, all subsequent work by contractors in that area was under a permit to work system. In the closing stages of the project we moved from a completely closed site to a completely open site.

Despite the efforts of the Museum and the Design Team to provide a smooth transition from building site to gallery, the Museum found it a continuous uphill struggle to manage the risks arising from the activities of the contractors. The contractors were mostly too polite to say that they found it a continuous uphill struggle to complete the building in the face of the Museum's attempts to control them. However, no serious injury, damage or loss occurred, and the galleries were eventually completed to a generally good overall standard. Giving each of the contractors a financial incentive in the finished product (rather than just the delivery of their particular component) might have made a difference.

Preparing deliverables The project deliverables included: conserved and mounted objects, period rooms, mounts and fixings, labels, low-tech interpretive devices and high-tech multimedia interactives. The necessary activities of conservators, photographers, curators, technicians and others were established as early as possible, so that we could identify the size of the task and its implications and the processes by which work would be managed. Estimating the resources required was carried out thoroughly by using aggregated historical records and also setting up trials of small batches of objects and using benchmarking of individuals' performances as a guide. It was most important to agree how, and how frequently, progress would be measured against these targets. Frequency of review is commonly known as control interval.[8] Initially, we set most control intervals at two weeks, until we were reasonably confident that a process was working, and then monthly. At later stages in the project, when complex mount-making processes were being carried out against tight installation deadlines, the control interval was weekly. In the final stages of installation it was daily.

Preparation of deliverables was linked to installation, which in turn followed the sequence determined for construction and fit-out and the production of design information needed to support them. It was arranged at the beginning of the project that all work would start in the gallery space furthest away from the point of entry to the site and that work was to be completed in phases on a gallery-by-gallery basis.

Phased deadlines were set for tasks to coincide with installation; therefore, the amount of time available was known and, by-and-large, fixed. The issue then was to use the available resources to best effect, setting priorities for the most urgent work, allocating resources on the basis of the size and importance of the task. For example, the first objects to go back would be those in the galleries in which construction was completed first. Within each gallery, large wall-mounted items would go in first. There were also requirements for particular items to be photographed for publication well before installation. Some of these required conservation, so this had to be done first.

The very largest items had to be ready in time to be brought on site using the site hoist. The hoist would need to be removed some months before completion of the galleries, so that windows removed to provide access to the galleries could be put back. For some objects, particularly textiles, conservation would need to be completed before mounts could be prepared (so their precise size would be known), and there would then be a further stage to be completed of mounting the conserved object before the object could be installed. There were many other such considerations to be taken into account. However, a balance had to be struck between carefully targeting resources and simply getting on with the job. Different approaches were adopted for the preparation of each deliverable; only a few important themes can be illustrated here.

Although every Museum object that would go into the galleries would need to be photographed, the most pressing requirement at the beginning of the project was to obtain photographs for the major publication accompanying the gallery.[9] These images were required far in advance of the gallery opening, and it was therefore decided to concentrate photography exclusively on these. Just after this decision was made, a form of trend analysis was adopted that allowed the whole status of photography for the project to be monitored in a matrix on one page of A4 paper (fig. 10). This was based on the known capacity of the studios to photograph particular types of objects. The matrix contained information about the numbers of each type of object photographed in each month, the numbers that needed to be photographed, the available time remaining and the absolute maximum capacity of the studio. It was therefore possible to see whether we were likely to achieve our targets at the current rate of progress and whether we still had the available capacity to do them at all. This demonstrated to us that the rate at which we were proceeding by specifically targeting the flagship publication was not fast enough overall and that we were not using the full capacity of the studios. The strategy was therefore changed, and we began to target any objects selected for the galleries, provided that their appearance in a photograph would not be altered by conservation treatment. Later in the project, this ability to see clearly what had been done and what remained to do allowed us to target more precisely areas of outstanding work, such as cataloguing or conservation.

Although the clock was ticking on the time set aside for object preparation, final decisions about object lists always take longer than expected. The generally preferred conservation approach was to work on the most demanding things first, as less demanding things could be included with reduced treatment if time got too tight. The risk that work would be wasted

Figure 10.
Photography Progress Chart,
December 1999.

Collection	Total no. A objects needing an approved CT	Total no. requisitions sent to date for all objects	Total new/ approved CTs (A objects)	Overall % complete	Objects photographed in December	No. of A objects remaining to photograph	Max studio capacity (per month)	Current monthly trend
Ceramics	638	432	390	61%	59	243	80-100	41
Far Eastern	90	52	28	31%	6	62		3
Furniture	339	198	100	29%	15	238	20-40	6
Indian	22	18	6	27%	5	16		1
Metalwork	557	367	190	34%	22	360	80-100	22
National Art Library	78	53	24	31%	14	54	200	5
Prints drawings and paintings	464	379	299	64%	34	155	400	41
Sculpture	123	75	42	34%	7	77	20-40	5
Textiles	381	171	127	33%	13	252	40-60	9
THM-BGM	19	19	0	0%	0	19		0
Total	2711	1764	1206	44%	175	1476		

if objects fell off the list as it matured was mitigated by careful selection of the objects to be worked on first. As far as possible, they were the ones that it would have been inconceivable to leave out. Once the object list became firmer, the principal concern was with volume. Trend analysis of both inputs and outputs was done to enable rates of progress to be assessed against the overall task to ensure the feasibility of completion. As a result of this, several actions were taken to improve the capacity and performance of some of the studios.[10]

Once confidence in our ability to do the whole job was established, our focus narrowed towards more specific conservation targets related to photography, mounting and installation. As we progressed towards installation, our approach became progressively more fine-grained. The interval of control was shortened (milestones became 'inch pebbles'), and tactics were changed as necessary in order to achieve targets. A system was adopted to show, on a single sheet of paper, the remaining work required by each conservation section to complete each gallery. We then moved from a situation in which conservators were giving us dates when items would be ready (supply-led) to one in which the project set detailed target dates for conservation to be completed (demand-led). To ensure consistency in quality, steps were taken to ensure that the remaining time available was spread evenly across the remaining objects. In the final stages of the project, the completion of objects was tied in detail to the availability of mounts and the schedule for installation.

As work on the design progressed, objects were changed. Some were omitted and new ones were included. It was possible to absorb some of this change, but in some cases it became necessary to set a capped limit to the resources available and ask those requesting the change to do so within those limits. Based on this and similar experiences, a useful guideline might be to allow 5–10% additional (restricted) resources for object preparation to allow for the inevitable process of refinement in the object selection during the life of the project.

The project started with established procedures for much of what had to be done. Roles and responsibilities had to be agreed as to what would be carried out by the project team members and what would remain the responsibility of individuals working elsewhere in the Museum. Some new procedures also had to be worked out. For example, the production of text for graphics and the British Galleries Online database had to be carefully controlled to ensure a quality product that was approved by all stakeholders. At the beginning of the project, processes were not necessarily geared up to project timescales or to harnessing the energy of such a large number of people as would be required.

Improving performance while engaged in the process of delivery has been likened to changing the gearbox while driving. Ideas (sometimes demands) for improvement were generated by customers (i.e. those making use of a product or service), by those responsible for supply and through the numerical information that was collected during performance measurement. Although these told us about the need for improvement, they did not necessarily tell us how to go about it

In all areas of the project it was possible to observe things that would tend to move the project forward and things that would tend to hold it back. While every project will have some different experiences, a few of the more general conclusions about what we would recommend to do and not do, based on the British Galleries experience are given below.

Clearly defined tasks and processes helped to move the project forward.

Clear statements about progress had the same effect. In the instance of text writing, league tables, the possibility of naming and shaming, peer group pressure, pressure in the management line, and good examples set by senior colleagues were all helpful in moving along the process of text writing. Appeal to an individual's good nature and their value to the project as well as an understanding ear all proved helpful too.

Sometimes, the sheer size of a task was a serious obstacle to progress. At one point, it seemed that we might never get together the material our graphic designers needed to allow them to start work in earnest. By waiting for all the text to be ready in order to manufacture the graphics for one whole gallery, we missed opportunities to progress in other areas, by finishing all the subject panel texts at one go, for example. Breaking tasks down into smaller, more manageable steps and making explicit decisions that we could all agree to were very important to making progress in this particularly complex area.

People were much more likely to give of their best if they felt really committed to the overall aims and objectives of the project and not that they were just supplying a product or service anonymously. At the beginning of the project a degree of isolation helped to insulate the project team from other distractions. However, it was not infrequently suggested that this might lead to the development of a silo mentality that would ultimately work against us. As a result, we may have found it more difficult to secure the delivery of some of what we needed from Museum staff who were not part of the project team. However much maligned, meetings can, and did, help to break down such barriers, especially when it came to justifying the need for additional resources. Visits to conservation studios and mount workshops also helped to foster a team spirit.

The availability and flow of information was vital to all areas of endeavour, both in terms of specifying what had to be produced and when, and in sorting out dependencies. To make this easier we made a basic assumption that work would be organised on a gallery-by-gallery basis. I think we believed that this was explicit and that everyone had signed up to it. However, the manufacturers of display cases and the makers of mounts and fixings found it necessary to diverge from this principle and to manufacture in batches. This required drawings and specifications to be made available and decisions about displays to be made out of the planned sequence, thereby upsetting the rhythm of the project and putting more pressure on those involved. On the other hand, forcing manufacture on a gallery-by-gallery basis would have made the particular items of work stated above very slow, inefficient, expensive and, in the case of mounts and fixings, disruptive to other work. Although we found ways to get round these problems, life would have been much easier if we had made sure that we were all working according to the same method.

We could and should have made more use of a review of each aspect of the decant, construction and fit-out during the life of the project, when they were first completed. Although we did make use of prototyping, its scope was generally limited to the production of trial items, such as object supports. We could have learned a lot by following through a complete process for a limited area of the gallery to help us anticipate problems and deal with them while they were still small. Instead, we learned many lessons slowly, in less formal ways – the difficulties that we experienced caused by people working in different ways eventually enabled us, in the closing stages of the project, to ensure that we were ready to complete all the tasks involved in installation in the right order.

Installation　A document outlining the requirements for installation was produced in September 1999 and used as a basis for discussions with all stakeholders. It continued to be developed until installation started.[11] A range of generic method statements for installation was developed as an aid to more rapid quantification of the task and more detailed scheduling that followed. Installation was planned to follow the same gallery sequence as construction. Large, heavy and difficult objects were installed first, followed by other fixed items (fig. 12). Smaller, free-standing items were installed later. Joint meetings were held between the technical services and design teams to confirm the suitability of the approach proposed and to enable the designers to develop mounting and fixing methods for objects. Paper templates were used to refine the positions of objects within each display area (see chapter 8). Details of the proposed installation process were added to the shared database.

As installation became a new focus for the project, the composition of the teams and the reallocation of project members to new activities also became an issue. An offsite residential team-building session was held for the whole team in February 2000 to review all aspects of the project and team members' perceptions of strengths, weaknesses, opportunities and threats to successful completion. As a result, new ways of working were proposed and agreed. An extended matrix of roles and responsibilities was drawn up covering all aspects of the preparation for installation and later extended to the actual installation process itself.

At the beginning of the project installation had been scheduled to start in late autumn 2000 and to be complete by the end of August 2001. As opening had been scheduled for 20 November 2001, this would give us three months to make final adjustments to allow finishes and materials to settle and to promote the galleries. All our early plans were based on having a single installation team following in the footsteps of contractors working on construction and fit-out. Galleries were to be completed in a predetermined order and the Museum given beneficial occupation to install objects. As construction and fit-out became increasingly delayed, it became necessary to revise our ideas and plan to have two and then three teams working in parallel on different galleries. However, this hugely increased the complexity and difficulty of organising and completing the work. The sequence and methods of working had to be constantly revised, and additional equipment had to be made available before we could really get going. It will be obvious that there are limits to the idea of the person week. Fifty people working for eight weeks is a very different proposition, for example, to ten people working for forty weeks.

By summer 2001, installation having been delayed by five months, it was necessary to have several teams working in parallel, each composed of a lead curator, a lead technician and an Operations Team member with additional resources allocated as necessary. Rather than setting out in detail what should be achieved each day, targets were adjusted to allow the teams themselves the flexibility to decide what could be achieved. The team planning the installation worked hard to identify critical steps that would hold up the operation if not completed in time.

In use, the system set up to monitor installation did not work as well as expected. A very simple revision was therefore created that would establish simple targets and monitor progress against them. The targets were numbers of objects and numbers of hours that were required to be completed per week. Progress was shown to the project team as a simple graph of actual progress against targets (fig. 11). If we were above the line we were on target and would succeed; if we were below the line we were off target and

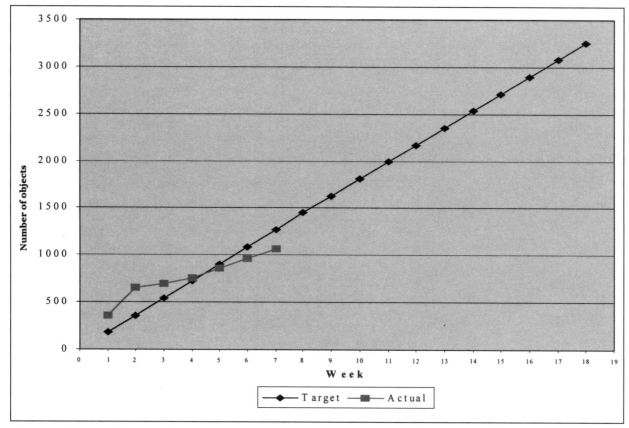

Figure 11. Object Installation graph,
June 2001

needed to take action to recover the rate of progress. A great deal of work in the summer of 2001 went into much more detailed analysis of the figures from which the simple graph was drawn, and this led to numerous changes in working practices, including such areas as mount-making, conservation and installation sequences.

Regular weekly reviews of progress were held in the galleries. Detailed plans and elevations of each area were put up along with display case status sheets to indicate the stages of installation, the stage reached and notes on approvals and other actions required. This helped to improve local communication and decision-making. At this point also, the project acquired many more mobile phones, and this also played a big part in cutting down the time required for approvals on site and the solving of problems as they arose.[12] The end result of all this endeavour to communicate and remain flexible in putting resources where they were most required was that we succeeded in getting the galleries to the stage where they could be opened on time, despite the delays described above. It is nonetheless true that a considerable amount of finishing off was needed after opening.

Nobody wanted to admit that there might be any part of the installation which might not be complete by the time the galleries opened. However, realising that we might not be able to complete absolutely everything on time, we determined what others have called a minimum public offering. The installation plan in the last six weeks was to complete everything possible in a priority order, recognising that some items would have more impact than others if they were missing. Some tasks that would preferably have been carried out before opening, such as the installation of a large part of the interpretive devices, revised graphics, and adjustments to the lighting had to be completed afterwards, out of hours. Some tasks that were delayed beyond the official opening, because of the passing of that incentive, took a very long time to be completed.

Resources The requirements of working in the public sector and with lottery funding are arduous. We had to estimate accurately exactly what the undertaking would cost before we had a definite project plan; we had to develop a business plan for galleries which were part and parcel of an operating museum; and we had to persuade both our institution and the Heritage Lottery Fund to take risks, when both are essentially risk-averse institutions. But any large building project is a risky business. The British building industry is attempting to reform itself, following reports by John Egan.[13] The idea is to move from an adversarial atmosphere, where the contractor and client are frequently in opposition, to an obligational contract, where both sides are partners in an endeavour to produce a high-quality project within the stated budget.

We decided to procure the building work through construction management (see also chapter 6). Under this system a firm of construction managers organises the site and divides the work into a series of discrete packages (e.g. enabling works, structural steel work, dry lining and display metalwork; see appendix 11). The firms who carry out each work package are then contracted directly by the museum, rather than all the construction work being carried out by one firm with a series of subcontractors under their control. Construction management gives the client more control to take action if anything goes wrong with one package. It also allows the detailed designs to be prepared for the contractors over a longer period of time. However, this approach requires rigorous control by the construction manager, and the co-ordination of the individual packages is important.

A great deal of effort was put into familiarising the construction management firm (Exterior) with the project and Museum protocols. Much of this initial effort was wasted, as the project suffered from rapid changes in personnel in the construction management team. Delays in construction occurred, which meant that the site was not clean and clear for the installation of the display cases. This gave us a series of problems in trying to construct large cases in a building site and led to some conflict on site. However, the various members of the management team worked well together to adapt the project plan, sometimes on a weekly basis, and this approach eventually worked.

Construction delays caused subsequent delays in the handover to the Museum for installation. This carefully planned operation had to be carried out much more quickly than anticipated. The fact that it did not work according to the detailed plan, but instead within the very broad initial parameters, was a learning experience, one which we are now applying to other projects in the V&A. The key success factor was flexibility and having a firm enough understanding of what had to be achieved to make adjustments – sometimes on a daily basis.

The initial cost plan was for £31 million – this included over £3 million for inflation. Despite delays on site and some unforeseen problems, such as having to replace all the double glazing, (due to a manufacturing defect) we were able to bring the project in for £29.45 million because inflation was less than expected. The cost breakdown is given overleaf (£ millions).

Construction	**10.0**
Enabling works/site set up	2.8
General building work including double glazing, flooring etc.	3.2
Mechanical and electrical works (including lifts)	4.0
Fit-out	**8.4**
Screens/decoration/finishes etc.	3.0
Display cases	2.0
Display lighting	1.0
Graphics	0.45
Security	0.40
Furniture	0.35
IT interactives	1.2
Period rooms (including movement, reinstallation and restoration and other large object movement)	**3.0**
Professional fees	3.8
Museum costs (including project teams, conservation and mounting, hands-on interactives, marketing and education programmes)	4.25
Total	**29.45**

Just over half of the funding for the project came from the Heritage Lottery Fund, with most of the remainder from private donations (see appendix 10). If there was one aspect we did not foresee, it was the level of advocacy required to sell the project to potential funders and opinion formers. For the last year, during installation, there was continual pressure to show people around the site, while still working to complete on time.

Conclusion In managing the project, our aim was to ensure that we knew what tasks had to be completed, that we had a workable process to achieve the task and a means to check progress against schedule. As a general principle, we tried to ensure that appointed co-ordinators understood the tasks, processes and schedules and then left them to get on with it, leaving us to deal with unplanned or deviant items by exception as required. Processes and schedules were reworked and roles/responsibilities clarified as necessary to overcome blockages in the system.

We tried to strike a balance between telling people what to do and telling them what result was required so that they could decide with local knowledge the detail of how it would be achieved. This allowed everyone to add value. As managers, we needed to see that controls were in place but recognised that in a project this size we could not directly control everything. The more other people determine their own controls the better, but there have to be controls. Experience confirmed that a quantitative approach that allowed progress to be measured was necessary. We believe that management through application of correct principles alongside individual autonomy best suits major projects at the V&A.

Notes 1. For the description of a machine bureaucracy, see Mintzberg, Henry, *Strategy Safari: A Guided Tour through the Wilds of Strategic Management* (London, 1998) and Morgan, Gareth, *Images of Organisation* (Thousand Oaks, California and London 1997).

2. At its peak the Operations Team consisted of eight people. Over the five years of the project Sally Merriman and Rachel Johnston were Assistant Project Managers (programming), Julie Taylor was Assistant Project Manager (Operations). Ananda Rutherford was Project Co-ordinator. Alexandra Corney, Annette Wickham and Christine Bradley were Assistant Project Co-ordinators. Victoria Humphreys, Charlotte Cadzow and Denise Drake were Administrative

Assistants. Claire Partington was the British Galleries Technical Services Team Manager. Rebecca Naylor, Lois Oliver and Edel Brucciani were Curatorial Assistants to the Concept Team. Verena von Langen was British Galleries Project Assistant. Mary Guyatt and Rebecca Milner assisted installation during the autumn of 2001. Working in conjunction with the Operations Team, Sue Liley and Barbara Joseph were Project Accountants; Vicky Oakley acted as Conservation Liaison for the Project.

3. Nick Brod was the Multimedia Manager, Sarah Stallard managed the production of low-tech devices.

4. The Steering Group was responsible for the highest level of monitoring of the project within the Museum. It consisted of Project Director (Chair), Chair of Museum Trustees Building Committee, Project Curator, Museum Project Manager, Programme Manager (Bovis), Construction Manager (Exterior), Architects (GA Associates), Designer (Casson Mann), M&E Consultant Engineers, Structural Engineers, Quantity Surveyor.

5. See Timothy Carpenter and Vicky Oakley, 'A Concise Approach: Managing Information for the British Galleries Conservation Programme', in *V&A Conservation Journal*, no.39 (Autumn 2001). For damage categories, see Keene, S., *Managing Conservation in Museums* (London 1996).

6. Period rooms were disassembled into many hundreds of separate components for removal and transportation. Each period room component was photographed and automatically given a unique number. The position and number of the components were then marked on plans and elevations of the room to show where the item had come from. A spreadsheet was used to record the component numbers, crate numbers and location of crates in store so that both contents of crates and locations of separate components could easily be determined during the re-installation phase.

7. Partitions were two-hour fire rated.

8. If two years has been allocated for a task and the control interval is monthly, then there are 24 occasions of review and 23 opportunities to make changes to process if things are not going right.

9. Snodin, M. and Styles, J. (eds), *Design and the Decorative Arts: Britain 1500–1900* (London, 2001).

10. For example, additional staff were brought in to some studios, movement of objects into and out of studios was improved, and steps were taken to reduce non-British Galleries work, such as loans and other projects going on at the same time. The aim was to focus more of the available time on the project.

11. Regular meetings were held to agree detailed procedures for handover of galleries to the Museum, including sequences of gallery handover, inspection of prepared spaces and showcases, and arrangements for protection, access and security once the Museum had been granted beneficial occupation of each area.

12. The use of mobile phones enabled decisions to be communicated and acted upon much more quickly. It also meant that key individuals whose approval was needed for exact positioning of objects on display, for example, could be located and summoned to the particular point where they were needed. They could thus be active across a wide front. Meanwhile, as individual mounts or objects became available, this could be made known to the teams doing the installation.

13. Sir John Egan for the Department of Trade and Industry, *Rethinking Construction: The Report of the Construction Task Force to the Deputy Prime Minister, John Prescott, on the Scope for Improving the Quality and Efficiency of UK Construction.* http://www.rethinkingconstruction.org/rc/report/ (consulted 10 February 2004).

*12. **Wall Painting** Psyche and Her Sisters, 1700–20, awaiting installation in Stuart gallery (54), July 2001. Photo by Stephen Johns.*

Chapter 6　Designing the galleries

Dinah Casson

Introduction
Christopher Wilk

The selection of designers for the project provided the Museum with a test of its commitment to abandon business as usual. In May of 1996 we interviewed numerous architectural, as well as exhibition and interior design, firms and found the decision difficult to make.[1] We rejected what we considered to be the safe choices, designers whose work showed a belief in traditional exhibition design and who employed historical pastiche. We also rejected several architects because they demonstrated insufficient interest in the specifics of displaying objects and were more concerned with the architectural setting. It was interesting to note – as it always is – the lack of true understanding of the differences between designing spaces for the hanging of essentially two-dimensional pictures and undertaking the design of galleries which must accommodate three-dimensional objects of varying sizes and with complex display requirements. Only one firm – Casson Mann – clearly demonstrated an understanding of the demands and matched our ambition to communicate directly and vitally with our audiences. Their work was interesting, quirky and very contemporary. It included exhibitions (one in which video screens were installed in a series of faux-hedges), public museum spaces and offices for lawyers and public bodies.

Casson Mann impressed us by their attention to the needs of visitors and by the freshness of their approach, both in their written submission and in their interview. They were, however, a very small firm with limited experience of displaying historical objects and no experience of designing a project of this scale, though, indeed, few firms, small or large, had such experience. One other concern about Casson Mann had to be weighed. One of the cornerstones of the design brief was that we wanted to use colour throughout the gallery, both to enliven the visit to such a long run of galleries and because it can provide a sense of historical setting, even within a modern design. We had also assumed that we would end up with designers familiar with the vocabulary of historic design, knowledge which would inform the gallery design overall, as well as the choices of colour. This was, inevitably, an impossible demand in view of the fact that we had very clearly said we also wanted a contemporary design overall and had specifically written that 'an over-reverential attitude to the interior architecture of the building [was] undesirable and would amount to cowardice' – hardly the sort of demand that normally encourages designers passionate about historical accuracy.

With this in mind, and keenly aware of the extensive amount of work that would be required on the five complete historic interiors to be included, we took the unusual step of hiring a second designer from among those interviewed: David Mlinaric of Mlinaric, Henry and Zervudachi. We proposed that Mlinaric, along with the team he had assembled for the project (chapter 7), work as consultant on historic decoration and the period rooms. Mlinaric was best known for designing the interiors of grand houses, both private homes as well as those open to the public – including Beningborough Hall, outside York, and Spencer House, London. He had also decorated the interiors of art galleries, including the National Gallery and the National Portrait Gallery, demonstrating his sensitivity to historic buildings and his ability to use colour and texture in ways sympathetic to historic works of art. He had not, however, had to deal with museum cases or the labelling of museum objects.

Although, in retrospect, this collaboration between Casson Mann and Mlinaric was a genuinely successful one, at the outset we were aware that it was a high-risk decision to hire design companies with such different approaches, experience and personalities, and fundamentally different attitudes to the past. But the demands we required were so varied that, following much discussion among ourselves and with those involved, it seemed worth taking a chance. Both designers departed from their normal patterns of work to undertake this project and we were grateful for the considerable efforts they made to make the collaboration work.

In addition to the interior elements the public would be most aware of we would also need an architect to handle the construction side of the project, including the installation of two new lifts, an air-conditioning system and the incorporation into the galleries of what had been less accessible storerooms along the interior walls. For that we hired

Alastair Gourlay of GA Associates who, while at Arup Associates, had designed the much-praised transformation of London's Imperial War Museum (where Alan Borg had been director). With that appointment, we had our three design protagonists who worked for the duration of the project. Today, what the public sees is largely the work of Casson Mann, crucially informed by Mlinaric's contribution. Architect Gourlay acted in a central and largely unseen role, coordinating the work of the wider Design Team.

In this chapter, Dinah Casson writes about the process of designing the galleries, including the contributions of other designers and consultants. The chapters on the organisation of the project (chapter 5), on content development (chapter 8) and on interpretive devices (chapter 9) also touch on aspects of the collaboration between designers and the Museum. The chapter on colour (chapter 7) highlights the work of Mlinaric and the Historic Decoration Team.

The Museum appointed the three core teams of designers in May 1996: the team of Historic Decoration Consultants led by David Mlinaric, GA Associates as architects and Casson Mann as exhibition and interpretive designers. The rest of the team, consisting of nine different consultants, followed later (see appendix 12). The process of selection was unusual and astute: normal practice for museums at the time was to ask prospective designers to produce design schemes in advance of any knowledge of either the contents or the ambitions of the curatorial teams. Instead of this approach, in addition to a portfolio of work, the V&A asked for a short text from applicants setting out their views on how the Museum might approach the redisplay of the British Galleries. This allowed them, and us, to establish a degree of understanding before the project began and there was a blank sheet of paper between us: it meant that anything would be considered.

Prior to this project, Casson Mann had no experience in the world of historic objects – although we had designed exhibitions, some with objects and some without. In many ways, although risky, this lack of experience turned out to be an asset as it meant that we questioned everything and took nothing for granted. The task was, nonetheless, daunting: so many objects, all of such quality, to be presented in a manner that would be effective for 25 years. The scale of the project was so large that it was almost impossible to grasp it and certainly one anxiety was how to retain freshness of approach during the five years required to design and build the galleries.

Developing designs for projects as large and as complex as the British Galleries requires the designers and the client to invest time early on in the process to discuss ideas, many of which are subsequently rejected. This is a crucial period for all projects, and if it is compromised, time can be lost later through misunderstandings. It enables the teams to get to know each other, to find ways of working together, and ways of communicating: it is also a way to develop trust. Without trust a project of this scale and ambition cannot work. The three teams of designers had never worked together before, but, as can happen with casts in the theatre, this was turned to advantage. After an initial anxiety that 'too many cooks spoil the broth', we eventually found that approaching the project from different angles was proving to be beneficial. The success of such teams is very dependent on the skills of the casting director (in this case, the client), who needs to have a clear overview of what skills will be needed.

Architecture: preparing the rooms

The programme of work inevitably meant that the architects, chronologically, would be working in front of us, but their work needed to support the basic concepts of the exhibition design. As this took some time to develop, it was vital that we worked together very closely and that they were able to build in as much flexibility as possible.

The option to phase the opening of the galleries over a period of months, or even years, had already been considered and rejected. This decision was based on the need to complete the work as cost–effectively as possible and avoid the possibility that later phases could be delayed owing to any financial shortfalls; the disadvantage, however, was that there was no possibility of a second phase incorporating the lessons learned from the first. The fitting out and object installation was planned to work from one end of the galleries to the other, roughly in parallel on the two floors, ending with the entrance closest to the main Museum doors.

In contrast to the highly decorated interiors already in the Museum, the Aston Webb galleries in which the British Galleries are located (built 1899–1909) anticipated many logical needs of the twentieth century (see chapter 1). Webb's own description of his galleries, apart from the lighting, demonstrated an extraordinary congruence with late-twentieth-century thinking about the needs of the museum visitor:

To the right and left of this vestibule are the staircase[s] leading to the three floors of side-lighted galleries … The walls of the galleries and courts … are kept perfectly plain and free from architectural features of any kind. On the other hand, an attempt has been made to prevent weariness to the visitor by avoiding galleries of undue length, by providing vistas and glimpses through the building in passing, and by varying the sizes, proportions and design of the various courts and galleries.[2]

Although strong in character, these 'side-lighted' galleries have been able to house the changing fashions in curating and design with remarkable dignity.

The principal tasks therefore facing the architects, GA Associates, were:

- to find a method of improving and controlling the environment in the galleries;
- to improve the visitor facilities in the galleries;
- to improve physical access to and within the galleries;
- to convert some adjacent storage areas into usable spaces for display.

All of these adjustments had to be accomplished within the restrictions of a Grade 1 listed building and a museum that was to maintain normal access to the public, with minimum disruption, throughout the project. To enable this, a large hoist was erected on the main façade of the building to provide access to the galleries through temporarily removed first- and second-floor windows, through which all construction materials, contractors and objects were to pass (fig. 13).

The designated rooms on each of two floors consist of four long, narrow galleries, of approximately 30 × 9m, with smaller, rectangular galleries linking them. The sequence of rooms wraps around the corner of the Museum with one of the linking galleries marking the corner. By creating an oculus here (formed by cutting a hole in the lower floor ceiling), the architects formed the only, and crucial, visual link between the two gallery floors. Since there were no existing internal staircases, the architects also installed two new lifts capable of carrying objects as well as visitors, and two much-needed suites of lavatories.[3] Both of these additions have made an enormous difference, not only to the previous difficulties of disabled access to the British Galleries, but also to access from the British Galleries to other parts of the Museum.

The large windows running around the perimeter wall presented two major problems. The first was that they were designed to let in the maximum amount of light. Whilst this created a pleasant sequence of spaces, particularly when the windows were not masked as they were in parts of the old galleries, it represented a problem in terms of the many light-sensitive objects which were to be displayed in the new galleries. The second problem was that the highly polluted street environment outside did not allow fragile objects to be displayed. Both of these problems were mitigated by the installation of secondary glazing units with integral, and adjustable, venetian blinds. These have successfully created a treble glazed barrier that protects the objects both from dirt and ultraviolet light. The installation of a carbon-filtered air-conditioning system was the final part of the strategy to ensure the environmental integrity of the rooms. The difficulty of inserting an air-conditioning system into a listed building with concrete floors and decorative plaster ceilings was solved by raising the gallery floors by half a metre, creating a plenum floor, a raised floor filled with filtered air under positive pressure.

This filtered air is fed from a new plant room on the roof of the Museum (fig. 14) into the galleries via carefully positioned floor grilles.[4] The air is then extracted at high level through visible round ducts cut into interior walls and then recycled back to the plant room (fig. 15). The raised floor provided an accessible space for the distribution of electrical and data cabling as well as the housing of lighting projectors (fig. 16).[5] The upper levels of reclaimed storerooms running alongside the main galleries accommodate much of the ducting and result in a series of new side galleries with three-metre-high ceilings (colour plates 45–46). Created from the leftover spaces between the perimeter galleries and the major courts, these curiously shaped areas became a useful foil to the rigorous rhythm of the main galleries with their imposing ceiling heights of five-and-a-half metres.

Decisions had to be made about the degree of restoration that could be done to the existing building fabric. The rooms were in reasonable condition and, although there were areas that needed minor repairs, it was decided for reasons of cost to do the minimum necessary. The Design Team agreed that the new installation would be uncompromisingly modern and 'loose fit', allowing the visitor to see clearly where the old galleries stopped and the new interventions began; the design would stand independently from the Aston Webb architecture and would not therefore be compromised by its condition.

The result of the architects' work was a series of 14 air-conditioned galleries, with a grid of data/electrical outlets, looking remarkably unchanged from the original rooms (though half a metre less high) thanks to some careful attention to details such the reinstatement of skirtings around the architraves of the reduced doorways (fig. 17) and the careful matching of additional steps to all staircases leading up into the galleries. Sets of distinctly modern steel and glass portals lead out to neighbouring galleries. One common problem associated with air-conditioned galleries is the need for closed doors and this can put potential visitors off; because of the positive air pressure in these galleries, the doors can remain permanently open, automatically closing only when the fire alarm is triggered.

As lead consultants, the architects were also responsible for co-ordinating the work in the galleries by all the external consultants and they worked closely with Casson Mann to ensure that their work anticipated the requirements of the objects. The exceptional height of the Norfolk House Music Room in Gallery 52 (colour plate 24), and the panelling from Haynes

Grange in Gallery 58 (colour plate 1), for example, meant that these had to be recessed into the raised floor and positioning these within the sequence became a vital early decision. Similarly, areas of the floor had to be reinforced to take particularly heavy exhibits, such as the Roubilliac statue of Handel weighing 2000 kilos (colour plate 17). The positions of air outlets needed to relate to display cases and plinths (colour plates 68 and 70).[6]

Designing the exhibition The present writer, one of the two senior partners of Casson Mann, started working closely with the Concept Team in 1996, with the early weeks given over to discussion, visiting other museums together in the UK and overseas, agreeing processes and programmes and, most importantly, starting the examination of as many of the objects as possible.

The Design Team were reliant on photographs and data sheets for each object, which filled 40 or so lever-arch files. The data sheets accompanying each object contained all the information required for their display: dimensions, weight, medium, likely mounting method, light sensitivity and some indication of their desired position relative to the other objects in the same display. Each object entry was cross-referenced with the Framework Document (see chapter 8). The Framework Document, continuously up-dated and published fortnightly throughout the project (the last issue was number 81) acted as a working brief: it described why each object was relevant to its display or subject, the interpretive ideas that might accompany the display and, crucially, it monitored deletions and additions.

At the end of the first nine months, we had, together, written a design brief. The design brief is the document to which designers work. It co-ordinates and sets out the requirements from all parties: curators, engineers, conservators, access consultants, architects, lighting designers, graphic designers and educators. It provides a form of checklist of everything that has to be considered for each of the design stages, with each stage generating the design brief for the next stage.

At the end of 1998, we, at Casson Mann, appointed three designers in the studio to work opposite the three Gallery Teams at the Museum, with one designer, Jon Williams, having further responsibilities as the project designer. This meant that each designer was only responsible for holding information on one section of the galleries, and the intention was that each designer would remain with that group of objects through to the final installation.[7] We also appointed an in-house project manager, Richard Hill, in 1999, an architect by background, to co-ordinate our work with the Museum's project manager, construction manager and the other consultants. Later, in 2000, we appointed another designer to work across all the galleries on metal components, video housings, audio housings, benches, etc. At its peak, the Casson Mann Design Team for this project consisted of six designers and one administrator.

The first stages of the design process had six continuous working threads. The first was discussion with the curators about the proposed objects: where they should go, what they should be next to, what they were to 'say' and how they might 'say' it. This process continued throughout the five years of the project, gradually moving from big, strategic decisions to the question of how each object would actually be held in position. The second was with the teams of educators, developing interpretive ideas: what form should they take, where they should go, how they should look. The third was with the team of Historic Decoration Consultants working on colour and the development of the period rooms (see chapters 7 and 10). The fourth was in the studio, developing the architectural language of panels, plinths and display cases that would hold the design of the galleries together. The fifth was with the architects and building engineers, folding the decisions from the other threads into the fabric of the shell they were preparing. A sixth thread quickly evolved once the lighting and graphic designers had been appointed.

Discussion with curators The work with the objects began with the distribution of the 104 individual, titled displays proposed for the galleries by the curators, relating each to the available space and identifying essential juxtapositions. The number of displays changed as the project developed, as new topics were introduced, merged or eliminated. Their positions were affected by their probable size, their theme, the scale and significance of the objects within them, and their place in the chronology.

We also identified:

- objects suitable for being the focus of a vista;
- objects, temporarily nominated as 'star objects', highlights that all visitors would want to see and that had to be placed along the main route through the galleries; and
- objects that could be lit with natural (i.e. unpredictable) light.

Originally, the brief asked for two performance spaces, a seminar space, a temporary exhibition space and a café. Gradually, all of these had to be omitted as the scale of the core displays developed and it became clear that pressure for space would not allow these more general museum needs to be accommodated.[8]

All of these 'geographical' decisions were integral to the placing of the five period rooms (see chapter 10). As well as needing to connect with the chronology of the galleries, these had to be positioned so that their considerable bulk did not interfere with the flow of visitors through the spaces. Placing large rectangular objects, such as historic rooms into gallery rooms presents a simple geometric problem in that the space left over inevitably feels like a corridor. Sometimes it was possible to lose this by turning the axis, as for Bromley-by-Bow in Gallery 58 (fig. 52); in Gallery 52, however, we were able to use the corridor as a gentle ramp alongside the exceptionally wide Norfolk House Music Room (fig. 18); but the placing of the Henrietta Street Room has created an unavoidably tight area in Gallery 54.

Where the Museum possessed rooms where only certain elements were authentic, it was decided to remove the later construction and show only what was authentic. The Adam ceiling, for example, is shown as a ceiling suspended within the gallery – with no walls but with the footprint on the floor directly underneath expressed in polished oak boards (colour plate 26); only a section of the Haynes Grange panelling is shown, with the walls 'cut' through to show a true section; the Northumberland House drawing room is shown as an area of panelling only, with a scale model alongside (colour plate 25). This suggestion of deconstruction was extended to the exposure of small areas of rooms showing the rear of the panelling in order to demonstrate construction (fig. 19). These were ideas that came from the continuous designer–curator dialogue, where issues of display, information, entertainment, trust and historic integrity were explored in some detail.

The larger and heavier objects were then located around these first markers: the Great Bed of Ware, the large tapestries, the marble tables and wall monuments. Two of these were particularly difficult to position. The Melville Bed, over five metres high, retains its exceptional original silk and velvet hangings and requires a micro-climate of its own, but it was clear that a freestanding display case over five metres tall would call inappropriate attention to itself. This was finally resolved by fitting a controlled environment into the 'elbow' of the galleries in a reclaimed storeroom at the corner of Galleries 56 and 54 (colour plate 12). Here we were able to create the micro-climate and suggest the relatively small-scale panelled room in which it stood at Melville House. This placement of the bed, without the plinth that traditionally supports the case, reduces the sense of enclosure and separation from the visitor.[9] The other potentially difficult object was the seven-metre-long embroidery from Stoke Edith, requiring support from a backboard of equal size (colour plate 13). After some deliberation, the Museum decided that it was robust enough to be displayed outside of a display case, but with the proviso that, should environmental monitoring suggest that further protection was needed, it would be possible to glaze it at a later date. A structure has therefore been installed to receive the glass should that become necessary and the processes required to install it have been documented.

Discussions with educators Work with the educators focused on ways in which interpretive devices could be placed alongside objects (see chapter 9). The success of this strategy depended on them being treated with the same level of care as museum objects. Traditionally, visitors to the V&A have not expected to find things to touch, videos to watch, objects to pick up. It was important that these activities were clearly endorsed by the Museum as a valuable experience for adults and not just added on to amuse children. We wanted them to be perceived as extensions to the texts, as an alternative route to understanding. One particular difficulty was making it clear what was touchable and what was not. This was overcome by the setting out of touchable objects on a consistent style of panel with a small 'hand' symbol attached (fig. 20).[10]

We also worked on how the three Discovery Areas could be made to have their own identity and yet hold a family of activities that would link them together. This was achieved by repeating activities that visitors could recognise on their way through: for example, in each Discovery Area it is possible to sit at a computer and create something – a bookplate, a coat of arms – that is connected to the period. It is also possible to try on a garment and to try to identify 'Mystery Objects'. Each area, however, has wall colours and a floor finish redolent of its period (colour plates 4, 36 and 56).

Discussion with Historic Decoration Consultants It was not clear, initially, how the work of the Historic Decoration Consultants would connect – and relate – to the more general design work in the galleries. Whilst much of their work was centred on the presentation of the five period rooms, they were also heavily involved in the selection of colours for the galleries and the displays (see chapter 7). As the galleries were built to last 25 years, it was clear that the selection of colours in particular should not, if possible, be colours of the moment; instead we needed to find colours of historic integrity and the team worked hard for two years on this problem. In all there were about 70 different colours used on the gallery walls and displays, and 38 different textiles used in the cases. This large palette of precisely selected tones has given the galleries the warmth and accessibility that a more obvious, perhaps more nervous, contemporary solution might not have created.

Work in the studio In the Casson Mann studio a design vocabulary began to develop from a period of research, and some self-imposed rules quickly began to emerge. The first group of rules were concerned with the experience of the visitor. Everyone was aware that 3400 sq metres of exhibition space densely packed with 3000 of the richest objects in the Museum could become indigestible and exceptionally tiring to view. The problem of fatigue was therefore taken very seriously. Apart from supplying as much seating as possible, we made studies to determine how modulations in light, sound, colour and density could create sufficient variety for the journey through the galleries to be a series of smaller, manageable experiences, each different from its predecessor (figs. 21–24). We likened this to consuming food at a banquet, which is only possible, and enjoyable, if the menu is planned for contrasts in texture, taste, smells, piquancy and quantities. Changes in floor finishes, spatial variety, variations in densities and methods of display were aimed at keeping the menu varied.

Other causes of fatigue were identified as lack of orientation, inability to understand the scale of the journey ahead and too much work for the eyes. These were eased by ensuring that visitors were aware of the outside world, and, wherever possible, by creating vistas through the galleries that would indicate what was ahead. In addition, the programme of interpretive devices ensured that the pressure was not only on the eyes, as visitors were invited to touch, to lift, to write, to listen, to pull, to push, to dress up, to smile – in other words a mix of the active and the passive. Activities are sometimes quite minimal, but the act of lifting a torch to examine a miniature, or opening a drawer can be enough to relieve the strain of looking without rest (colour plates 10–11).

The other group of rules concerned the architectural installation itself. It was agreed that the integrity of the Aston Webb rooms should be respected and that the new installation should be visibly 'loose', with the new and the old clearly distinguished. This provided a platform for the very different demands of each display and enabled each to have its own colour and form within the bigger, more neutral envelope of the gallery. We were also sure that it was important that the visitors could trust what they saw: in other words, apart from within the period rooms, there was to be no pastiche and no mocking up of historic context beyond an abstract suggestion.[11] The Museum had requested an uncompromisingly modern installation; one way of achieving this was to make it clear what was an exhibit and what was a support for an exhibit.

Many of our early decisions were connected to the themes, each of which was to be presented using a distinctive design vocabulary. *Who Led Taste?* displays such as *The Great Exhibition* were to be spectacular set pieces, suggesting the irresistible nature of the new (colour plate 35); the *Fashionable Living* displays, such as *Grand Tour*, were to express the rather passionate chaos that followers of fashion can get themselves into (colour plate 70). The *Style* displays, such as *French Style*, were to be essentially didactic, arranged to dislodge the objects from their function, layered rather than composed, focusing attention on details in order to make their decorative features easy to identify and compare (colour plate 72). *What was New?* displays such as *New Technical Skills* were to be cooler, more overtly technical in character (colour plate 9).

We felt strongly that, since all of the objects were now away from their original context, the galleries provided an opportunity for visitors to be encouraged to look at them differently, more analytically. By supporting a portrait, or a mirror, on legs – away from the walls on which they are conventionally hung – it can be seen afresh, as a designed object (fig. 25). One of our objectives was to give visitors a slight jolt – enough to encourage them to see things as if for the first time.

An important part of our working strategy was, perhaps surprisingly, to delay the introduction of images of how the galleries might look until quite late on – much to the frustration of the Museum. This was partly a belief in the need for projects to have time to 'cook' or even marinate, but it also represented a reluctance to allow discussions, which were correctly well-focused on content development, to become sidetracked by aesthetics. It was also our concern that, should the aesthetic be established too early in the five-year process, it would become stale.

Discussions with the Architectural Team

Close collaboration with the architects and engineers continued through to the end of the project. Much of their work would be on site whilst the galleries were still being designed, and one of our joint tasks was to ensure that options were left open for as long as possible. This was not only for the sake of our developing proposals but also for the sake of the long-term future of the galleries. Understandably, most museums are keen on the idea of flexibility as it leaves options open. However, this had to be carefully discussed as flexibility can be expensive to design in and the reality is, frequently, that the 'options' are never taken up simply because of a shortage of resources. The possibility of a new object being introduced at some point has to be considered, but, however ingeniously conceived, changing galleries is expensive and time-consuming. Casson Mann needed regular meetings with all the other members of the Design Team, in addition to the architects and the Historic Decoration Consultants. Once the weekly meetings with the Architectural Team were added to the schedule, the programme of meetings began to feature more heavily than time in the studio. Managing meetings, deciding who should attend, focusing their length, and ensuring their clarity of purpose became a core activity.

Discussion with lighting and graphic designers

Once the graphic and lighting designers were appointed, it was essential for their work to be fully integrated. It became increasingly important for the graphic designers to be involved at an early stage in the development of the interpretive devices as well as with the core graphic elements. The former in particular involved the sourcing and testing of resilient materials that were receptive to text, as well as the creation of the visual identities of the various devices, dividing them into series that could be readily recognised and pleasant to use. How big these should be, how they should be fixed, how they should maintained, what colour these should be were all issues for discussion.

With the lighting designer, a balance was sought between the differing requirements of conservators and visitors – the former keen to minimise the amount of light and the latter keen to maximise it. The important thing was to create a cohesive journey from one area to the next which nonetheless offered some variety in colour and intensity. The early decision to install only one lighting raft carrying mainly fibre optic lighting worked well in most situations, but there were areas where we had difficulties in finding suitable substitutes; any group of fibre optic fittings required projector positions as well as 'ducts' for sizeable fibre optic tails. Lighting the period rooms proved to be particularly difficult as light positions had to be hidden, not damage the fabric of the rooms and produce a quality of light comparable to the original candlelight – or indeed daylight.

In October 1998, after two-and-a-half years' work, we had most of the displays in their final positions and were able to submit Scheme Design (RIBA stage D).

The temporary gallery, 'Best of British' By the autumn of 1998, we were ready to build a prototype section of one the new galleries within the temporary gallery, 'Best of British', in order to test out some of our ideas (see colour plates 74–77 and chapters 7 and 11).[12] This enabled assessment of the qualities of window panels, plinths, lighting from the raft, footlighting, labelling, colour and security. This was invaluable; as a result, the proportions of the window panels were adjusted, the 'colour' of the lighting was adjusted, decorative techniques such as polished plaster and timber plinth finishes were tried and assessed. Important decisions about text size and label colours were taken. Most of the work done in the temporary gallery was for objects on open display. In retrospect, we could have used this facility more extensively and, for example, done more work with testing out the fittings and arrangements inside display cases. This might have enabled us to streamline or modularise the fittings for the cases and the object mounts; it might also have highlighted some of the problems we encountered later with lighting some of the case interiors.

Communication with the Museum Methods of communicating design ideas with the Museum emerged as a surprisingly complex issue. The majority of the Museum team had no experience of reading drawings, and finding ways to communicate design ideas quickly and accurately became increasingly important as the project progressed. Although every object was drawn on computer, the resulting computer-generated drawings were hard for non-designers to understand (colour plates 49 and 53). If they were only showing structure, without any objects, they were particularly impenetrable. The use of free-hand drawings that are inherently negotiable (colour plates 51 and 55–59), in conjunction with CAD drawings that appear to be non-negotiable, became a preferred method and, indeed, an essential tool. Ultimately, it was clear that the most successful medium was the 1:25 scale model (figs 26 and 27). Started in early 1997 and initially used as a design tool in the studio, it was completed by 2000, when all the larger objects had been made to scale (in white card) and positioned. This assisted the whole team – as well as potential funders – to understand, probably in many cases for the first time, the full implications of the design.

The exchange of information between Museum and design studio was also an initial difficulty as it took some time for the Design Team to find ways of explaining what information was relevant to the design process and what was not. The dimensions of paintings that included frames were vital to the designers, for example, whereas the dimensions of the canvas itself were more important to the Museum. Equally, it took the Design Team some time to understand fully the implications of the conservation requirements: why, for example, all dress and upholstered furniture had to be cased, whereas tapestries could be on open display, or why vibration can cause such difficulties for objects as diverse as ceramics and chalk drawings.

Lighting Richard Aldridge was appointed to join the Design Team in 1997. In addition to lighting objects according to their individual conservation requirements, his ambition was to reduce the overall electrical loading in the galleries and to reduce the number of different types of spare lamps that would have to be held in stock by the Museum. These goals were achieved.[13]

Aldridge's scheme was conceived around the principle of creating an infrastructure with enough flexibility to allow the lighting to be created on site once the objects were in position. He proposed to light the majority of the objects with fibre optic lighting. This was a radical proposal, as fibre optics had not hitherto been used for the more general illumination necessary for objects on open display, although they had been used in display cases for some time. There were a number of reasons for his proposal:

- It is possible to change the lighting to suit any alterations in the gallery layout with very limited disruption. The light rafts installed in the long galleries have extra holes cut in order to allow for the repositioning of the fittings.
- The light source can be mounted well away from the objects on display, with no danger of the heat from the lights, or the projectors, affecting them.
- Light intensity and colour can be adjusted with simple gel filters and/or frosted lenses fitted at the tail end. With conventional lighting the gels would burn out.
- Projector lamps can be changed by the maintenance team without affecting the focus of any of the lights, ensuring that the required illumination is kept constant.
- Light intensity can be controlled by the proximity of the tail end to the object, as well as the diameter of the fibre. The larger the quantity of fibre, the more light it can transmit.
- The size of beam can be varied, and changed, by the selection of 26mm, 18mm or 12.5mm lenses, depending on the displays. In some instances the tails were left bare, with no lenses, providing a softer, wide beam.

The main run of galleries, therefore, is lit from the asymmetrically positioned lighting raft that lies over the plinths in front of the windows (colour plates 7, 30, 31, 37, 42). The inner areas of the room are lit with 'masked' spotlights, still sourced through fibre optic tails, that focus on particular objects from behind a small metal screen fitted to the top of some the wall panels (colour plate 68).

Richard Aldridge also proposed the installation of footlights along the front edge of the plinths for the larger objects on open display, in order to provide an upwash of light on to areas that are normally in shadow and hard to see.

The only objects on open display that are not lit with fibre optics are the large wall hangings: these are lit with asymmetrical fluorescent lamps that provide a wide but uniform illumination across large, flat areas (colour plate 13 and see note 13).

Lighting in the display cases Where possible, the display cases were lit from outside; this, along with the lack of any internal structure to support the fittings, ensured maximum visual transparency. This was particularly useful for the 'lift-up' family of cases (figs 37 and 42). Otherwise the cases have integral lights top and bottom with the projector housed either in the base of the case or in an adjacent position under the floor. Some cases have a mirrored film applied to the underside of the top surface and these reflect light thrown up from the base of the case.[14]

The level of light within the cases varies depending on the contents. Textiles and paper are lit between 50 and 70 lux; for oil paintings and wooden objects this can be increased to 250 lux. Although metals, stone and ceramic objects can tolerate even higher levels, it was decided that these should not differ too much from the 250 maximun lux level, as this would break up the harmony of the galleries. Because of their particular fragility, miniatures are shown within shadowed recesses at under 20 lux, and visitors can use a fibre optic torch (colour plate 10) to view them or, in one instance, trigger additional light on a timer.

The Design Team were keen to ensure that visitors were aware of the presence of the natural light outside wherever possible. However, as natural light can vary in colour temperature from 5500°K to 7000°K it was decided that, with the exception of the Study Areas in the two corner rooms (colour plate 22), this should be allowed in as light reflected off the ceiling. This gave the ceilings a cooler feel without impinging on the white light of the display lighting. All the galleries register changes in natural light owing to the design of the window panels, but in three places changing natural light was deliberately sought: the Study Areas in the two corner rooms, the *Great Exhibition* display in Gallery 122, where glass panels carry full-size prints of the original engineering drawings (colour plate 35), and the light fluctuates with the weather outside – as indeed it would have done in the real Crystal Palace, and on the ramp outside the Norfolk House Music Room (fig. 18).

In retrospect, it is possible that too much was demanded of the fibre optic concept and some areas in the galleries are darker than they should be. This could have been remedied with the installation of a wider selection of positions for light fittings, had the infrastructure been sufficiently developed in time. There is a balance to be achieved between an over-complex infrastructure that is capable of doing anything, most of which is never utilised, and one that is too restricted. Finding accessible positions for all of the projectors proved to be difficult and some are awkward to access for maintenance. Owing to a mixture of technical factors, there are unsatisfactory variations in the colour temperature of the lighting over time, although this is mitigated when lamps in the projectors are changed before they burn out – a standard of maintenance not easy to achieve.

Graphics In 1998 Rose Innes Associates (RIA) were appointed to design the graphics. In addition to the design of the labels and text panels associated with the displays, they were also responsible for designing the graphics for the interpretive devices and for the signage (figs 29–34). The appointment was made because of Rose-Innes' considerable track record of working within large museum projects and their classic modernist approach.

Typeface and legibility RIA had to find a typeface for use throughout the galleries that would work equally well on a wide range of materials and components and that would be legible at all sizes with well-proportioned characters and perfect kerning (letter spacing) characteristics. Sans serif typefaces generally lack legibility when text is set in large blocks, whilst true serif typefaces frequently suffer when reproduced in smaller sizes, particularly when silk-screened. Having found nothing entirely suitable, the solution was the development of a new typeface (appropriately named 'V&A'), a 'transitional' face mid-way between serif and sans serif that is pleasing to read and capable of good reproduction in digital and conventional methods (i.e. silkscreen) in both large and small point sizes (fig. 28).

There are instances where case labelling is difficult to read as a result of inconsistent light levels, particularly at the bottom of cases. With hindsight, some of these problems could have been avoided with more tests at prototype stage. In the event, it was impossible to bring together prototypes of cases, lighting and graphics in one place at the right time. It is possible that testing would have led to greater use of dark text on the pale grey background colour as it seems to be more widely legible under low light conditions.[15]

Additionally, there were instances comparatively late in the design process when it became clear that there was insufficient space for labelling along the front of cases, the preferred position, and some labels had to be enlarged and relocated to the back walls of cases, among numerous wall-mounted objects. In future it would be prudent to identify early those showcases needing a lot of labels, and consider alternative methods to provide information graphically, such as showcase catalogues. Overall, our experience reinforced the importance of integrating exhibition design, graphic design and lighting design as early as possible in the design process.

Colour Given the wide and varied colour palette used in the galleries, RIA proposed a discreet, easily recognisable palette of grey for the graphics, one which would ensure simplicity, consistency and legibility. According to the context, dark grey type on a pale grey background or light grey type on a dark grey background would be used throughout. For the other graphic components they proposed a more colourful palette. The orientation panels, for example, required a stronger, more immediate presence and brighter colours were used as highlights for the special interpretive devices described below.

Materials and techniques Variety was to be achieved by using different materials and methods of application for each of the graphic components according to position, form and function. As some of the subject panels were likely to be vulnerable to touching, these were made from silk-screened, folded aluminium and were designed as tall monoliths positioned within each display (fig. 29 and colour plates 5, 9, 19, 41, 50 and 68). Silk-screening was also used for orientation panels, directional signing and individual wall-mounted object labels.

Digital printing on to paper that was then mounted and laminated was used for all plinth and showcase labels, as this allowed for the inclusion of colour photographs and other illustrative material. In comparison to silk-screening, digital printing is relatively cheap and allows for simple and quick replacement. All materials, paints and inks used inside display cases had to be tested alongside the paints, mounts and textiles to ensure that they would not harm the objects.

Object labels The locations for the labels were varied: some were to be mounted on to plinths and gallery walls, some inside showcases and others on the front of and inside drawers. Typographic variations were designed in different formats depending on their location and height above floor level. Those labels fixed to barrier rails at low level had to be considerably larger than labels inside showcases viewed at waist level. The content of the labels also differed enormously; some were very brief, others were long and detailed. A versatile typographic discipline had to be established, therefore, that maintained a clear, standardised hierarchy for text information. The Design Team preferred the use of long strips of digitally printed labels for plinths and showcases. Wherever possible, we wanted to avoid the use of individual label units, which over time lead to unsightly joins and colour discrepancies (fig. 32). While individual labels are undoubtedly easier and cheaper to replace, it was agreed (after much discussion) that the contribution of strip labels to the look of the gallery was significant enough to warrant their inclusion.

Large-text books for each display contain the complete text of each subject panel together with all related object labels in extra large type. These were printed in-house on heavyweight paper and ring bound in polypropylene folders and can be easily updated. Six books form the 'Questions of Design' series. The binding and covers are of hardwearing polypropylene. The illustrated texts are litho-printed in full colour on to heavy-duty laminated card. Showcase catalogues are provided for densely packed showcases where individual object labels could have overwhelmed the objects themselves. Covers and pages are made of hard-wearing, silk-screened polypropylene.

Display cases The selection of the display case manufacturer was made in 1999. Many factors determined the decision, but a major one was Goppion's ability, and willingness, to work with us to find new solutions to old problems. The galleries would need 180 cases. Some were to be recessed into walls, some freestanding; the largest would be 2.5m high and nearly 4m wide, and the smallest would be 70 × 50 cm. A variety of internal finishes was proposed – some painted and some lined with textile. There were to be several different cladding materials: slate (rough and smooth), stone, painted metal, timber. Some were to have drawers, and some were to have torches. Some were to have internal fibre optic lighting, and some were to have none. All cases had to meet the conservation requirements of the Museum and, if possible, give 100% opening access, allowing the staff to work with the case completely open.[16] This breadth of specification was part of the strategy to build in variety to the galleries, and although the range of different case sizes caused logistical difficulties, a more restricted range of dimensions would have meant reducing the number of objects on display or limiting the diversity of objects.

Work started with Goppion in January 2000 on the basis of a set of Casson Mann drawings for the 180 cases. These set out the required dimensions and finishes for all the cases (some of which were to change as the designs developed), but did not specify construction or opening details. Ultimately, the contract was extended to include some of the walls and panels where these were structurally integral with the display cases. Of all the museum projects undertaken by Goppion, the British Galleries proved the most complicated, both for the volume of work and for the number and variety of display elements. The exceptionally tight programme and stringent demands of the Museum and the designers led them into a programme of research and manufacture beyond anything they had undertaken before.

One of the demands of the contract was that Goppion should collaborate closely with Casson Mann during the development phase of the project, so that the outline designs for the display cases could be developed in parallel with the other architectural elements. This involved many hours of collaborative design and, because of the constraints of the programme, much of the development work had to be done quickly during extended sessions in London and Milan.

Company structure and production process Goppion works through 'work groups' and 'production units', which are combined together according to the technical skills needed for each new project undertaken. This gives the company a high level of organisational flexibility, enabling teams to break up and re-form according to the evolving objectives of each project, and permits them to undertake a large number of different tasks at the same time. This inherent flexibility makes development work fast and efficient. It is a typical structure for an Italian manufacturing company and very different from most of their competitors.

The main production unit in Milan carries out research, experimentation and testing, while the peripheral units, each with its own technological specialisation, carry out basic engineering and technical work, such as precision joinery, mechanics and glazing. Each of these peripheral units has highly advanced specific equipment and skills, equipped with CAD work stations capable of creating 3D models, while the machine shops are equipped with machine tools with numerical control and laser metal plate cutting machines.

The development of a design from its proposal to the point where it is fully detailed is a demanding job requiring precision and patience; each physical component and construction detail involves a technical drawing, and any mistakes in this phase will inevitably be carried over into the production and installation phases. Here Goppion describes the scale and complexity of the project:

5000 technical drawings and thousands of hours of designing were needed to complete the British Galleries project. The initial set of 5000 drawings became 40,000 drawings of construction details, generated by the selected 'work groups'. Once these drawings had been made, design changes became very expensive. Checking and cross-checking these drawings was a crucial and time-consuming process for all parties.

Goppion divided up the production between the associated workshops according to their specialisation, equipment and production capacity. As with all industrial activities with a decentralised organisation, production quality control became vital: materials and work were checked and assembly tests carried out at the individual production units. The parts produced by the peripheral workshops were then taken to the central workshop on the Trezzano sul Naviglio (Milan) site, where each showcase was assembled and tested. During this assembly and testing period, 189 metal structures, 800 sheets of glass totalling 1600 m², 205 slabs of slate, 95 slabs of *pietra serena* and 22 different types of fabric were fully co-ordinated before dispatch to London. This involved two trucks making 60 trips between Trezzano and London, covering a total of 90,000 km. The cases were then assembled and installed on site by eleven men over 100,000 hours. The entire process was carried out to ISO procedures.[17]

Design development The crucial part of the development phase was holding on to the initial ideas that we at Casson Mann had started with – namely that the cases should be as discreet as possible and that they should be fully integrated with their surrounding structures. We pushed Goppion hard, and they responded with many ingenious devices and structural ideas to allow these concepts to remain as the main linking element throughout the installation. They were unusually responsive to these demands, regarding them as part of the legitimate process of design development:

We quickly understood that the showcases we were to make were almost excluded from the basic idea: the articulation of space, panels and plinths to support the objects suggested a search for the closest possible relationship between the object and the visitor, without the interruption of a showcase in between. Here was a museum designed without showcases – where they had been added, it was out of necessity because of the demands of security and conservation. They were conceived as glass boxes with minimal structure, fully integrated into the architecture of the installation.

Much of the time spent in the long series of meetings between Goppion's technical staff and Casson Mann's designers centred on the issue of 100% access and the opening mechanisms that would allow this. The main problem was how to achieve this, given the ambition to design a glass box with minimal structure but with airtight seals. The solution lay in developing five types of cases – each with its own method of access – with some special ones designed for specific pieces (figs 35–41 and 42–46).

The display cases are fabricated from epoxy-coated sheet steel, and all linings are either in stone, slate, Hexlite Dibond (aluminium–polythene–aluminium sandwich) or sheet steel. For conservation purposes, the desire was to have display cases with all parts of the interior constructed from inert materials; at the same time, the Design Team were keen to achieve as much variety within the cases as outside. After many trials and tests, the interior panels were finally lined in fabric, mirror glass or sprayed with Nextel (a special suede-like paint developed by 3M) or emulsion paint. All of these were tested (see p. 111). The programme for the design, development, manufacture and installation of the cases was very tight, given that four out of five of the designs were new rather than ones Goppion had previously manufactured. This meant that the cases were, in effect, hand-made prototypes, and teething problems took correspondingly longer than normal to resolve.

An evaluation of the cases must take into account the stated design intention that the cases minimise visible structure, as well as the original performance specifications for stability, dust control, materials, access and security. In respect of the former, the cases fit the overall design idiom very successfully, mitigating the visitors' sense of separation from cased objects. It is an aspect of the galleries that many visitors gratefully comment upon. The five types of case design have provided considerable flexibility and variety to the display of objects as diverse as portrait miniatures and very large textiles.

In respect of the performance specification the cases have, overall, performed well. The quality of air seals on the cases is high and visible dust levels low. Vibration from the floor or during case opening has not been a serious issue, and where a few objects have been found to 'creep' along glass shelves the problem can be remedied. Extensive time and effort has gone into refining the smooth operation of drawers – some of them large, over 100 cm wide – incorporated within display cases. Obtaining large drawers that require little physical effort to open, yet which can be closed by most visitors without a jolt, proved surprisingly difficult. Drawer design is an area that we would approach differently in future.

In general the cases provide excellent access when open but they are not particularly straightforward to operate, partly because of the diversity of opening mechanisms, and partly because of the relative complexity of security and compression arrangements. The infrequency with which most cases are opened means that it is not practical for all curators to be trained in operating all cases and that, instead, a few trained staff have to be relied on to open cases. Depending on which type, case opening usually takes 2–15 minutes, and, while it is possible for one person to open most cases, it has always been Museum policy for two members of staff to be present when a case is opened. The cases set a new standard in the Museum for the use of passive materials. Construction materials are either known to be passive (steel and glass) or tested and proved to be so before use (adhesives, seals, paint finishes, textile linings). Fixings are made almost entirely using aluminium, perspex and Hexlite Dibond rather than wood.

Recurring elements of the design

In addition to the display cases, a number of recurring elements define the final design of the galleries. A lighting raft runs through all the large galleries and carries the projectors for the fibre optic fittings and security cameras (colour plates 7, 30, 31, 37, 42). Its height allows the Aston Webb ceiling to be visible above and yet allows the fibre optics to illuminate all the objects displayed along the window wall. The linking galleries – 57, 53, 119 and 123 – have a free-floating ceiling panel that fulfils a similar function (colour plate 3). Changing the lamps of the projectors on the rafts requires a mobile hoist, and the gallery layouts had to ensure that this access was always possible.

The floors of the galleries are made from a reconstituted stone bonded to a raised accessible floor system (fig. 16). The selection was determined by the need for resistance to heavy weight on any single point (point loading), surface durability with minimal 'tracking' (there is a tendency for reconstituted stone containing resin, after a while, to show which areas have had heavy use), and available colours that would fit in with the general concept of the galleries – namely, that the fixtures and fittings would be as neutral as possible in order for the panel colours and objects to stand out strongly. When applied to the gallery walls, this strategy of neutral colouring allows the Museum to change the objects and change the panel colours without concern for the bigger surfaces. Towards this end, two colours were selected for the floor, a pale and a dark grey, and these alternate according to the historical period and desired atmosphere of the gallery. At certain points, dates are set into the floor panels to remind visitors were they are in a chronological run of galleries (colour plate 33). A number of timber floors provide essential variation in sound and texture underfoot (colour plates 4, 12, 22, 26, 35, 36).

The window panels are the main rhythmic devices running through all the galleries, screening harmful daylight from the objects but permitting the presence of the outside world to leak through. Many studies were made to establish the proportions and scale of these in relation to Aston Webb's rooms.

The display panels support the objects and define the perimeter of a display: detached from the architecture and painted (or occasionally covered with textile) in highly-tuned colours, these, together with the plinths, create the main structure of the interior design (colour plates 30–31). The plinths are basically modular but have a variety of finishes – paint, polished plaster, timber, slate, stone. Some are rough and some are smooth. All support low-level lighting, graphics, security devices and allow the filtered air to enter the galleries from underneath. It was felt that a great majority of visitors would understand that the 20 cm plinths demarcate, *per se*, areas for objects, out of bounds to visitors (fig. 47).

The desire for objects to be shown out of display cases whenever possible meant that, if there were no plinth, protection from touch was required. This led to the development of a system of robust, removable barrier rails that are connected to the raised floor but easily removed, and capable of supporting graphics and lighting (colour plate 2). The design for these was similar to that used for the supports for the free-standing interpretive devices and, indeed, some of the objects themselves.

Housings for the audios, videos and computer interactives had to be capable of being connected to a variety of different supports, wall surfaces, display cases, plinths, benches and work surfaces (colour plates 27–28). These had to be discreet, durable and allow easy access for servicing. Like the ends of the benches, these are finished in Nextel paint that is warm to the touch but remarkably resilient to wear and tear. The interpretive devices form a family of related activities, particularly those adjacent to the displays, and are made from the same materials as the rest of the installation. They are deliberately not treated differently. All can be easily removed for maintenance.

Benches were designed by Casson Mann specifically for the British Galleries (colour plates 13 and 27). We searched for but failed to find a product on the market that would satisfy all our requirements. These were that the benches had to be:
- designed with no exposed wood (as they were to be surrounded by exquisite examples of wood craftsmanship, and nothing within our budget could have looked anything other than poor);
- modular and available in various sizes (the largest bench is just over two metres and the smallest is just over one);

- comfortable – preferably upholstered, but in a non-organic fabric;
- capable of accommodating a variety of books and audio points;
- accessible for the mechanisms and technology associated with the audios;
- easy to clean, maintain and repair.

The Museum was keen to have arms and backs to improve visitor comfort, but these lifted the overall height of them above an acceptable level. The final designs are made as a modular system that can be reconfigured depending on where the benches are placed. Pockets for gallery books or audios can be added at either end. A removable unit, upholstered in Kvadrat 'Glove' fabric, covers a steel frame bolted to the gallery floor. The frame houses the sound players for the audios and the recoiling devices for the handsets.

The Film Rooms

These were designed with sound-proof entry boxes. In fact, visitors appear to need the sound of the film to draw them in, so the doors are generally left open. The walls are designed to absorb as much of the sound as possible and the 'linen fold' patterned timber panels, cut by laser, are a deliberate reference to other, historic panelled rooms in the galleries (colour plate 21). The benches are a standard product adapted to our needs and covered in the same fabric as the gallery benches.

The Cornelia Parker sculpture

The oculus created by the architects at the corner of the galleries offered the opportunity to hang an object to lift the eye through to the upper floor – or direct it down to the lower floor (colour plates 20 and 22). This is an important moment, as it is the only place in the run of galleries where the visitor is aware of another level. A historical chandelier was considered, but there was a desire to underpin the fact that the corner rooms were essentially contemporary rooms with no exhibits, twenty-first century spaces where the past, visible from both doorways, could be viewed and read about. The work of several contemporary sculptors was therefore considered by the Project Team, and Cornelia Parker's work, focused as it is on memory, on objects that hold memories or on narratives related to objects, was thought to be a perfect fit. She was commissioned in 1999 and her piece *Breathless* was installed in 2001. The gallery text for *Breathless* is reproduced in appendix 13. Visible through the windows to the outside world at night, it is a gentle reminder of the larger political implications of the British Galleries and the objects they contain.

Programme

The first programme, created in 1996, allowed a period of three months between completion of the galleries and their official opening in November 2001. During this time it was envisaged that the galleries would be tested, snagged and marketed. Photographs would be taken for publication and publicity, inevitable IT problems would be resolved, lighting adjusted, text errors corrected. The opening date of November 2001 was met, but, unfortunately, this 'settling time' was lost.

The programme of completing such a project in five years, including this snagging period, was always ambitious, but nonetheless realistic, if every aspect of it had worked perfectly. As it was, most aspects worked reasonably well, but with each element, particularly building elements, slipping a little, the cumulative time lost amounted to three months. In addition, it has to be admitted that the knowledge that the three months was there probably permitted more leniency than one, harder deadline might have allowed.

The design period, after a calm start, was intense. In October 1997, the application was made to the Heritage Lottery Fund. Stage C of the design programme, 'Concept Design', was not submitted until May 1998, two years after our appointment. Thereafter the speed of work increased dramatically with Scheme Design (Stage D) and Detail Design (Stage E) following at six-month intervals. During the summer of 1998 the decision was made to use construction management as the preferred method of procuring the galleries, and Exterior was appointed as construction managers. This method divides up the work into packages of work according to trade, and each package is separately tendered. By this means, costs are easier to control than with a more traditional method of procurement whereby the project would be tendered and awarded to one contractor who would then be responsible for sourcing and controlling all the subcontractors.

In theory, construction management should allow more flexibility for the finalising and issue of design details. In our case it required the early release of three of the 12 'packages' of work (period room frames, structural metalwork and the lighting raft) that required a number of fast design decisions that were unconnected to the sequence of galleries and our own programme of work. At this stage, Detail Design (Stage E) was not complete and considerable pressure was put on the Design Team to keep the flow of information within the programme. The Museum decided to procure two of the packages themselves: the IT equipment and the object mounts. Procurement of the IT was postponed to the last moment because of the hope of a fall in prices and improved performance of equipment. Object mounts were usually made in-house, and for this reason there seemed little point in putting them through the full tendering process. This decision made both packages vulnerable to the weaknesses of parallel management, with co-ordination and responsibilities not being clearly allocated.

The construction management route was probably the only way that the galleries could have been delivered on time, but, once on site, any delays incurred by one contractor had inevitable knock-on effects, so that if one contractor ran late, the effect on the others following on seemed to be hard to control. It also created a phenomenal quantity of paperwork for all parties. The merits of construction management for this type of work continue to be a point of discussion, with some museums fully committed to it, and others anxious to revert to more traditional processes.

Conclusion Looking back on the redisplay of the British Galleries, there were many lessons well-learnt. Some were practical – concerned with management, keeping meetings short and focused, being clear about priorities. Some were connected to the client – to do with understanding the decision-making process and establishing a common language. But the most useful concerned the design process. These centred on the idea of keeping faith in early responses – the ones that come from deep down and are hard to explain until later when they tend to clarify themselves – and on learning how to hang on to them through the inevitable beating, crushing and stretching as they are put through the machinery of implementation.

We should probably have tested more of our ideas through prototyping. We should perhaps have tried to exclude more objects, so that there would have been more long-term flexibility in use of the gallery spaces. But one unexpected difficulty was how to balance our cool objectivity as outsiders against the seductiveness of the objects. As time went on, we felt late omissions almost more keenly than the Museum team. Our five-year relationship with the objects became almost personal. In the end, it was the objects that became the clients, with all the smiles and complaints that one would expect during a process of rehousing. Now, when we visit the galleries, we are visiting old friends with the normal mixed feelings of delight and reservation that such encounters provoke. But, generally, there are still more smiles than complaints.

Notes I would like to thank Richard Aldridge, Sandro Goppion, Crispin and Grita Rose-Innes, Christopher Wilk and Nick Umney for information towards this chapter.

1. The interview panel consisted of Alan Borg, V&A Director, Gwyn Miles, Head of Major Projects, Robin Cole-Hamilton, Head of Public Affairs and responsible for design at the Museum, and Christopher Wilk, then Chief Curator of Furniture and Woodwork.

2. Quoted in Physick, John, *The Victoria and Albert Museum: The History of Its Building* (London, 1982), p. 224.

3. The possibility of installing a staircase between the two floors in the corner rooms was investigated but proved unfeasible.

4. In a normal air-conditioning system where air is pumped in from the edge of the room, the movement of air could have been too vigorous. This system allows the air to move slowly. It also aimed to lessen the amount of dust that might enter the galleries, as air flows up, not down.

5. My anecdotal view is that, contrary to expectations, the raised floor appears to have reduced the amount of vibration transferred through the raised gallery floors. The original concrete floors of the Aston Webb rooms are not as solid as one might expect, indeed they are surprisingly 'lively'.

6. This level of co-ordination was one of the keys to the success of the project and was achieved through the extensive experience and patience of Alastair Gourlay and Christopher Beaver, who, together with Ross Shute, project manager for Bovis, were able to hold the team to account and keep the design work on programme.

7. In the event, Jon Williams and Philippe Haag, working with the Hanoverian and Victorian Teams, remained, whilst the Tudor and Stuart Team, for no particular reason, had a sequence of four different designers. Although some information was inevitably lost during the handover periods, and the Museum co-ordinator for the Tudor and Stuart section had to be particularly patient owing to changes in designers, it highlighted the importance of maintaining a high quality of documentation, particularly within the design studio.

8. The Concept Team ultimately made the decision that the British Galleries could not alone provide services and spaces which has to be considered on a museum-wide basis.

9. This solution has another advantage that we did not foresee. A bed in a glass case may allow the visitor to look closely at details of embroidery and trimming but the bed is effectively imprisoned. By showing it in its own room, scholars can be taken into the space to examine the bed, stepladders can be erected for inspection and all sorts of routine maintenance can be carried out as and when needed.

10. Visitors appear to understand this, except that the addition of the words 'Please Touch' alongside the hand symbol suggests to many that the symbol itself needs to be touched. This is a good example of why extensive testing is essential if the full range of interpretation and misinterpretation is to be anticipated.

11. As, for example, was created for the Melville Bed.

12. The temporary gallery 'Best of British' was opened to the public on 29 January 1999.

13. The main sources of light for the larger objects are 150w metal halide lamps with 16 size-24 tails 3 metres long. The sources for the display cases and the areas with lowered ceilings are 100w halogen lamp with varying quantities and lengths of size 14 or size 8 tails. Large flat objects, such as tapestries, are lit with recessed asymmetrical 18w compact fluorescent lamps. The ambient/emergency lights for side galleries are recessed downlighters fitted with compact fluorescent lamps and covered with a frosted filter.

14. A few selected cases dedicated to the display of a single object were fitted with a block of frosted acrylic. When lit from underneath, this created a glowing plinth that lights as well as supports the object. This is particularly effective under glass objects such as the decanter designed by William Burges.

15. Our testing was not conclusive on this point. In limited evaluation of subject panels with the visually impaired, we found a preference expressed for light text on a dark grey background over dark text on pale grey.

16. The V&A requirements set out in the tender document for supply and fixing of freestanding display cases listed: stability and vibration (conforming to the requirements of BS Code of Practice BS 6399); construction (using inert materials, and obtaining performance as good as that achieved with welded steel bases); use of laminated low-iron content 'white' glass; air seals (giving an air exchange rate of 0.1 air exchanges per day, and with very good ability to exclude dust); access (to a minimum of 75–90% depending on case type). It was also specified that cases provide for an air sampling port, a facility tray to contain, for example, absorbent material,

and that they accommodate the Museum's preferred security locks, fibre optic tails and building monitoring system sensors.

17. Certification under ISO 9001: 2000 regulations represented a significant achievement for Goppion, who had developed very quickly during the 1990s from a small, family-run business based on traditional practice to a company based on recognised standards for commercial and production processes. See *International Organization for Standardization ISO 9000 Quality Management Principles,* http://www.iso.ch/iso/en/iso9000-14000/iso9000index.html, consulted 10 February 2004.

13. Main entrance to the Museum in November 1998, showing the British Galleries hoist behind hoarding.

14. Museum roof showing the British Galleries plant room, June 2000. Photo by Stephen Johns.

15. Typical gallery section, showing displacement ventilation principle, 1998.

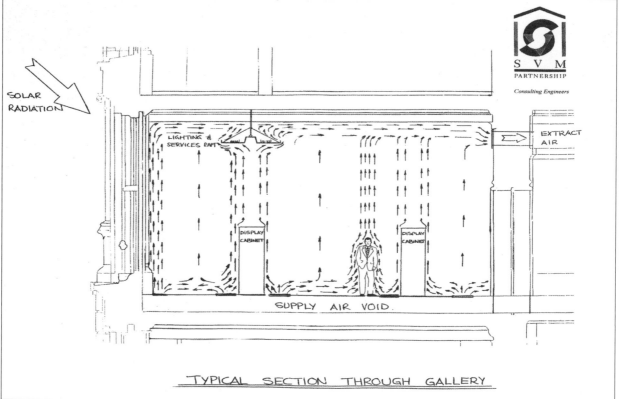

TYPICAL SECTION THROUGH GALLERY

16. Regency gallery (120) showing installation of raised floor, June 2000. Photo by Stephen Johns.

17. Tudor gallery (58) showing portal with integrated fire doors and reinstated marble skirting around the architrave of the reduced doorway.

18. Georgian gallery (54) showing ramp outside Norfolk House Music Room looking towards Chinoiserie.

19. Georgian gallery (54) showing area of cutaway panelling outside Norfolk House Music Room.

20. Touch Object *with associated graphics and pull-out braille panels, gallery 122.*

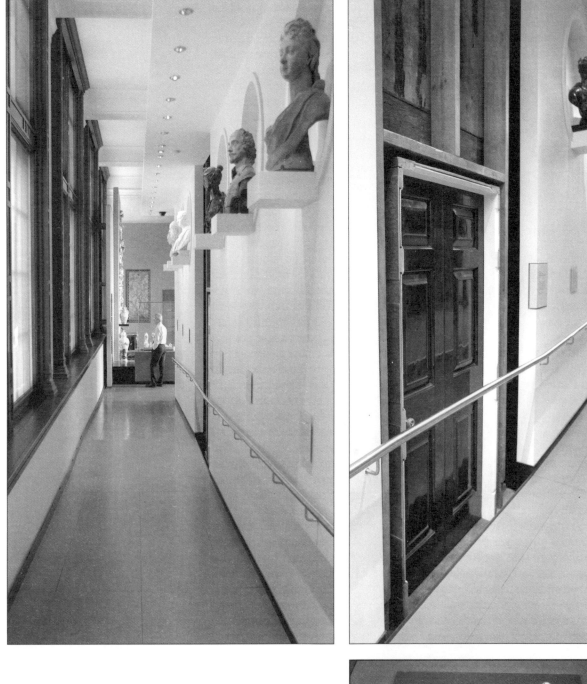

21. *Study of level 2 showing extent of natural light in the galleries, Casson Mann 1998.*

22. *Study of level 2 showing variation in noise levels generated by areas of activity, e.g. Discovery Areas, Film Rooms and displays*

likely to appeal to school groups, Casson Mann 1998.

23. *Study of level 2 showing how the galleries are divided into a series of perceived 'rooms', Casson Mann 1998.*

24. *Study of level 2 showing 'fast track' visitor route through the galleries with major objects alongside, Casson Mann 1998.*

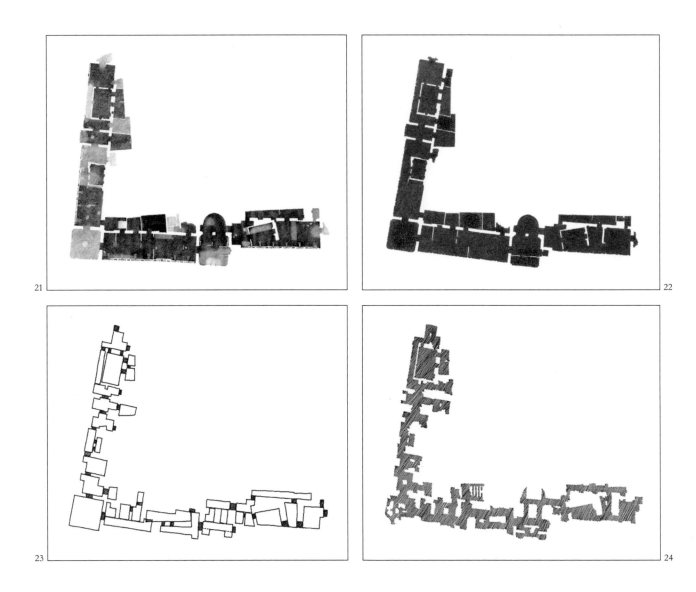

25. Supporting metal structure for mirror in Stuart gallery (56).

26. *Scale model of British Galleries at Casson Mann studio, May 1998.*

27. *Scale model showing Victorian gallery (125).*

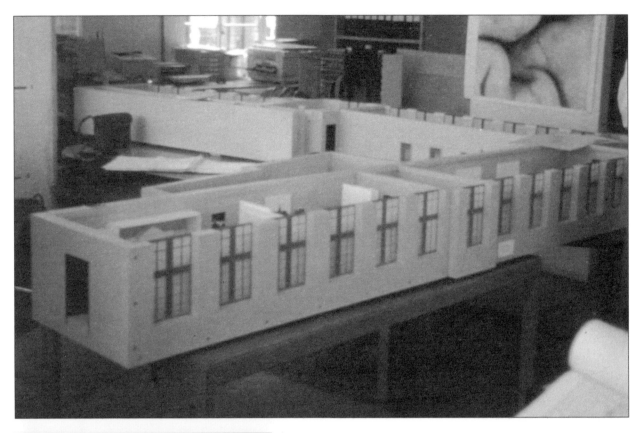

28. V&A typeface (above) with a Serif typeface (below). The V&A typeface requires less space. Supplied by Rose Innes Associates.

Opposite page:

29. 104 subject panels were positioned either on open display or inside showcases. Photo by Dennis Gilbert/View.

30. Didactic panels provide more background information. They were produced as digital prints mounted on to aluminium. Photo by Dennis Gilbert/View.

Chinoiserie 1745–1765

Chinoiserie was a form of decoration fashionable between 1745 and 1765. People were fascinated by the exotic nature of luxury products such as porcelain and lacquer that had been flowing into Europe from East Asia since the early 16th century.

Chinoiserie 1745–1765

Chinoiserie was a form of decoration fashionable between 1745 and 1765. People were fascinated by the exotic nature of luxury products such as porcelain and lacquer that had been flowing into Europe from East Asia since the early 16th century.

31. *Orientation panels are located at all the principal points of entry. Photo by Dennis Gilbert/View.*

32. *The Design Team preferred the use of long strips of digitally printed labels for plinths and showcases.*

33. *Large-format books supported on fixed pedestals provide information for each period room and for the panelling from the Northumberland House Glass Drawing Room. Each page is made of scratch-proof, rigid acrylic and is bound with an oversize nylon hinge. Photo by Dennis Gilbert/View.*

34. *'Handling Collection': research revealed that Braille readers dislike reading Braille from cold metallic surfaces. Labels and tactile drawings were produced as warm-to-touch, rigid and brightly coloured polypropylene sheets that pull out from under the related text labels. Photo by Dennis Gilbert/View.*

35. Box rotation and normal rotation case. The structure comprises a frame fixed to the wall and a glass-shell, front-closing system. When the glass shell is open, the interior of the case is fully accessible. The front, mobile part of the case is supported on a wheel, which defines the opening arc.

A compression seal, recessed into the metal frame of the opening section, creates an air-tight seal once the case is closed. Fibre optic lighting is threaded through the structure of the case and can be positioned at the top, and/or the base of the case (see details A and B).

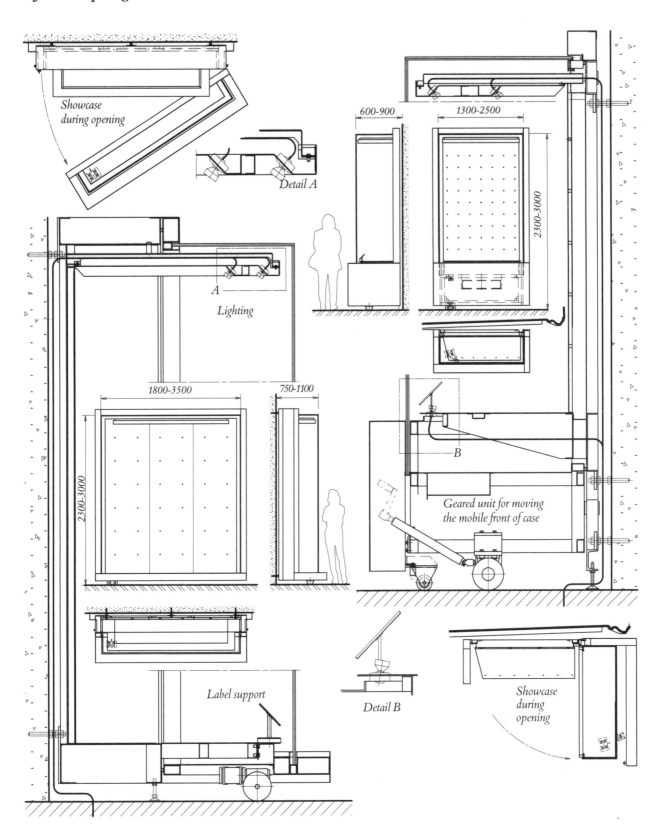

Showcase during opening

Detail A

600-900

1300-2500

2300-3000

A

Lighting

1800-3500

750-1100

2300-3000

B

Geared unit for moving the mobile front of case

Label support

Detail B

Showcase during opening

36. Free-standing pull-out case. The structure comprises a fixed base with a rebated solid (or glazed) panel within a supporting structure, and a mobile section upon which a glass hood (three glass sides and a top) is placed. The hood pulls away from the main structure leaving the base and interior of the case open.

A simple, mechanical system uses wheels that run along portable tracking (see detail A). A compression-seal system seals the case. Fibre-optic tails come through the base or hood (see detail B), and mirror foil can be applied to the underside of the glass top to reflect light.

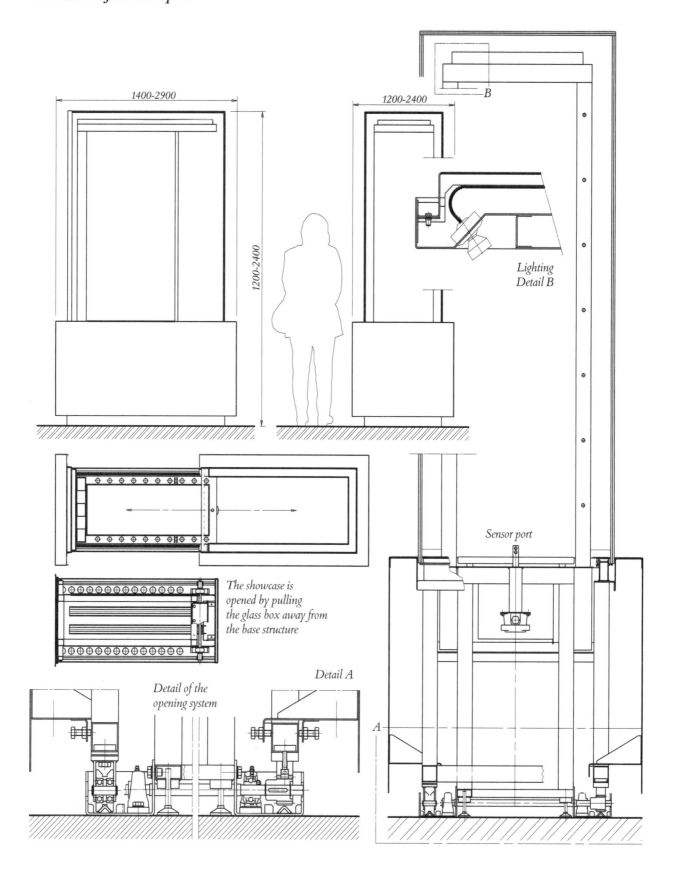

1400-2900

1200-2400

1200-2400

B

Lighting Detail B

Sensor port

The showcase is opened by pulling the glass box away from the base structure

Detail A

Detail of the opening system

A

37. *Free-standing lift-up case, working on a rack or pantograph. A metal base contains the mechanical parts for lifting the glass hood.*
Type A, rack consists of four rack and pinion mechanisms with a reduction gearbox at each corner, pushing the hood upwards as the geared handle is turned (see detail A).

Type B, pantograph consists of one or more pairs of scissor arms which, when closed, are contained within the base.
The mechanism is used when the hood has to be lifted to a height greater than that allowed by ratchets fitted within the base of the case.
In both designs, a compression

seal, fitted between the base, and the metal profile attached to the bottom edges of the glass hood, seals the case. Fibre optic tails come through the base and mirror foil can be applied to the underside of the glass top to reflect light (see detail B).

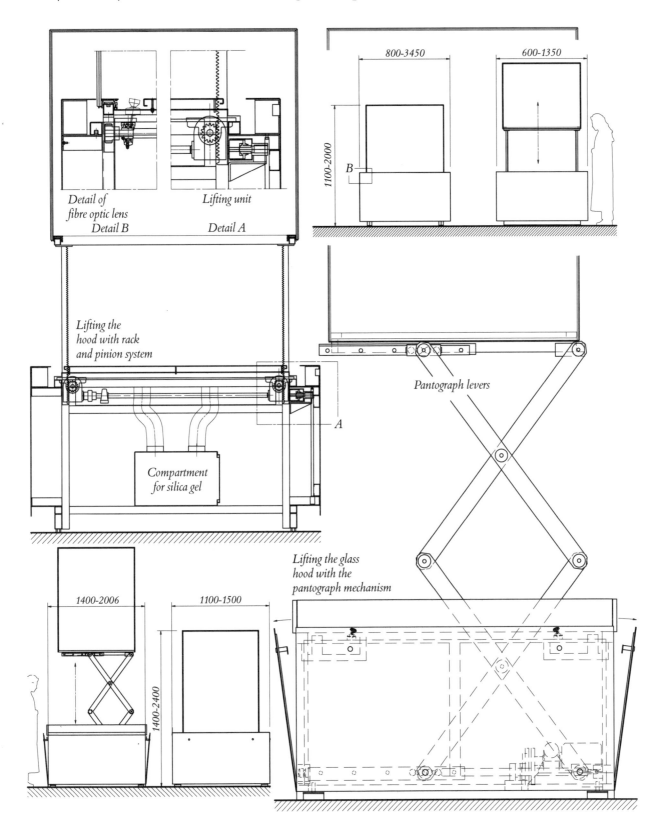

Detail of
fibre optic lens
Detail B

Lifting unit

Detail A

Lifting the
hood with rack
and pinion system

Compartment
for silica gel

Pantograph levers

Lifting the glass
hood with the
pantograph mechanism

800-3450

600-1350

1100-2000

B

1400-2006

1100-1500

1400-2400

38. Fitted case. *The structure is built to fit the gallery wall. One glass panel is stepped forward from its closed position so that it slides over the adjacent panel (see detail A). There are compression seals at the top and bottom of the doors, and manual compression seals on the vertical edges of the glass. Lighting can be positioned along the base and the top of the case (see detail B).*

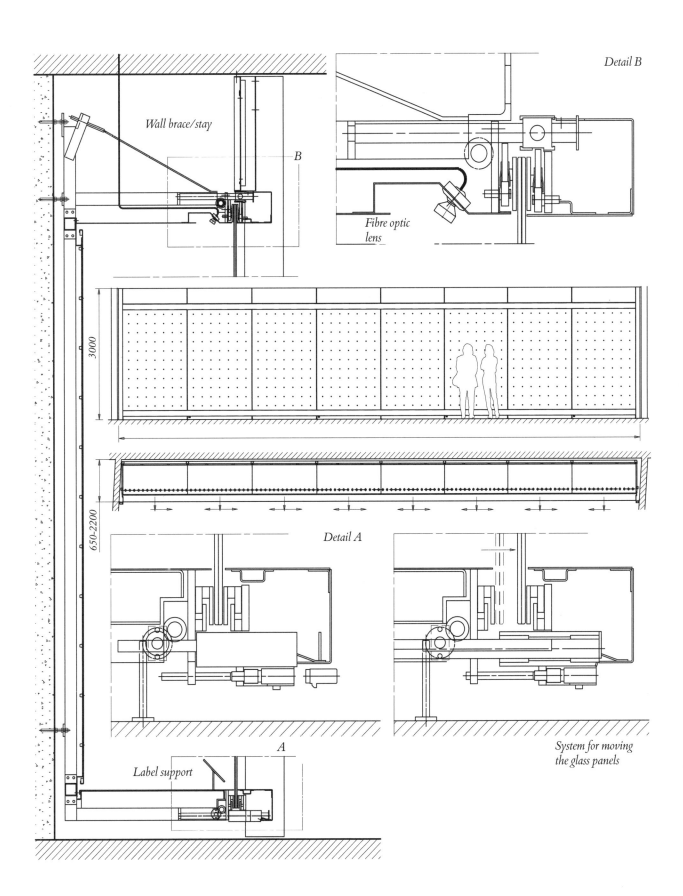

Detail B

Wall brace/stay

B

Fibre optic lens

3000

650-2200

Detail A

A

Label support

System for moving the glass panels

39. Free-standing frame case. The steel profile that surrounds the glass doors and the glass structure of the case itself is shaped to retain the seals (see detail A). The edges of the glass panels are protected by L-shaped steel profiles, which reinforce the glass panels. They hold the hinges (see detail C) and locks, and hold the seal compressors (see detail D) which press the door against the frame. Hinged glass doors are opened using a specially designed adjustable trolley. The case can be lit from the base and/or the top with fibre optics. Within the plinth is a tray to hold silica gel (see detail B).

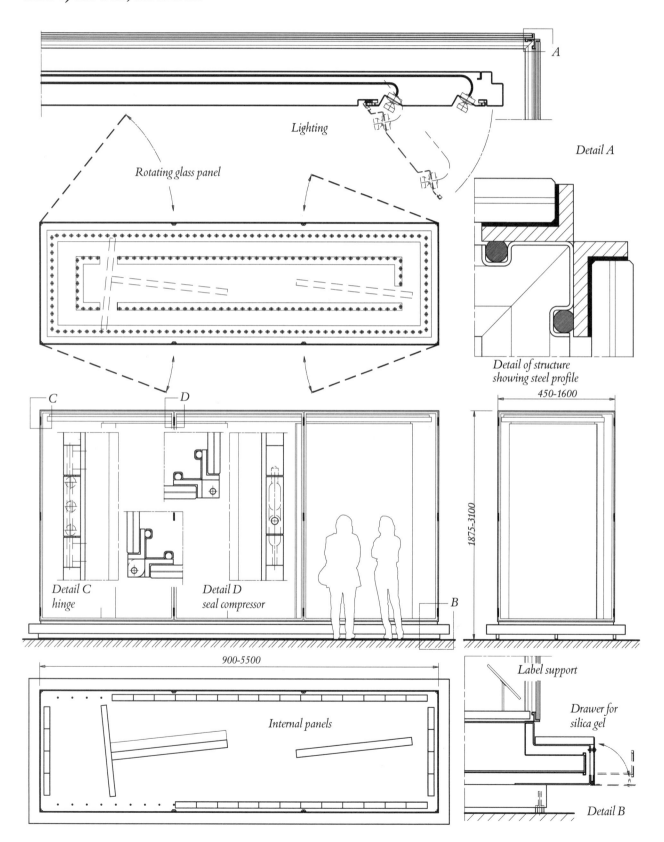

Detail A

Lighting

Rotating glass panel

Detail of structure showing steel profile

450-1600

1875-3100

C

D

Detail C hinge

Detail D seal compressor

B

900-5500

Internal panels

Label support

Drawer for silica gel

Detail B

40. Special cases. These were designed in conjunction with V&A conservators for especially vulnerable objects requiring an unusual degree of physical support or environmetal control. The case for the Sackville Pedigree, for example, had to provide a microclimate that would be very stable in terms of relative humidity, yet still allow easy monitoring of the internal environment. It is withdrawn from its wall niche by rotating the entire case around one of its vertical sides. A wheel helps to support the weight. Once it has passed through ninety degrees, the back panel of the case is opened like a book cover for the installation of the object (see detail D). A monitoring port (see detail BB) and a conditioning panel inside the case (see detail A) can be accessed without fully exposing the object to the air. Compression seals (see detail C) maintain an air-tight environment.

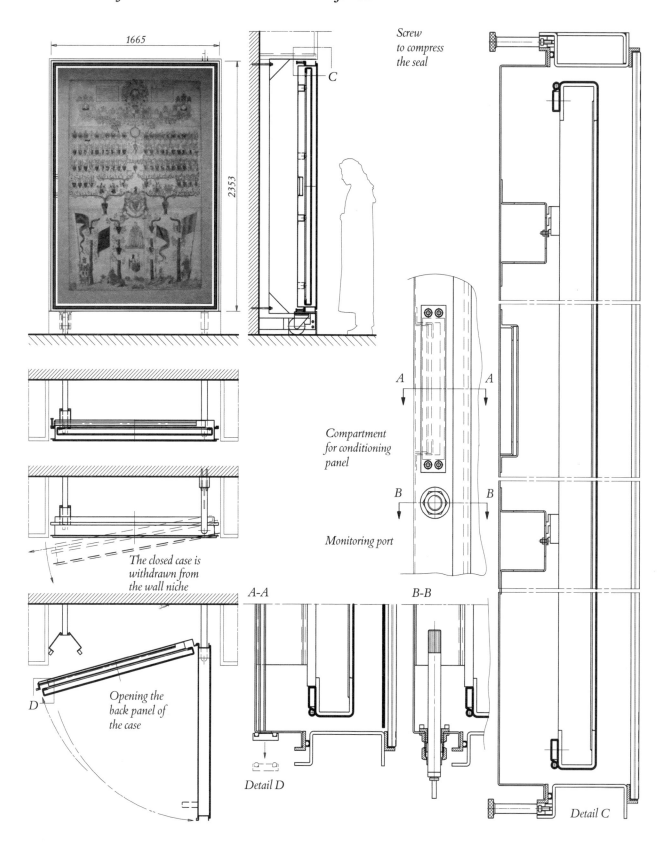

1665

2353

Screw to compress the seal

C

The closed case is withdrawn from the wall niche

D

Opening the back panel of the case

A   A

Compartment for conditioning panel

B   B

Monitoring port

A-A

B-B

Detail D

Detail C

41. Drawers. Generally these are housed in the bases of the cases. Each drawer is fitted with a removable tray, an integral caption holder and a tray for silica gel to absorb moisture. The top of the drawer is fitted with a low-reflective glass panel that is hinged at the back allowing access from the top (see detail A). The steel front is hinged at the bottom so that the tray can be removed without opening the glass top (see detail B). There is a compression seal between the glass lid and the drawer sides. A version of the drawer was developed and produced with an electronically controlled motor to limit vibration when opening and closing.

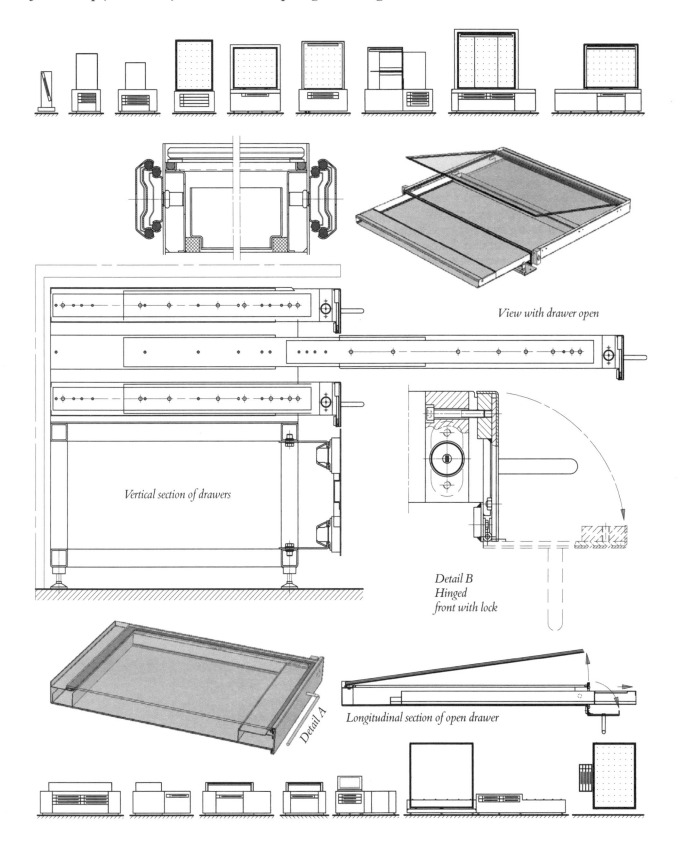

View with drawer open

Vertical section of drawers

Detail B
Hinged
front with lock

Detail A

Longitudinal section of open drawer

42. *Lift-up case in Tudor gallery (58).*

44. *Frame case in Tudor gallery (58).*

46. *Fitted case in Victorian gallery (125).*

43. *Rotation case in Stuart gallery (56).*

45. *Pull-out case in Stuart gallery (56).*

47. Early drawing showing modular construction of plinths, display panels and window panels. Plinth surfaces would vary but all would be fitted with removable metal front edge for protection. Front areas of plinths are designed to house fibre optic lights by projectors under the floor and are fitted with threaded holes for label supports, Casson Mann 1998.

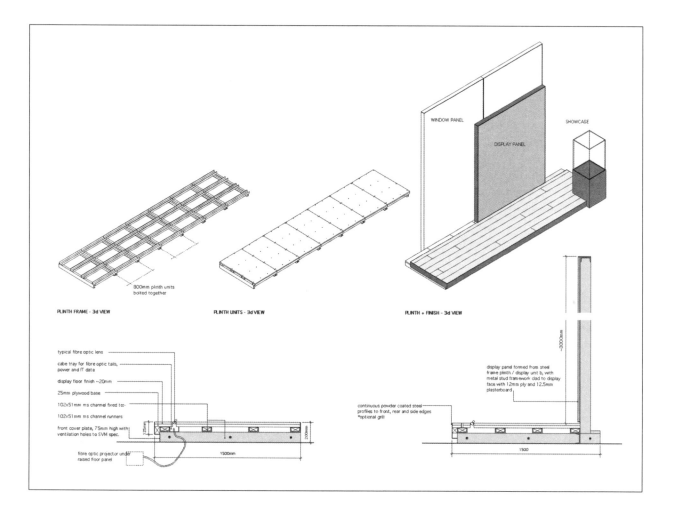

Chapter 7   Colour, Texture, Pattern and Light

Sarah Medlam

Choosing the colours   At the head of the very first piece of paper on which we recorded our aspirations for the presentation and design of the galleries we wrote a motto for ourselves: *Blandness is not an option.* In the course of many visits to art museums in Europe and North America, we had been wearied by the infinite shades of grey and off-white that had dominated the design of so-called permanent galleries in art museums for so many years. They leached colour and splendour from the objects shown in them and offered little stimulus to the visitor. We also feared that a monochrome series of galleries would date more quickly and would, in a very few years, appear old-fashioned and unappealing.

The variety of colours, textures and patterns used in the British Galleries was one important weapon in this campaign against blandness. We wanted to demonstrate that all three were important elements of historic decoration. Many of the objects that were to be shown were originally highly coloured, even if they are now faded, and the 'safe' option of showing them against neutral colours often diminishes them even further. We also had a very practical concern that was addressed by the use of colour. In such a large run of galleries, variety would be essential to enliven the journey of visitors and prevent museum fatigue, and we recognised that colour was a key element in providing variety. We tried to use colours as evocative of different historic periods, rather than seeking archaeological correctness in every case. Though the approach was appropriate in choosing colours for the period rooms (see chapter 10), in areas of formal museum display we used colour with greater freedom, using historic colours to inform our choice of modern paint finishes and the selection of fabrics for display use.

For more than 18 months we met weekly to create the changing palette of colours used throughout the galleries. Christopher Wilk and the present writer were the regular Museum representatives on what became known as the Historic Decoration Team, with curators from the three teams attending occasionally. David Mlinaric, an interior decorator noted for his particular sensitivity to historic interiors, worked with Dinah Casson, the main exhibition and interior designer, to direct the work of the team. Jason Roberts, of Mlinaric, Henry & Zervudachi, undertook much of the work of getting our ideas off the drawing board, supervising colour mixing and trials of paints. His colleague Mary Ellison was responsible for sourcing many of the fabrics required. Additional members of the team were John Cornforth, whose expertise in the history of interior decoration in Britain was unrivalled; John Harris, the architectural historian; and Christopher Gibbs, a collector and dealer who has exceptionally wide knowledge of different periods. This team not only chose colours, finishes and fabrics for all the galleries, but also advised on the decoration of the period rooms.

The displays span 400 years and extend through 16 galleries. We aimed to create a sequence of colours for each period, which would give a different character to succeeding areas of the galleries and carry the visitor through with a sense of changing rhythm and pace, even though they might be unconscious of colour as the method used to achieve this. The intention was to develop a scheme using predominantly simple, painted surfaces, with only occasional accents of glazed paint, polished plaster or fabric.

Almost all the colours in the sequence grew out of a consideration of the historic colours used and favoured at particular periods. They also reflect the colours of the wide range of objects shown in these galleries, now including dress as well as textiles. Some choices were influenced or confirmed by reference to individual objects or to groups of objects. Some objects, and in particular ceramics and enamels, offer glimpses of the vividness of early colouring. Others have lost much of their original colour, and the choice of subtler shades to bring out what remains of splendour proved a firm discipline. The process was very much one of responding to the objects rather than imposing a single scheme. We worked with colour photographs of objects to make a preliminary selection, then checked our ideas against the objects themselves, often having to take colour boards into store to set them behind large tapestries or paintings that could not easily be brought out.

In considering colour, lighting had to be constantly borne in mind. Many of the objects, particularly the textiles, watercolours and miniatures, required low light levels for conservation reasons. Colours for low-lit rooms and cases had to be selected with this in mind and tried out, where possible, under similar lighting. Consideration of light levels also affected colour choices more widely, as visitors' eyes need to adjust slowly to reduced levels of light. Changes of light level between galleries had to be carefully managed and the colours used for walls and display boards can affect visitors' perception of light levels. At the same time that we wanted to control light, we had no wish to exclude all daylight. Casson Mann's design of window 'screens' meant that daylight was visible in most areas, at high level, moderated by blinds. At certain points, where the material on show allowed it, we were glad to use the blinds to let in higher levels of daylight, as in the displays on Vauxhall Gardens (Gallery 52) or the Great Exhibition (Gallery 122) (colour plate 35). In the Study Rooms (Galleries 55 and 121), where no museum objects are on show (colour plate 22), the blinds are set so that the visitors may orientate themselves by looking across the junction of Cromwell Road and Exhibition Road to the finest Victorian building of South Kensington, the Natural History Museum.

The scheme evolved as a series of layers, following the hierarchy of screens devised by Casson Mann. For the shell of the original Aston Webb building we chose generally more muted and neutral colours (stone colours or grey-greens). These were historically colours for everyday use, hard-wearing colours derived from cheaper earth pigments. For the same reason, we generally avoided white, as this too was a luxury colour for most of the period under consideration, a colour that was, historically, always prone to yellowing and discoloration after a very short time. A few galleries were painted more strongly. In the Rococo gallery (53) a greyish mid-blue (sugar-bag blue) was used (colour plates 16, 17), reflecting contemporary colours for papers or fabrics, and in one of the Victorian galleries (123) we painted the walls a greyish lilac, typical of the lighter colours used before 1850 (colour plate 38). Doorways and the plaster surrounds of the windows were painted a dark grey throughout, to tone with the black marble door surrounds that appear in most but not all of the galleries. With the dark grey powder coating of the cases, these served to provide continuity throughout the galleries. Ceilings were also treated similarly throughout, in an off-white. For the large window panels that follow the Aston Webb fenestration in their regular placement, we generally chose a similar colour to that of the walls, with slight tonal variation to reflect the fact that they were not part of the original structure.

In addition to colours for walls and window panels we also chose individual colour schemes for each display. For the display panels and cases, the choice of colours ranged from broken whites and elegant pale greens to intense blues and even a shocking acidic yellow (in the display *French Style* in Gallery 122) (colour plate 72). It is in these smaller areas that we were able to introduce greater variety in types of finish and also to use fabrics in a way that would not have been appropriate or affordable in larger areas of the galleries. In these areas, we used commercially available fabrics, avoiding specially woven or dyed fabrics except in the period rooms. These individual areas of display on a single subject are the most likely to be changed during the life of the galleries, to accommodate new objects or new displays, or simply to refresh areas as they become worn. Polished plaster, stippled paint and marbling, used in small areas, can add different textures and suggest the variegated colours that are so often evident in historic objects or interiors and which are so difficult to replicate in the thick, even colour of modern, mass-produced paints. Textiles offer variety of colour and weave, but also introduce pattern. The idea of pattern has been very unfashionable in recent years and so is often forgotten as a vital element of historic decoration, though interest in the subject is showing signs of revival.

One aspect of decoration that it is easy, quite literally, to overlook, is that of floors. Experience of museum visiting had made us very aware of the importance of floors in offering variety in a visit, and of the pleasure of hearing the change of footfall over wooden floors as against ceramic tiles or marble. As with the journey of colour, visitors may well enjoy the effect of such variety without being at all aware of it as a deliberate choice. It was one of our principles in the consideration of the period rooms that we would try to reinstate suitable flooring, because none of them (except the Victorian room from The Grove) retained their original flooring. We then looked for other areas where it would be appropriate to interrupt the standard floor finish, a grey resin tile giving the appearance of ceramic, that was used mostly in a mid-grey-green, but with a lighter grey version used in the eighteenth-century galleries and occasionally elsewhere.

Opportunities for wooden flooring occurred in areas such as the small room used to show the Melville Bed (Gallery 56) (colour plate 12). Here, pale, scrubbed floorboards were used to give the visitors the sense of walking into a room, and suggest continuity between the visitor space and the cased area where the bed stands. To those brought up on fitted carpets, the contrast of unfinished pine boards with the elaborate embroidery and fringing of the bed is a shocking one, yet it is one that is verified both by the evidence of inventories and by reference to illustrations of interiors.[1] In the Discovery Area placed in the sequence at about 1740, off Gallery 52, panels of parquet were used, following an eighteenth-century design for floors. Similar parquet was used in both the Study Areas (Galleries 55 and 121) (colour plate 22), and in the re-creation of the National Gallery of British Art of the 1860s in Gallery 122.[2] In the Great Exhibition display (Gallery 122) the floor was laid with unfinished pine boards of exactly the width (9 ins) of those used in 1851 (colour plate 35). Only modern health and safety legislation prevented us from laying them with the same 3/8 ins wide gaps that were, in the Crystal Palace, used to let dust and rubbish be swept through at the end of the day.[3]

The process of choosing Many people expressed great surprise that the selection of the colours should prove so lengthy. Indeed, the amount of work it required surprised us. It was important from the beginning that the work was undertaken for all the galleries by the same team, with the curators of particular periods joining meetings when necessary. Only in that way could we ensure that the balance of the whole was maintained. Week by week, individuals might be absent from discussions for one reason or another, but after the first months we had established very firmly the particular strengths of individual members of the Historic Decoration Team and would schedule work to allow for this. John Cornforth brought particular knowledge of historic sources to the discussion and frequently provided stimulating new ideas. David Mlinaric and Jason Roberts were immensely skilled in understanding how different colours and combinations of colour would work in such large spaces, and the subtle variations that could depend on exactly how a colour had been mixed. Their experience of managing large decorating projects was a useful skill.

Initial discussions of a gallery would take place with files of illustrations being shown and discussed (see fig. 48). The creation of a temporary gallery (open for nearly two years from January 1999) not only served to keep some important items on show, but also offered us an opportunity to try out aspects of the design, from label layouts to prototypes for interpretive devices (colour plates 74–77). One area was set aside for trials for colours and lighting. A weekly programme soon developed of paint trials on ceilings, walls and on mock-up versions of wall and display panels. A contract painter patiently painted and repainted these areas as we worked. Jason Roberts modified colours when shade-card samples proved unsatisfactory when seen in a large area, and once a week we met for review. This system was very important, and it is likely that it will be followed in future Museum projects. However, progress at this stage was hampered by the failure to get in place an adequate mock-up of the proposed lighting for the galleries. The dynamic relationship between light and colour is a vital one and every effort to replicate the likely lighting needs to be made before final decisions on colour can be made with certainty.

Early on we took the decision that colours for the walls and ceilings of the galleries, and for the large window panels, must be chosen from standard, commercially available paints, from the largest paint manufacturers. We took this decision for reasons of economy, to allow for rematching when redecoration is needed. In a project of this size, such discipline is essential if the work is to be completed. Discussion of colours can be prolonged endlessly and pleasurably, and timetables needed to be used to ensure that decisions were made in a useful order and to a reasonable schedule. We also recognised that certain colours were particularly successful and useful, and these were used at several different points in the galleries, often looking quite different because of differing lighting conditions. Wherever possible we used ready-mixed colours, but certain objects and certain displays required colours to be mixed specially for us.

When colours had been agreed in principle, sample boards 60 cm square were painted up and annotated with the gallery number and the name of the display. Later, these boards were cut in two and half given to contractors as a control for their work. This allowed us to assess samples painted up in the final galleries for final approval just as painting was due to start. However, it occasionally proved necessary, even when the samples on the gallery walls matched the sample boards well, to modify the colours further, perhaps moving up or down a shade to allow for local lighting in the particular gallery. Because the building programme suffered slippage, the time allowed for this in the original schedule disappeared, so that changes were undeniably aggravating to the contractors, who, by that stage, had a demanding schedule to keep to, but it was vital in a few cases to balance the final effect. The success of the team's work reflected not only the months of weekly meetings but also its committed willingness to follow through inspections during the decoration and fit-out period, with site meetings at 8 am when required by the schedule of the contractors. With project managers nervous about progress and contractors hustling for a slot in a schedule, it can become a delicate matter to insist on modification at a late stage, and designers and curators need to be disciplined in keeping such changes to a minimum. It is important also, as work progresses, to have in place systems for recording the colours as finally used and for archiving small amounts of paint for touching up or repair as necessary.

From the start, the designers recorded every decision for galleries and for each display on a spreadsheet. This became a particularly important tool, as it was not possible to move through the sequence of galleries making every decision for one area at a time. Fabrics for case lining in particular proved tricky. After an initial suggestion of colour and type of fabric was made, sourcing could take several weeks and the team might have to revisit sections several times before completing them. An additional problem was posed by the Museum's need to commission testing of materials proposed for lining cases. This was a conservation requirement, to make certain that the chemical composition of the fabrics or papers, or the dyes used to colour them, would not release gases that might harm objects, metals in particular.[4] Such testing was expensive and time-consuming and for this reason the team considered carefully the use of such problematic materials. We had to accept several disappointments when particularly beautiful fabrics simply failed their tests. There was nothing to do but to search again, and test again when necessary. Powder-coated metal backboards, matched to paint samples, were used in many cases. However, the impact of, say, a rich, red silk velvet behind Elizabethan miniatures was such that it was worth all the effort of sourcing and testing.

Just as we had to return several times to some areas, so occasional review of the whole was an important factor in the success of the scheme. In particular, we needed, from time to time, to look up, mentally, from the plan and the spreadsheet to 'walk' through the galleries in our mind's eye. What is it here that will serve to pull your eye through to the next gallery? What will this look like if you come in by the other door and walk in the opposite direction? How will this colour in the foreground work with the other colour glimpsed across the room? These were exercises that were extremely helpful. From time to time we highlighted large objects on plans to see how they were spaced and placed in the galleries. At one point we even marked plans with the objects that offered glimpses of red to visitors and the areas where we had introduced red into the display materials, to establish that the enlivening effect of this colour appeared regularly throughout the displays.

When the plans of all the galleries were laid out in sequence, with samples of each of the colours painted on the edge, it was interesting to see how the different galleries had developed a distinct character and yet formed part of a rhythmic pattern, with light and strong colours predominating in turn. For the visitor, we hope that little of this is obvious, that what they notice and enjoy is simply the variety and that all the complexities of colour, texture and pattern remain as a discreet support to their enjoyment of the objects. It is also true that many visitors will not follow the whole sequence detailed below, as they would in a temporary exhibition. There are more than ten entrances and exits to the sequence of galleries. Visitors choose exactly how much they want to see on any visit and it was important that the galleries should feel harmonious individually, in sections and as a whole.

A walk through the galleries   After the two flights of stairs panelled in chilly white and black marble that lead to the galleries, Gallery 58 starts with a strong colour statement. The choice of a golden yellow ochre for the walls (colour plate 1) was inspired by the frequent references in contemporary inventories to ochre being used in grand sixteenth-century interiors (colour plates 68 and 69).[5] This colour is stronger and warmer than most of the colours used on walls in other galleries and provides a rich background for the wall of dark wood panelling from Haynes Grange and the tapestry of *The Story of Esther* in the display on *The Court of Henry VIII*.

There are several impressive and richly coloured objects here, such as the crimson and gold velvet cope lent by the Society of Jesus from Stonyhurst College, and the painted and gilded writing box known as 'Henry VIII's writing desk'. Even so, it has to be recognised that colour and light have a more vital role to play in this early section of the galleries, because the rare surviving objects cannot fully convey the lavish splendour of Henry VIII's court. Decisions on colour for individual displays also had to take account of the faded appearance some of the most important pieces. The Leicester armorial tapestry of 1585 (colour plate 5), for instance, is a grand design but is now quite soft in colour and argues strongly for a warm, neutral background. For this we chose not a cold grey, but mid-tone greenish drab, a colour that was to prove useful in several places in the galleries.

It is frequently as much the texture of a material as its colour that ensures its success as a background for a display. Polished plaster and fabric both offer subtle nuances of colouring that can be very supportive to a variety of objects, as can be seen in the first display on the *Renaissance*, with objects shown against a deep, blood-red, polished plaster, with its natural varying tones (colour plate 68).

With five full period rooms in the galleries, we decided not to resort to the creation of elaborately reconstructed or faked backgrounds elsewhere in the displays. One particular area of concern was how we might create sympathetic settings for the four beds shown in the galleries – large objects that naturally dominate the areas in which they are shown. In Gallery 57, the Great Bed of Ware is no longer set against panelling. We took a risky decision to use a semicircular apse, created by Aston Webb for his 1909 galleries, as the enclosure for the bed (colour plate 3). The grey-green chosen for the wall not only serves to reduce the impact of the curved walls but also reflects the earth pigments that dominated paint colours for interiors in the sixteenth century. The immediate source for this colour was an early seventeenth-century miniature showing a member of the Brathwaite family of Ambleside, Cumbria, in a green-hung bed.[6] With no surviving hangings for the bed and no record of how it would originally have been hung, we took the decision to dress the bed entirely in reproduction textiles, following the advice of the specialist consultant Dr Charles Kightly. His research in sixteenth-century inventories revealed the fact that alternate panels or 'panes' of red and yellow were the most popular colour combination in southern England in the late sixteenth century.[7] 'Say' (a popular twilled cloth of wool) was dyed with the natural dyes of madder (for the red) and weld (for the yellow). The result was breathtaking in its brightness, and we were happy for visitors to be shocked and enlivened by this meeting with historic colour.

Gallery 56 covers most of the seventeenth century. The wall colour here is soft stony white (colour plate 44). The colours for the displays are also quieter. The large Mortlake tapestry from the *Venus and Vulcan* series dominates the display on the courts of James I and Charles I, but this is also an area where we felt that a hit of colour in the decorative scheme was required. This is provided by a panel of dark red polished plaster behind the ebony and hardstone cabinet that once belonged to the diarist John Evelyn (colour plate 7). In the cases dedicated to a display on *The Civil War Years* the background is grey but the objects are far from dowdy. On one side of the case is a brightly-painted clavichord and, on the other, the deep plummy pink and gold of a soldier's silk sash, echoing the painting of one in a portrait by Dobson, borrowed from Tate Britain (colour plate 44).

After the Civil War period, the objects themselves survive in greater quantity and tend to become richer and bolder in texture and colour. In the display on *Britain and the Indies,* a small room is filled with black and gold lacquer, a red japanned chair, painted wall panels in *chinoiserie,* lustrous blue and white porcelain and printed and embroidered textiles (colour plate 8). With careful lighting these colourful, smooth-surfaced objects now shimmer luxuriously within a small, smart box of a room, the walls of light drab colour, but scarcely visible behind the rich array of objects. We specifically wanted the shimmering effect to draw visitors into this small side gallery. At the end of Gallery 56 a case displaying *The Role of the Upholsterer,* is lined with a deep blue moleskin fabric. This strong but discreet colour does not overpower the faded purple glory of Bishop Juxon's chair, used at the coronation of Charles II, but serves to show up the vibrant yellow silk from Leeds Castle, Kent, and the polychrome cut velvet provided for Queen Anne's bed at Windsor in 1714. It also provides a foil for the intricate workmanship of the tassels and fringes that were such an important element in upholstery at that period.

The Study Room (55) at the corner of the L-shaped run of galleries, is a calm space where people will sit and rest, use computers and enjoy Cornelia Parker's sculpture *Breathless* (colour plates 20 and 22). The choice was therefore made to use a light stone colour for the walls, one with no particular historic resonance. Beyond this area, Gallery 54 opens with a view of a lacquer-veneered mirror and table, set against bright red fabric, suggesting the strong colours used for fabrics in the grandest interiors in the late seventeenth century. To the right the visitor can look through to the Melville Bed, a splendid survival of the upholsterer's art of about 1700. This is set within a glazed 'room' similar in size to its original setting at Melville House, Fife (colour plate 12). Rather than embark on re-creating oak panelling for this room, we had the walls stippled brown, to provide a suggestion of the original tone against which the Earl of Melville would have viewed his bed. This stippling also provided a sympathetic background for the Soho-made *chinoiserie* tapestry, woven with small figures set against a tobacco-coloured ground. Historic photographs of the rooms at Melville House record just this sort of tapestry in the room that originally contained the bed.

Further along the gallery, the Earl of Macclesfield's silver fountain, cistern and wine cooler are shown within a recess that suggests a marble-lined buffet of the late seventeenth century.[8] The marbling itself is modelled on the black-veined white marble chosen by the architect Aston Webb for the main hall and staircase of his new building at the V&A. It is similarly divided into panels with the figure of the marble running in different directions. Opposite the buffet niche, the enormous embroidery showing a formal garden and orangery of about 1710–20, known as the Stoke Edith hanging (colour plate 13) has been mounted on a soft blue fabric that serves its faded colours very gently. As the visitor moves into the eighteenth century, the Palladian display is simply painted in a light stone colour, evoking the typical colours of the hall of a great country house. In deliberate contrast, the Rococo display in the adjacent gallery (53) uses clear green panels set against a strong blue wall colour (colour plates 16–17). Colours for the two period rooms in this area were also carefully considered. For the Henrietta Street room we wanted to use a plain wool cloth, rather than the more frequently reproduced woollen damasks. For this we chose blue, as a colour of lesser importance than either red or green (colour plate 15). This gave us a clear contrast of colour and status of fabric with the Norfolk House Music Room, where the survival of the original inventory dictated a green silk damask (colour plate 24). At the end of gallery 52 (the last gallery of the lower sequence) a clear, brighter blue is used to set off the gilded frame of a *chinoiserie* mirror. Opposite this, the subtle colours of the japanning on the Badminton bed are well supported by the soft putty colour, known as 'drab' and mentioned so often in eighteenth-century inventories and accounts for the decorating of houses.

In the upper level of galleries, the palette lightens. The walls of the first gallery (118), showing the large displays on *Neo-classicism* and *Robert Adam and his Rivals*, are in very light stone, with light greens and blues. The sky blue against which plaster casts are shown at the beginning of this gallery (in the display on *The Grand Tour*) is an idea lifted from the wall colour shown in the painting by Zoffany of *Charles Townley and his Friends* in about 1781–83, supposedly showing the library of Townley's house in Park Street (now Queen Anne's Gate) (colour plates 70–71).[9] In the smaller space of the adjacent gallery (118a), Horace Walpole's objects are shown against a purplish colour inspired by the original wallpaper in the Holbein Room at Strawberry Hill.[10] At the other end of this small gallery, furniture from the workshop of Thomas Chippendale, or made to his published designs, is set against drab (colour plate 27). Drab would have been called a 'common colour' or everyday colour in the eighteenth century.[11] Here it was designed to evoke the plainness of a cabinet-maker's workshop, in which such a variety of furniture (carved mahogany, carved giltwood, veneered and painted furniture, and upholstered pieces) might have stood together, as it never would have done in any single fashionable interior.

The suite of bedroom furniture supplied by Chippendale for the actor David Garrick and his wife in the 1770s is shown against a green distemper paper, the paper produced as small sheets in the eighteenth-century manner and then painted *in situ* with tinted distemper. This sort of finish, which readily rubs off on clothes, could not be used in the general space of the galleries but enhances this area, which is beyond public reach. Its soft, chalky surface provides a lively background to the screen-printed reproduction of an eighteenth-century Indian chintz, which we chose to replace the fragile surviving pieces of the chintz that Garrick originally received as a present from friends in Calcutta.[12] We spent several months attempting to re-create the painted chintz, but when this proved unsatisfactory, we sought and found a commercially available, screen-printed chintz that was both affordable and a good approximation of the original.

Throughout the project, we were very aware of the cost of specially woven or printed fabrics and chose off-the-peg versions, except for the period rooms, where historic authenticity was vital. Alongside the choice of colours for the gallery displays, another large task was the sourcing of appropriate fabrics with which to reupholster various chairs. Most of these projects required only a metre or so of fabric, and it would not have been economic to have these specially remade. Instead, we confined our choices to the leftover lengths of fabrics woven by specialist firms for other projects, and we relied very much on the goodwill of these specialist suppliers in helping us to acquire historically correct fabrics in the most economical manner.

Beyond the displays devoted to the great entrepreneurs, Wedgwood and

Boulton, is an entire small gallery (119) which centres on the Canova sculpture of *The Three Graces* (colour plate 29). It is shown against a curved screen of soft orange polished plaster, evoking the shape and colour of the scagliola-faced wall of the curved rotunda in which the group was originally installed at Woburn Abbey. Because *The Three Graces* is owned jointly with the National Galleries of Scotland, we had to plan for its periodic absences. The green scagliola plinth on which it now stands is designed to be removed to reveal a wooden frame, from which the group can be moved with mechanical assistance. The green was chosen to complement the orange plaster, but we had also to consider the effect when Canova's *Sleeping Nymph* takes the place of *The Three Graces*. That plinth is in deep purple scagliola, imitating porphyry, and will show to equally good effect against the polished plaster.

In the next large gallery (120), which covers the Regency period, there is a marked contrast, with all the colours becoming stronger, richer and darker, as they did in that period (colour plates 30–31). The walls of this gallery are painted a raw sienna and the displays use a variety of reds, from the stippled purplish red imitating porphyry in the section on the collector Thomas Hope, to the crimson silk velvet showing silver-gilt in *Marketing Art and Design*. One important source for colour choices here was the scagliola used in the decoration of Lancaster House in the late 1820s by the firm of William Croggon.[13]

After pausing in the Study Area (Gallery 121) to look down this time on Cornelia Parker's sculpture, or to use the computers, visitors move into another strongly coloured area, the Victorian Galleries (122–25). The opening display on *Gothic Revival* is full of highly coloured objects, from encaustic tiles to painted and gilded cabinets. Equally strong colours are used for the display panels, like the deep blue used to show a painted cabinet by Burges, a blue taken from the painted decoration of the object itself (colour plate 33). Following this, the section on *The Great Exhibition* is full of daylight, with a wall of glass printed with a full-scale design for the ironwork of the Crystal Palace (colour plate 35). The red plinths here echo those shown in contemporary lithographs of the exhibition. Further down the gallery, the grey-green for *The National Gallery of British Art* is based on records of the original 1860s gallery in the South Kensington Museum (as the V&A was known until 1899). The display on *Classical and Renaissance Revival* uses another popular decorating colour of a slightly later date, a terracotta imitating the figures on Greek pots (colour plates 37 and 65). Opposite this display, the bright yellow of the *French Style* display reminds the visitors of the more garish colours that had dominated the commercial world of furnishings since the 1840s, relying on new chemical dyes for their startling splendour (colour plates 72–73).

Gallery 123 is painted a light, greyish mauve, suggesting the lighter, prettier colours of the early years of Victoria's reign (colour plate 38).[14] As a staircase leads up from this gallery to ceramic galleries above, it was important that the wall colour should not cause an abrupt break with the colours visible on the upper part of the staircase. The balustrade here is a greenish polished limestone and the colour chosen had also to work with that.

The final gallery (125) covers the last quarter of the nineteenth century. It starts with a powerful display on the effect of Japan on British design (colour plate 40). The innovative design of the objects is reflected in the colours chosen for the display, which underline the strong impact that Japanese art had when first seen in Europe after Japan emerged from centuries of cultural isolation in the 1860s. A wall covered entirely with gold leaf, on which are hung Japanese prints, suggests revolutionary interiors such as J.M. Whistler's Peacock Room of 1869.[15] An adjacent wall, painted a glossy black, echoes the ebonised furniture that rapidly became fashionable and the fine black frames so frequently used to display the newly discovered Japanese prints. Next door to this, the display on *Aestheticism* uses a strong grey green that, like drab, appears several times in different parts of the galleries. It derives from the quieter earth-based pigments seen at the time as a fashionable escape from the cruder and brighter chemical dyes of the preceding 20 years. In this display it offers an excellent foil to the subtle colours of the woven silk and wool furnishing fabric designed by B.J. Talbert in the 1870s, and the olive green plush and brocade of the Liberty gown of about 1895–1900.

In the side gallery (125a), displays on the influence of Islam, India and China on British design use strong reds and pinks as a foil to their brightly coloured exhibits and to differentiate the three sections of the display. Here, the objects themselves gave references for many of the colours, including the iron red of Isnik tiles and the softer pinky reds of woollen shawls from Kashmir and from Paisley. In the main gallery (125), the complex patterning and colouring of a William Morris tapestry, his carpet for the house Bullerswood, his tiles and wallpapers, offer powerful evidence of his importance to British design in the nineteenth century (colour plate 41). Rather than use reproductions of his wallpapers and textiles and risk confusing the visitors, we have set these rich pieces against simple backgrounds of rich cream. At the end of the gallery, the *Arts and Crafts* display shows its colourful textiles and ceramics against an off-white background suggesting limewash (frequently used in Arts and Crafts interiors) (colour plate 42). Opposite, the objects in the *Scottish School* display are shown against a sharper, more elegant white (echoing the work of Charles Rennie Mackintosh). Having followed this journey of colour from 1500 to 1900, the visitor emerges once more onto the black-veined white marble of the staircase designed between 1899 and 1909 by Aston Webb, which here fits perfectly with the chronological sequence of the galleries.

Notes This chapter draws substantially on the material in a paper prepared during the final year of the project by John Cornforth for the Concept Team.

1. Daniel Marot's engravings, for instance, showing designs of interiors dating from the 1690s, show very sparse carpeting or none. One such engraving (Thornton, Peter, *The Authentic Interior* [London, 1978], pl. 50), shows the bed surrounded by a 'bed carpet', three narrow strips of carpeting placed around the bed.

2. See Carwitham, John, *Various Kinds of Floor Decorations* (London, 1739), illustrations reproduced and discussed in Gilbert *et al.*, *Country House Floors 1660–1850* (Temple Newsam House Studies, 3, Leeds City Art Galleries, 1987), pp. 13–17.

3. As reported in the *Illustrated London News*, 4 January 1851 and 11 January 1851.

4. All such testing was undertaken by the laboratories of the British Museum.

5. We are grateful to Claire Gapper for providing references to the use of ochre on both plaster and timber, from ch. 1 of her thesis *Plasterers and Plasterwork in City, Court and Country, c. 1530–c. 1640* (unpublished thesis, University of London, 1998).

6. See Harding, Robert, 'The Brathwaite Bible Miniature', in *The British Art Journal*, vol. 1, no. 1 (Autumn 1999), p. 16.

7. Dr Charles Kightly, *The Great Bed of Ware in the Victoria and Albert Museum: Suggestions for Dressing the Bed with Replicated Historic Textiles and Other Fittings* (report to the Victoria and Albert Museum, June 1999), p. 31. Dr Kightly's suggestions were based on a study of approximately 1500 inventories from the late sixteenth and early seventeenth centuries.

8. For this display we looked at the surviving buffet in the Marble Parlour at Houghton Hall, Norfolk and at illustrations of other late seventeenth- and early eighteenth-century buffets lined with marble.

9. Illustrated in Saumarez-Smith, Charles, *Eighteenth-Century Decoration: Design and the Domestic Interior in England* (New York, 1993), fig. 305.

10. Illustrated in Cornforth, John, *English Interiors 1790–1848: The Quest for Comfort* (London, 1978), pp. 105–07.

11. Bristow, Ian, *Interior House-Painting Colours and Technology* (New Haven and London, 1996), p. 158, discusses the term and gives references to eighteenth-century sources for it.

12. The original hangings came to the Museum in 1917 with the bed. They date from about 1775, although the bed and its hangings were altered in the 1820s. The full history of the hangings is recorded in John Irwin and Katharine B. Brett, *The Origins of Chintz* (London, 1970), pp. 78–83.

13. Yorke, James, 'Better than Any Original', *Country Life* (1 April 1993), vol. CLXXXVII, no. 40, pp. 54–55.

14. At Frogmore lilac was used in 1860 to redecorate Queen Charlotte's dining room (later the drawing room) for the Duchess of Kent. See Cornforth, John, 'Frogmore House, Berkshire', *Country Life* (31 July 1997), vol. CXCI, no. 31, pp. 52–55.

15. This and other rooms in a similar style are discussed by Charlotte Gere, in *Nineteenth-Century Decoration: The Art of the Interior* (London, 1989), pp. 328–33.

48. Members of the Historic Decoration Team at David Mlinaric's studio with samples of colours, fabrics and decorative finishes on the wall. From left to right: John Cornforth, David Mlinaric, Dinah Casson, Mary Ellison, March 1999.

Chapter 8   Developing the Content of the Galleries

Sarah Medlam

One of the questions most often asked about the making of the galleries has been 'How did you make the selection of subjects and objects?' Colleagues from other museums understand the process of choosing items for an exhibition, with the choice being made by a single curator or a very small group. However, to research, choose and prepare 3000 objects for such a highly structured programme in so many galleries necessarily required the development of working practices that involved many more people. The British Galleries Team benefited from the decision by the Trustees and the Director that this was to be a flagship project for the Museum. The team was given a free hand in proposing objects from any of the galleries in the Museum for transfer to the new galleries.

Traditionally at the V&A, the development of new galleries had been undertaken by teams that represented every department which might have an interest in the project, headed by senior curators with a particular specialism in the field. Senior curators at the V&A carry a heavy load of administration and government advice, in addition to commitments to research, writing and lecturing. Seconding such colleagues to work full-time on such a large and lengthy project would have had a serious impact on the Museum's whole programme of work. Instead, we decided to use such colleagues as part-time advisers to the project, as Senior Subject Specialists, either one or two to each period.[1]

To deal with this large number of galleries, we created three period-based Gallery Teams, each responsible for roughly one third of the whole. We appointed younger curators who could be relieved of departmental duties to work full-time on the project, and designated them as gallery co-ordinators. Each had several years of experience in the V&A and understood the structure and administrative processes of the institution. The co-ordinators were chosen as having an interest in and general knowledge of the various periods, and as curators of exceptional energy and commitment. Each worked with an educator and a curatorial assistant. These teams were formed in October 1996. Later, in 1997, they were joined by research assistants, recruited on temporary contracts from outside the Museum.[2]

The teams, with their Senior Subject Specialists, began to work from a number of directions in developing the subjects for their section of the galleries. Each team met at least twice a week in the first months of the project, with full-time members of the team following up on decisions made at those meetings and setting up new appointments to discuss matters with individual departmental curators and to view materials in store (fig. 49). Initially, there was considerable scepticism amongst our curatorial colleagues, who felt, in some instances, that this vast project was a threat to their own particular hopes and aims, often cherished and worked at for several years already. This conflict was unavoidable. It is a testimony to the generosity of colleagues that they turned cheerfully to contribute to the British Galleries; their work on identifying and cataloguing pieces and advising on conservation and display was essential to the success of the project. Several were so generous with their specialist knowledge that they took on overall responsibility for certain displays, becoming what was known in the project as 'subject parents'.

One method of developing the initial plans for the galleries was the 'textbook method', a consideration of the subjects that one might want to cover in writing about design and consumption at a particular period. This produced some of the most fertile thinking at the start of the project and encouraged the teams to think as widely as possible. Though practical considerations later 'edited' some of these ideas quite severely, much of the thinking that could not be well represented in the galleries nonetheless contributed to plans for the book that was published at the time of their opening.[3] The book could, for instance, cover much more about architecture than the galleries. Faced with the difficulty of representing architecture in the galleries, two responses were to commission a small number of high-quality models, and to use the opportunities of film to address the subject.[4] The constraints of interpreting ideas through gallery design might have been seen merely as a difficulty but in fact they often served as an impetus to more creative thinking about how we could present different subjects.

A second line of development worked entirely from a close scrutiny of the Museum's collections, which presented subjects for which we simply had such wonderful objects that it was unthinkable that we would not present them to the public. For instance, no other museum could illustrate as richly as the V&A the importance of the Spitalfields silk trade in the eighteenth century, or the wide range of the work of William Morris in the nineteenth. Sometimes, the 'book method' and a review of the collections converged on the same material, as in the case of the Great Exhibition display. Not only was the Great Exhibition an essential element in a discussion of nineteenth-century design, but the V&A also contains an unrivalled collection of objects bought directly from the Exhibition – everything from Pugin's great armoire to ladies' machine-knitted vests. We were certain from the first that the display on the Great Exhibition should be a large one. This decision was reinforced by the knowledge that the Victorians are currently one mandatory historical subject for study in primary schools in Britain, a fact which also encouraged us to make the exhibition the subject of one of our longer films to be shown in the Film Rooms.

Close investigation of the collections was not confined to subjects where we knew we had substantial holdings. The teams also had more wide-ranging discussions with curators throughout the Museum to investigate all aspects of our extensive collections. New research was undertaken on pieces that had been in the Museum for many years and particular attention was paid to stored collections and to items in study collections. We were very keen that these galleries should present a fresh look at the subject, incorporating pieces that had never before appeared in what used to be called the Primary Galleries.

However, a third consideration, of which these two strands of thought had to take account, was presented by certain objects that were just so well-known that it would be impossible to redisplay these galleries without incorporating them. The example usually cited was the Great Bed of Ware, famous from the 1590s as a tourist sight and continuing in this role ever since. It had long been said to be the single V&A object most asked for by name by visitors, and every guidebook that covers the V&A leads its readers to this piece. It was unthinkable that we would not include it.

The V&A is the only museum that could have mounted such a comprehensive display of British art and design in such a wide variety of materials. Even so, it was not possible for the V&A to provide every single object that we might have wanted to show. We started from the premise that we would look first at our own collections and that we would only borrow when it was absolutely essential. Of course, the V&A has always benefited from some wonderful long-term loans, such as the Drake Jewel or the clock/barograph possibly designed by Robert Adam, and the lenders were kind enough to allow us to include several of these in the galleries. Benefiting from a new initiative of co-operation between the V&A and Tate Britain, we were able to borrow a number of paintings from their collections, sending miniatures, paintings, and sculpture from the V&A collections to the Tate as a reciprocal benefit.[5] Other museums throughout the country provided particular pieces, as did other organisations such as the Society of Jesus, who lent a cope from their collections at Stonyhurst College, Lancashire. This vestment had been used by priests serving the court of Henry VII and had travelled with Henry VIII's household to the Field of Cloth of Gold in 1520. Ultimately, we borrowed 90 objects out of a total of 3000 shown in the galleries.

Early on in the project, the Gallery Teams were asked to list the large objects that might be included in each display, such as large-scale textiles (figs 50–51) or sections of architectural woodwork which were inordinately greedy of space. The inclusion (or not) of these individual pieces could seriously affect the size of a display and they had to be considered carefully at an early stage. These lists were essential for the first round of planning with the designers, when different displays were allocated to different galleries.

Certain categories of object, and in particular textiles and works on paper, need to be taken off show and rested every few years, to minimise the effects of exposure to light. In proposing objects for the galleries, the teams were very aware of such matters and wherever possible two objects were chosen, one noted as a 'rotation' object, which would replace the first after an agreed number of years. Identifying these at the beginning allowed the Design Team to design in the changes, although they may not be activated for several years. Many of the CAD drawings showed, in ghostly, dotted lines, the shapes of alternative tapestries or embroideries and how they would fit into the display. In a few cases, no alternative was available, and the Museum will have to decide whether it wishes to keep these items on show. Strenuous discussion between the curators and the Design Team came up with a variety of design ideas that can lessen exposure to light. These include: items shown in drawers; items shown behind doors; and miniatures in shadow boxes with light 'torches' that visitors can pick up to examine them in detail (colour plates 10–11).

As soon as discussions began on the actual choice of objects, we had to think of a way of capturing the thinking of the moment, to ensure that work moved forward and that the teams did not repeat work or discussions unnecessarily. Two main tools were used. The first was the Framework Document, which expanded from about 50 pages in its first edition to nearly 250 by the end of the project (see appendix 7). This listed every display subject and all the objects agreed for it, together with notes of design ideas and ideas for interpretation (later developed more fully in other documents, as described in chapter 4). Each team updated this once a week and it became the universal record of thinking so far in the project. Once a month a new version was printed and sent to the designers. At the time we started work on this project, the Museum's ability to share large documents 'live' was still relatively unsophisticated. Now, such a document would sit on the Museum's intranet, to be read by anyone who might be interested.

The second tool that was developed for this project was the British Galleries Database. The Museum's central inventory and cataloguing database (the Collections Information System or CIS) could not at the time be used to manage the sort of information on objects that we would need to collect for this project. We needed a tool to hold and sort information in a variety of ways, both intellectual information (cataloguing data, including free text) and administrative information used, for example, to schedule conservation or photography, or the writing of labels (see also chapter 5). The British Galleries Database became an invaluable tool. It did not entirely supersede such old favourites as the file of studio photographs and amateur snapshots, but it is unlikely that any electronic system could have done so. Teams still need the opportunity to spread out images and to shuffle them about and see them in different groupings. It is not possible to overestimate the usefulness of the image (however imperfect) to curators, conservators, educators and designers. In subsequent projects digital photography plays an increasingly important role, but prints currently remain the foundation on which new displays are created. Building up the database and image files took immense amounts of time in the early part of the project but was an important investment. Two copies of the relevant information about objects were made in printed form, one for the teams and one for the designers, who were working on the other side of London. Once the British Galleries Database was set up, we hoped to allow the designers to have electronic access, but this proved too difficult, though it will certainly be the way that we progress in future projects. The database also became the method by which we captured and stored all text written about the objects (both for labels and for the British Galleries Online program) and the database is now the engine by which British Galleries Online is supported (see chapter 9).

The British Galleries Database was not just a tool for the Gallery Teams. Colleagues around the Museum could use it at any time to check which objects had been definitely selected, which dropped, and which might yet be used if space permitted. As objects were chosen for displays, staff in all curatorial departments used it for the strenuous programme of cataloguing each piece, undertaking research where necessary and entering descriptions and notes that would be used later by those writing labels. It was the BG Database that also kept track of the process of the cataloguing, conservation and photography of each of the nearly 3000 objects. Staff in many departments helped with this work and each of the Team Co-ordinators took on managerial responsibility for one aspect of the work overall (cataloguing, conservation or photography). The database also recorded all the items chosen for display with interpretive devices, requested for loan or chosen as rotation objects. It also recorded objects that needed to be photographed for the main publication associated with the galleries, *Design and the Decorative Arts: Britain 1500–1900*, but which would not be displayed in the galleries. The database could also accept basic codes to record whether conservation was due, in progress or completed. At the same time the Conservation Department was developing its own database, CONCISE, which could record conservation in greater detail. By 1999 the two databases were linked.

At the same time as decisions about objects for inclusion were being made, the teams were also working on ideas for the interpretation of these objects. Right from the start, the educators on each team were at work educating curator colleagues in the needs of the visitor (see chapter 4). Early editions of the Framework Document carried not only lists of objects and ideas about display for each subject, but also ideas for interpretation, which were developed and changed in just the same manner as object lists. From summer 1999, as ideas for interpretation were developed and agreed, a third document was developed, recording all the briefs for various interpretive devices (see chapter 4 and appendix 8).

At the beginning of the process, one of the Concept Team curators sat in on each individual Gallery Team meeting for several weeks, to ensure that the principles agreed in the first stage of the Concept Team's work (see chapter 2) became embedded in the thinking of the Gallery Teams as they set about the detailed work of developing subjects. Throughout the project the three team co-ordinators met once a week with the Concept Team to discuss progress. As the teams worked on their displays, the Concept Team from time to time undertook reviews of particular aspects of the displays. In particular, our task was to ensure that there was continuity between the different sections and some degree of uniformity in the approach to certain aspects of the plan. We reviewed the balance of subjects within themes, ensured that one team was not proposing vastly more subjects than the other two, and tried to ensure continuity. In some cases, we advocated repetition (so that *Birth, Marriage and Death* or *The Church* would occur at more than one point in the galleries). It was the Concept Team's work both to encourage the development of certain subjects and to wield the axe when it was clear that a subject was not going to yield a good display or that there was simply not enough space in that part of the galleries.

Design work had started well before the first application was made to the Heritage Lottery Fund and the discipline of considering how it was all going to fit was an important factor in pushing forward decisions about what was to be shown. Within the chronological framework, the teams had begun to propose subjects and to suggest groupings of those subjects (so that, for instance, *The Court of Henry VIII* should be somewhere close to the display on Renaissance style (fig. 52), and the *Rococo* display to that on Vauxhall Gardens). The information about groupings of subjects was important to the designers, but sometimes multiplied their problems in trying to fit the displays into the long, narrow galleries designed by Aston Webb between 1899 and 1909.

The effect on teams of working with the designers from such an early stage was vital in making them understand the factors that would turn their ideas into concrete displays. Providing dimensions for gallery displays rather than catalogue records was one vital lesson, but it was equally important for everyone to understand the importance of recording any information out of the ordinary – 'Is this item particularly heavy?', 'Can it only be shown closed?', 'Is it more light-sensitive than one might deduce from its appearance?' At the first Christmas of the project, the team were given pocket tape measures. At the second, the present was scale rulers, for use as curators gradually developed the ability to read plans and drawings accurately and finally to be able to estimate available space on plans by eye. The floor grid of 600 mm became an important aid to such estimates, which were often needed to allow the team to suggest an alternative place for an object. Every measurement had, of course, to be carefully checked.

The series of period rooms (originally six, later reduced to five) and some of the largest items, such as the beds and the largest tapestries and embroideries, became important focal points of the galleries. In some cases, the options for these were limited and, in particular, the Norfolk House Music Room could finally be placed in only one of two places because of demands of its height. The panelling from Haynes Grange suffered from similar constraints as to where it could be shown, while other large objects, such as the Stoke Edith hanging or the section of panelling from Northumberland House, had to be considered before smaller displays in the same areas could be given their place.

Although much of the work on content and design development was undertaken with the three Gallery Teams working together or individually with the Concept Team, there were occasions when it was necessary for the Concept Team to undertake its own surveys of work so far and to issue both deadlines and diktats to move the work along. In the course of three years we reviewed such issues as the balance of materials shown in different parts of the galleries and whether the four themes were represented roughly equally in the three periods. We looked at whether the role of women in design and making was as well represented as it could be. We also looked at how far we should represent the process of design and making, given that the Museum also offers whole galleries devoted to the materials and techniques of different kinds of object. Given that these galleries are not about British Design and Art, but about Design and Art in Britain, we needed to consider how we represented imports at different periods and whether this reflected history accurately. We also needed to consider the impact of designers and makers who came to Britain to work, a regular pattern of enrichment to British design.

One vital review came after more than a year's work, at the suggestion of Gail Durbin. We asked the Gallery Teams to write a 'Purpose Statement' for each display, a declaration of what they thought visitors would understand after looking at the display with its related interpretation. At first there was strong resistance to this. It was seen as an unnecessary task. However, once the teams had started on the process, many changes were made and the displays certainly became simpler, stronger and easier to understand as a result.

It was the responsibility of the Concept Team also to review the developing content in terms of how successfully it addressed the various audiences that we hoped to interest in these galleries. This involved review of the plans for interpretation, which, in some cases, affected the choice of objects. Our decision to treat of import and trade allowed many points of reference to Asian cultures. Although there is one display in the late eighteenth-century gallery on export, it was harder to find material that directly related to this. We spent many months investigating the possibility of creating a display on the export of British design ideas and their reinterpretation by cabinet-makers working in the Caribbean, which was to be called *Being British Abroad*. Although this subject would have been immensely rich, and we may sometime take it up as the subject of a temporary exhibition, it proved impossible to do in the time available. The V&A has few examples of furniture made in the Caribbean, and good examples are now so rare and so sought after by Caribbean collectors and museums, that it would be difficult to purchase pieces and long term loans would be hard to negotiate.

Two members of the Concept Team (Christopher Wilk and the present writer) were intensively involved in design work with the Historic Decoration Team (see chapter 7). That team met every Tuesday for nearly two years. The team co-ordinators joined the group from time to time, often to talk through objects selected and at times to discuss substitution, supplement or removal, when the design required it. Christopher Wilk and Sarah Medlam also worked with specialist suppliers on certain aspects of design that were more closely related to individual objects, and, in particular, to the development of mannequins and wigs for display of dress.[6] This work was done in partnership with the curators specialising in historic dress and was reviewed by Dinah Casson. The development of designs for the three architectural models in the galleries was overseen directly by Christopher Wilk, working with the appropriate curators, with Dinah Casson and with the model-makers.

As designs became more fixed, it was clear that we had to develop a method of testing these drawings at full size in three dimensions. It was never going to be possible, as it might be with smaller displays or exhibitions, to assemble all the objects and try out layouts. The alternative was a lengthy templating exercise with photocopies, cardboard and rulers (colour plate 48). William Beckford's lacquer box was made up out of old cardboard boxes, and Wedgwood teapots cut out of foam. The making sessions could be fun but the intent was serious. Only at full size (occasionally in three dimensions, but more often in two) could we check sight lines and explore the real relationships between objects in a particular layout. This review process involved tremendous amounts of work for the Co-ordinators and for the designers, who had to return from each review Session to transfer the lessons learned to the British Galleries Database and to the CAD drawings, but those late improvements demonstrated how vital the process was.

It was at this relatively late stage that we all became aware of the seriousness of the conflict between the objects to be included and the space required for labels. Work on graphic design had been going on for months at this point (see chapter 6, pp. 78–80), and much diplomatic work had been required to persuade curators throughout the Museum that our stringent guideline of 50 words of commentary for an object label was achievable. But even at 50 words, and often with lengthy 'tombstone' or caption text, labels for nearly 3000 objects required a lot of space, if we were not to retreat to the tiny font size that is so often adopted as the solution to the space dilemma. At the templating stage, the full problem became apparent and at times it was only resolvable by removing objects from a display or, as had already been planned for certain intentionally dense displays, by providing individual object labels in hand-held books. With hindsight, this was one aspect of the design that did not work as easily as we might have hoped. Curators and designers (both graphic designers and exhibition designers) need to work together from the earliest possible moment, with very realistic understanding of what space and lighting provision the labels will require.

There was great pressure to complete the templating stage as soon as possible, because other staff were waiting to start work on making and commissioning the object mounts and fixings needed to install the displays. Some mounts were made in-house, but many had to be commissioned from outside suppliers. The Museum's technicians oversaw the commissioning of all this work but the gallery co-ordinators were heavily involved in the detailed discussions of what was needed. Some mounts, such as those for design drawings or engravings, could be standardised in design and ordered for each piece to precise measurements. Others, and there were many of these, had to be devised for individual items. Inevitably, because work on the fit-out stage of the project was shortened by delays in building work, the last nine months of work was particularly pressured. At this stage, the Gallery Teams were working almost entirely reactively with the designers, reviewing drawings to make sure that no detail had been omitted ('Does that need a block?', ' Has this been shown the right way round?') and providing new information where necessary to those working on mounts and fixings.

Most team members were also, by the end of 2000, heavily involved with the writing of gallery text. Much thought on this had been undertaken at an early stage in the project. A small working group had grappled with the issues surrounding gallery text and produced the first draft of text guidelines for the project.[7] The Gallery Teams and other curators involved with the project had undergone training in writing for particular audiences and, most important of all, in writing for an audience who would read text standing up, rather than in an armchair. Most of those who undertook the training found it very stimulating, and the project identified some exceptionally skilled writers in all departments of the Museum and amongst the teams. It also identified some who found it very difficult to write within the constraints of the guidelines. Nonetheless, this project has taught us to accept the discipline of short labels and to be very conscious of the variable knowledge of our visitors.

The writing of text panels for each display benefited from the Purpose Statements that the Gallery Teams had produced for the Framework Document (see appendix 7). We took the decision early on in the project to allocate the writing of labels for each complete display to a single writer, in contrast to the tradition of having, say, one curator write all the sculpture labels and another all the metalwork labels, for the same display. We felt that it was important that each object label should be written in relation to the subject of a particular display. If the subject was *Mr and Mrs Garrick, a Fashionable Couple*, a label on a silver tea service should concentrate on matters of consumption, rather than on the technicalities of how the silver was worked or decorated. By having all labels in a display written by one author, it was much more likely that we would avoid repetition and could use the label text to give a fully rounded view of the subject.

With hindsight, it is clear that we spread the load amongst too many writers and thus made the task of managing the text-writing unnecessarily difficult. In any future project, we would advise using fewer writers. From the beginning, we were very aware that we would need an editor to ensure the quality of all the text. We were slow in appointing the editor, and she did not come into post until May 2000. With hindsight, we should have tried to get writing done earlier and allowed more time for editing and rewriting where necessary. We also set up a programme with too many layers of review for texts and would simplify this for any future project. Reducing the number of writers must strengthen the bond between editor and writers and create the kind of solidarity that existed between the Gallery Teams and the Concept Team. It is that kind of solidarity that gets such large projects done.

Many of the activities of the last year, that looked so neat on the programme as set out in 1997, necessarily crumpled over each other like geological layers during 2001. The Gallery Teams and the Installation Team had to work over and around each other and exercise considerable good humour in doing so. More experienced team members were philosophic about this and younger colleagues learned from it the reality of carrying out such a large project.

It might have been predicted that the role of the Gallery Teams would dwindle towards the end of the project, but in fact they played a vital role until the moment before opening and beyond (fig. 53). Although templating had been a vital exercise, even at the moment of installation it was necessary to make slight alterations in the arrangement of objects and to be cheerfully pragmatic about such modifications. As cases were installed, both the gallery Co-ordinators and the two curatorial members of the Concept Team were constantly on call to advise and adjudicate on the final appearance of the cases. They worked very closely with the Design Team, who also spent long hours on site during the last few months of the project. Nor could the work of the Historic Decoration Team be considered over once all their decisions had been made and recorded. Both for the period rooms and for the decoration of the galleries and of cases, regular weekly sessions and intermediate 'emergency' consultations were essential, in particular to judge and approve paint colours as they were applied to the walls.

In such a highly designed and carefully organised project, it would be too easy to think that the teams' task ended with the day of opening. Wise programming had, in fact, allowed for a period of nearly four months (from opening in mid-November to the beginning of the next financial year in

April 2002) when a diminishing team, drawn from the original Gallery Teams and installation team, continued to work at snagging, adjustment and final installation tasks. This team was also charged with tidying up the project documentation, before handing over responsibility to the teams who were have to have different on-going roles in running the galleries.

Case study: developing a display
Nick Humphrey

In order for readers to understand how some of the tasks described above worked in practice, the following pages record in summary form the development of a single display. The display, titled *Achieving Splendour 1500–1600*, falls into the theme *Fashionable Living*. It is located in Gallery 58 (colour plates 5–6), and consists of 30 objects shown both on open display and in two cases. Appendix 7 provides a full description of the display as recorded in the Framework Document of May 2001. The introductory text for the subject that appears in the gallery is as follows:

FASHIONABLE LIVING

Achieving Splendour 1500–1600

Nobles and rich merchants used luxury goods to increase the comfort of their surroundings and as symbols of their status and wealth. They built ambitious houses and filled them with extravagant furnishings. Rich textiles were used to add colour and comfort, though few now survive in their original settings.

Great sums were spent on silver and silver-gilt plate for domestic display. Rare and beautiful materials such as mother-of-pearl or porcelain from Asia were enhanced still further with mounts of precious metal.

The social standing of individuals and families was clearly displayed in their portraits or incorporated into their houses in the form of stained glass windows decorated with coats of arms.

On starting work, the Tudor and Stuart Gallery Team was presented with the overall chronological and thematic framework worked out by the Concept Team. We were asked to develop a series of displays, at the same time developing interpretive ideas for them. A first draft was required quickly. Faced with a blank page, headed only by the dates '1500–1714' and the titles of the four themes, the Team Co-ordinator (the present writer) and the Subject Specialist, Philippa Glanville, spent one long session, sketching ideas for specific displays that matched museum objects with design history.

Our first draft for the Tudor and Stuart gallery read like the title page of a textbook. Among the sub-headings under the theme *Taste and the Consumer* (later retitled *Fashionable Living*) were three that pointed towards the display that eventually became *Achieving Splendour 1500–1600*:

Cultural Authority: Large Houses and the Second Tier of Authority
The Role of Objects in Social Ritual: Entertainment
The Domestic Interior

Beside each was a generalised statement of the intended purpose for the display (not yet the detailed Purpose Statements that were to be part of a later review), a list of 'essential and large objects' and some generalised interpretive ideas. At this stage the team suggested appropriate types of museum objects that we expected to find rather than specific items.

Cultural Authority: Large Houses and the Second Tier of Authority
plate and buffet, clock, pewter, expensive textiles, jewellery, renewing objects (objects showing re-use), family portraits, miniatures, stained-glass armorials, maps, andirons, panel-back armchairs, swords, horns.
Essential objects: a salt belonging to the Vyvyan family and the Thomas More family portrait.

The Role of Objects in Social Ritual: Entertainment
tableware (silver, pewter, wooden roundels); objects for banquets, e.g. for guild or mayor; musical instruments; buffet; objects related to civic corporate, military procession and pageantry; hunting and weapons.
Essential objects: the Great Bed of Ware.

The Domestic Interior – (about the specialisation of objects and spaces, and about the 'relative *lack* of things' compared with later interiors) bed and bedding; hangings and scarcity of furniture; dress for different activities; tapestries; drinking vessels, andirons.
Essential objects: none.

This document was prepared before the Museum's collections had been examined closely and necessarily represented a 'wish-list'. It is worth noting that some object types, such as buffet plate, appeared more than once, although the Museum has very limited collections of this early date, while others (e.g. dress, or objects related to military procession and pageantry) are barely represented in the Museum at all. The finished display conflated aspects of all three draft sub-headings of this early document, but equally some aspects suggested in the initial draft were not, in the end, dealt with at all.

Initial ideas on content Alongside discussions with curators about the strengths and weaknesses of the Museum's collections, the Gallery Team (including an educator, research assistant and curatorial assistant) began the longer process of systematically reviewing all the collections and assigning objects to displays. In the absence of a computer database that could provide us with convenient lists of all the relevant Museum collections, we built up our own lists using photocopies and snapshots. We used published catalogues (far more useful when illustrated) and department lists of various kinds (some of which had been prepared for earlier schemes to redisplay the British Galleries); we saw stored material with curators and surveyed objects in the V&A's galleries.[8] As we started to specify individual objects rather than types, we realized that some of our ideas were unsustainable. The Museum simply did not possess sufficient sixteenth-century jewellery, musical instruments or dress to create a display centred on these. However, we learned that it did possess wonderful embroideries of the right date. Although some of these could be French or English, a French origin did not preclude their having been used in English houses – and indeed contributed to a useful point about the desirability of imported objects.

Store visits were particularly important. What were especially inspiring were the opportunities to handle objects and appreciate them (even in storerooms that provided less than ideal viewing conditions) as intricate, textured objects that had been fashioned, purchased and used – in short, to appreciate them in ways that are difficult when such objects are presented statically in a display case. While it would be impossible for visitors to handle most objects, it was possible to translate something of the tangible experience that we enjoyed. One method was to show objects in the galleries from an unfamiliar angle, another was to offer a close view of a vivid, pristine detail instead of a wider view of the whole worn and faded object. This is in fact the method we used in *Achieving Splendour* to show a particularly vibrant red embroidery which had been made up at a later date into an ecclesiastical chasuble.

It was vital when viewing dozens of unfamiliar objects (usually without secure attribution) to photograph them in colour, as the visual condition of some objects had changed considerably since acquisition, when the only available photographs (black-and-white) had been taken, if they existed at all. We also recorded details of existing mounts and fixings of the objects, and tried to take accurate and consistent measurements reflecting the way that the object would need to be displayed in the new gallery. To our surprise, objects of great interest came to light during these visits. Some of these had only been acquired by the Museum relatively recently, such as the blackwork panels, later shown as part of a woman's smock (fig. 54). Others, such as the heraldic glass panel (fig. 55), had become relatively unknown since first published 70 years before.[9]

Basic information for each object considered was recorded on the British Galleries database, without images. For daily use in meetings we used printouts and our various photographs in two sets of ring binders. These had to be kept constantly up to date, one for our use and one for the designers to work from. These cumbersome files were our primary resources, carried from office to meeting room and unpacked and spread out over tables, then annotated and spattered with post-it notes. Our knowledge about many of the objects first seen in store was limited; they needed to be researched, but full catalogue entries were completed only after a decision had been made to include them.

As potential objects were identified, the team also tried to refine a written Purpose Statement of three or four sentences for each display. It was important that this statement used simple language and realistically expressed what was possible with a grouping of objects in museum galleries, avoiding generalisations in academic language. Thus we refined an early statement, '[This display will show] How conventions of formal social behaviour and entertainment required certain objects to be used as indicators of status…', to 'The purpose of this display is to show the luxury and imported objects that were essential to express status…'. We also experimented with the title of the display, aware that this would appear in the galleries, and would be an important signpost for some visitors: over a period of two years *The Pleasures of Life* became *How did wealthy people live?/In the new fashion*, then *Spending for Effect*, and finally *Achieving Splendour 1500–1600*.

At this early stage we also included ideas to help the designer understand the mood or appearance we wanted to evoke in the display, including notes such as 'Textiles should be low enough to be studied… Many of these objects are … richly worked and intricate'. We also specified the need for proximity to other displays: the Bromley-by-Bow period room would contextualise some of the furnishings shown in *Achieving Splendour*. We thought that a separate display looking at heraldry would benefit by being located near by.

Interpretive ideas   Throughout the process of selecting objects we explored ideas for interpretation. Many of these, such as audio extracts from Philip Stubbes's puritanical *The Anatomy of Abuses* (1583) or sugar sculptures to accompany objects for Tudor banquets, were initially concerned with conveying the colour and vigour of sixteenth-century material culture. However, ideas gradually focused on interpreting the objects we had chosen. Some of these were abandoned as over-elaborate (and potentially distracting), while others found their way into other parts of the galleries. Others might have worked well, such as a video examining the design, function and decoration of a multiple salt cellar but, with a limited number of videos for the entire run of galleries, had finally to be rejected . We learned to become sceptical of interpretive ideas that required lengthy contextual explanations. The principal interpretive device in *Achieving Splendour* is the *Explore a Painting* computer interactive, devoted to the miniature portrait of the family of Sir Thomas More. First conceived of as a video 'to provide information about daily life at a high level in society', it was developed into a much more elaborate form that uses the visible elements in the picture to provide a huge amount of more general information about life in a Tudor household.

Team working Given that the Tudor and Stuart Team was simultaneously developing over 40 displays for the period 1500–1714, and considering objects that might be appropriate to several displays, meeting deadlines often meant shutting ourselves away to meet as a team for half-days at a time, even while each of us was working individually on various aspects of the plan. Individuals reported on their own work-in-progress. It was possible for the team to meet regularly only because staff were wholly dedicated to this project. Team meetings were chaired by the co-ordinator and decisions made by consensus. Beyond the requirements of team roles, there was considerable overlap in skills. We all learned to ask each others' questions – 'How will visitors understand what is meant? Does this new object really contribute to the purpose of this display? How can we convey the excitement aroused in Tudor England by rarities such as porcelain?' In addition, each team member brought to the process of developing content his or her wider experiences and interests, such as the history of gardening or music, engineering, the concerns of ethnic minorities. The Concept Team stipulated deadlines to all three Gallery Teams for developing content, and this was a powerful engine, as were Concept Team decisions that brought to an end lengthy debates. As far as possible, each member of the team would be consulted, but a decision had to be made even if team members were absent.[10]

Every few months we invited a group of curators with specific knowledge in the Tudor period to view progress and respond to the developing content. Seven of these individuals became 'subject parents' about half-way through the design process, joining the Tudor and Stuart Team to help develop a particular subject display, and eventually writing the gallery text for it. In the instance of *Achieving Splendour* where textiles play such a prominent role, the subject parent was Linda Woolley, curator of textiles and dress. Periodically we sent the Tudor and Stuart Framework Document to colleagues outside the Museum with specialist knowledge of the period or met with them, seeking their responses and guidance as the written content of the displays developed.

Developing content After about six weeks' work, the proposed display was very large and shapeless, with at least four subsections sharing common ground. The Bromley-by-Bow period room was removed from the proposal and treated as a separate though associated display (in the finished galleries, the two are side-by-side). A sub-section about novelty and new fashions was incorporated into the main 'status' narrative since both required many of the same object types. Another idea about housekeeping and the role of servants in caring for luxury objects was removed from the display and put to one side temporarily. This was later taken up again and developed into the independent display *Protecting Possessions*.

Over the next five to twelve months, the list of proposed object types was gradually turned into a list of specific objects, supplemented by new additions suggested by our ongoing research or fortuitous finds in the National Art Library and Print Room of the Museum. Some objects that could have worked well in the display, such as the inlaid weapons from Belchamp Hall or the Holbein miniature portrait of Jane Small, were removed as we decided that they would be shown to better advantage in other displays. Some of the potential textile exhibits were designated as rotation objects to be shown in place of others after several years. The Museum has nothing directly comparable to the More portrait miniature, which is also highly light-sensitive, but, as an extremely popular object and the subject of an elaborate interpretive device, we accept that it will stay on long-term display (fig. 56). In briefing the designer, it was important to make careful provision, in terms of light and physical support, for all such fragile objects.[11]

Building up a display was essentially an imaginative process, relying on photographs of objects (some colour snapshots, others black-and-white museum prints), which we would spread out across a table or the floor. It was quite impractical, even at a late stage, to bring together all the objects being considered, to see how silver-gilt would sit beside faded embroideries. The large case of embroideries and plate in *Achieving Splendour* was represented as a computer-aided image drawn up by the designers using scanned colour images – an aid that we had expected might be widely used in the design process, but which proved prohibitively laborious. The CAD line drawings by which we represented planned groups of objects were accurate in terms of dimensions but inexpressive of the colours and textures of objects (fig. 57). For the purposes of presentation to the HLF panel and other sponsors, these were supplemented by evocative gallery views done in watercolour (fig. 58), and the three-dimensional gallery model (see chapter 6), which was, however, more useful for conveying the proposed designs to others than it was for us in developing displays.

Design I   Our initial meetings with Dinah Casson and the Concept Team, planning the allocation of space in the Tudor galleries and discussing the distinctive character of individual displays, encouraged us to embrace the principle that 'less is more', that visitors would be better able to appreciate didactic points made succinctly, and that objects should have 'space to breathe'. Dinah Casson's suggestion of varying the scale and character of displays led to a much larger and bolder display of heraldic stained-glass panels, rather than the use of one or two inside a case, close to other luxury objects. We took the surviving great chamber window at Gilling Castle, Yorkshire (fig. 59), as a model for the arrangement of these panels as a massed display, forming a foil to the textiles that dominate the adjacent case.[12] This meant selecting nine panels from the twelve in the Museum to create a symmetrical group and agreeing with the Museum's stained glass conservator how best to remount these panels into frames of a uniform size evocative of Tudor window framing. A particular concern was that stained glass be back-lit more softly and subtly than in the old galleries.

Finding an arrangement for the 30 disparate objects that would encourage visitors to make their own links between them was a long job. Moreover, the display was to stand at a crossroads where visitors could choose one of two routes. Our intention had always been to limit the casing of objects. However, embroidery and goldsmiths' work had to be cased, the fragile textiles to protect them from dust and the smaller items so that they could be seen closely yet securely. We liked the idea that, with precise lighting, these two object types representing the most expensive luxury goods of the time could be seen together to mutual advantage. We imagined the display as rich, with layers of texture and with light shimmering over the metal threads and silver-gilt, making a stunning impact. In the previous English Primary Galleries, a similar combination of textile and plate had been undermined by thick glass and bland, fluorescent lighting (fig. 60). The

Leicester armorial tapestry, which had formed the background to that earlier display, had suffered particularly from poor lighting and the design had been unreadable. *Achieving Splendour* needed tapestry, the most prestigious of Tudor textiles. We had initially planned to use the *Judgement of Paris* (now hung in the Bromley-by-Bow room). As it became clear that the larger and higher quality Leicester tapestry would not fit into the planned display *The Court of Elizabeth I*, *Achieving Splendour* seemed the obvious place for it. In this display there was room for it to be fully visible on open display, complementing the best of the Museum's Elizabethan embroideries.

Early hopes to include linen damask and a table carpet in the display required modification. The most expensive linen damask of the period, woven to order with the owner's arms, requires extremely delicate, oblique lighting if the design is to be visible and we could not find a way to do this in the limited gallery space available. Eventually we had to forgo the display of the linen. Similarly, to show the Turkish table carpet on a flat table-top (as it would have been shown in sixteenth-century England), yet to keep it out of the reach of tempted fingers, would have required considerable space in a gallery already overfull. It would also have required a table of the right size and, were we to have shown it in that manner, we would have had to resolve the problem of stress for the textile where the corners would have hung in folds. Even if all these problems could have been overcome, we would have faced the difficulty of casing the object to prevent dust collecting on the flat surface. Our compromise solution was to show the carpet on open display, but mounted flat on the wall, where we hoped its strong design would evoke the bold appearance of such carpets in portraits of the time. Attentive visitors could make a link between the carpet in the gallery and the one depicted in the More family portrait shown nearby.[13]

The pairing of portrait and chair (colour plate 6) was an idea that Dinah Casson conceived as a repeating motif throughout the galleries. Time and research were needed before we could identify suitable pairs. Doubts were raised over the authenticity of four other early oak chairs being considered, as they were re-examined by curators and conservators. Before seeking possible loan portraits from other institutions, it was vital to know more about the V&A's modest portrait (at that time in store) now believed to depict Captain John Hunnynge.[14] Archival research by the team research assistant discovered so much interesting material about the likely sitter and his involvement in the English military campaign in the Netherlands of 1586 that we decided to show this portrait rather than seek another of grander status. As it happens, the Earl of Leicester, whose grand armorial tapestry hangs behind the portrait, was the disastrous leader of the military expedition in which Hunnynge may have died. The Bromley-by-Bow room behind *Achieving Splendour* dictated the size of the partition wall on which the tapestry hangs, so that there was little room above or below. The canopy above would contain some top lighting, but more significantly would serve to draw together the various elements of the display (case, tapestry, stained glass) into a closer relationship.

In many ways the most taxing problem in planning the space was positioning the More portrait in relation to the interactive touch-screen in such a way that the technology would not overwhelm the object. Indeed, we wanted the device to encourage visitors to look more closely at the portrait. Initially we favoured a bench in the middle of the space (3–4 m. from the More portrait), from which all the objects in the display would be visible, and which would support an interactive screen and its accompanying hardware (fig. 58). Yet we were concerned that a bench would congest a busy area (especially if a wheelchair-user were at the screen), and that the link between screen and portrait would be lost if they were not side-by-side. This latter factor, one of the founding principles of the interpretive strategy, eventually led us to abandon the bench and put the interactive beside the portrait, shown in its own small case (colour plate 6). The design proved much less intrusive than some of us had imagined.

Administration to support the project

As proposals for each display became clearer, we sent printed object lists to each curatorial department so that they could confirm that the objects were available for display or indicate potential difficulties, such as new doubts over authenticity or other display plans. In time, the British Galleries database became available all around the Museum to those who chose to use it, but the number of queries raised by our active and systematic checking, object by object, demonstrated the need to ask colleagues directly. The database tended to be used only by those who were directly involved with the project or, occasionally, by other colleagues to check specific matters. It would be unreasonable to expect all Museum colleagues to use it and contribute to it as proactively as we, the team members, did.

As outline designs for the gallery were agreed, we carried out a similar laborious checking process with Museum conservators after they had made preliminary physical assessments. We discussed the conservation treatment and likely gallery mounts needed for every object under consideration. This confirmed the vast amount of work needed in most cases to prepare large textiles, such as tapestries,[15] for long-term display, or the delicacy of embroidered cushion covers or panel paintings. It also enabled us to give the Design Team broadly consistent guidelines for the light levels appropriate to each object type. The process also presented to conservators the thinking behind many of the unorthodox display strategies being considered, such as layering embroidered textiles vertically in a large, shallow case so as to suggest a richness of effect belied by the scarcity of surviving objects.

What needs to be stressed about this period of 18 months spent developing the displays is the iterative nature of the work. Each display was revisited over and over, as the selection of objects was polished, and the design or the interpretation refined. Each of these elements was affected by changes to the other two, and all three needed to fit the physical gallery space.

Design II

As described elsewhere (see chapter 7), the choice of colours and fabrics for each display was made by the Historic Decoration Team in close consultation with Concept Team members, following paint trials in the Museum and laboratory tests on materials that were to be used in cases. Two specific design decisions concerned the panelled armchair and the painted portrait – whether to show a reproduction cushion on the chair, to show how it would have been dressed, and how (if at all) to reframe the portrait. We decided against the cushion, following a Museum predisposition against reproduction items mixed with historic objects in gallery displays. We arrived at this decision in part because we would need some reproduction set-dressing in the Bromley-by-Bow room next door (where a cushion would be shown with an armchair) and partly, given the heavy load of other work still to do, because we could always add one after opening. The issues involved in removing (and storing) the nineteenth-century giltwood frame on the Hunnynge portrait were considered at length, and we decided to reframe it in a modern version of a late sixteenth-century Anglo-Dutch frame.[16] A new frame could also be made to take the low-reflective glass that would provide additional environmental buffering for the fragile panel support.[17]

In a second round of meetings during the spring of 2000, Dinah Casson sketched a layout for each case as we discussed the physical requirements and appeal of each object to be shown, and the lighting and labelling that would be needed (fig. 61).[18] This sometimes allowed us to add a new object in a vacant space, but more often entailed removing an object that could not be shown adequately. It also highlighted more clearly how mounts for particular objects needed to be anchored to the case structure – leading in turn to further discussions with conservators and mount-makers, as with an embroidered valance that is cantilevered over the larger textile behind it. Then followed the process (described earlier in this chapter) of paper templating as many cases as possible at full size in 2D or 3D (fig. 62) and updating the CAD drawings (fig. 63). Every change of object at this stage required written notification to at least seven separate groups (designers, Concept Team, Installation Team, conservation, curatorial department, cataloguer, photographic programmer), sometimes more. Research into the objects as they were being catalogued (sometimes for the first time since they were acquired by the Museum) also occasionally highlighted problems. For example, a false hallmark might be recognised, casting doubt on the authenticity of a silver cup, or there might be new discoveries, as when a portrait in an adjacent display was newly attributed to Hans Holbein.

Installation Installation was a phased process starting with the large Leicester tapestry and stained-glass panels on open display. Earlier ideas of supporting the tapestry from a pulley system from the overhanging canopy (to be able to lower the tapestry easily in future) were rejected in favour of the simpler method of fixing on a batten directly to the wall. With the tapestry hung, the metal barrier and supporting frame for the portrait could be installed into the floor. The height of the portrait had been decided long before, when the metal supports had been designed and manufactured, but for isolated wall-mounted objects like the Turkish carpet we could make small adjustments by eye when positioning the object itself.[19] With technicians following a detailed schedule of work and bringing crates of museum objects into the gallery every hour, spot decisions were often required. Mobile telephones were useful but constant attendance was obligatory, even had it not been natural to want to watch the results of five years' work taking physical shape. Questions cropped up constantly. Should we centre this object or follow the design drawings? Should we seek a spare perspex block to raise the height of a cup in relation to its companions? Should we install a case although all the requisite labels had not yet been delivered? There were other factors to consider: organising the opening of a large case takes time; when using heavy equipment and moving irreplaceable objects the teams of technicians need to rest regularly; museum objects should not be left unsecured in a space where contractors may still be carrying out urgent remedial work.

Once the inner glass had been checked for smears and cleaned, the first objects to be installed in the large case were the uppermost, wall-mounted textiles. In most instances, the distances between wall-mounted objects were so finely judged that the grid system of fixing holes was insufficiently flexible and new fixing holes were made as necessary. Where possible we used split-batten type fixings, to avoid visible mirror plates that would need to be painted-in to match the wall colour afterwards. After all this meticulous preparatory work, placing the goldsmith's work, freshly lacquered from conservation, was in some ways the easiest part of the whole job (fig. 64).

Given the labour and disruption involved in opening such a large case, we installed the labels on their metal mounts (screw-fittings and split-battens prepared in advance) as soon as the objects were installed. Ideally, the focusing of case lights would have taken place at the same time, but the contracted schedule of installation meant that it was impossible for one lighting designer to adjust the lighting in the three or so cases open at any one time. We reopened the case for this late in the afternoon, and left him behind the stained glass panels experimenting late into the evening with translucent screens to obtain the gentle light effects we wanted. The final stages of work that actually took place on *Achieving Splendour* were the adjustments to security equipment and the installation and checking of software for the More family portrait interactive.

Notes

1. For the Tudor and Stuart Team, Philippa Glanville played this role at the beginning of the project. After she left to become Director of Waddesdon Manor in 1999, we were grateful to Professor Maurice Howard of Sussex University for taking over this role and extending his secondment to the Museum until 2002. Malcolm Baker and Michael Snodin shared the role for the Hanoverian Team at first and were later joined by Hilary Young. The Victorian Team started with a similar sharing of the role between Paul Greenhalgh and Linda Parry, but after Paul Greenhalgh left the V&A in December 2000, Linda Parry continued as the single Senior Subject Specialist.

2. The Tudor and Stuart Team was led by Nick Humphrey, with Colin Mulberg as the Educator (later Celia Franklin), Sara Pennell as the Research Assistant and Richard Dunn as the Curatorial Assistant (later Dinah Winch, who then moved into the role of Research Assistant and was replaced by Kate Best). The Hanoverian Team was led by Leela Meinertas, with Morna Hinton as the Educator, Martin Myrone as Research Assistant (later Rachel Kennedy), and Kate Newman as the Curatorial Assistant (later Andrew Spira). The Victorian Team was led by Karen Livingstone, with David Judd as Educator, James Cheshire as Research Assistant, succeeded later by Laura Houliston; the original Curatorial Assistant, Sally Merriman, was succeeded by Suzanne Fagence, then Laura Houliston, followed by Eleanor Tollfree. The teams received invaluable assistance over a period of years from dedicated volunteers Jill Bace and Joan Dekker, to whom we wish to extend our hearty thanks.

3. Snodin, M., and Styles, J. (eds), *Design and the Decorative Arts: Britain 1500–1900* (London, 2001).

4. Models included a traditional architect's model in wood of Chiswick House, for the display on Palladianism, a finely-detailed and fully furnished model of the Glass Drawing Room from Northumberland House for the display on Neo-classicism (giving life to the splendid but fragmentary survivors of the panelling, displayed alongside), and a large-scale model of one section of the Crystal Palace, to give visitors a chance to appreciate the revolutionary, modular system of building devised by Paxton. The architectural models were made by Network Model Makers. The wish to show architecture, both for its own sake and as the context for many of the objects on display, led directly to the decision to make the longer (15-minute) film on country houses and their interiors.

5. It was this joint initiative that allowed us to show, amongst other paintings, James McNeill Whistler's *Nocturne: Blue and Silver – Cremorne Lights* as the centrepiece of our display on the influence of Japan in the nineteenth-century galleries, and William Morris's only surviving painting, *La Belle Iseult*, amongst the rich products of his design talent.

6. The mannequins were supplied by Garry Hall, the wigs by Kevin Powling with Bodyline, Inc.

7. The group consisted of the present writer, Morna Hinton, Nick Humphrey, Michael Snodin and Hilary Young, later joined by the project editor, Lucy Trench. The guidelines have been revised since the opening of the galleries and adopted as text guidelines for the V&A. They will form the basis for decisions about labels and text in forthcoming projects.

8. The number of surviving Tudor and Stuart objects in the Museum meant that it would have been physically possible for us to see every potential object for display, although we certainly did not achieve this thoroughness in terms of the Museum's prints, designs and books. For our colleagues in the Hanoverian and Victorian Gallery Teams such a comprehensive survey would, of course, have been impossible. In making selections from thousands of objects, they had to define more precisely the types of material that they sought, before making store visits.

9. V&A: C.335-1930, published in *Review of the Principal Acquisitions, 1930, Victoria and Albert Museum* (London, 1931), and featuring in 'Verre Eglomisé' by F. Sydney Eden, *Connoisseur*, 89 (June, 1932).

10. During the five years of project work there were three changes in the Tudor and Stuart Team as individuals left the Museum or changed jobs, so that only the Co-ordinator was involved throughout.

11. For the More portrait we specified a maximum light level of 70 lux, falling evenly on the painted surface. The question of a mount was straightforward as the portrait was to remain in its own eighteenth-century free-standing, wooden frame.

12. This was one of many helpful suggestions made by John Cornforth, a member of the Historic Decoration Team.

13. Following curatorial advice we planned to show the a set of blackwork panels made up into a partlet (a woman's upper garment with detachable sleeves) low down in the case where the fine embroidery could easily be appreciated. Mid-way through the design process, research suggested that the panels would have decorated a woman's smock, a much longer garment. Rather than exclude this exceptional object from the gallery, show it too high to permit close study, or show flat panels only, we decided that the lower part of the made-up smock could be draped on the floor of the case, as would have been impossible with a garment 400 years old.

14. V&A: 176-1880. The internal research report was written by Sara Pennell, March 2000.

15. For example, the Mortlake *Vulcan and Venus* tapestry (V&A: T.170-1978), shown in Gallery 56, required over 3200 hours of conservation.

16. Over a two-year period a small working group investigated the histories of existing frames, their suitability to new subject displays and glazing needs (as glazing might well require a new or stronger frame). For display under the *Style* theme, a new frame in an appropriate style might be chosen, whereas for a display about collecting, under the *Fashionable Living* theme, the existing frame fitted by an earlier collector (though stylistically inappropriate) might be retained. John Cornforth acted in an advisory role in the detailed choice of reproduction frames or frames based on historic precedent. We are also very grateful to Jacob Simon of the National Portrait Gallery for his advice.

17. Tim Newbery provided all the new frames for paintings in the galleries.

18. The design and sizes of all the cases had to be calculated as part of the whole case contract before these detailed layouts were prepared. These crucial calcuations were therefore based on the data prepared for each object by the Gallery Teams and handed over in ring binders months earlier. It is salutary to remember that very large sums of money were spent on the basis of simple measurements. Collectively we spent hundreds of hours, making, checking, recording and updating the measurements of objects.

19. The carpet (on its supporting board) was to have been angled out slightly on a block to mitigate the sense of it hanging flat on the wall like a picture. When it came to installation, we discovered that the narrow block had not been produced or delivered. Insisting that the block be remade would have put other necessary work at risk and we therefore decided to hang the mounted carpet flat.

49. *Store visit to inspect elements from the Northumberland House Glass Drawing Room, July 2000.*

50. *Carpet on backboard being wheeled through the Stuart gallery (56) prior to installation in Jacobean.*

51. Installation of carpet in Jacobean.

52. Detail of level 2 floor plan showing early grouping of displays in Tudor galleries (58 and 57), 1998.

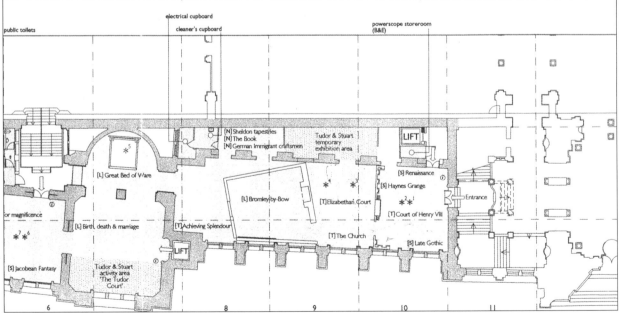

53. Members of the Gallery and Installation Teams installing **Developments in Ceramics** *(Gallery 56).*

54. Woman's smock incorporating blackwork panels, English 1575 en 1585, V&A: T.113 and 114–1997.

55. Heraldic glass panel, English, about 1570, V&A: C.335-1930.

56. Miniature of **Sir Thomas More and his family,** *by Rowland Lockey, 1593–94, V&A: P.15-1973.*

57. *CAD drawing for* **Achieving
Splendour,** *Casson Mann,*
February 2001.

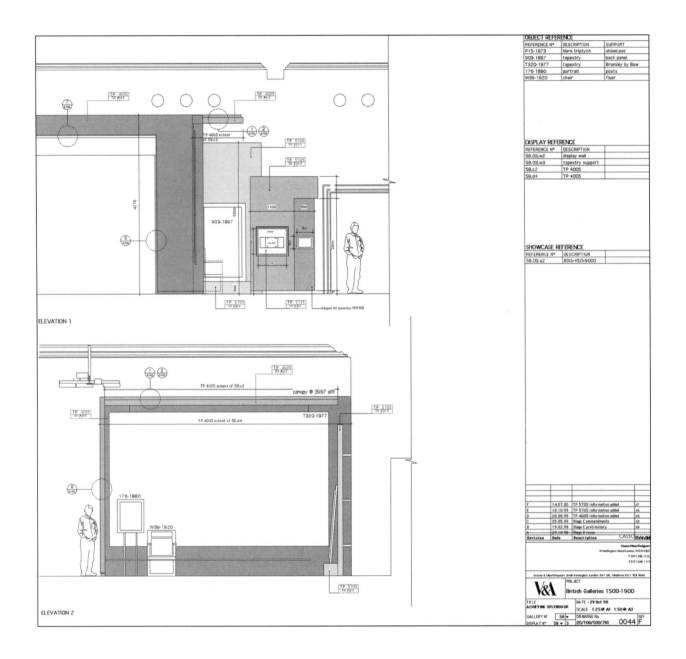

58. Watercolour sketch for
Achieving Splendour *showing
proposed position of seat and
touch-screen interactive, by Dinah
Casson, spring 2000.*

*60. British Art and Design
Galleries with the Leicester
armorial tapestry as displayed
behind plate glass, 1988.*

61. *Sketch for case in* **Achieving Splendour,** *by Dinah Casson, spring 2000.*

62. *Full-size templating exercise for case in* **Achieving Splendour,** *July 2001.*

63. *CAD drawing of case in* **Achieving Splendour,** *Casson Mann, August 2001.*

64. *Installing the case in* **Achieving Splendour,** *October 2001.*

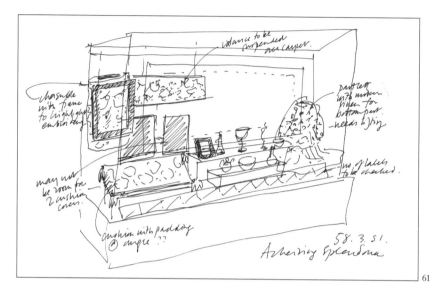

61

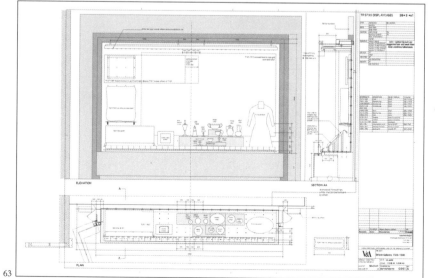

62

63

64

Chapter 9   Interpretation in the Galleries

David Judd, Morna Hinton and Frances Lloyd-Baynes

Low-tech interpretive devices
David Judd

All the interpretive devices in the British Galleries had one common aim: to engage the visitor with the objects. Producing over 100 low-tech interpretive devices for the galleries relied on all members of the Project Team understanding the value of interpretation for the visitor. Good relations between educators, designers, production manager, graphic designer and curators were essential, as was working to clear design briefs.

During the design phase of the project, suggestions for low-tech and high-tech interpretation devices were recorded in the Framework Document as part of the detail on each display.[1] As it became apparent that too many interpretive devices were being proposed, the merits of each device were discussed amongst the educators and within the teams, and selections were made. These discussions could be animated, with concerns voiced that some devices were too simplistic and others too complex.

The low-tech devices were developed as a number of series (see appendix 6). The main ones were divided into: construction activities (e.g. assemble a replica eighteenth-century chair) (colour plate 61); drawing activities; facsimile books and designs; gallery books which engaged visitors with the displays through open questions (such as *Questions of Design*); handling collections (colour plate 62); lift-the-label activities; mystery object displays; replica costume (colour plate 60); raised rubbing; spot the difference activities; touch objects (specifically provided for sight-impaired visitor to find out about style); touch plates for visually impaired visitors; and visitor response activities (colour plate 67).

In order to reach our various target audiences (see chapter 4), we knew that we would have to develop types of interpretation not used at the V&A before. Selection was based on the device's direct relevance to display objects, clarity of purpose and location. Positive feedback from the public during prototype testing helped settle a few nerves. Rough ideas were then developed into more detailed briefs. In order to create standardised briefs, a template was devised, which was used for all the interpretive devices. Information included:

Aim: what the purpose of the activity is.
Audience: which audience/s the device is targeted at and what learning style it might appeal to.
Format: what the visitor will be presented with. An outline of what the device consists of – objects/ samples/instruction text, etc.
Content: exact details of what the devices consists of – stating sizes, museum numbers where appropriate and whether there will be instructions/diagrams.
Design: where the device will be located, which object/s it relates to and an idea of what it might look like.
Text/Graphics: types of text required/Braille.
Drawings: to be commissioned for instructions/panels.
Photography: to be commissioned for use on panels/labels.

As the briefs were developed, the educators, designers and Gallery Teams discussed the location of the devices within displays and their proximity to featured objects. Logistics such as the space required, maintenance and accessibility all had to be resolved.

To ensure consistency in content and design, the three gallery educators each took on responsibility for several series of devices across all the galleries. One device from each series was prototyped and tested with the public. Any changes suggested by the prototyping were implemented across the whole series. Testing proved especially useful for finding out what visitors wanted to know about the object or manufacturing process, and how effective the instructional text was. If the evaluation showed that there were major problems, either in the text or the design of the device, then modifications were made and it was retested. For example, the text for a handling collection relating to encaustic tile-making was rewritten after testing because less than 65% of visitors understood the process of making (fig. 65). It was retested with new text, and 93% of visitors could explain the process. The design of an interpretive device could also be modified as the result of testing, for example the replica crinoline was made shorter as young children tripped up on the prototype (fig. 66). The two side-ties were also changed for one central one so that it could be more easily fastened by a visitor on their own trying it on.[2]

From the outset of the project, the aim was to cater consistently for the different needs of different visitors, throughout the run of galleries. One way to ensure this involved plotting all the interpretive devices on a set of gallery plans. This allowed us to see the spread of interpretive devices throughout the galleries. Some changes were made to avoid bunching of similar devices in the same area.

To cope with the ever-increasing amount of information collected for the briefs, a separate briefs document was produced and circulated monthly (for a sample, see appendix 8). Eventually, a final list of devices was signed off by the Gallery Teams and Concept Team. An additional document contained all the text needed for devices, including titling, captions and instructions. This was circulated, edited and then sent off to the graphic designers, one series at a time. The final graphics were signed off only when all those involved with the device (series educator, Concept Team, Head of Major Projects, copy-editor, production manager, graphic designer) were satisfied. As will be clear from this account, a great deal of work had been completed before designing the associated graphics and the presentation of devices in the gallery. In future, the gallery design and graphics would be established even earlier in the process, and the devices developed to fit within this framework.

In order to get the devices made and installed, a production manager was employed. Her role was to liaise with the educators, Concept Team, designers and graphic designers, and to identify manufacturers. Using the briefs, the production manager was able to sketch designs for the devices. However, the design process often raised questions that required further development and research to resolve, and the educators frequently needed to talk directly to the manufacturers to fine-tune the design briefs. The production manager obtained samples of the devices and proposed materials from manufacturers. These had to be agreed by the Concept Team before the devices were produced. The whole process was a lesson in compromise, as the various team members expressed their opinions and decisions were made. One particular concern was that devices would detract from the displays if they were obtrusive and disrupted sight-lines, so their size, location and design were discussed in great detail. With hindsight, reducing the number of people involved in the signing-off process would have helped speed up the process. Having many people involved at the beginning helped create a sense of group ownership, but did not facilitate decisions on manufacture and materials.

The low-tech devices demanded expertise from within and outside the Museum. Obvious issues regarding securing, mounting and protecting the handling and touch objects were resolved by Conservation and Health Safety departments inside the Museum. Outside advice was sought from a disability consultant, who produced guidelines on how to modify devices to give maximum access.

From the start of the project there was great concern that interpretation should be as authentic as possible. Most of the touch objects and handling collections are museum objects, although some objects and samples, such as the historic fabrics, were purchased especially for the galleries because they would have to be discarded and replaced in due course. For the replica garments, modern fabrics as close as possible to the original were sourced. Compromises did have to be made, for example with the replica ruffs. Originally the ruffs would have been starched and held together with pins, but the replica ones are tacked together, to avoid obvious hazards. The ruffs are regularly washed, restarched and retacked. This costs £55 per ruff, and needs to be done on average every four to five weeks.

In planning the interpretation, it was important to take account of maintenance issues. Multiple copies of some devices, such as facsimiles, were made or purchased as part of the original brief. However, it is only now, a couple of years after opening, that we have a realistic idea of how long things will last. Many of the interpretive devices have survived in the galleries longer than we had anticipated. This is despite the unexpectedly large volume of people using them. We have found that the replica costumes which have to be pulled and tied, such as the corsets, crinoline and hoop petticoat, need small general repairs regularly on a monthly basis.[3] The replica books that had been impregnated with fine-grade plastic lasted over ten months, while those pages where no coating was added to replicate an authentic feel lasted six months, although the books on the lower, busier floor of the galleries have had to be replaced twice during the first year. The reference books bought for the Study Areas on average have lasted nine months.

From the handling collection series, all the objects on display are still the original ones, except the silk and crêpe samples from the nineteenth-century fabric collection, which need to be replaced about every seven months. One general point that we have learned is that anything near the entrance to the galleries tends to suffer much greater wear and tear than devices further on in the historical sequence. With hindsight it would have been useful if the exact costings for each element of each device had been established and recorded at the time of commissioning, making the process of obtaining replacements for worn-out elements later on much simpler. During the fit-out of low-tech devices we should have arranged for a member of the Museum's technical staff to be involved, who could have taken a direct role in any maintenance required after opening. As it was, we had to spend considerable time trying to resolve minor problems with suppliers and sub-contractors.

Initial concerns that interpretive devices would be damaged deliberately have fortunately proved unfounded. One major fear was that the handling objects, especially the tethered ceramics sherds, would soon get broken. There is wear, but two years after opening, only one touch object has had to be replaced. Another concern was theft, but, given that the Museum attracts over 2 million visitors annually, relatively little has been stolen over the two years – 8 replica cravats, a torch, a magnifying glass, 27 books from the Study Areas (154 are on display at any one time) and 3 large-print books, 3 label books and a *Question of Design* book.

A maintenance manual for the interpretive devices was devised and produced by an educator and the production manager. This has been maintained by the gallery manager. The document contains details on the manufacturers, suppliers, number of duplicates, and original costs etc. It has proved invaluable. There was so much emphasis on getting the devices completed for the opening, that assumptions were made about who in the Museum would maintain them, without formal agreements being made. These have had to be negotiated after opening, as has the question of funding. Maintenance and other issues relating to the ongoing life of the galleries were one of the most problematic areas for the project as a whole. Though the need to identify budgets for post-opening maintenance and further development of devices was discussed and agreed in principle, such costs could not be made part of a project budget which would, within months of opening, cease to exist. Instead funds had to be bid for as part of the Museum's annual budget planning cycle. The unsatisfactory nature of this arrangement has led to delays to repairs and modification of devices, as well as a gap in funding for the development of new interpretive devices. This has proved a valuable lesson for the future.

Audio programmes and videos
Morna Hinton

Like all the interpretive devices, the audio programmes and videos were conceived as a number of distinct series, each with their own character. A single firm, The Edge Picture Company, was contracted to produce both the spoken word audios and the videos. One observation of such a collaboration is that the working styles of a film production company and a museum are very different. Film-makers work intensively on one project at a time, making quick decisions. Museums work on many projects running in parallel and need time to consult colleagues and check for accuracy. Both sides need to know what motivates and constrains the other party. Over two years, the V&A and The Edge developed an appreciation of each other's needs and priorities. One of the things that helped the relationship was that a single person (the present writer) acted as the Museum's 'producer', co-ordinating its contributions and liaising with the film-makers.[4]

Videos

There are three series of short (2–5 minutes) videos shown in the galleries, together with three longer films (10–15 minutes) for the Film Rooms. The *How was it Made?* series deals with techniques; *Object in Focus* videos examine single objects whose original function is hard to understand from a static display, for example a complex seventeenth-century lock. A third series of gallery videos deals with broader topics relating to individual displays, such as *Taking Tea* in the eighteenth-century galleries (colour plate 18).[5] All the short videos are positioned next to the objects or display they relate to and have subtitles in order to avoid the intrusions of ambient sound in the galleries (colour plate 33).[6] The films shown in the Film Rooms (colour plate 21) have narration and a soundtrack and provide a broad historical context for the exhibits through the following topics: *Country Houses*; *Art, Design and Empire*; and *A Day at the Great Exhibition.*

Members of the Project Team were assigned individual videos to manage, working with one of the three gallery educators as a manager of the whole series (see chapter 4). While numerous Museum staff contributed to each video, the device and series managers carried particular responsibility for developing content, reporting to and obtaining approvals from the Concept Team. The first thing we did for the videos was to write a brief describing each film's aims, content, length and target audience. There were three key variables in terms of making the films: objects, locations and presenters. For the *Object in Focus* films it was very straightforward, as each film usually involved only a single object, filmed at the Museum with no presenter (we used subtitles). With hindsight it is clear that the filming became less manageable as the script became complicated with additional objects, locations or featured commentators. A film such as *Art, Design and Empire* included a large number of objects and also had several different locations and presenters. In future we would try to do all the filming at the Museum if using many objects and several presenters.

For the short films, where we were clear about what we wanted to say, we drafted storyboards for The Edge. For the longer films we provided an outline of the areas we wished to cover, together with background material. The script was then refined in collaboration with the director of the film. There were usually more than four drafts but less than ten.

For some of the films we needed props, such as writing materials for the video about a sixteenth-century royal writing box or costumes for actors in the Vauxhall Gardens film. The Edge had to be gently disabused of the notion that they could just delve into the V&A's stores and use museum objects as props – 'But you've got loads of dresses!' they cried, unfamiliar with the principle that once historic dress enters a museum it is never worn again. In the end we obtained costumes and most of the other props from commercial prop houses, although sometimes V&A staff purchased or borrowed suitable items from more specialist sources.

When it came to the filming, long days were the norm because film crews are paid by the day (fig. 67). After a set number of hours, overtime was paid but it was still usually cheaper to work one long day than two short ones. We filmed on location, in the Museum and at a 'rostrum house', a specialist facility for shooting flat objects (in our case, paintings and works on paper) using a special camera that can be pre-programmed to give smooth shots, adding liveliness and professionalism to the finished film.

One important rule that we established early on in the filming was that no one except V&A staff was to touch or move a museum object. There was always one person on a shoot whose sole job was to ensure that the objects were safe. Another important rule that we learned to observe was that all comments to the director of the film or the cameraman were to be channelled through The Edge. It was explained to us that there is a distinct chain of command on a film set and that to ignore this leads quickly to chaos.

The editing process was divided into two stages: off-line (lower quality 'rough cuts') and on-line (the high quality final edit). We generally needed two rough cuts before the final edit. This was to avoid making expensive changes at the on-line stage. It was important to vet any music being suggested for the soundtrack before editing. Later changes mean substantial re-editing because the pace of the music determines the timing of cuts and other transitions that are put in at the editing stage. We learned this the hard way after discovering that the original music suggested for the *Great Exhibition* film was a modern pastiche rather than authentic nineteenth-century music, and in future we would vet soundtrack music before the editing stage.

All the British Galleries videos (20 short films and 3 long ones) were produced within about 18 months, from start to finish. The costs were as follows:

Object in Focus: eight films for £54,000 (all filmed at the Museum).
How was it Made?: six films for £52,500 (including location work).
Other gallery videos: six films for £74,570 (some location work plus animations).
Film Room videos: three films for £150,000 (extensive location work for one film).

Audio programmes   There are three different series of audio programmes: two series of the spoken word and a music series. The first spoken word series, *Telling Tales*, focuses on the stories depicted on objects, such as *Achilles and Patroclus*, (fig. 68), or stories about objects, for example a screen painted by Lawrence Alma-Tadema, who fell in love with his patron's daughter.

The second audio series, *Talking about Art and Design*, is divided into two different formats. Some programmes are based on historical quotations that relate either to the actual objects in our galleries (e.g. *The Three Graces*; colour plate 29) or more generally to the work of the artists and designers on display. For the third format of this series we asked contemporary practitioners to talk about objects from the point of view of their own work. We deliberately chose people from a wide range of disciplines, including the poet Benjamin Zephaniah and the gardener and writer Anna Pavord, in order to demonstrate to visitors that a personal connection with objects need not depend on specialised historical knowledge.[7] The music series aims to provide atmosphere as well as relating to individual displays. Thus a programme of songs and other musical pieces of the type performed at Vauxhall Gardens is designed to complement the gallery display on Vauxhall. All the audio programmes use telephone-style handsets next to the relevant object or display (colour plate 64).

As was done for the videos, the first stage in the process of making the audios was writing a brief outlining purpose, content, audience and so on. For programmes that told the story depicted on an object, we provided original material (such as translated extracts from the *Iliad* for the story of Achilles and Patroclus) that could be used by The Edge in developing the scripts. Each of the speech-based audios was to be between 90 seconds and two minutes long. The music programmes have five individual pieces, each of which is about two minutes long.

For the *Talking about Art and Design* programmes based on historical sources, such as the writings of the architect Robert Adam, we researched the accent and manner of speaking of the subject. With some figures we made educated guesses so that the production company would be able to brief the actors and voiceover artists who would read the scripts. The most problematic 'voice' for us was Charles II, because we could find no evidence about his manner of speaking. We therefore asked for a 'regal' voice but the initial attempts sounded too modern. The first actor came over as an upper-class airforce pilot of the 1940s, and the second was also felt to be unsuitable. Our final choice was an actor who had recently played Charles I on stage and who could use the voice he had developed for that role. It was important that members of the Museum team attended the recording sessions because questions inevitably arose that needed an immediate answer, such as the pronunciation of unusual names or words (fig. 69).

Shortly before the opening of the galleries we experienced technical difficulties with the hardware for the audio programmes. Custom-made handsets quickly broke, and static in the gallery interfered with the electronics. Although we chose to persevere with the custom-made model, we would in future reconsider very carefully the use of an off-the-shelf solution.

The total cost for the speech-based audios was £21,470 for 21 short programmes. The copyright on music can be prohibitively high, so the Museum engaged a commercial company, Classical Communications, to source suitable tracks for the music programmes. They charged a relatively small fee in exchange for the right to produce and market a set of three CDs linked to the British Galleries.

High-tech interactives
Frances Lloyd-Baynes

From the beginning of the British Galleries Project, the Concept Team had decided to utilise hi-tech interactive devices within gallery spaces as a means to enhance the visitor experience. Research carried out for the Museum in 1998 established that information communication technologies (ICT) within the British Galleries framework could

be used as [a] tool to create a varied, dynamic and personalised educational experience; enable visitors to engage in an exploratory relationship with the objects in the collection, one that encourages creativity and response; allow the V&A to build community among its visitors; be used as a navigational tool to open up the richness of the entire V&A collections; [and] be used only when it is the most appropriate means of achieving the stated aims of the project.[8]

On a practical level, the Project Team laid out a set of guiding principles in the 1996 Development document (appendix 1) and in the 1998 Feasibility Study, of which all but one (web delivery) were met in the development of the interactives. These principles stated that

- interpretation would be close to the object in the gallery, except in the case of Reference Databases in the Study Areas;
- no prior computer experience would be necessary to use the interactives in the galleries;
- the gallery interactives would augment the visitors' experience of and navigation through the galleries, and would not require the visitor to engage in a deep and detailed dialogue in order to derive benefit and information from the experience of using the interactive;[9]
- there would be variety among the interactives: the user experience for each, though part of an overall look and feel, would vary according to the application;
- the interactives would offer a quick, enjoyable and easy-to-initiate dialogue. Equally they should be easy to disengage from;
- where appropriate, a web-based version of the interactive would appear on the V&A website, with the proper alterations to enable lower bandwidth accessibility from a dial-up modem;
- interactives would be linked technically and conceptually where appropriate;
- there would be a mechanism to maintain profile information for each user, providing a personalised gallery experience;[10]
- wherever possible, there should be seating for at least two people at an interactive;
- where there is sound, this should not be audible round the galleries.

In defining the hi-tech interactives, the Concept Team sought a balance of interpretive ideas to meet the needs of the widely varied audiences and learning styles identified by the project (see appendix 5). Of about 200 gallery interpretive devices, 18 were web-based applications served to 40 gallery points or kiosks.[11] These included the *British Galleries Online* object database, the *Date a Design* database, *Visitors Online*, nine *Style Guides*, four *Design a...* devices, and two *Explore* programs. In addition, an Interactives Management System was developed as an underlying application content and kiosk management system.

The British Galleries Online (BGO) database aims to allow the visitor to approach objects via the individual gallery displays or via the four main gallery themes (fig. 70). Visitors can also search by time, place, people or object type. Each of the 3000 objects in the galleries is described within an individual record that can be associated with extensive contextual information in a variety of media formats (images, video, animations, text, audio), as well as being presented alongside biographies, place descriptions, and narratives. The program is visually led, primarily utilising images and brief text to guide visitor choices.[12]

Date a Design, originally called the 'Registration Marks' database, shows visitors how to date a nineteenth-century design through its registration mark (fig. 71). It also introduces visitors to the additional information on the patent registration scheme available from the National Archive (formerly the Public Record Office), such as drawings or fabric samples, and details of designers or manufacturers.[13]

While a variety of historical styles are shown and described within the galleries, it is not possible to explain the basics of a given style every time it is mentioned in the 104 gallery displays. In visitor evaluation we discovered that an overwhelming majority of visitors did not understand the terminology of style (see chapter 11). This directly led us to propose the Style Guides as the most numerous interactive in the galleries. The nine Style terminals, covering 21 styles, such as *Gothic Revival*, *Palladianism* and *Aestheticism*, act as a reference point for visitors, providing a simple description of a style supported by visual examples (fig. 72). The program shows visitors what motifs and other details to look for to identify a style and gives examples of the style within historic interiors, as well as providing examples of links with other styles.[14] Visitors who want to test their ability to identify styles can opt for a quiz.[15]

The two *Explore* interactives enable visitors to explore not only the pictorial content of featured paintings, but also the cultural context in which they were produced. The programs focus on the portrait of *Sir Thomas More and His Family* (attributed to Rowland Lockey) (fig. 56) and *The Opening of the Great Exhibition by Queen Victoria on 1 May 1851* (by Henry Courtney Selous)(fig. 73).[16] The program terminals are positioned within five feet of the paintings to allow visitors to examine the painting via the interactive without obscuring the actual work (see chapter 8, pp. 132–3).[17]

The *Design a…* terminals encourage learning by asking visitors to apply what they have learned in the gallery to solving a design problem. Visitors can:

- design a coat of arms using authentic heraldic motifs (fig. 74);
- create a monogram from their own initials;
- design a Victorian bookplate; and
- design a textile by choosing a set of floral motifs, a colourway and the way of repeating the pattern.

Each interactive draws on the V&A's extensive collections to offer design elements as templates for the visitors' designs. Special print options also exist, for example the textile design can be printed in colour or in outline as a colouring sheet. The design activities, available in the gallery Discovery Areas, are linked, allowing the design created for one activity to be accessed and used in another. For example, a monogram and a coat of arms can be saved and later incorporated into a bookplate design. Visitors are able to use their own designs or those of other visitors using this facility. Visitors are also able to email or print their completed designs.

The intention of the final interactive, the *Visitors Online* program, is to stimulate discussion between the Museum and its visitors, as well as between visitors, facilitating a broader and faster dialogue than the methods available to visitors in the galleries (i.e. paper and pencil) (fig. 75). Visitors can engage in an online debate, sign an electronic visitors book and contribute to a series of online history projects. A guest 'critic' is used to start a new thread to the debates on offer. The debates are moderated and as time passes the number of threads that visitors can tap into will increase. The *Visitors Online* program is available to visitors on the 16 Study Area terminals as well as on the V&A website (www.vam.ac.uk/visitors_voices).

The Interactive Management System (IMS) allows the V&A to create additional ICT applications in the British Galleries and to update existing ones from scratch. It also allows a chain of editorial systems to control the *Visitors Online* program, enabling change and management of debates and online history projects. The system further contains the 'validator' for the object database (*British Galleries Online*), a program which periodically extracts data from the British Galleries project database and inserts it into *British Galleries Online*. The main function of the IMS, however, is to manage the day-to-day operation of kiosks throughout the British Galleries. Kiosks can be assigned new applications and printers, or be shut down and restarted in the event of any software failures. This allows gallery staff without great technical expertise to handle all the first line support of technology in the gallery spaces, a process that has worked well during the galleries' first two years. The creation of this management system also freed the Museum from the costly and binding maintenance of the software by its outside software supplier. This was instrumental in achieving the goal of incorporating the British Galleries systems into the day-to-day running of the Museum by its staff.

Interactive design and development

At the outset of the project the Project Team generated a great many ideas for high-tech activities and creative approaches to engaging with a wide variety of audiences, but we lacked a proven structure in which to set them. Because the high-tech issues were complex and costly, we put a great deal of effort into establishing such a structure. Our computer services department worked with external consultants Momentus New Media to develop a technical strategy for the use of digital media in the gallery. One important decision was that everything should be connected to the Museum's computer network and centrally managed.

Once we had determined the technical strategy we had to structure our many ideas for content. For this we employed consultant Karen Donoghue, who had experience of visitor interactives in North America.[18] An important decision was to organise our varied ideas according to shared characteristics and create seven distinct series, each with a common structure. This was set out on paper and tested before development work was started. This gave us a 'routemap' which was subsequently followed by the Multimedia Project Manager (Nick Brod), who joined the team in 1999 and delivered the entire system for the opening of the galleries, and whose role was to manage both the internal museum requirements and external service providers.

The Multimedia Manager began by translating the Gallery Team's concepts into a brief for tender, which served as the basis for a cross-Europe tender process (April–July 1999). Of 30 interested firms, the Museum selected Oyster Partners (London) from a shortlist of five.[19] To initiate the work before confirming a contract, the Museum and Oyster undertook a one-month contractual development stage that provided the base documentation of the project (a requirement of both the V&A and the Heritage Lottery Fund). Discussions then ensued which resulted in the principal project documents:

- an Evaluation Strategy (to ensure consistency and delivery of overall project objectives throughout). This defined usability (how easy it is for visitors to use), technical performance, and audience relevance criteria;[20]
- a Creative Prototyping Process and timescales (breaking the project into three main phases: prototyping, full development, and acceptance/commissioning);
- a Deliverables list (written reports and software, tied to each project phase as well as to the developer's payment schedule); and
- a Quality Plan (defining means of communication, documentation standards, issue and risk escalation procedures, and sign-off authorities for each aspect of the project).[21]

Prototyping   The public testing of the interactives formed part of the prototyping phase, but it is worth noting that, in terms of software development, prototyping has a specific technical meaning – to define the technical architecture of the interactives and to begin establishing the look and feel of each. As part of the prototyping, British Galleries team members took responsibility for the development of the seven proposed interactive prototypes that had been selected to represent the full scope of the final applications.[22] The team member was responsible for explaining and iterating the concept and content of each device to the developers.[23] Criteria were established by which the interactives' effectiveness could be assessed. Consistent vocabulary was agreed both for the content and navigation.

The prototyping phase was broken down into a number of stages. The first stage (Global Design) aimed to ensure that both Oyster and Museum staff were approaching the project concept in the same way. We organised a series of some 20 lectures, seminars, workshops and presentations for Oyster's design and technical teams, V&A staff and relevant consultants such as the gallery designers. This initial phase served to inject new ideas and new expression into the project, allowing team members on both sides to think freely about proposals, thus opening up all the interactives to a wider range of possibilities. Concurrently, the V&A's Information Systems Services Department (ISSD) worked with the technical team on explaining to Oyster the Museum's complicated technical architecture and systems, and producing a technical strategy that was carried through to final product delivery.[24] The point of these technological discussions was to ensure that any solution created for the British Galleries was consistent with the Museum's wider IT strategy, and could be maintained under existing systems once the galleries opened.

During the subsequent Concept Phase, Oyster worked up screen designs, navigational and creative concepts. These were realised with paper prototypes, which were subsequently assessed with the V&A team member responsible for the device.[25] Several variations of screen designs were made, with up to three generations of design. With hindsight we could have planned more paper prototyping in order to make necessary changes before they became more expensive and difficult. As it was, the Museum extended this phase beyond its allotted period to allow these variations to be generated and the multimedia manager to work up detailed navigational paths, or 'device maps', for each device (fig. 76).

The first design phase aimed to develop a framework within an overall style and consistency guide to define a look-and-feel across all the devices. Oyster then used the device maps to build working prototypes following the agreed technical architecture.[26] The prototypes were installed in a system mock-up that matched the proposed technical architecture. They were then prepared for the first round of public testing (see chapter 11).

The public test results required the redesign of many elements of the prototypes.[27] New versions were made to resolve each design problem, which were in turn tested and agreed with the British Galleries Project Team. A second version of the prototypes was built using the new screen designs and reinstalled to the system mock-up where they were prepared for a second round of public testing. The resulting evaluations were again discussed jointly by the Project Team and Oyster to develop a clear brief for the final phase of prototyping.

Having gathered all the knowledge gained during the prototyping phase, the multimedia manager developed final specifications for all gallery devices. Oyster, meanwhile, completed their technical evaluation of the prototypes to enable final definition of all common design elements, fonts, colours and image sizes, as well as other requirements. They also prepared the technical architecture report in what would almost be its final version. The V&A, working jointly with Oyster, made final specifications for client hardware and infrastructure technology so that this could be in place for the development phase ahead.

By this stage the V&A had begun to prepare all final content for the interactives, a massive undertaking for staff from across the Museum working to a very tight timescale. This involved identifying, digitising and formatting some 13,000 internal images for the interactives, some 25,000 images for the *British Galleries Online* database, and writing all associated text. The BGO database in particular involved over 70 members of the Museum's curatorial staff in writing entries for each of 3000 objects. These entries supplement the gallery labels, expanding on whatever information was relevant to the object, such as the artists and associated people, the object's history, or the social and historical context in which it was made. The texts were then reviewed by the educators and Gallery Team co-ordinators for content and readability, copy-edited and separately checked for issues relating to ethnic diversity.

Other devices, such as the *Explore* series, involved in-depth research over several months, which was taken on by individual team members. The prototype *Style Guide* had been initially developed by one of the project educators, but full development of the interactive was handed over to a curator outside the main Project Team who could dedicate herself to the *Style Guide* more or less full-time. This program required extensive picture research in order to identify interiors and buildings that exemplified particular styles. Negotiating copyright of these external images for use in the interactive was a major task in its own right.

Strict deadlines were set for the completion of the content development. Oyster began the final construction of all gallery software in around March 2001, based on a schedule of phased delivery with devices being delivered in time for content written by the V&A team to be loaded into them prior to the galleries' opening. The *British Galleries Online* database was on a much longer content development phase, which ran from mid-2000 to November 2001 and ultimately delivered over 700,000 words of text.

Commissioning and installation

Despite a smooth end to the software development, the commissioning stages of the project proved frantic. Delays in completing the physical gallery spaces compressed the planned six-month installation of equipment into just six weeks. As each application was completed, various people at the V&A tested it (over the internet) to see that it worked.[28] Three waves of tests were run for each interactive with the last wave of testing completed once the system had been commissioned to the galleries. An agreed project closure process ensured that the work was completed on time – just eight days prior to public opening.

Although a guiding principle of the British Galleries interactive development plan was that web-based versions of the interactives would appear on the V&A website where appropriate, at the time of the gallery opening in November 2001 no interactives were yet ready for web delivery. Widely different bandwidth was available to the web and to the V&A's internal network – the two main delivery channels for the British Galleries interactives. This meant the Museum would have to create different formats of the interactives to support gallery and web delivery. The additional development time and cost of producing the two formats meant that it was not feasible to create web material within the project timeframe. The *Visitors Online* and *Explore* interactives went live on the V&A website in 2002, while the *Style Guides* went up in November 2003.[29] Work to deliver the complete range of British Gallery interactives to the website, including *British Galleries Online* with all its special features, is in progress at the time of writing.

Work on the British Galleries interactives has taught us a number of lessons for future projects:

1 Different interactive devices suit different gallery spaces. The careful design of the gallery interiors as well as that of the computer housings offers the possibility that the inclusion of interactives may enhance particular displays or exhibits.

2 The development of different types of interactives, conceived as series (e.g. *Style, Explore…, Design….*), can yield a large number of programs for limited budgets. Such types can then later be reused in other galleries if the systems use the original program structures as a form of template.

3 The development of interactives should be done according to an iteration-based project plan, with each stage of the project leading towards set deliverables. Such development should frequently refer back to the actual needs of museum visitors using public usability testing. By organising a project in this way museums, which tend to work at a slower pace than commercial interactive developments, can hopefully avoid schedule and budget overruns, which are common on long projects.

4 Vital to the success of any project-based plan is the correct organisation of management structures. If museums are to work with external commercial contractors, they should understand that such companies work to fixed schedules and consequently lines of reporting, management and authority are vital to the successful delivery of a project. Management of a large-scale multimedia project requires an internal qualified staff member to understand and manage the relationship between museum and contractor.

5 Maintenance of technology can be one of the most expensive and problematic aspects of gallery management. Consequently, museums should consider the maintenance, both day-to-day and long-term, of their interactive projects from the start.

6 Inherent to most modern museums is a web presence. It would be prudent for any museum undertaking high-tech interactives to consider how such technology can be reused on the museum's website. The redevelopment of gallery interactives for a website at a date later than the initial launch of a gallery itself is likely to be far costlier (if handled externally) than if performed concurrently with the initial development.

Conclusion
Morna Hinton

There are a large number of gallery redevelopments in progress at the V&A at the time of writing, ranging from the Medieval and Renaissance Galleries, which is a project on the same scale as the British Galleries, to small galleries like Sacred Silver and Stained Glass. The Museum is in the process of developing an interpretation policy based on the British Galleries and our experience on other projects. The policy sets out principles and highlights issues that need to be considered, such as the provision of interpretation for visitors with disabilities and the need to plan for adequate maintenance of interpretive devices.

One of the key principles carried forward from the British Galleries is variety of interpretation. Even in small galleries, the intention is that labels and panels should not be the only method of engaging the visitor. Bearing in mind the most important principles of learning style, we are striving to ensure that there is some sort of hands-on interpretation in every part of the Museum, so that visitors who prefer active participation will find something to interest them.

Each type of interpretive device found in the British Galleries may be considered for future use, but it is clear that not all will be suitable for all galleries. Maintenance issues are important and although the newly established role of gallery assistant (as opposed to warder) is being expanded to deal with day-to-day maintenance, it will not be possible to have high-maintenance activities such as drawing and replica costume in every gallery. In addition, certain types of gallery lend themselves to particular interpretive devices. For example the *How was it made?* videos that we developed for British Galleries are ideal for materials and techniques galleries. We will commission new videos using this format as well as reusing British Galleries films where appropriate.

There is a tendency for every new project team to want to refine and improve on forms developed in the British Galleries. This is only natural but it is also important to put energy into developing new types of interpretation whenever possible, thus extending the 'menu' available to future projects. Where the computer interactives are concerned, the aim is to use the digital 'architecture' of the British Galleries interactives as templates for those in other projects. This means that the Museum would be able to add content with only minor adjustments to potentially expensive design. It is also important that web and gallery versions of the interactives be developed in parallel, and alongside the templates needed to support them.

The excellent resourcing of the British Galleries Project, both in terms of budget and staff, enabled us to research, develop and test an enormous range of interpretation. This investment will pay dividends for the V&A in decades to come, as future projects build on the firm foundations the British Galleries have provided.

Notes

1. See appendix 7 for a sample display.
2. The full prototyping reports for the encaustic tiles and replica crinoline activities can be viewed on the V&A website at http://bg_lowtech (consulted 27 August 2003).
3. Replacements for the crinoline (wear) cravats (theft and wear) and ruffs (theft and wear) were made within the first year. The Inverness Cape has required almost no maintenance, except for replacing buttons and regular dry cleaning.
4. For a more in-depth analysis of working with film companies, see Hinton, Morna, 'The Screen Test', *Museum Practice* (Spring 2003), issue 22, pp. 53–57.
5. All the short gallery videos can be viewed on the V&A website at http://www.vam.ac.uk/bg_video (consulted 27 August 2003).
6. Before making further videos, we would review the use of subtitles, in particular the possibility of keeping them on screen for longer periods of time.

7. The *Telling Tales* and *Talking about Art and Design* audios can be heard on the V&A website at http://www.vam.ac.uk/bg_audio (consulted 27 August 2003).

8. 'Feasibility Study on the Use of Information and Communications Technology in the British Galleries', incorporating advice from Karen Donoghue, Donoghue Halliday Associates (V&A internal document dated 5 October 1998, held in the Intermediate Records Store of the V&A Archives and Registry), p. 7, hereafter as Feasibility (1998).

9. In planning future interactives, we would probably investigate ways to make them more open-ended, so that users can contribute their own creativity at the same time as assimilating information.

10. Feasibility (1998), pp. 7–8.

11. See Brod, Nick, *Diving in at the Deep End: The British Galleries at the V&A* (2002) (http://www.archimuse.com/mw2002/papers/brod/brod.html) (consulted 11 December 2003), hereafter as Brod, the source of much of the information on high-tech interactive development for the British Galleries Project presented in this chapter.

12. The Museum originally hoped to feed the BGO from its Collections Information System (CIS) database, but technical problems forced the development of an Oracle and Visual Basic system (known simply as the British Galleries database) to provide this service. This database has gone on to provide the core of a more widely used project database in the Museum.

13. Visitors either choose from a selection of objects provided or may seek information on the registration details of an object that belongs to them. The result of this search gives them the design registration date of the object and the option to see any related material lodged at the National Archive, or they are told how to set about further research.

14. On each terminal, the styles represented in the galleries near that terminal are offered as the first choice to explore. By navigating deeper, users can access styles displayed further away in the galleries. The program is also available in the gallery Study Areas, where any style can be selected.

15. Much of the content prepared for the Style terminals was used, in adapted form, for Jackson, Anna, with Hinton, Morna, *The V&A Guide to Period Styles: 400 Years of British Art and Design* (London, 2002).

16. The interactives are entitled 'Explore the More Family Portrait' and 'Explore the Opening of the Great Exhibition'. Each painting is assigned five categories in the program, such as 'People', 'Possessions', and 'Royal Court and Foreign Officials' (they are different for the two paintings). Using touch-screen technology, visitors can scan the painting for features that interest them, zoom in to see the details of the painting, and access further information or pictures of related objects in the collection, via an index option.

17. 'Explore the More Family Portrait Interactive Concept Document' (V&A internal document, held in the V&A Registry, held in the Intermediate Records Store of the V&A Archives and Registry), p. 1.

18. She took the Gallery Team's initial ideas and structured them, describing the interactives' basic format.

19. Oyster's selection was based on proven performance using the Oracle database platform (the Museum's preferred software format at that time), their interface design capabilities and understanding of the Museum's needs.

20. A number of audience objectives were specified for each device, and these were assessed informally throughout the prototyping phase against the usability, technical and audience criteria, and finally, formally assessed against their original objectives.

21. The Museum chose the Dynamic Systems Development Method (DSDM) – an approach to delivering interactive systems that should allow iteration at each stage and throughout the life-cycle of the project, tied back to the original audience/business objectives.

22. Design a Coat of Arms, Design a Bookplate, Visitors Online, Registration Marks (later 'Date a Design'), Explore The More Family Portrait, and two Style terminals: Rococo and Palladianism.

23. Iterating content meant repeatedly testing and redefining it on the basis of the results.

24. The technical team consisted of the multimedia manager, the head of ISSD, and the ISSD systems development manager. Oyster were represented principally by Oyster's senior software architect and technical director.

25. 'Some project participants from the technical side were reluctant to work on paper while developing ideas. The habit of going straight to computer means that ideas and structures get fixed too early, and not enough allowance [exists] for change' (written communication from Gail Durbin, 27 May 2003).

26. The device maps were also useful in explaining to senior project staff how the devices were to work.

27. The problems identified were, on the whole, specific usability issues related to the ways that the screens worked. In one case, a device was redesigned from scratch with an entirely new structure (Brod).

28. Acceptance tests were run by the Multimedia Manager, a volunteer student and, in some cases, device managers.

29. *Visitors Online* and *Explore…* are identified on the website as 'Visitors Voices' and 'Explore a Painting' respectively and can be found at http://www.vam.ac.uk/visitors_voices and http://www.vam.ac.uk/explore_painting. The Style Guides can be found at http://www.vam. ac.uk/understanding_styles/ (consulted 12 December 2003).

From the time the galleries opened, object-information from the British Galleries Online database has been delivered to the V&A's website by SCRAN (the Scottish Cultural Resources Access Network), who are hosting the data. Since April 2003, the BGO object data has also been delivered directly from the V&A's Collections Information System via the Museum's Access to Images initiative.

65. *Prototype testing* Encaustic Tiles, *February 2000.*

66. *Prototype testing* Replica Costume, *July 1999.*

67. *On location filming Michael Snodin presenting the* Country Houses *video, June 2001.*

68. Thetis and her nymphs rising from the sea to console Achilles for the loss of Patroclus, *by Thomas Banks, English, about 1778 (V&A: A. 15-1984), the subject of one of the* Telling Tables *audio programmes.*

69. In the recording studio for the audio programmes, Spring 2000.

70. British Galleries Online *homepage.*

71. Registration Marks Database *screen.*

72. Style Guide *screen.*

73. Explore the Opening of the Great Exhibition, *'scan' option.*

74. Design a Coat of Arms *sample page.*

75. Visitors Online *home page.*

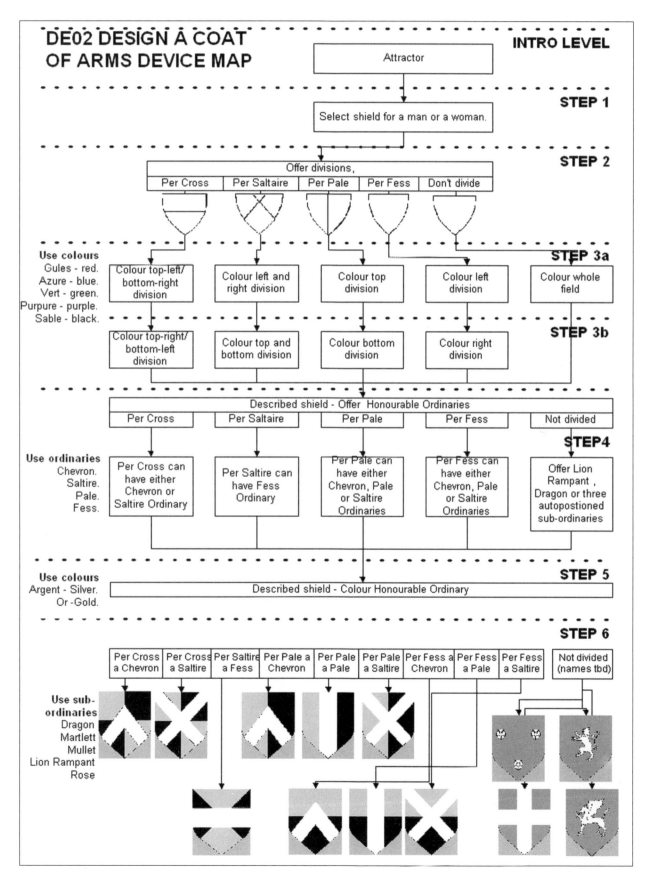

Chapter 10 The Period Rooms

Sarah Medlam

For a museum concerned with the history of design, and which counts architecture as one of its main subjects, the five period rooms in the new British Galleries provide a powerful experience of historical architecture in three dimensions. For many visitors who may have little historical knowledge and for whom museum displays may be difficult to understand, period rooms can usefully suggest social context. For those who find abstracted museum objects dry or distant, such rooms can evoke a different atmosphere from that found in museum galleries, suggesting aspects of the lives of previous occupants and connecting with the visitor's own experience of domestic life. Visitor research conducted in the old galleries in 1997 highlighted the continuing popularity of period rooms and that they were of particular value in tracing the evolution of domestic styles. Rooms – so different in mood and appearance from typical museum galleries – also provide variety and change of pace within the gallery setting.

Of all the objects in the galleries, the period rooms were the most complex to install, conserve and present, and certainly the most expensive. This account of what we did to each room, and of some of the difficult decisions that we faced, is an attempt to give our colleagues in museums and historic houses a fuller account than is possible for museum visitors standing in the galleries. Decisions were made often after long and very complex discussions or disagreements. Historical research was vital and highly illuminating but it was equally important to be able to accept compromises when necessary and to realise that archival work, though essential, could not answer all the questions or direct all the decisions. Though reams of paper recorded the process, from first research reports to the final processes of making curtains and chair-covers, we very soon recognised the paramount importance of giving one person overall curatorial control for the period rooms throughout the galleries. Simultaneous work on so many varied rooms required a single person to keep a constant involvement with the larger issues of conservation and display and also to take responsibility for pushing forward the myriad decisions, large and small, that had to be taken for each room. It was also important to develop fruitful working relationships with the multifarious people involved, whose interests, particularly in the latter part of the project, might well conflict. The Gallery Teams were naturally interested only in those rooms that fell within their particular period, but it was important that experience from dealing with one room and one set of problems could inform subsequent work. The curatorial responsibility for the period rooms was taken by the present writer as Deputy Curator of the British Galleries, working with Albert Neher of the Furniture Section of the V&A's Conservation Department, who provided technical expertise and agreed all proposals put forward by conservation contractors. Detailed reports of work undertaken, together with formal photographs and hundreds of snapshots, are now held in the Information Section of the Furniture, Textiles and Fashion Department at the V&A, where they can be consulted.

Period rooms in the V&A, 1869–1998 The V&A's collecting of period rooms has mirrored the rise and fall of the fashion for such exhibits almost since the Museum first opened. Its acquisition, in 1869, of the exquisitely gilded and painted cabinet or boudoir made in 1779 for the Hôtel Megret de Sérilly, Paris, represented an initial wish to acquire items that demonstrated the highest technical excellence in their design and execution. Whether or not this panelling was seen as 'a room' or as a highly decorative object, is not clear. It also brought an example of continental design (then thought to be innately superior to British) within reach of artisans in London, thus furthering the aims of an institution that had started out as the Museum of Manufactures. The second half of the nineteenth century was a period when the European markets were flooded with architectural woodwork and panelling, sometimes in the form of complete rooms but more often as fragments of earlier grand interiors, set adrift as the result of widespread demolition and development throughout Europe. Further continental rooms, including French and Swiss rooms, were acquired by the Museum occasionally until the first decade of the twentieth century.

However, by the 1890s, the main focus of museum collecting, whether of rooms or other types of object, had turned to material that represented British (or, more narrowly, English) cultural history. The emphasis on particular techniques of construction and decoration had become secondary and the Museum followed general collecting taste in Britain in turning from the elaborate forms and techniques of European furniture to an admiration of the restrained design and decoration of English furniture made during the seventeenth and eighteenth centuries. This concern with nationalist cultural history gave rise to a wish to 'save' particular rooms from destruction, as historic houses (particularly in London) increasingly faced demolition for development and their rooms faced export. Though the Museum did buy several of its rooms from dealers, three of the five period rooms chosen for the new British Galleries are from London houses and came directly to the Museum at the time of the demolition of those houses. This reflects a growing concern, which was to last until after the Second World War, about the loss of the English architectural heritage. During the three decades from 1890 to 1920 this concern was so powerful that the emphasis changed to a more active policy of creating an encyclopaedic series of English rooms. The idea was that these should illustrate every major style and many of the important techniques used for the decoration of rooms at all periods, including inlay, carving and plasterwork.

The pre-1999 English Primary Galleries, installed in the space now occupied by the British Galleries, included eight period rooms. These were intended to give context to what was planned as a comprehensive display of English decorative arts from the sixteenth century to the nineteenth, a major element of the reorganisation of the Museum into 'Primary' and 'Study' Galleries, that has survived, in modified form, to the present day. From that time onward three factors began to affect the Museum's attitude to period rooms. First, as more houses opened to the public, more rooms were available elsewhere for people to visit. Secondly, as the pace of demolition slackened, with the development of more powerful planning controls, the Museum no longer had to take on the role of saviour of threatened rooms. Finally, with the expansion of the Museum's collections to include Apsley House, Ham House and Osterley, as fully furnished interiors, the focus of curatorial work and experiment with historic decoration shifted to those houses. Curators were by then more concerned with supporting the preservation of surviving buildings and interiors than in benefiting from their break-up.

Changes in fashions in presentation had also led to profound debate about the possibility of achieving authenticity in the presentation of period rooms in museums. With new knowledge, panelling and fittings acquired in the early twentieth century as a single room might be discredited and recognised as having been assembled or made up by a dealer. Period rooms had already begun to fall out of fashion with curators before the Second World War, though their popularity with visitors continued to be high. Since the Victorian room from The Grove came to the Museum in 1963, only one other room has been acquired, the wood-panelled office designed in 1935–37 by Frank Lloyd Wright for the department store magnate Edgar J.

Kaufman in Pittsburgh. When discussion on the new British Galleries started in 1996, there were many debates on how many (if any) period rooms we should include and on how they should be presented. It was their popularity that ensured their survival, together with the quality and authenticity of those rooms that we chose to include, but it was valuable for us in making our plans that we had to argue for the inclusion of each of them and assess their likely value and impact.

Rooms no longer on view

There are five complete rooms in the new galleries (see gallery plans), with substantial fragments of five others, shown simply as objects. In the old galleries (originally installed 1947–52) there were eight complete rooms, with substantial sections from four others forming part of the displays. Of the eight, one, the room from Sizergh Castle, Cumbria (V&A: 3-1891), was successfully returned on long loan to its original location. In 1891 the owners of the castle had sold the panelling to the V&A and for nearly a hundred years it was a much-admired exhibit. However, in 1950 Sizergh Castle passed to the National Trust and since that time there had been periodic discussions about the desirability of reinstating the panelling. For many years this project could not proceed because of the costs of removing the room and creating displays to fill the space that it would leave. However, when the British Galleries Project launched a complete redisplay of the galleries, which included, in any case, the dismantling of all the period rooms, negotiations opened once more. The Heritage Lottery Fund generously funded the reinstatement of the room at Sizergh and it opened to the public in spring 2000. The V&A was delighted to be party to this repatriation of the panelling.

Of the other rooms in the old galleries, one, the room from Hatton Garden (V&A: W.4-1912), traditionally dated about 1730, was found on examination to have been moved about and altered in arrangement so often by dealers before it came to the Museum in 1912, and again when it was installed by the Museum staff, that no clear plan of its original arrangement could be arrived at. For this reason it was decided that it should not be used. One other room, the oak-panelled room from Clifford's Inn, of about 1686–88 (V&A: 1029-1903), featured in our plans until quite a late stage, until pressure of space forced it out. One wall of this panelling, including two of the fine carved door-cases, is now shown in the display on Restoration style in Gallery 56.

The panelling from Haynes Grange, Bedfordshire, possibly of about 1580–90 (V&A: W.1-1929), could not be displayed in the old galleries, owing to its height, but it had for many years been shown as a room in Gallery 40, now the Fashion Court. This is one of the most intriguing of British rooms, chiefly because so little is known about its origins, although it is accepted as one of the most important early examples of the use of full classical orders in British architecture. There were a number of vociferous lobbyists pressing for its re-erection, and this was carefully considered. It finally proved impossible on two grounds: first, the height available in the galleries was not enough to accommodate the full room; and secondly the single, very narrow door, meant that visitors could not have entered the room. One wall of panelling, however, was included as an example of Renaissance design, prominently facing the visitors as they enter the galleries (colour plate 1).

Principles and problems of redisplay

From the start of the project we identified the over-arching principle in all our work with the period rooms as that of returning to the rooms a sense of their architectural integrity. Wherever possible, we would re-create the fourth walls. We would also display them in such a way that visitors, when possible, could enter the rooms and experience the architectural space, providing the opportunity for them to sit down in the rooms wherever possible. As early as 1907, a commentator writing of the Bromley-by-Bow room had lamented the lack of window walls and the use of barriers to keep visitors out of the 'viewing box' that he deplored as the standard method of presentation for period rooms.[1] A third method of re-establishing architectural integrity was to be the installation of historically appropriate flooring. In all but one case the original flooring of the room had not survived, and the historic panelling just sat on Aston Webb's parquet flooring of 1909. This lack of appropriate flooring seriously diminished the visual impact of the rooms. We also decided that each room would be treated differently, some more abstracted than others, some more fully furnished, to give variety to the presentation. We would provide not only information on the history of each of the rooms but also information that would allow visitors to understand the conservation and restoration undertaken on each room, so that they could judge our work for themselves. In some cases we would leave uncovered areas on the outside of rooms or at the edge, to demonstrate their structure to the visitor.

The people involved

The management of the project meant that four main contracts were involved in the reinstallation and conservation of the rooms, in addition to separate contracts for electrical works, and plasterwork for the cladding of the outside of the rooms. The demounting and packing of the rooms, their reinstallation and making good were undertaken by Momart, working with the conservation firm Taylor Pearce. The dismantling and re-erection of the frames made in the Museum to support each room when first installed in the twentieth century was undertaken by Westminster Partitions and Joinery Ltd. In the three rooms from the eighteenth century, paint analysis was undertaken by Oestreicher Davies, with subsequent consultation with Patrick Baty. Finally, the firm of St Blaise won the contract for the creation of the fourth walls and the redecoration of the rooms. St Blaise used a number of specialist firms as subcontractors, notably Weldon Flooring to supply the floors of salvaged timber and the firm of Hare & Humphries to undertake specialist painting and gilding. The work was co-ordinated by Richard Hill, working for Casson Mann.

The Historic Decoration Team (see chapter 7 for a full listing of all those involved) took all decisions relating to painting, decoration and furnishing, in consultation with Museum staff. Lighting for the rooms was specified by Richard Aldridge and installed as part of the general lighting contract by Museum and Gallery Lighting of Bury, working with Profile Glass of Derby. Wilkinson plc of London undertook specialist work to rewire the original sconces in the Norfolk House Music Room. Other firms which undertook specialist work in one or other of the rooms will be mentioned in the appropriate section. Many of the Museum's own curators and conservators provided advice, information and detailed specifications on particular aspects of work in the rooms, and advice from colleagues in the Furniture and Woodwork Department (as it was then known) underpinned much of what was done.

Practical considerations

Requirements for conservation and restoration were described in detail for each room in the initial document prepared for the tendering process. In each case we had also to specify the services required for each room. Provision had to be made for lighting and for any power necessary for audios or any interpretive devices or for occasional power for microphones – even vacuum cleaners. The provision of all wiring for security devices had to be considered at planning stage, as did any fixings or solid fixing points required for museum objects or such furnishing items as curtain pelmets, etc. Each room required a security camera, and we were at first concerned about these, but in practice they are now so small and discreet that most visitors are scarcely aware of them. We left consideration of them until quite late in the process and then discovered that plans for curtaining created problems in terms of sight lines. These issues then had to be dealt with on an *ad hoc* basis, but it would have been better to consider them at the point of planning.

When we wrote the initial specification for the work, we believed that we had covered every detail of the process of reinstallation and conservation. It was sobering to realise just how many decisions remained to be made at the last minute. This inevitably caused tension with contractors and project managers and the lesson learned was that we should have established this early on as an essential part of the process and have allowed more generously for it in the allocation of time in the final stages.

Thousands of photographs were taken in the course of the work, and detailed surveys were prepared by Momart as part of the process of dismantling and storing the panelling. Regular progress photos were taken by the Project Managers, Bovis, as the work of rebuilding the rooms progressed, but it always seemed that some crucial work took place at a time when no one was around to photograph it. The importance of good photographs cannot be stressed too much and, although formal progress photos may appear more impressive, it is often the immediate snapshot (if it is properly annotated and dated) that is both more useful and more powerful as evidence of what was done.

Parlour from the Old Palace, Bromley-by-Bow 1606

The house at Bromley-by-Bow, just to the east of London, was probably built by a merchant, but almost nothing is known for certain of its origin. It may have been built by the master builder John Thorpe.[2] This room (colour plate 2) was on the ground floor, at the back of the house (fig. 77). A room in that position was often called a parlour. It was less grand than a Great Chamber, which commonly stood on the first floor, but like the Great Chamber it would have been used for entertaining. At Bromley-by-Bow the Great Chamber on the first floor boasted an even grander plaster ceiling than this room.

The ceiling (V&A: 51-1894) of this oak-panelled room carries the initials IR for of James VI of Scotland, who was also James I of England. The overmantel is carved with the royal arms. Elsewhere in the house, a carved stone carried the date 1606 (V&A: 430-1895), and this has always been taken as the date of the panelling. The ceiling medallions show three of the Nine Worthies (each shown twice) – Joshua, Hector and Alexander. The designs are based on a series of engravings of the Nine Worthies by Nicholas de Bruyn, published in Antwerp in 1594. The designs appear on other ceilings in England and Scotland.[3]

The house remained in continuous use, as the area gradually became less rural. It was altered and partly refitted in 1660–70, and it was probably at this time that the owner inserted a door on each side of the chimneypiece. These doors were removed at the time that the panelling came to the Museum. In about 1750 the building was divided into two and given more up-to-date sash windows. By the mid-nineteenth century the building was used as a club and lodging house. Despite its lowly use, it acquired a romantic history as a hunting lodge built for James I. The arms over the chimneypiece were interpreted as a mark of royal ownership rather than, as is more likely, a declaration of loyalty by someone who did not possess his own coat of arms.

In 1893 the building was acquired by the School Board for London, who wanted the site for a new elementary school and sold the house to a firm of house-breakers for £250. The fate of the 'Old Palace' became one of the first publicly fought battles for the conservation of a historic building and the Arts and Crafts architect C.R. Ashbee (1863–1942) led the protest over its demolition.[4] The School Board was shamed into buying back the chimneypiece of the parlour for use in its new school, though it was finally given to the Museum, after the latter purchased the panelling and wooden overmantel from the house-breaker. The Museum's files detailing the acquisition of the room include a drawing by Ashbee of the chimneypiece of this room and its flanking doorways (fig. 78).

Once demolition became certain, there was strong support for the then South Kensington Museum to purchase the parlour, the best-preserved interior in the house. The house was already in the hands of the demolition contractors, and the South Kensington Museum had to purchase the ceiling from one owner, the panelling from another and the chimneypiece from the School Board itself. Some pieces had wandered earlier. It was not until 1901 that the figures of Peace and Plenty from the overmantel were given to the Museum (V&A: 859 to 861-1901) by a woman whose family had lived in the house in the middle of the nineteenth century. When the room came to the Museum in 1894, it was not thought necessary to bring the three sash windows or the two pine door-cases of the later seventeenth century. The partition that ran across the room at the end opposite to the chimneypiece was also left. Although the form of the door-cases is dimly evident in a contemporary photo (fig. 79), there is no record of the window wall.

At first the room was displayed in the galleries to the east of the Museum garden. The room was shown as a three-sided box and panelling from the window wall was used to fill areas formerly occupied by door-cases. By the time that it was pictured in place in the Museum in 1901, the 'window' wall had been moved from the right of the chimneypiece to the left, presumably to allow some light from the actual windows of the Museum.[5] It was said that an arch, originally outside the room, was used on the wall opposite the chimneypiece when it came to the Museum, but this is not evident in the 1901 photograph.

By 1907 the room had been moved to the new Aston Webb galleries at the south-west corner of the museum on the raised ground floor and it remained here until 1998. Once more it was erected with a panelled wall to the right of the chimneypiece, with visitors viewing it as if from the window wall opposite, through large, floor-length openings, later glazed. No flooring had been acquired with the panelling and the room was placed directly on Aston Webb's parquet. It has always been said that the panelling was stripped of many layers of graining when it came to the Museum but there is little evidence of this remaining.

Evidence for decisions in redisplaying the room

Despite the declaration of principle that we would reinstate the fourth wall of each period room, we had to accept defeat in this instance. No evidence survived of its form in 1606. Plans of the room and the few photos of the exterior showed only the sash windows of the eighteenth century, and even for these the evidence was scant. The only photograph traced of the room (fig. 79) showed clearly that the windows were to the right of the chimneypiece but nothing about their form. We knew from written sources that the panelling had been pieced out and supplemented with new plain panelled sections to cover the spaces lost when the seventeenth-century doors were removed. Close examination of the panelling certainly confirmed that some sections are newer than others, but it was difficult to establish exactly how much had been renewed on the two short walls and how much of the wall had been made up from elements of panelling from the window wall.

What was done The ceiling was cut into sections following the saw cuts made when it was originally moved from Bromley-by-Bow. It was largely possible for saw cuts to follow the edges of the decorated ribs, and cuts through decorative areas were kept to a minimum. In the specification we had asked for the ceiling to be limewashed but this would have caused problems with earlier generations of emulsion paints that had been used on it and, as the surface was sound, we decided in the end to paint it with contract emulsion in an off-white, leaving archaeological evidence of earlier layers in place for our successors.

We were clear that we wanted to hold fast to our second aspiration at least, that visitors should be able to enter the room and experience the space. Casson Mann's solution to the lack of evidence for the window wall and to the need to provide easy entry for visitors was to create an abstract fourth wall, and to hinge it out, as it were, from the south-west corner, allowing visitors to slip into the room at the south-east corner and to exit through a door space in the short wall opposite the chimneypiece. This avoided the creation of an unpleasantly narrow corridor alongside the room but does gives a sense of enclosure to the space. This fourth wall is not panelled. Instead it is painted a brownish grey and is used to show one of the Museum's spectacular embroidered table carpets, known as the Bradford Table Carpet (V&A: T.134-1928). This is the sort of colourful textile that would have been used in such a room but which is now too rare and fragile to be shown unframed. It complements the tapestry of the *Judgement of Paris* (V&A: T.310-1920), from the Sheldon tapestry workshops, that hangs on the opposite wall.

Our approach to the panelling itself was conservative. We decided that, although we would reorientate the wall opposite the windows so that it returned to its correct relationship with the chimneypiece wall, we would leave the earlier replacements of panelling in place. The movement, of course, was not as easy as it might seem; short sections of the horizontal 'frieze' against the ceiling and other mouldings had to be replaced with reproductions in order to allow the room to be fitted exactly without cutting into any of the original panelling at the corners. At a late stage, replacement sections in the horizontal frieze also proved useful in providing secure fixing points for the bar from which the tapestry was hung. The same measure was adopted in dealing with the cornice of the fourth wall and its junction with the end walls. On the wall opposite the chimneypiece, where a section of panelling had been let in above a created arch, we chose not to reinstate this panelling but to leave a simple floor-to-ceiling gap between the two sections of wall panelling, through which visitors could pass.

Once the panelling was in place in its new formation, it required very little work other than light cleaning and waxing. Originally we had decided that the edges of the panelling visible at the south-east corner and in the opening on the west wall should be left unfinished to show visitors something of the structure of the panelling. At a late stage, we changed our minds about the reveals of the doors, feeling that the transition here to the gallery walls would be disturbing if not lined and painted.

It was clear that the installation of correct flooring would greatly enhance the visitors' experience of this room. With no precise visual evidence, except a brief glimpse in the one surviving photo, we asked Weldon Flooring, a firm specialising in replicating historic floors, to source historic, wide oak boards of variable width, to replicate the variety of widths seen in houses of the period. When we first started to work with Weldon Flooring we asked them to prepare sample boards for the floor of each room, based on a written specification. Immediately, it became clear just how difficult it is to brief others on such matters (particularly on matters of colour and degree of ageing). With hindsight we should have set up visits to the properties on which we based our specification as a way of establishing exactly what we wanted. Verbal descriptions and even photographs are too open to personal interpretation and prejudice. It is fatally easy in the course of such a project to believe that one does not have time for such visits with contractors but they often save time in the long term.

One problem that inevitably occurs with the choice of recycled timber is the speed with which batches of timber come in and out of the salvage merchants, making the question of producing samples for approval very difficult. Finally, Weldon's solved the problem of the floor for this room by sourcing an exceptional consignment of old oak, the widest board of which is 42.5 cm across. The planks are nailed to battened joists as they would have been in the original house. The use of recycled timber inevitably means that planks have at least one extra set of scar marks from old nailing and this must be balanced against the naturally-aged colour of recycled timber. The polishing up of the floor produced the patinated look of the floor in an old house and it has survived two years of heavy visiting remarkably well with no further polishing. The floor is now remarkably atmospheric and gives out satisfyingly realistic creaks as visitors pass through.[6]

Together with the wood for the floor, we also had to source a new hearthstone. The pattern for that was the very pale limestone of the chimneypiece itself, identified by V&A conservators as Reigate limestone. Portland stone was chosen as the nearest match. The hearthstone was cut in sections as large hearthstones frequently had to be.[7] Each step of the process raised new questions. Once we had decided on the form of the hearthstone, we had to establish the details of jointing between the hearth and the boards. In this case, no edge framing was used, the boards just running into the hearthstone, as at Haddon Hall, Derbyshire, and Chelvey Court, Somerset. In its last incarnation no depth for the hearth had been allowed and the fireplace appeared only about 15 cm deep from front to back. This was now remedied and the hearth cavity lined with reclaimed Tudor bricks, set in English bond, following the form of the recorded fireplace at Eastbury Manor, Barking.[8]

The chimneypiece itself was conserved by Museum staff while the room was dismantled. Early texts had suggested that there was originally painting and gilding on this, but no evidence was found. The lower edges of each jamb had been lost and replaced in wood. These were replaced again in the Portland stone that was used for the hearth. The panel carved with the legend 'Better is a dinner of herbs where love is', visible in the pre-1893 photograph, was part of the later, inner section and was not reinstated.

Lighting Lighting for this room proved particularly difficult, in that the abstract 'window wall', used as it was for display, could offer no light, real or artificial, via windows. The most radical option would have been to cut into the plain sections of the ceiling, in the shadow of mouldings, and to insert small fibre optic lights. There was understandable unwillingness, however, to cut into the historic fabric and to alter it so radically, with no surety of success, though this was the subject of vigorous discussion amongst the Historic Decoration Team, the curators and the lighting consultant. Some lighting could be introduced via the barrier, at low level, but there was no opportunity for introducing convincing visible artificial light (as we were able to in the Norfolk House Music Room by using the original wall sconces) into a room that would, at best, have been lit by firelight and very few candles.

Lighting from the open edge of the panelling along the south side was also possible, though care had to be taken in order that visitors coming in an easterly direction through the room (i.e. against the chronological flow) would not be blinded by spotlights. Finally, David Mlinaric suggested the use of modern uplighters and Casson Mann designed a version of these, rising from the barrier. These help to light the ceiling, but there are still problems with the overall light in this area, especially on gloomy winter afternoons. It is likely that we will have to return to the problem in the future, to address in particular the lighting of the label book. This difficulty resulted in part from the programme for the installation of the galleries. Gallery 58 was one of the last to be installed, and so there was little time to experiment or to revise proposals for lighting the most problematic room of all those shown.

How the room was presented We knew from the very earliest planning stage that this room would be of great interest to primary school groups visiting the Museum. Although it was, strictly speaking, just outside the Tudor period, which is one of the two mandatory periods for study by primary school children in Britain, it was likely that it would be used for work on that subject. There was a strong feeling that it should be shown as much as possible as a furnished room. Three problems presented themselves. One was the practical one of furnishing a room that visitors walk through. Whereas for the other period rooms, visitors choose to divert from the main galleries into the spaces, the Bromley-by-Bow room is on a main through route.

A second problem was posed by its likely use by school classes: any class visiting the room would need space for 25–30 children to gather with their teachers and other adults. Initially we had discussed placing a reproduction table in the centre of the room to provide an anchor piece, on which gallery books could be consulted, but we had to abandon that idea because it was likely that it would make the room too crowded. The third problem arose from the Museum's own collections of sixteenth-century furniture. Much of the V&A's early furniture had been collected in the nineteenth or early twentieth century and was doubtfully authentic or had undergone extensive alteration and restoration. Even from those pieces that were indisputably authentic, it was not easy to assemble the furnishings of a credible room from pieces of slightly different dates and sometimes very different social origins. We were also faced with the question of how to represent the textiles element of furnishings, which would have been so strong in such rooms.

Our decision finally was to set up a display area to one side of the room, behind a barrier, in which we could show examples of the main types of furniture of the time. One advantage of this arrangement is that it does not suggest a too literal or fixed furnishing scheme. A Jacobean parlour would have been used in different ways at different times, for dining, entertaining or private business, with furnishings being moved in and out as appropriate. We debated long about the question of using reproduction textiles in this room, to increase the representation of textiles in the domestic interior in line with what might have been there in the early seventeenth century and to allow us to 'dress' the furniture. The display does include an important tapestry from the Sheldon workshops in Worcestershire or Warwickshire, showing *The Judgement of Paris*, opposite the framed Bradford Table Carpet. Other original textiles, where they survived at all, were excluded on the grounds of rarity and fragility, but in the end we chose to use a reproduction cushion on the chair and reproduction cloths on the cupboard.[9] For dressing the cupboard itself and making clear its function, we also turned to reproductions, using electrotypes of famous early pieces of silver and silver-gilt, that had been made for the Museum in the nineteenth century, together with modern pewter plates. It would clearly not have been possible to use original pieces of that rarity and value without casing them, which would have destroyed all sense of a domestic interior. They are shown together with original stoneware pieces. In the hearth area we have used a fireback (V&A: 685-1899) and a pair of firedogs dated 1576 (V&A: M.1-1985), these firmly fixed down and loaded with elm logs, less likely than oak to react adversely with the iron.

Following the decision in principle to allow visitors to sit down in the rooms, a reproduction bench was made by the firm of Richard G. Philips Ltd, London, using the turnings and mouldings of a contemporary stool from the Museum's collections (V&A: W.223-1923) as a model. This is placed in the south-west corner of the room, allowing visitors to sit while using a handset to listen to music contemporary with the room. The book of labels is set on a stand forming part of the barrier, close to the historic furnishings that it describes.

The parlour from 11 Henrietta Street, London 1727–28

This room (colour plate 15) was the single main entertaining room on the first floor of a London terraced house built and decorated in 1727–8 to the designs of the architect James Gibbs (1684–1754) (fig. 81). Number 11 was one of four houses built to Gibbs's designs in Henrietta Street (now Henrietta Place), just to the north of Oxford Street. He leased four plots and built one (number 5) for his own use and three, including number 11, for investment.[10] The whole area between Oxford Street and Marylebone Road was under development at the time by the landowner Edward Harley, 2nd Earl of Oxford and Mortimer (1689–1741), who had inherited the estate through his wife, Lady Henrietta Cavendish-Holles (1693–1755). Gibbs worked frequently for the earl and designed the local church for the estate, St Peter's in Vere Street.

The main decorative effort expended on the house was concentrated in this room and chiefly in the fine plaster ceiling. The incorporation of painted panels into such an elaborate scheme of plasterwork decoration is unusual.[11] As a parlour this room would have been used as the main entertainment room, and the incorporation of garlanded heads on the frieze decorated alternately with grapes and flowers indicates that it would also have been used for dining. At this time dedicated dining rooms were still uncommon and found only in the largest and finest houses. No detailed archival records have been found for this house, so the maker of the ceiling remains uncertain. However, James Gibbs enjoyed particularly close links with a group of Swiss plasterers active in Britain from about 1720 and used them for his country houses and churches. He recognised their skills and their superiority in draughtsmanship and left them free to create their own designs. The most likely modellers of this ceiling were Giuseppe Artari (1692/1700–1769) and Giovanni Bagutti (1681–after 1730). Equally, the painter of the central panel is unknown, but it may be the work of Antonio Bellucci, who is known to have worked with Gibbs on the chapel at Canons, Middlesex.[12]

During the eighteenth century the house had a number of tenants of gentry status but gradually the area fell out of fashion, and by the middle of the twentieth century the house was divided into offices and this room was used as the fitting-room for a firm offering ladies' tailoring (fig. 80). This gradual slide down the social scale meant, at least, that little was changed in the room, though it was repainted from time to time. When proposals for development in the Henrietta Street area were made in the 1950s, the house was scheduled for demolition. By that time the importance of this house, and of this room in particular, was well-recognised by scholars. The owners, Debenhams Ltd, offered the ceiling and woodwork to the Museum. The costs of moving it and installing it in Gallery 57 were met by a benefactor of the Museum, Dr W.L. Hildburgh FSA.

Evidence for decisions in redisplaying the room

The removal of the room directly from its original setting to the Museum meant that it did not undergo the cutting about and alteration often suffered by rooms when they are made to fit new spaces. Colour plate 14 shows the room as displayed in 1994. Nonetheless, the moving of rooms in the 1950s was generally done in a more cavalier manner than would be done now, and we had to accept that much of the evidence that we would like to have seen had disappeared in 1956. For instance, the windows and the woodwork of the shutters and window seats were not brought to the Museum as there was no intention to recreate the window wall. At that time it was the plasterwork that was regarded as the most important element of the room. The ceiling was cut into sections and removed to the Museum relatively intact. The paint layers on many areas of the ceiling had remained undisturbed and analysis of these was possible, giving evidence for a much simpler scheme than the one that was actually carried out in 1960.[13] The entablature had suffered much more alteration, reflecting the lesser importance that it had always been given. When it came to the Museum it was in fragments. In 1959 Messrs George Jackson & Sons were awarded the contract to re-erect it and repaint it.[14] They used surviving fragments as models in replacing the moulding around the central oval panel and the architrave below the frieze. They also replaced the plain outer frame of the ceiling and cleaned sections of the cornice and recast the whole from those. Initially, they thought that all but two or three of the heads in the frieze should be dispensed with but eventually they found they could reinstate 16 of the heads as in the earlier room, although they modelled and made up casting patterns for the swags in between the heads.[15] It is recorded that they 'pickled' or cleaned the heads but even so both Jo Darrah in 1960 and Oestreicher and Davies in 1998 found some traces of surviving colour on the masks, although the disposition of it was hard to interpret.

The decorative door-cases and the chimneypiece and overmantel were also rescued, but all plainly moulded woodwork such as the dado rails were left in situ; the current woodwork in these positions dates from 1960 when the room was re-erected. Even on the historic woodwork there is little archaeological evidence of paint layers, as everything but the oak-leaf frieze of the chimneypiece was chemically stripped before being redecorated by the V&A in 1960. The walls of the room, being plaster rather than panelling, were demolished with the house and no recording or analysis of their paint layers was thought of at that date.

The windows and shutters had not been salvaged and had to be entirely re-created. Initially we were confident of this process as we knew that two sets of detailed survey drawings had been made for the National Buildings Record (forerunner of the National Monuments Record) in 1946 and for the Historic Buildings Division of London County Council in 1955 (fig. 82).[16] The pitfalls these put in our way illustrate the need for most careful checking in such projects. It was only at a fairly late stage of work that we noticed that there were discrepancies between the two in the detail of the panelling of the shutters. The 1955 drawings showed a square panel at the top of both the lower and the upper shutters, as well as a square panel at the level of the window seat. The drawing of the chimneypiece wall from the earlier set, however, showed a section through the window reveal that showed only three panels to each shutter, with the lower shutter consisting of a single long panel only. We chose to follow the four-panel format in re-creating the shutters as this was the most likely to have been Gibbs's original intention, the three-panel pattern being more typical of an early nineteenth century design. The 1955 drawing also included the most detailed and informative sections through the shutters and through the window reveals, and gave us a strong pattern to work to.[17]

Other evidence for the colours and materials used to decorate the room were taken from an analysis of more than 40 inventories of London houses of this quality built between 1720 and 1750. From these it became apparent that certain combinations of textiles were often used together and, in particular, a wool and mohair cloth for the walls (known as 'mohair'), with 'lustring' curtains (see p. 175). Such curtains were often lined with tammy (a light woollen cloth of plain weave) and we followed this precedent. It appears that mohair schemes were one step below those that hung walls with silk damask and it is likely that the sheen imparted by glazing mohair (a finish we chose) was designed to reflect light in imitation of a silk.

Our decisions for the hanging and furnishing of the Henrietta Street room were made with a conscious wish to point up contrasts with the splendour of the Norfolk House Music Room (see below) for which we had precise evidence for the use of green silk damask. We wanted to show how 'polite' interiors might range from the magnificent to the simply genteel, with a variety of colours and finishes.

What was done The dismantling and re-erection of the room was straightforward. The main painted panel of the ceiling was faced up with paper and cut out as one panel. The rest of the ceiling was cut into sections, working along the lines of cutting established when the room was first moved. The wooden frame made for the room at that time was dismantled and moved by Westminster Partitions and Joinery Ltd. In making up new walls of plywood (which proved an easier and therefore less expensive option than moving those that had been created in 1960), care had to be taken to ensure that the battening for the hanging of the proposed fabric was allowed for. It was important that not too much discrepancy should be seen between the wall planes above and below the dado. It was also important to avoid the effect of 'sinking' the door-cases too far into the upholstered walls from the dado upwards. This matter is difficult to explain except on site, but required careful mental arithmetic to arrive at the correct positioning of the false walls on the different levels. Above the windows, it was necessary to provide, in the battened structure, sufficiently firm fixing points for the pulley boards for the curtains.

For the new window walls, elevations were carefully drawn up by an architect, Charles Peel, working for Casson Mann. He worked from all available archival material and the careful survey drawings that Momart had done of each room before it was dismantled. Entrance to the room was to be by an opening in the space of the window furthest from the chimneypiece, which was cut through at window-seat height with no pretence of creating a door-case. This decision may initially be seen as bizarre, given the presence of three apparent doorways into the room (the one nearest the chimneypiece had been, in fact, a dummy door when the house was first built). However, we were concerned that such an orientation would have given the visitor a first view of what was a substantially new wall structure, rather than of the original eighteenth-century carved door-cases.

Models for the carving of the window architraves were available in the door-cases opposite, and Gonzales & Harms and the joiners working for St Blaise supplied us with a full range of carvings and moulding for approval and to act as quality control samples. The models for the glazing bars for this room were taken from those in buildings by Gibbs and were supplied by the architectural historian Dan Cruickshank. The glass in the windows is modern. Subsequent to the opening, people have asked why we did not insist on crown glass, but as the windows were to be artificially lit from behind, we did not think at the time that this was vital.

The floor was to be of pine boards of even, wide width, to be presented dry-scrubbed rather than polished, according to the fashion of the time in houses of this quality. Weldon Flooring produced a fine consignment of salvaged timber for this, all 22 cm wide and very little damaged by past use. Similar flooring was also used in the Lee Priory room, later in the galleries (see below). One pre-1956 photo (fig. 80) clearly showed the room with boards laid from the windows to the doors, so this orientation was followed, although there was some debate about this. It would have been unusual for the joists to run (as they must have done) the length of the room, i.e. across the width of the house. This orientation of planking helped, however, in one matter of housekeeping: access was needed across the floor for wiring in the sub-floor space, and the use of boards running in this direction avoided the need to cut ugly access panels into the floor.

When the elements of the room had first been erected in the Museum, a new chimneypiece had been created out of wood, in place of the nineteenth-century one that had been inserted below Gibbs's carved frieze. At that time, one element of the chimneypiece had been omitted, and it was clear from a socket under the ends of the cornice, that the surface of the chimneybreast should be built out slightly at that point. This detail is clear on a Gibbs drawing for a very similar chimneypiece in the Museum's Print Room (V&A: E.3633-1998). In the new arrangement, this element was reinstated. One advantage of a chimney opening created entirely in new wood was that we could cut it back as required to provide the exact size and fixings needed for the painted chimney-board that we wished to show in it. No hearthstone had come to the Museum, so a new one was inserted, of salvaged white marble. The hearth was set into the floorboards with a narrow, mitred frame around it, as was common practice in the eighteenth century.

The walls of the room were hung with a wool/mohair mix in a plain weave. Despite the frequent reference to 'mohair' in eighteenth-century inventories, no sample of furnishing weight mohair has yet been absolutely identified. The lack of pattern on such fabrics has meant that they were not thought worthy of collection by museums in the nineteenth century. The V&A itself, until a few years ago, concentrated only on collecting fabrics with interesting texture or pattern. Surviving fragments of plain textiles are now very rare. The Museum has a single example of a lightweight mohair (V&A: T.331-1998) that may have been used for either dress or furnishing. The fabric made up for the walls was a plain-weave fabric, with worsted warp and mohair weft, a heavier version of the Museum's sample and possibly reflecting the form of mohairs popular in the eighteenth century. This was an experiment entered into enthusiastically by the textile consultant John Miners and Ian Dale of Angus Weavers.

It was John Cornforth who led us away from the now much more commonly reproduced figured woollen damask into this new line of research and experiment, and it was he who introduced the idea of glazing the fabric – again something that is recorded frequently in eighteenth century inventories. Angus Weavers had produced a glazed mohair a few years earlier for a private client in Bavaria and were easily persuaded to carry the experiment further. The glazing process involves the fabric being passed through rollers. This produces a very subtle lustrous finish, which in candlelight would have glistened softly. One challenge we could not have appreciated until the process was replicated, was that with each passage through the rollers the fabric pulls slightly out of true. The maker has to choose carefully the number of finishes that will give the highest gloss without causing too many difficulties to the upholsterer who has to seam and hang the fabric. The fabric was woven to a modern width, then halved to a traditional eighteenth-century width of about 21 ins before glazing. It was seamed by machine. The walls were prepared by being battened out and lined with black Bolton twill (a heavy cotton fabric) by the firm of R&M Curtaining. The fabric was attached with staples rather than the traditional tacks, and the edges were covered with a woollen braid made by Context Weavers at Helmshore, Rossendale, Lancashire. After consultation, it was Anna Benson and Neil Warburton of Context Weavers who came up with the suggestion of using a braid with a 'laddered' pattern, an enlargement of the pattern of a woollen braid used to trim an eighteenth-century bed valance now belonging to the Society for the Preservation of New England Antiquities in America, and certainly imported from Britain at the time.[18]

Lighting The re-created windows in this room offered an important opportunity for lighting, and the decision was taken that this should be seen as a daylit room, in contrast to the night-time scheme offered in the Norfolk House Music Room (see below). The plan was to use fluorescent tubes in the recess behind the windows, with an opalescent diffuser, rather than using frosted glass in the windows. Controls for the lights were fitted into the window seat areas, which were made with lift-off 'lids' and access to the tubes for replacement is through the fully-opening sash windows. Inevitably this scheme did not run as smoothly as we had hoped. There were problems with the brightness of the fluorescent tubes and with the dark edges of the diffuser panels being visible from the visitor area. This last was dealt with by judicious edging of the panels to one side and the use of the shutters in a slightly open position, which serves to cover any awkward view of edges.

Lighting of the Hogarth prints on the back wall and of the label and label book was done by means of fibre optic heads mounted on the upper surface of the pulley board of the curtain over the entrance. With hindsight, some form of lighting fitted to the label book support would probably have been preferable, as the problem of visitors standing in their own light is not fully resolved.

Although no inventory survived for this particular room, the work on comparative inventories, together with the survival of illustrations for similar interiors, encouraged us to make this the most fully furnished of the period rooms, protected from visitors by a barrier.

A number of contemporary illustrations also helped us in deciding on elements of the furnishing.[19] We also took a conscious decision to treat the Henrietta Street room and the Music Room from Norfolk House in very different ways. As we knew that the room from Norfolk House had always been intended for ambitious evening entertainments and should be seen by candlelight, we took the decision to show the more modest parlour of the Henrietta Street house lit by daylight and dressed for more domestic entertainments.

As with all the rooms, soft furnishings presented many questions for consideration. In this case we decided to follow general inventory evidence and create festoon curtains of lustring, a lightweight silk similar to taffeta, with a glazed surface that reflects light particularly well.[20] The lustring (called lute in modern terminology) was woven by Richard Humphries at Castle Hedingham, Essex, the silk being dyed to tone with the mohair of the walls. At the same time we had extra silk noils (spun silk) dyed and this was supplied to G.J. Turner & Co of London, who used it to make the silk line and tassels for the festoon curtains (curtains that draw up rather than pull sideways). Annabel Westman acted as consultant to determine the form of the curtains, which were made by R&M Curtaining. It was she who provided the idea for the form of the tassels, the upper part with an open trellis of silk over a round core, based on a marble tassel carved on a chimneypiece in the Blue Velvet Room at Chiswick House, which was roughly contemporary with the Henrietta Street room. The curtains were lined with a light, glazed woollen tammy, woven by Context Weavers. The pulley boards for the curtains were made exactly as they would have been in the eighteenth century, with boxwood pulley wheels. They were made by the workshop of Hugh Routh and John Hartley, in Petersfield, Hampshire, following a pattern provided by Annabel Westman. The simple brass hooks to which the curtain lines are fastened were provided by Edward Bulmer Ltd, Pembridge, Herefordshire.

We still had to face the major difficulty that museum collections are not usually formed with the idea of furnishing rooms. The V&A has almost never collected sets of furniture and only rarely acquired pairs. For this reason we took the decision to furnish the room as it might have been at about 1745–60, rather than at the time of its first letting in 1732, because the V&A collections offered more scope in this later period. This allowed us to use a set of walnut parlour chairs covered in woollen needlework, one of the few sets in the V&A's collections (V&A: W.14 to W. 18-1938). Chairs and covers were roughly contemporary although it is likely that the covers were put on to the chairs in the nineteenth century. The chairs are of quite ordinary quality but they do illustrate the use of embroidery in fashionable drawing rooms, parlours and bedrooms throughout the first half of the eighteenth century.

In the furnishing of the Henrietta Street room we decided to break with the principle we had held to elsewhere in the galleries, that we would not show historic textiles on horizontal surfaces, to avoid damage from dust. We did so here, encouraged by the opportunity to show such decorative seat covers, by the well-regulated light levels in this room and by the additional protection afforded by their enclosure within a room, within the larger, air-conditioned gallery space. Given these conditions, we decided to show two of the chairs with their embroidery uncovered. The other four would be shown with replica case covers of woollen serge, in a colour matching that of the walls and the curtains, to demonstrate a housekeeping technique that was rigorously adhered to in the eighteenth century, when seat furniture was kept under case covers except on the very grandest occasions. The set can thus be rotated on a two-yearly cycle, with 'new' chairs being shown and others rested under covers.[21]

This plan also allowed us to use exactly the same covers on four reproduction chairs on the visitors' side of the barrier, on which they would be encouraged to sit. These chairs were made to the pattern of the eighteenth-century chairs by the Edwin Turner Partnership in Gislingham, Suffolk. Four of them are placed against the wall opposite the chimneypiece. Between the centre two is a low stand with handsets, allowing interested visitors to listen to the contemporary interior designer, David Mlinaric, talking about the process of choosing colours and furnishings for the room. Serge was woven for the chair covers by Stuart Interiors of Barrington Court, Somerset, with the addition of 10% of nylon to the wool. This will improve the wearing qualities of the covers to the public seating but is not enough to alter substantially the appearance of the serge. The seams of the seat covers were bound with a strong cotton tape bought off-the-peg from John Lewis and Partners. With a view to the future we have made up three sets of covers to allow for dry-cleaning and eventual replacement.

Card tables and tea tables were found in many of the eighteenth-century inventories that we studied. These were easily found in the V&A's reserve collection and the inventories fortunately gave us frequent evidence for the use of mahogany and walnut in the same room. Paintings were more problematical and we spent much time in discussion with Tate Britain without finding anything suitable. The two portraits currently in the room will be supplemented when suitable ones are found. On the wall opposite the chimneypiece we were however able to hang a full set of engravings of *The Harlot's Progress* by William Hogarth, shown in a set of original subscriber's frames (Engravings: V&A: F.118:36 to 41; frames: V&A: E.2882 to 2887-1995).

Another rarity which we were pleased to show was the painted chimney-board of about 1730, painted in trompe l'oeil with English copies of Dutch Delft tiles lining a hearth that is set for the summer with a vase of flowers (V&A: W.12-1994). We were pleased also that this absolved us from the difficulty of finding a suitable grate for a chimneypiece of this quality and of this particular size.

An early aspiration had been to replace the modern mirror panel in the overmantel with a painting of ruins in the style of Panini. Such paintings were often shown in contemporary illustrations of such double-height chimneypieces and were advocated by Gibbs.[22] Although it was possible that the frame had been modified at some time, we wanted to work to the dimensions that it offered. After a long search, a suitable painting in the manner of Panini was found in the collections of the Maidstone Museum and Bentlif Art Gallery, Kent, and we are grateful to them for allowing us to borrow this for the room. This painting of *Classical Ruins with a Soldier* was almost certainly purchased in Italy by Sir Thomas Twisden of Bradbourne, Kent, between 1733 and 1736, so it is particularly appropriate for this room. It fitted almost exactly, the difference between painting and frame being covered by a narrow gilded fillet.

The most difficult problem we had to overcome was that of a carpet for the room. English carpets of the period are so rare as to be out of consideration. Carpets from the Middle East of a correct pattern to have been available in Britain in the 1740s are equally rare; added to this we had the problem of the particular size of the room and the need to find a carpet that was correctly proportioned for it. We also had to consider carefully our principle not to show historic textiles horizontally. Just sometimes in such a project, luck comes to one's aid. In this case we were grateful to find amongst the Museum's collections an Ushak medallion carpet dating from the seventeenth century, that was ideal in terms of size and colour (V&A: 528-1903). This carpet, which had been acquired in 1903, is in sound condition but has several large areas of loss that have been made good with painted canvas patches. Because of this damage, it is unlikely that the carpet would ever be displayed in the Museum's galleries. Its contribution to the furnishing of the room was very strong and the decision was taken to use it, with regular vacuum-cleaning and monitoring. The carpet has been placed centrally under the oval of the ceiling, with the nearer edge rolled under on a padded roller, so that it is clear of the barrier, and the painted patches at the far end, where they are scarcely visible. The visitors walk on bare boards.

The colouring of the carpet, with large areas of mid-blue, is particularly sympathetic to the overall scheme of the room, and the juxtaposition of the carpet with the embroidered covers of the chairs is enlivening. As we deliberately took the decision not to dress the room with, for example, pens, paper and books, or a candlestick, the colour is a particularly important contribution to the overall effect. We did, however, take a late decision to add to the room a dummy board of a man dressed in the manner of about 1745. The origin of dummyboards is not fully understood but they may, as here, have been valued just for the way in which they people a room.

The Norfolk House Music Room 1756

The Music Room (colour plate 24) was the first in an enfilade of entertaining rooms along the entrance front of the first floor of Norfolk House, built in the south-east corner of St James's Square between 1748 and 1756 for the 9th Duke and Duchess of Norfolk.[23] The rooms formed part of a circuit for guests to parade (a new idea at the time for London houses) and each room exceeded the last in the richness of its decoration. From the ante-room at the head of the stair, the guests passed into this room, the first of the three large rooms that overlooked St James's Square (fig. 83). From the white and gold carving of this room, they passed into the next room (the Green Damask Room), from there into the Flowered Red Velvet Room, before turning to the left, into the Great Drawing Room or Tapestry Room. It is not surprising that on the opening party in February 1756, Horace Walpole described the scene as follows: 'You would have thought there had been a comet, everybody was gazing in the air and treading on one another's toes. In short you never saw such a scene of magnificence and taste.'[24] The Music Room follows precedence in such suites of rooms, where the first was often fully panelled, as a prelude to rooms that were hung with textiles, with the richness of decoration increasing as the visitor progressed.

The building history of Norfolk House is complex and has been the subject of much research in the last 40 years. The shell of the house was designed by the Palladian architect Matthew Brettingham for the 9th Duke of Norfolk and his francophile wife Mary Blount. They travelled frequently on the continent and the Duchess in particular showed her interest in contemporary design by buying engravings by Just-Aurèle Meissonier (1695–1750).[25] When the shell of Brettingham's building was completed in 1751, it seems likely that it was her decision to go elsewhere to find a suitable designer to decorate the room. The main outlines of Brettingham's panelling are still discernible, and the door-cases, dado and the main divisions of the ceiling must all follow his designs, made in a workmanlike, Palladian manner. However, it is worth noticing that the main panelling of this room is not strictly symmetrical and slight differences are visible at, for example, the right and left edges of the window wall, where one side shows a complete moulded frame and the other shows one truncated for lack of space. The single door in the wall opposite the windows is also not strictly centred on the wall.

Overlaid on the Palladian scheme is a much more decorative and dramatic scheme of carved decoration with ebullient fanfares of foliage, complex trophies of musical instruments, ribbons and flowers, the ceiling with eight compartments decorated with trophies of the arts and sciences, with a central trophy of arms. The design of this was by the Italian architect and designer Giovanni Battista Borra (1713–70), who had worked for the court in Turin and came to London in 1751 and worked in England for almost a decade.[26] The carving and gilding was carried out by the carver John Cuenot, who had come from France to work in London and who worked in the house between March 1753 and February 1756.[27] His detailed bills for the carving and gilding give an important view of this room from the point of view of a tradesman engaged in its construction.

The ribbed outline of the plaster ceiling (based on the layout of panels designed by Inigo Jones for the ceiling in the Banqueting House, Whitehall) probably survived from Brettingham's original scheme but Rococo cartouches were added. Although these cartouches and the central trophy of arms laid aside are of extremely high quality, no reasonable attribution has ever been offered for the plasterer responsible, though it seems unlikely that Clarke (the only plasterer recorded as working in the house) could himself have produced such free modelling.[28]

The house remained in family use until the 1930s. During the nineteenth century it was decorated on a number of occasions and altered in detail. Between 1817 and 1819 the house was closed up for two years for a major overhaul. It is possible that some of the plain panelling in this room was renewed at that time, because the plain areas carry two fewer layers of paint than the high relief areas. It must have been at that time that a Regency register grate was inserted into the chimneypiece, although no record exists of what was done. The room was reworked again in 1842 for the 13th Duke and Duchess, when the portico was added to the house by R. Abraham and the sash windows of the Music Room replaced by French windows giving on to the balcony formed above the portico.[29] It is the cypher of the 13th Duke and his Duchess that is carved over the single door on the long wall. Other redecoration must have taken place during the nineteenth century, but archival evidence survives only partially. Charles Nosotti did work in the house in 1869 and 1875 and, as a decorator who specialised in carving and gilding mirror frames, might well have been the man responsible for adding the additional mirror opposite the chimneypiece, but there is no firm evidence, and it is also possible that this was added in the 1842 work, at a time when white and gold schemes with looking glass were once again highly fashionable.

In 1938 the house was sold for development and demolished. At that time the panelling and ceiling of this room were presented to the Museum by the 16th Duke of Norfolk, in conjunction with the Norfolk House (St James's Square) Syndicate Ltd. The sections were removed directly to the Museum and, like the Henrietta Street room, this room has not suffered serious alterations, although one element of plain plaster immediately below the frieze was taken out to allow it to fit into the height of the V&A galleries.[30] The shutters and soffits from the windows were put in store, with the frames of the pier glasses between the windows, while much of the moulding around the windows was reused to make a large proscenium arch, through which the room was viewed. The frames of the French windows were not removed and must have been demolished with the house. The ceiling was repainted and partially regilded to make good the damage of transit and the walls were touched up, but nothing further was done.

Evidence for decisions in displaying the room

Visual evidence for the form of the window wall was limited. Concrete evidence survived in the form of five of the six shutters and the soffits for two of the window openings, together with the dado panels from beneath the pier glasses. These gave us some verifiable evidence for the size and detailing of the window embrasures. Although the mirror plates from the two pier glasses did not survive, extensive elements of the carved frames did. Of the right-hand glass about 80% of the frame and trophy survived but the left-hand glass had fared worse: of the trophy for that glass only the violin, the bow and the base of the lyre survived.

Fortunately, and most rarely, *Country Life* had photographed the window wall (fig. 84) in 1937, when it published an article on the house.[31] Window walls are rarely photographed because of the difficulties of shooting against the light. This photograph became the single most consulted document for the reconstruction of the wall. Frustratingly, it was the right-hand glass (the best preserved) that could be read most clearly. The trophy on the left-hand glass was slightly out of focus and confused by reflections in the glass but, with the help of computer scans and enlargements, it provided the best source we had. Of course this photograph showed the French windows added in 1842. Although a plan of the room survived, there were no elevations of the front of the house in the eighteenth century except an engraving of St James's Square, which included a diagonal view of the house front (fig. 85).[32]

What was done

There was much early discussion amongst the designers about the siting of the room in the galleries, but in the end the decision was made for us. There were only two positions in the galleries where the full height of the room could be accommodated under the dropped beams that divide the ceilings of the galleries into sections. As one of these would have placed the room far too early in the chronological sequence, the present site at the north end of Gallery 52 became the only possible one. Even in this position, we needed to drop the raised floor of the new galleries to the old level to fit the room and its ceiling. To accommodate the new floor that we wanted, it was even necessary to remove the wooden blocks of Aston Webb's parquet and to store these.

Casson Mann also had to design a long, easy ramp to run alongside the Music Room, to take visitors from the main floor height of the gallery down to the lower level to enter the room (fig. 18). We needed to place the room so that entrance from the lower level was possible through the original doors on the short wall opposite the chimneypiece. This meant that the chimneypiece wall had to remain at the south end, setting the new window wall on the opposite side from the actual windows of the gallery. Placing the ramp against the window wall of the gallery also allowed us to use the ramp area for some display, rather than having it as a dark tunnel through which visitors must pass quickly. With the blinds on the windows of the gallery set slightly open, we were able to use daylight to display a number of portrait busts in this area. Coincidentally, these now present a fine view from street level outside.

The only drawback to this scheme for the ramp was that we could not bring visitors into the room by what had been the original entrance door, on the long side of the room, because that door was now blocked by the ramp. Instead, we had to make use of what had originally been a blind door, leading only to a cupboard. The second entrance/exit could not be by the other door on the short wall closest to the windows, because it would have led directly into the space beside the entrance from the lift into the main gallery and would have created an uncomfortable bottleneck. The secondary entrance/exit is by the window space into the side gallery, which has the added benefit of preventing that small space from becoming a cul-de-sac off the lift lobby. As in the case of the Henrietta Street room, this opening is simply cut through, with no attempt to disguise its original use as a window.

The dismantling of the room was relatively straightforward. Panelling, by its nature, is relatively easy to separate into sections. The plaster ceiling and entablature were cut into sections along the lines that had been cut in 1938. One factor that did make the movement of these ceiling sections difficult was the fact that the rafters had been cut through in 1938 and the whole sandwich transferred to the Museum. Although this thickness of the ceiling contributed to the difficulty of fitting the room into the available height, we wished to retain all this historical evidence and so had to make allowance for it in the new setting.

The frame of the room was to be clad on the outside with plasterboard and used for displays. However, following our assertion that we wanted to show process where possible in the galleries, Dinah Casson suggested that we leave some sections unclad, so that visitors could examine the back of the panelling and understand its non-structural role as 'wooden wallpaper'. With this in mind, we originally left unclad the area above and just to each side of the single door in the long wall, and an area behind the door that would be used to enter the room. In the course of completing the galleries, we felt that this second unfinished area, seen as a backdrop to the extravagantly carved door-case from another room at Norfolk House (colour plate 19), was simply confusing to visitors and we finally left only the area around the door on the ramp unfinished (see fig. 19). This shows the back of the large overdoor panel, with its complex joinery and repairs using pitch and hessian.

The 1756 inventory of this room listed a 'A Wilton Carpett to cover the floor' (i.e. possibly a fitted carpet). The one shown in the 1937 photograph was presumably the 'very handsome Axminster' supplied by Nosotti in 1869, rather than the original, but we did not want to reproduce any carpet as none could have withstood the kind of visitor traffic that we foresaw in the room. The original floor, which had been offered to the Museum with the panelling, could not then be installed and was sold, as recorded in Museum files. Unfortunately, no record had been made of board widths or other detailing. We decided to create an oak floor from salvaged timber, with planks set randomly in three widths (between 6 and 8½ ins), following the pattern of floors at Spencer House and other eighteenth-century houses of this status. From the first we knew that we would have a problem with the depth left for the floor and that it would be impossible to lay a conventional floor on joists. Weldon Flooring came up with the solution of laying a floor directly on the concrete, with a thin (less than 1 cm) facing of oak giving the surface. Salvaged timber had to be taken down in thickness from the back to provide a suitably oxidised surface. The oak sourced for this room does show evidence of bruising and damage and, although the colour of the final floor is very mellow and very supportive to the panelling, with hindsight we might have chosen to do the floor in modern oak, coloured down, and possibly with slightly wider board widths. The polished oak here is in deliberate contrast to the scrubbed pine of the more modest room from Henrietta Street and encourages visitors to understand the diversity of levels of grandeur even within polite London society at the time.

The white marble chimneypiece had lost its original hearthstone. For this we also sought salvaged material and an appropriate slab was found from marble that had originally been used to line the Gentlemen's Steam Room in the Great Western Hotel, Paddington, then being refurbished. The hearth was surrounded by a mitred frame of oak, following eighteenth-century precedent. We debated at length about whether or not to keep the Regency grate, if we were, as we had already decided, going to re-create windows of eighteenth- rather than nineteenth-century form. Eventually practicality came to the aid of our decision-making. The only invisible way of drawing air from the air-handling system into the room was to bring it through the hearth area. For this reason the grate was not brought back from storage and a false hearth was constructed of black-painted MDF with a gap at the sides of the back board, through which air gently flows into the room. This arrangement works well, though it has the disadvantage of showing the cutting away of the back inner edge of the marble jambs that had been necessary to accommodate the Register grate.

Work on the fourth wall went through several stages. One of the first decisions we had to take was whether to re-create the 1938 form of this wall, with French windows that had been added in 1842, or whether to follow Brettingham's original plan. As no element of the nineteenth-century windows survived, we decided to revert to the sashes of the eighteenth century. This reflected our wish to show the room as an eighteenth-century interior but also offered practical advantages. It allowed us to use the lower half of the left-hand window as an entrance/exit and reduced the large areas of blank glass that might otherwise have drawn attention to the lack of natural outlook for the room. Initially the architect Charles Peel, working for Casson Mann, was asked to draw up the elevation of panelling, using all the surviving elements and archival information. Details of the glazing bars were provided by Dan Cruikshank, following the form that Brettingham had used for Holkham Hall, Norfolk, where he was working before 1748. We also made a decision to set the soffits and shutter panels about 10 cm forward of the window frames. Behind the shutters these gaps are filled in with plain wooden panels, but behind the soffits these gaps are left empty to provide a route for extraction for the air-handling system. This modification is only noticeable on close inspection but was essential to the functioning of the system of ventilation and heating.

Details of the mouldings for the outline panels on this reconstructed wall could be taken from other mouldings on the skirtings, architrave and other areas of the room. As in the Henrietta Street room, Gonzales & Harms provided samples of these mouldings and these were approved by the Historic Decoration Team and became control samples for the later work. Where possible, mouldings were salvaged from the window architraves that had been reused for the 'proscenium arch' in the last incarnation of the room, but some pieces had clearly been discarded when the room was first installed in the Museum.

At tender stage we commissioned the decorative artist Christopher Hobbs to produce full-scale drawings of the trophies, incorporating the surviving elements and using the 1937 *Country Life* photos to produce a reconstruction of what would have been there. This was an extremely taxing process but an important one in allowing tendering firms to price for this work. We also believed that it was the best way to get the result that we wanted. The carving in Norfolk House was always outside the usual pattern for English carvers, then as now.

The fourth wall was largely constructed in plywood on the wooden frame, with carved mouldings being produced off-site at Gonzales & Harms' workshops and applied on site. One shutter and one soffit panel also had to be made by joiners and the moulding carved complete. All the joinery elements and mouldings of this room are in pine, with the high relief carvings in limewood. Much discussion was given to the question of glass for the two pier glasses. The 1937 photos showed each glass with two plates, the join covered by a carved beading. It was not possible to establish the age of these mirror plates. They might possibly have dated from the eighteenth century or (as seemed more likely) have been replacements of the nineteenth century. The overmantel glass and the glass opposite were both composed of small plates with carved giltwood fillets covering the joins. Given the lack of clear evidence, we decided to reconstruct what appeared in the 1937 photo and to match the glass closely to the surviving glass in the overmantel mirror (although that dates from the nineteenth century), so that the new glasses would not look at odds with the one that was to be reinstalled. It was also necessary to balance the colour and finish of the pier glass plates with whatever glass we chose for the windows. We experimented with blackened glass to suggest the evening parties for which the room was designed, but finally settled on a slightly darkened mirror glass. We did not want a match between this and the pier glasses, which needed to be the most noticeable feature on the wall, and so the window panes are noticeably darker in tone.

The surviving elements of carving for the pier glasses were painstakingly pieced together and missing elements carved by Gonzales & Harms. In the spirit of the eighteenth-century work, much of the detail was invented by the carvers as they worked, drawing on the detail of the surviving work to establish the style of representation of leaves and flowers. On the three walls that have always been shown in the Museum, relatively little replacement carving was needed, except for the curving fronds of foliage that wrap round the frame of each main panel and disguise the metal fixing points for the wall lights. Clearly, in 1938, these had either been missing or very damaged and the decision had been taken not to reinstate them. However, the raw metal flanges that were thus evident at the ends of the wall lights were certainly not intended to be seen, and at first we thought that the wall-lights might have been mispositioned. However, on consideration, it became evident that they were in the right places (confirmed by finding only one hole per light for wiring, once the panelling came off the wall and the back of these sections could be examined), but that some element was missing. A twist of foliage made sense visually, and also symbolically, in a room for entertaining, if we took into consideration the classical tradition of using draped and entwined garlands to indicate a celebration or party.

One element was removed from the room as a result of discoveries made during the work. Inventory evidence from 1756 and later recorded only three mirrors in the room, and we presumed these to be the overmantel mirror and the two pier glasses. We speculated that the glass opposite the overmantel had been added in one of the nineteenth-century refittings. Indeed, when this mirror was taken down, the complete panelling was visible behind, the paint layer showing the outline of the main trophy which had been removed and replaced over a 'wallpaper' of mirror glass panels. Should we retain this mirror as part of the room's history, or return the wall to its eighteenth-century appearance? As often happens, the answer was compromise. We wanted to achieve as much as possible the visual effect of the eighteenth-century scheme but we did not wish to remove or damage the carved framing that had clearly been added in the nineteenth century to frame the outside edge of the new glass. If this remained, how were we to cope with the gap behind it left by the removal of the mirror sheets?

Eventually, we decided to fill the space left by the glass with a thin sheet of plywood. This allowed the raised framing to be read sensibly but also allowed us to leave unpainted the large area of panelling thus covered. In future years our successors may return to this for further archaeological examination. Considering this glass made us look carefully at all the large wall panels. Although the two opposite the pier glasses had never been recorded as being covered with mirror glass, a small stepped fillet inside the framing mouldings raised the question of whether there had ever been the intention to mirror these also. The effect would have been of a *Galerie des Glaces* and it might be that a decision was taken against this at a late stage in the scheme.

The question of the extent of redecoration, and particularly regilding, had exercised us from our first discussions. Two things were clear: first, that the paint and gilding we were looking at did not date from 1756 and, secondly, that both were in very poor condition. Both were very dirty and the gilding was cupping (lifting) severely. The gilded fragments of the pier glass frames were in even worse condition, heavily encrusted with dust acquired during removal from a demolition site and sixty years of storage in conditions that were far from ideal. Given the archive descriptions of the room from 1756, we were very keen to re-create some of the impact that it had on visitors at that date. We believed that only a full regilding could do this, but clearly the first step was to investigate the paint and gilding layers fully and establish just what might have survived.

Before the room was dismantled, a full analysis of the paint and gilding layers was undertaken by the partnership Oestreicher Davies to a specification agreed by the Museum's conservators.[33] This revealed that there were up to eight different layers of decoration, dating from the eighteenth century to the 1930s, though not all layers were discernible on all sections. In particular, samples taken from the flat areas of the wall panels lacked the initial two layers of paint apparent on areas such as the cavetto mouldings adjacent to the gilded egg-and-dart mouldings on the dado. It was extremely difficult to interpret this evidence, unless one posits the renewal of some flat areas of panelling at some point in the early history of the room, with carved mouldings being salvaged and reused. We do know that Norfolk House was closed up for a couple of years between 1817 and 1819 and that some substantial work was done at that time, but we have no record of exactly what that work was. Another piece of evidence that raises questions is the fact that the uprights of the framing of the panelling have been cut through at some time at dado height. This was clearly visible on the back of the panelling as it was installed but whether this was done in 1938 to extract the panelling from the house or at an earlier date is not clear.

The evidence of George Evans's original painting bill of 1756 only serves further to complicate the issue.[34] The bill clearly states that the painting of the room was to include:

> 218 Yards of 5 times in oil party colour'd
> & a clear cole white lead including Pilas
> ter pannels, rich Moldings, Trophys, &
> other loose Ornaments lay'd on after
> pannels were finish'd   ....at 2s 2d yd   £ 23.12.6

and

> 36 sash squares party Colour'd........at 5d Sqr   -15.-

The 'sash squares' of course disappeared with the remodelling of the windows in the nineteenth century, but, even on the walls, no evidence of 'party-colouring' (painting in more than one colour) was found in the sampling. Slight differences were found in the whites used on the frame and bed of the ceiling and on the different elements of the entablature but the colouring of these areas was not precisely described in George Evans' accounts:

> 108.4 [108?] ft run of Corinthian Entablature
> 3 times in Oil to Ornaments Gilt...... at 15d ft   £ 6.15.5

Given the discord between archive and physical evidence, we took the decision to follow the earliest scheme for which almost complete physical evidence existed. When investigation started, it seemed likely that this scheme dated from as late as the 1820s (because of the presence of a pigment thought to be cobalt). Subsequent re-examination by the paint scholar Patrick Baty suggested that it was more likely that the pigment was a Prussian blue (present in minute amounts) and that this scheme might date from the 1780s. Areas of this early scheme were uncovered and subjected to UV light to attempt to reverse the discolouring effect of years of coverage by another paint.[35] Although no archival evidence exists for work in the 1780s, it is possible that the room was redecorated a generation after it was built, perhaps after the 10th Duke inherited in 1777.

In the absence of any evidence on which to base a 'party colour'd' scheme, this second scheme did offer evidence for most areas of the room. It was a relatively simple scheme of white, tinted very slightly with blue pigment, with a flatting coat. It strongly contrasted with the gilded areas, which followed Continental practice in covering all areas of carved work, rather than in highlighting only certain elements of the carving, as would have been done in a traditionally English scheme. Sampling and microscopic examination had showed that the gilding was all done over a white lead ground, with no gesso or bole layer. This gilding directly on the white was followed in all areas of new gilding. Sampling from the ceiling suggested that the guilloche bands and entablature were painted in white without any blue pigment, the background to the paterae showing a deeper blue, a detail that was not replicated, for reasons of cost, in the final scheme.

The choice of this scheme had the advantage of allowing us to work back to the second scheme of gilding, which was substantially the first scheme, with some infill and repair. Although we had started work with little hope of retaining much of the early oil gilding and had resigned ourselves to the necessity of regilding the entire room, as work progressed it became apparent that, above door height, the second gilding did survive under later layers of paint and dirt. The second layer had been laid over with a red glaze and the effect of this had been to cause cupping in the subsequent layers. When these were picked off carefully, the gilding below remained in reasonable condition. Once the cleaning of this gilding had been accomplished, it was clear that we could leave this with only minor touchings-in, and that we could use it as a pattern for the toning of lower areas, which had been much more heavily worn and for which complete regilding was the only option. Final adjustments and balancing of the gilding and toning were done once the walls were repainted, and in a few areas at high level small areas of additional gilding were added to the highest relief carving to 'lift' certain areas. The Historic Decoration Team spent much time at this stage of work in sampling and approving the precise degree of glazing that was needed to tone the new work in with the old. This was another matter that caused contention, and we could only advise someone undertaking a similar project to be as generous as possible with the time allowance for this stage of the work.

The blue white of the first complete surviving layer was, of course, in lead white, with some coloured particles. Long discussions and trials were undertaken in the course of determining whether we should use lead paint for the new scheme. With the help of Patrick Baty, we undertook a number of trials with lead white paint but finally decided against the use of it for practical reasons, if the blue-white/gold scheme was to be maintained over many years. In the end, the painters, Hare & Humphries, used lead paint with the correct colouring agents to make trials of a suitable blued white and then we copied the result in a modern flat oil. Despite all the samples and analysis, of course, the final selection of a colour has to be done by eye. Samples can establish the colouring agents used but not precisely the amounts used and the effect achieved.

Below door height, most of the carved woodwork required total regilding to achieve anything like its original splendour. This included all high relief carving and most mouldings. On the window wall, all elements of high relief carving were cleaned back and regilded. This was necessary because of the additional degradation of the gilding that had occurred in store, and it also allowed a closer matching with the newly carved and gilded sections of the frames. Again, the upper areas of the other walls provided the sample for the new oil-gilding. The mouldings of the dado panels were particularly badly clogged with gold paint and successive layers of gilding. Given the crispness that could be revived on other mouldings by the dry stripping of later layers of gilding, we took the decision to strip the layers of gold paint from these with a chemical poultice, to reveal the carving.

The ceiling was repainted. It had been said to have been partially regilded (with oil-gilding) when it came to the Museum in 1938 and was still relatively fresh. Only two panels were now regilded entirely, having suffered greater damage or, perhaps, having been unsatisfactorily gilded at an earlier date.[36] A few other areas on the ceiling required new gilding to balance the effect overall. Work was undertaken on the shield of the central trophy, the canvas in the 'Art' panel and a few other places.

The curtain cornices were treated differently. Although these had been in store for 60 years, they had remained in relatively good condition. Whereas oil gilding had been used for all the carvings on the walls, these were water gilt and after repair of some breaks, the surfaces were cleaned and only small areas regilded.

In the finished room we left one narrow section as it had been in 1998, as a record and as a teaching aid. This sample area, on the long wall at the left end, runs down from shoulder height to the floor. At dado level some further work has been done: one third of the mouldings have been left as in 1998, one third stripped back to the bare wood to show the detail of the carving and one third is shown with the wood painted white in preparation for the gilding.

Lighting The question of lighting for the Norfolk House Music Room had been a major difficulty. In the old galleries the lights in the wall sconces had been supplemented with directional spots from the entrance arch. Once the architectural integrity of the room was re-established with the reconstruction of the fourth wall, any such modern intervention would have been extremely difficult, yet it was not until the painting had been done that we could assess how much light could come from the wall sconces. In the course of much travelling we had seen some absurd and ugly attempts to light period rooms, yet we knew that it was easy to scoff, but hard to come up with an acceptable scheme. We discussed uplighters but felt that they altered the balance of light so radically that they distorted any historical view of a room in which the ceiling would naturally have been in some shadow for most of the time. Yet people still had to be able to see the room, including the fine plasterwork of the ceiling, and to read the label books. In order to be certain of sufficient light, we asked the contractors to install provision for 12 fibre optic cables into the plain area of plaster just above the frieze, an area which had been modified in 1938 and in which we would therefore not be damaging eighteenth-century plasterwork. As repainting began, we rigged up makeshift tridents of lights to try them out in the positions where the wall sconces would be fixed. It was one of the most jubilant days of the whole process when it became apparent that these would suffice, aided by the reflective qualities of the white and gold scheme and the three mirrors. The outlets for the fibre optic cables were quickly filled and painted and work proceeded.

The wall-lights were wired by Wilkinson plc and new gilded metal candle holders in the form of leafy buds were modelled and made by the St Blaise workshops, to replace composition candle holders that had been made up when the room was first installed in the Museum and which were modelled on nineteenth-century originals. The sconces are now the sole light source, though electric sockets, hidden behind panels in the skirting board and behind the window shutters, allow reading lights to be plugged in for musicians and other performers using the room. The sconces are controlled by a dimmer and in fact the room can look more atmospheric when the lights are slightly dimmer, though modern eyes tend to demand a higher level of lighting.

How the room was presented Evidence for the appearance of the room in 1756 was provided by an inventory taken just after the house opened.[37] The list of the contents seems rather austere to modern readers, who might expect extravagant sets of matched furniture in such an interior. The main furnishings were 14 stools of different sizes, with green and gold frames, covered in the same 'Green and Silk Damask' as the three window curtains. No pier tables are listed, although '2 brass Rods' were in place 'before' the pier glasses and presumably to protect them from a press of people; the same purpose probably accounted for the '4 brass Rods Down the Sides' of the curtains. These entries are at the moment both intriguing and mysterious. Further research is needed to establish just what the function of these fittings could have been (possibly also protection of the fragile sconces). The inventory also included one carved and gilded card table and two in mahogany, and a dining table, suggesting furnishings that might be brought in to this room whose first purpose was for entertaining. More lavish furnishings would have limited the space for promenading. Despite the naming of the room, there is no evidence that it was ever used for musical entertainments.

We were conscious from the first that, in this room, it was the panelling itself that was the chief exhibit. All our decisions were made on the basis of encouraging visitors to look at the panelling with care and to feel free to move throughout the room to do so. At first we hoped to reproduce stools for use by the public but considerable research failed to turn up any suitable model, and so we limited the public seating to a simple modern bench that allows visitors to look down the whole length of the room. We were, in addition, wary of the fragility of carved, painted and gilded stools, if they were to be used by the public. It had always been our intention that the room should be used occasionally for concerts and readings, and modern gold-painted chairs are brought in for these occasions.

What we did decide to reproduce were the three green silk damask curtains. Research over the last 30 years has brought forward considerable evidence for the form of mid-eighteenth-century curtaining, and a number of suitable patterns of damask can be reliably reproduced. Annabel Westman advised the Museum on the form of the curtains suitable for this setting. The listing of three curtains, as well as the fashion of the date, suggested single festoon curtains rather than pairs of draw curtains. A suitable damask was woven by Richard Humphries at Castle Hedingham, to the pattern 'Pavia' in an eighteenth-century width of 21 ins. The curtains were lined with a glazed tammy, a light, plain-woven wool, dyed to a similar green. This was provided by Context Weavers. The curtains were edged at the bottom with a silk fringe, woven by G.J. Turner & Co. of London, using silk noil that had been dyed by Richard Humphries with the main silk for weaving. Turner & Co. also provided the silk cord for drawing up the curtains, woven from the same silk. The pattern for the fringe was taken from one woven for the rehanging of the bed in the State Dressing Room at Nostell Priory and based on a surviving eighteenth-century fragment in the collection of David Mlinaric.

The curving giltwood cornices presented a particular challenge in designing the curtains, as no precedent for them survived in English interiors. They required conforming pulley boards, which were made by the workshops of Hugh Routh and John Hartley in Petersfield, Hampshire, and covered with the tammy used to line the curtains. These boards were of beech, inset with boxwood pulley wheels.[38] The brass cloak pins round which the cords from the curtains were wrapped were supplied by Edward Bulmer Ltd, Pembridge, Herefordshire, the model based on a cloak pin visible in a portrait of Paul Sandby by Francis Cotes dated 1761, now in Tate Britain.[39]

The Strawberry Room from Lee Priory, Littlebourne, Kent 1783–94

This little room (colour plate 32) was built and decorated for the antiquarian Thomas Barrett (1744–1803).[40] After a short interlude in parliament, as MP for Dover, Thomas Barrett retired from public life and devoted himself to his antiquarian interests. He was a close friend of the well-known collector and writer Horace Walpole and was inspired by his friend's enthusiasm for the Gothic style, and in particular by the house that Walpole built at Twickenham from the 1750s, Strawberry Hill. Walpole was usually an acerbic critic of other people's efforts, but he was uncharacteristically generous in his comments on Barrett's new Gothic house, calling Lee Priory 'a child of Strawberry prettier than the parent'.[41] It was probably Walpole who introduced Barrett to the architect James Wyatt who designed Lee Priory. Walpole visited the house on several occasions and advised others to do so. It was in his honour that Barrett christened this room the 'Strawberry

Room' and had strawberries carved on the lower panel at each side of the chimneypiece. The room was at the end of a suite of rooms on the first floor that were the private apartments of Thomas Barrett and included his library (fig. 86).

Wyatt had a much longer career than his more celebrated contemporary, Robert Adam, and sustained his originality of design throughout the 45 years of his active life. It is also true that fewer interiors by Wyatt remain, and so this is a particularly rare survival. The room originally had an oriel window, as can be seen in an early engraving (fig. 88), but in about 1865 the house was remodelled and enlarged by Sir George Gilbert Scott (1811–78). A larger bow window replaced the oriel, together with a second door, opposite the original one. The wooden archway now opposite the mirrored bookcase in the room is thought to be George Gilbert Scott's work, the entrance to his bay window. Lee Priory was demolished in 1953, at which point the room was given to the V&A by Thomas Oakley and G. Jackson & Sons Ltd.

Evidence for decisions in displaying the room   As with the other rooms in the new British Galleries, this room came directly from its original house at the time of demolition. By 1953 local authorities and amenity bodies such as the Georgian Group were much more conscious of the need to document important interiors before demolition. A number of photographs of this room are available in the National Monuments Record at Swindon, amongst many of the house. One of these (fig. 87) provides the only visual evidence for the form of the rather plain doorcase inserted by Sir George Gilbert Scott in 1865 (and indicated on later plans of the house). Unfortunately, no photograph was taken of the window end of the room, perhaps because the altered window was deemed to be of less interest than the untouched James Wyatt sections of the room. Only the vaulted plaster ceiling and the woodwork of the room were removed from the house and no reliable evidence of the wall finishes was preserved.

What was done   Most of the woodwork in this room could be easily dismantled, and the lath and plaster vaulting was cut into eight sections, following the lines of cuts made in 1953. After the framework had been moved and re-erected, new walls were faced up with plywood and the skirtings and door-cases applied. A new doorway was created opposite the original Wyatt one. This was required for reasons of safety and public circulation, and although in Wyatt's time no such second doorway had existed, Sir George Gilbert Scott had inserted one at just this point when he had enlarged the house.

As no clear evidence for either the original oriel window or its nineteenth-century bay replacement existed, we decided that the area outside the arch should be treated in an abstract manner, with no attempt to re-create historic decoration. This area now provides a modern bench for visitors, where they can, if they wish, listen to a short audio programme with dramatised readings of Horace Walpole's enthusiastic comments on the room as it was first decorated.

The room was floored with wide pine boards (22 cm wide) and left unpolished to give the effect of sand-scrubbed boards of the eighteenth century. The floor was continued back into the seating area for visitors, to give a sense of unity to the space. A modern Perryfield limestone hearthstone was provided for the painted wooden chimneypiece and was set into the boards without a framed surround. Old photographs gave some clue to the size of the original hearthstone but this feature had not been considered important when the room was installed in 1953 and had not been transferred to the Museum. The edge of the hearthstone was slighly abraded so that it did not look too new.

As with all the rooms that included painted surfaces, an initial investigation was undertaken by Oestreicher & Davies.[42] They sampled all areas of the surviving woodwork and the evidence was clear that the distribution of gilding and painting had not altered since the first paint layer of the 1790s, although the paint in successive layers had moved from light stone to a lighter, broken white. As with Norfolk House, Patrick Baty offered guidance in the choice of final colouring and based his work both on the constituent materials found in the various samples and on examination of areas of the first painting that were exposed to UV light to reverse part of the discolouration caused by years of being covered by extra layers of paint. We took the same decision that we had taken for Norfolk House, to use lead paints and traditional colouring materials to establish the colour that we wished to use and then to replicate it in a safer and more resilient modern flat oil paint. The areas of oil-gilding were then replaced. For the arch that defines the window areas, we took a different course. We strongly suspected that this dated from 1865, and there was lively debate about whether we should omit this from the reconstruction. Eventually, for practical reasons, we decided to keep it *in situ*, but to mark its difference from the original room by painting it to match but not gilding the details of the arch, thus marking its ambiguous status.

The treatment of the wall surfaces was the most problematic consideration in this room. When the decorative woodwork had been removed from Lee Priory, no investigation had been made about the layers of decoration on the structural walls, which were just demolished with the house, though the area of 'wall' immediately below the traceried ceiling and as far down as the pendant bosses was of wood and had been removed with the ceiling structure. In the 1970s a small fragment of trellised leaf pattern wallpaper was discovered behind a piece of woodwork. Because of the small scale of the design it was possible to reproduce this and the room was hung for nearly 30 years with this paper, though it is now thought to date from the early nineteenth century.[43] In dismantling the room in 1999, further small samples of a plain paper were found at the top edges of walls, behind panels of hardboard on which the 1970s wallpaper had been mounted.[44] The papers appeared to be fragments of strips that had been placed above the two lines of tacks that outlined the tops of the walls below the vaulting. It is possible that they were remnants of border strips, of wallpaper or of lining papers. All bore traces of lead-white, with some colouring agent creating an off-white colour, but it was not possible to determine the date of this paper.

It is possible that the walls of this room were originally simply painted to match the vaulting or were painted and lined out as ashlar. However, in the absence of any sound evidence for a first scheme for the walls, it was decided that we should hang it with a verditer paper. Verditer paper (a plain paper coloured in greeny-blue with a copper-based wash) was very popular in the 1780s, but few examples survive.[45] As papers that are reproduced for historic interiors are often patterned, we thought that it would be useful to demonstrate the popularity of plain papers, just as we had chosen to use a plain fabric for the walls of the Henrietta Street room (see pp. 177–78). We were also encouraged to take this line by the recent discovery of a surviving verditer paper in a room by the same architect, James Wyatt, dating from the late 1770s, at Burton Constable Hall, East Yorkshire. In the Great Drawing Room there the verditer paper had survived behind the pier glasses, although the rest of the room had been redecorated in the nineteenth century. Because the later scheme survived, there was no proposal to reinstate this type of paper there but the Curator, Dr David Connell, kindly provided us with a sample, which is now held in the Print Room of the V&A (V&A: E.439-1999).

In recent years the re-creation of verditer papers has been pioneered by the wallpaper conservator Allyson McDermott, who has re-created verditer for a number of interiors.[46] Her team was commissioned to create the wallpaper here, hanging small sheets of handmade paper in an overlapping fashion as would have been done in the eighteenth century and then applying the verditer wash. The exact colour of a verditer wash was said, in eighteenth-century texts, to vary with climatic conditions, depending on whether it was made in summer or winter. If the mixture was made in warmer weather, it was said to be greener rather than bluer, though Allyson McDermott believes that the determining factors are more likely to be the exact composition of a particular mix. The presence of tacks along the wooden edges of the walls, just under the vaulting, suggested that on at least two occasions the room had been hung with paper in the eighteenth-century manner (i.e. with paper tacked to the walls). Allyson McDermott was of the opinion that such paper hanging would always have involved the use of paper borders. We were deterred by the difficulty of cutting-in borders round the Gothic pendants and for this reason we chose not to re-create a border for this paper, though this decision is still controversial.[47] The dull red stained glass in the spandrels of the doors of the bookcases was simply cleaned and replaced once work on the woodwork and walls had been completed.

Lighting   Lighting for this room had always presented grave difficulties because of reflections from the mirrored doors in the bookcases on the far walls, which reflected any but the most carefully placed light source. Without a reconstruction of the window, that source of light, coming from behind the visitor, was also barred to us. Fortunately, we had decided that in such a small room we must control the flow of visitors by the use of a solid barrier, which would confine visitors to the areas between the doors and the arched area. Following Horace Walpole's general admiration of 'gloomth' we were not over-concerned with brightness in this room, but it was important that the label book should be legible. Our lighting designer came back with a simple scheme of fibre optic tails set under the low barrier and carefully angled and set so that they offered least reflection. These were intended to be supplemented by further lights set behind the left-hand edge of the fireplace, invisible to visitors but adding helpful additional light to the end wall. As it happened, these additional lights were deemed unnecessary but it is possible that they will be put in place in the future.

How the room was presented   Although no archive material exists to record the furnishings of the room in 1794, a detailed list of the contents of the room in 1834 was available from the sale particulars published in that year.[48] The 'Strawberry Room' was furnished in ebony, with upholstery in blue silk, with a Persian carpet. This may represent what was in the room in the 1790s, in particular because it echoes Horace Walpole's predilection for ebony furniture at his own house at Strawberry Hill.[49]

The catalogue gave us the idea to show in this room two seventeenth-century ebony chairs from the Coromandel coast of India, one of which had belonged to Horace Walpole and one to the collector William Beckford, who also favoured these dark pieces, then seemingly often considered as British chairs of the Elizabethan period (V&A: IS.6-2000 and 413-1882). As Walpole frequently mixed black lacquer with ebony furniture, we also included a lacquered cabinet on stand, the cabinet made in Japan in about 1630, the stand probably made in the Netherlands 1680–1700 (V&A: FE. 38-1978).

The question of a carpet for this room involved lengthy investigation and discussion. The 'Persian carpet of the room' mentioned in the sale catalogue of 1834 did not offer much to go on. It might have been an imported rug or a fitted carpet made in the early nineteenth century in a 'Persian' design. We debated the making of a floorcloth or the purchasing of Tatami matting, but although there was woven matting in the Great Parlour at Strawberry Hill, we felt that something more luxurious would have been required by Mr Barrett in this small and comfortable room. An early watercolour of the Holbein Chamber at Strawberry Hill showed a coloured rug but it was not depicted with sufficient detail to allow us to identifty the type or pattern.[50] We investigated the possibility of weaving a modern rug using a pattern of the 1790s.[51] Eventually, it was the constraints of the awkward shaping required by the hearth and the barrier that led us to place a small rug made in Turkey during the eighteenth century (V&A: 528–1903) in front of the hearth. On the walls is a pair of framed engravings of Henry VI and Archbishop Henry Chichele. These engravings, which were published in 1772-23, retain the frames in which they were shown at Strawberry Hill, from where they were sold in the great 1842 sale (V&A: W.97 and W.98-1978). As with the Henrietta Street room, it is likely that additions to the furnishings will be made in the future. In particular the room needs appropriate pictures.

The Ante-room from The Grove, Harborne, Birmingham 1877–78

This small room (colour plate 39) was the ante-room or boudoir, attached to the Drawing Room in a large villa (fig. 89) built in a suburb of Birmingham in 1877–78 by the architect John Henry Chamberlain (1831–83) for the industrialist and local politician William Kenrick (1831–1919).[52] Mr Kenrick was a collector of Chinese blue-and-white porcelain and of contemporary paintings and art pottery, and a good amateur painter in watercolours. He was for many years chairman of the committee of Birmingham School of Art. He also presented many significant works of art to the newly founded city art gallery. His collecting is recorded in his own watercolour of the hall of The Grove, now in the collections at the V&A (V&A: W.217-1968). His artistic interests were reflected in the design of his new house, and in the design of this room.

Kenrick was a great admirer of John Ruskin and a keen promoter of Gothic for architecture and interiors. This room also shows the developing influence of Japanese design in its marquetry panels by the firm of James Barfield.[53] The plants depicted in the marquetry would also have appealed to Kenrick's well-attested love of nature. The house remained in the Kenrick family until it was demolished in 1962 after the death of its last owner. It was offered to the V&A by the family at a time when interest in Victorian decorative arts was undergoing a revival. The 1960s was also a time when the mechanics of rescuing and conserving historic interiors was considerably developed. Though we now regret that the window from this room was not saved, at least the floor was, in contrast to the rooms collected earlier, where the floors were simply not considered as worthy of note.

Evidence for decisions in displaying the room

The room takes the form of an elongated octagon. A plan of the house (fig. 91) shows how the room relates to the drawing room. Although the drawing room could be entered directly from the hall, when the house was first built this room was used as the only entrance, except when the family held large parties.[54] It was the most lavishly decorated interior in the house and provided an impressive ante-room to the drawing room. A watercolour design for the decoration, by John Henry Chamberlain, exists in the V&A collections (V&A: E.218-1968) and shows that the scheme has survived unchanged.

Photos of the room exist in Birmingham City Archives and elsewhere but these date from about 1911 and later and show the room furnished as a small sitting room. An inventory of 1911 lists the furnishings of the room at that date.[55] Despite the large amount of archive material that survives on the house, little directly relates to the furnishings of this room when it was first created, although clearly furnishings were likely to have been fairly sparse to allow free movement through the space. Though Kenrick would certainly have used the fitted shelves to show parts of his collection of ceramics, we do not know exactly what was displayed here. However, the historic photographs of the room did help us in one very vital matter, in that one photograph of the window itself survived, showing in some detail the large sash window and the wooden panelling surrounding it (fig. 90).

What was done to the room   In the previous galleries one of the long walls, including the second door, had been removed to create a viewing arch. As with all the other rooms, we were keen that visitors could enter and experience the space, but the small size of the room presented difficulties. It would never be possible for visitors to circulate in such a small space. All the remaining panelling and the second door of the room existed in store and we wanted to reinstate as much as possible of this, consistent with letting visitors stand, at least, within the room. We therefore reinstated the second door (which allows visitors to understand the original function of the room better). We also replaced the upper frieze of arched panels that runs right round the room, only omitting the panelling below this height to allow visitors to pass into the room as far as a fixed barrier. The panelling was generally in good condition and required only light cleaning and the reinstatement of minor losses.

The marquetry border to the floor presented difficulty if we were to allow visitors into the room. Our solution was to take out the panel where visitors walk in. Weldon Flooring did an excellent job in making a replica, which was almost indistinguishable from the original. Two years of public access has vindicated our decision, as the wear on the replacement panel is already evident. Between 1963 and 1998 the octagonal central panel to the floor was in pine boards. We were not certain whether these were part of the original floor or had been put in by Museum technicians at the time of the transfer. It may have been that the centre of the floor was covered with a specially made carpet, shaped to cover the elongated octagon, though no photographic evidence records this and the 1911 inventory is inconclusive, listing only 'Red ground bordered pine pattern Persian carpet'. Rather than embark on the re-creation of a carpet on such unconvincing evidence, we decided that the centre of the floor should be replanked in polished oak, matching the width and colour of the oak boards in the framing panels.

The most difficult work for this room was the re-creation of the sash window. Since 1963 the window space had simply been covered with different textile hangings. St Blaise's staff drew up a preliminary drawing of the window, with cross-sections of mouldings, basing their work on the surviving photograph (fig. 91). Many hours of discussion and comparison with other work by Chamberlain were required before we were satisfied that we had a respectable replica. Old photos of the exterior of the house were digitised and magnified for comparison, and Barbara Shackley, the case officer for the Victorian Society in the West Midlands, provided valuable snapshot evidence of mouldings in other buildings by Chamberlain. The lower sash was made to rise, as it did in the original house, though today it simply allows access to lighting controls and for cleaning. The pattern of leading for the small side glasses of the window was clear from the photo but there was much debate as to the colour of the glass. On the photo this appeared to be uniform throughout the panes, but whether it was clear or mauveish or greenish in the manner of 'Cathedral' glass could not be determined. A decision was made to use a grey-greenish glass with an uneven surface, to contrast with the clear glass of the window. The glass was supplied by James Hetley & Co. Ltd, London.

Because of the particularly high quality of joinery of the panelling of this room, it was decided that here too, as at Norfolk House, we would expose part of the structure of the panelling on the outside of the room for the visitors to see. For this reason, a narrow section to the left of the main visitor area has been left unclad and the complex jigsaw of the panels can be seen from the back.

Lighting From the 1960s the room, as displayed in the Museum, was lit by a small chandelier with electric fittings, but this was not original to the room. We decided that a diffused light from the windows should provide the main source, but additional fibre optics were added to the frame of the opening to allow lighting to be focused on the label book and the ceramics on the far side of the room.

How the room was presented The absence of clear evidence of the original furnishings of the room, combined with the exceptional quality of the joinery and the marquetry, led us to show this room largely unfurnished, so that visitors may appreciate it as a fine object in its own right. However, the record of Mr Kenrick's interest in Chinese ceramics did suggest the idea of furnishing the recesses with blue-and-white porcelain. We were fortunate to be able to call on the exceptionally rich collections in the Asian Department of the V&A to provide items not only of the right date and origin but also of the right size to make a decorative display in the shelved recesses. The only reproduction piece commissioned for the room was the green holland blind for the window, needed to screen the blank outlook. There is no archival evidence for the use of green blinds in this room originally but the colour was chosen to illustrate the practice of using coloured blinds, as documented in a view of his own dining room at St John's Wood in about 1880 by the artist G.A. Storey.[56]

Notes I am grateful to Christopher Wilk for allowing me to use the text of his lecture 'Period Rooms at the V&A: Changing Patterns of Acquisition and Interpretation', given at the conference on period rooms held at the V&A in November 1997 to coincide with initial thinking about the presentation of rooms in the new British Galleries.

1. 'The "Bromley Palace" Room', *Country Life*, vol.XXI (6 April 1907), pp. 478–81.
2. E. Goodman, *The Palace of Bromley-by-Bow*. Third monograph of the Committee for the Survey of the Memorials of Greater London, 1901.
3. Ceilings with closely similar decoration were also found in Sir Paul Pindar's House of about 1600 in the City of London (now demolished), at Mapledurham House, Oxfordshire, and at Thirlestane Castle, Berwickshire and other houses in Scotland. We were grateful to Dr Clare Gapper for much recent information about the room and the ceiling, notes for her thesis, University of London, 1998 (unpublished), *Plasterers and Plaster Work in City, Court and Country, c. 1530–c. 1640.*

4. C.R. Ashbee (ed.), *The Survey of London: Being the First Volume of the Register of the Committee for the Survey of the Memorials of Greater London*, vol.I, *The Parish of Bromley-by-Bow* (London, 1900). The members of the Survey Committee were amongst the most vociferous critics of the demolition of The Old Palace.

5. It is illustrated thus in Goodman, *The Palace of Bromley-by-Bow*.

6. One point to bear in mind, though, in a room with heavy visiting, is that you will almost certainly have to have at least one follow-up visit from the contractor after a few weeks or months. Certain nails will work loose or worm-eaten edges of boards will have to be patched as thousands of feet pass over them. This period of settling-in proved necessary in several of the rooms.

7. As at Chelvey Court, Somerset, see H. Avray Tipping, *English Homes, Period III*, vol. I, *Late Tudor and Early Stuart 1558–1649* (London, 1929), p. xliii, plate xxxviii.

8. We were grateful to Richard Griffiths, architect for the restoration of Sutton House, Hackney (National Trust), for this reference.

9. Angus Weavers provided a small piece of reversible wool and linen cloth in blue and green wool with natural linen, of the type known in the seventeenth century as Kidderminster cloth. For the cupboard, we used a piece of a grander version of a similar weave (including gold thread) that had been made by the same suppliers for the counterpane of the Great Bed of Ware, covered with a simple, fringed cloth of reproduction white linen.

10. For the best general account of the room see John Summerson, '11 Henrietta Street, Marylebone, and Its Associations with James Gibbs', in *London Topographical Record*, vol. XXI (1953), pp. 26–36. For more recent work see Gordon Balderston, 'Rysbrack's Busts of James Gibbs and Alexender Pope from Henrietta Street', *Georgian Group Journal* XI, 2001, pp. 1-28, notes 45 and 46 and Gordon Balderston, 'William Thomas, Steward, Scholar and Virtuoso', to be published in the *Georgian Group Journal*, XIV, 2004.

11. I am grateful to John Cornforth for this and many other illuminating comments on the rooms and their decoration. He cites Fairlawne in Kent, another house by Gibbs, as another example of this combination. Gibbs's drawings for Fairlawne survive in the Bodleian Library, Oxford.

12. The matter of the artist for this panel has been debated for many years. Alastair Laing has suggested that Vincenzo Damini (the Italian painter who worked in London from about 1720–30) and Francesco Sleter (1685–1775) should also be considered as possible painters of this panel, but in the absence of evidence believes that the attribution to Bellucci cannot yet be overturned.

13. Oestreicher Davies, *Gibbs Room, Henrietta Street, Victoria & Albert Museum – Paint Analysis Report*. December 1998. 179 samples were taken and a further 19 samples taken in 1980 by Josephine Darrah of the V&A were re-examined. This showed that there had been up to 11 redecorations of the room, though not all the elements were redecorated on each occasion. Gaps in the evidence for various schemes were inevitable with so many reproduction elements and the use of chemical stripping on others. Nonetheless, it was clear that the recent florid schemes of green highlighted with gold paint, had not appeared before the twentieth century, and that the schemes throughout the eighteenth century were generally versions of off-white and pale stone colours, with little gilding. Traces of blue-green distemper were found in places on some of the frieze masks of Bacchus, but the evidence was not sufficiently strong to establish whether other areas of the frieze or entablature were painted in this fashion or, indeed, any other areas of the room. The only gilding appeared to be in thin lines outlining the main painted oval and its surrounding roundels.

14. V&A Nominal File, Jackson & Sons Ltd, lists the work that they did.

15. V&A Nominal File, Jackson & Sons Ltd, letters of 13 May, 8 July and 22 October 1959, and 15 January 1960.

16. National Monuments Record. The 1946 drawings are numbered 1946/301 and 1946/302 (neg. nos. E.48/66 and E.48.67). The 1955 drawings are numbered M.D. 96/1880-1882 (neg. nos. BB 008607-008612).

17. Our preference for this version was supported by Dan Cruikshank, who examined these drawings when making his report on the likely form of glazing bars for the Henrietta Street room.

18. *Bed Hangings: A Treatise on Fabrics and Styles in the Curtaining of Beds, 1650–1850* compiled by Abbott Lowell Cumming, essay by Nina Fletcher Little. New introduction by Jane C. Nylander (Boston, 1994), fig. 51.

19. Charles Saumarez Smith, *Eighteenth Century Decoration: Design and the Domestic Interior in England* (New York, 1993) was used extensively, as was Peter Thornton, *The Authentic Interior* (New Haven and London, 1984). Of particular use in recording the arrangement of furniture in rooms of middling status was Francesca Scoones, 'Dr William Stukeley's House at Grantham', *Georgian Group Journal*, vol. IX (1999), pp. 158–65.

20. Florence Montgomery, *Textiles in America 1650–1870* (New York, 1984), pp. 283–85, describes

the making of lustring in Britain. The substance used to coat the silk, which was then heated, always remained a trade secret.

21. Since the opening of the galleries, the Museum has been grateful to have the support of the Leche Trust and the Idlewild Foundation in the conservation of a further two chairs that will take the place of the original pair displayed during 2004.

22. Several of the illustrations in John Crunden's *Chimneypiece Maker's Daily Assistant*, published in London in 1766, illustrate paintings of this type. James Gibbs himself, in *A Book of Architecture* (1739), refers to 'Three Draughts of Chimney-pieces, with Ornaments over them for Pictures', and in *Rules for Drawing the Several Parts of Architecture* to 'Three other Chimney-pieces with Frames for Pictures or Pannels over them'.

23. The best general accounts of the room are Desmond Fitzgerald, *The Norfolk House Music Room* (London, 1973), hereafter as Fitzgerald 1973; Desmond Fitzgerald, 'The Norfolk House Music Room' in *Victoria & Albert Museum Bulletin*, vol. II, no.1 (January 1966), pp. 1–11. Norfolk House was described in detail in the *Survey of London*, vol. xxix, *The Parish of St James Westminster, Pt. I, South of Piccadilly*, general ed. F.H.W. Sheppard (London, 1960), pp. 192–201.

24. Mrs P. Toynbee (ed.), *The Letters of Horace Walpole*, vol. II (1903) p. 396, quoted in Fitzgerald 1973, p. 5 (see note 23).

25. *Rococo: Art and Design in Hogarth's England* (exhib. cat., Victoria and Albert Museum, London, 1984), pp. 23–24. For a discussion of the 9th Duke and Duchess's works at Norfolk House see also John Martin Robinson, *The Dukes of Norfolk* (Chichester, 1995) pp. 154–59.

26. His name was linked to the scheme only in the 1960s, when Geoffrey Beard discovered a bill in the archives at Arundel Castle (ref. MD. 18/9) from the plasterer Thomas Clarke for work 'according to Mr Bora's Directions'. Quoted in Fitzgerald 1973, p. 10 (see note 23). We are grateful to His Grace the Duke of Norfolk for permission to quote from archival material held at Arundel Castle and to John Martin Robinson and Sara Rodger for their help in accessing material there.

27. Geoffrey Beard and Christopher Gilbert, *Dictionary of English Furniture Makers 1660–1840* (Leeds, 1986), p. 217. His main account for the work at Norfolk House is in the archive at Arundel Castle (MD 18/1).

28. Fitzgerald 1973, pp. 7–10 (see note 23) had suggested William Collins (1721–93). More recently it has also been suggested that the cartouches might be by Bartholomew Cramillion, whose Rococo work in Dublin is recorded in Joseph McDonell, *Irish Eighteenth-Century Stuccowork and Its European Sources* (Dublin, National Gallery of Ireland, 1991), although no evidence for this has emerged.

29. Christie, Manson & Woods, sale catalogue of contents of Norfolk House, 7 February 1938, p. 3.

30. In pre-1938 photos of the room, three plain bands are clear at this point, though now there are only two.

31. Oswald, Arthur, 'Norfolk House, St James's Square: The Town House of the Duke of Norfolk', *Country Life* (25 December 1937), vol. LXXXII, no. 2136, pp. 654–60.

32. J. Bowles, *Vue de la place de Ste Jacques à Londres* (c. 1760), a detail illustrated in Fitzgerald 1973, p. 8 (see note 23).

33. Oestreicher Davies, *Norfolk House Music Room: Victoria and Albert Museum*, Paint Analysis Report, December 1998.

34. Archive, Arundel Castle, MS MD 18/6.

35. Patrick Baty points out that it is probably impossible to get back to an 'original' colour by this method, but that it can support other methods of analysis in trying to determine the original appearance of old paints.

36. The panels that were regilded entirely in the present project were those representing *Music* and *Astronomy*.

37. Published in full in Fitzgerald 1973, p. 53 (see note 23).

38. The specification for the boards was given by Annabel Westman.

39. Tate Britain, accession number 1943.

40. The best general account of the room is to be found in Hugh Honour, 'A House of the Gothic Revival', *Country Life* (30 May 1952), vol.CXI, no. 2889, pp. 1665–66.

41. Mrs P. Toynbee (ed.), *The Letters of Horace Walpole*, vol. xv (1903), p. 309, letter 2943, to Miss Mary Berry, 27 September 1794.

42. Oestreicher Davies, Architectural Paint Analysis, *Lee Priory (Strawberry Room and Library Bookcase), Victoria and Albert Museum*, Paint Analysis Report, December 1998.

43. Hannah Eastwood, *Analysis of the Lee Priory Wallpaper Fragment, Museum no. W.48:2-1953*. V&A Science and Information Report No. 98/64/HJE. This showed that the blue pigment was cobalt and thus could only date from after 1828. The predominantly pink and blue scheme of this paper mirrors the colours painted on the bookcases of an adjacent room during the 1865 refurbishing of Lee Priory by Sir George Gilbert Scott and it is possible that this paper dates from that period.

44. These were inspected by Merryl Huxtable of the Paper Conservation Section at the V&A and analysed by David Ford from the Science and Information Section of the V&A Conservation Department. David Ford, *Analysis of wallpaper fragments removed from the Lee Priory Room during Dismantlement, W.48-1953*. Science and Information Section Report no.99/35/DJF.

45. Gill Saunders, *Wallpaper in Interior Decoration* (London, 2002), p. 41.

46. Recent experimental papers of verditer have been hung at Temple Newsam, Leeds and Woodhall Park, Herts.

47. Allyson McDermott did offer examples of eighteenth-century schemes with borders cut in what to us appear very clumsy manner to go round chimneypieces or other shaped items. It may have been a twentieth-century weakness to omit this border and our successors will decide this.

48. *Lee Priory, Kent, catalogue of all the superb antique and modern household furniture (heir looms excepted), extensive and valuable library, containing upwards of 5000 volumes of books . . . will be sold by auction by Mr W. Sharp, on the premises, Lee Priory, near Canterbury on Monday August 11*[th] *and eleven following days ... 1834.*

49. Clive Wainwright, *The Romantic Interior* (London, 1989), pp. 71–108.

50. John Cornforth, *English Interiors 1790–1848: The Quest for Comfort* (London, 1978), pp. 106–07.

51. We are very grateful to Woodward Grosvenor & Co. Ltd, Kidderminster, for allowing us to search their archive, and in particular to Mr Brian Mottram for his help. A small Gothic pattern of the 1790s was located, but the irregular shape needed to cover the floor between the barrier and the hearthstone meant that a new carpet would have drawn attention to itself excessively.

52. The best general account of the room is found in Barbara Morris, 'The Harborne Room', *Victoria and Albert Museum Bulletin*, vol.IV, no.3 (1968), pp. 2–15, hereafter as Morris.

53. All we know of Mr Barfield's work is from a note titled 'Mr Barfield's Carvings', published just after his death in *The Birmingham Post* (17 September 1887), which describes his work in several buildings in Birmingham.

54. Morris, pp. 4–5. The information presumably coming directly from surviving members of the family. The room was only later used as a small sitting room.

55. Birmingham City Archives MS 400/93.

56. Susan Lasdun, *Victorians at Home* (London, 1981), p. 110. The blind was made by Sun-Ex UK Ltd of Bognor Regis.

77. *Plan of the ground floor of the Old Palace, Bromley-by-Bow. Plan prepared by Rose Innes Associates.*

78. *Drawing by C.R. Ashbee of the chimneypiece, made during the campaign to save the house in 1893.*

79. *Photo of the room before 1893.*

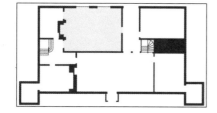

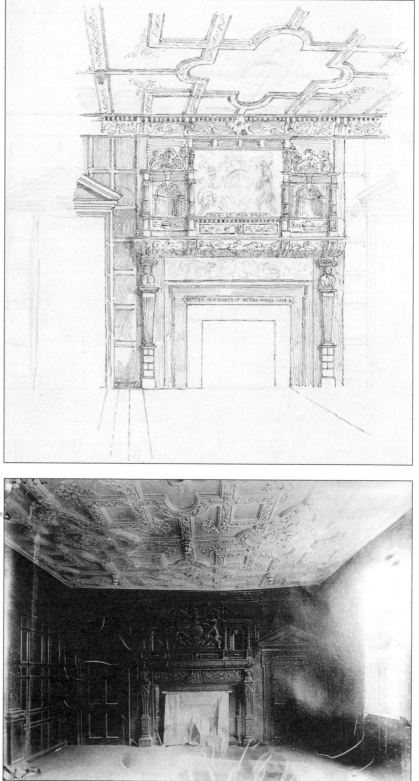

*80. Photo of the parlour from
Henrietta Street just before the
demolition of the house in 1955.
Copyright National Monuments
Record.*

*81. Plan of the first floor of the
house, London. Plan prepared by
Rose Innes Associates.*

*82. Elevation of the chimneypiece
and one window, from the 1955
survey. Copyright, National
Monuments Record.*

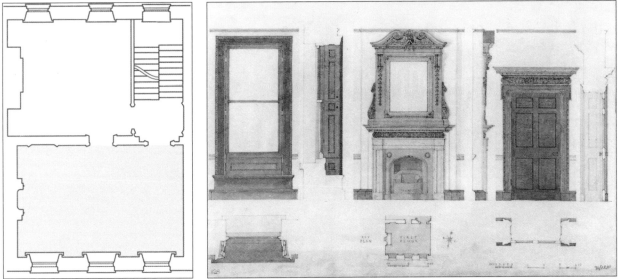

83. *Plan of the first floor of Norfolk House, 1756, showing the original entrances to the room. Plan prepared by Rose Innes Associates.*

84. *The window wall, 1937. Copyright Country Life Picture Library.*

85. *St James's Square, about 1752 from an engraving by J. Bowles. Norfolk House is the double-width house on the far right.*

Vüe de la Place de S.te Jaques a Londres.

86. *Plan of the first floor of Lee Priory before its enlargement in 1865, by Sir Gilbert Scott. The Strawberry Room is at the lower left of the drawing. Copyright British Architectural Library, RIBA.*

87. *The Strawberry Room in 1953. This photograph is the only evidence for the form of the doorway on the right, inserted by Sir George Gilbert Scott in 1865. Copyright, National Monuments Record.*

88. *Lee Priory in 1819, from an engraving. The 'Strawberry Room' was on the first floor at the right-hand end.*

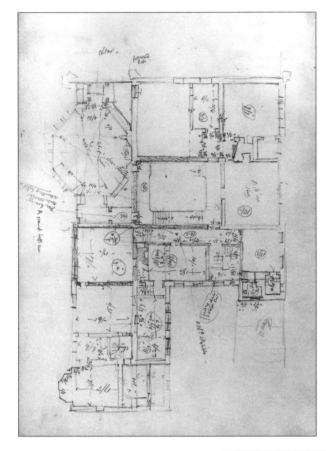

LEE PRIORY,
(SOUTH WEST VIEW.)
KENT.

89. The Grove, Harborne,
Birmingham, 1955. Birmingham
Museums & Art Gallery.

90. Photograph of the window,
before demolition. Birmingham
Museums & Art Gallery.

91. Plan of the ground-floor of
The Grove. Plan prepared by
Rose Innes Associates.

Chapter 11 Evaluation – Before and after Opening

Morna Hinton

At the start of the British Galleries Project the institutional understanding of evaluation and visitor research at the V&A was patchy at best. An annual visitor survey had been conducted over a number of years, so the Museum had good basic demographic data, but it was essentially a marketing tool that gave us little information on what visitors got out of exhibitions and displays, or their learning needs. Various small-scale studies had also been carried out for individual projects. A survey of all the visitor studies from 1986 to 1996 was commissioned from the Institute of Policy Studies in 1998. This 'Survey of Surveys' provided a useful summary of what was known about our visitors.[1] However, enthusiasm for this approach was by no means universal. The suggestion that visitors might be consulted about new galleries was dismissed by some as the tail wagging the dog. There was a sense that the Museum possessed sufficient cultural authority to determine what was displayed and how it was presented.

The British Galleries Project, with its commitment to a visitor focus, provided the opportunity to integrate evaluation into a major project. Evaluation was allocated a budget of £96,000, which permitted a full cycle of research through the lifetime of the project, pre- and post-opening, resulting in a unique museological case study.[2] In addition, there was a separate budget for prototyping various aspects of the designs, including around £15,000 for prototypes of interpretive devices that were tested with visitors. Since the Museum lacked in-house expertise, it was necessary to hire consultants and specialist research companies, whose work was managed by a member of the team. The very first piece of research was managed by Gail Durbin as part of her role on the Concept Team. The management of subsequent studies was handed over to the present writer, one of the educators working full-time on the project. Working with different evaluation experts required us to develop a critical understanding of the methods employed. We needed to brief the consultants clearly and then work with them on every stage of the process. It meant commenting on questionnaires, asking awkward questions and demanding further analysis of data when necessary.

Part-way through the project it became clear that it was necessary to agree action points after each piece of evaluation. The early studies on the old British Art and Design Galleries and on the recently opened Silver Gallery had yielded some interesting results, but with hindsight the issues raised were not all addressed as rigorously as they could have been. The need to agree actions was particularly acute for the prototyping phase, when it was essential that all those involved knew what changes were going to be made as a result of the testing. As part of the regular reporting cycle we were required to submit all the prototyping reports to the Heritage Lottery Fund (HLF), to which were added the actions resulting from each piece of research (although the HLF declined to fund any of the evaluation).

The involvement of Project Team members and other Museum staff in the evaluation process was a key factor in developing understanding and acceptance of the process. For example, when we ran focus groups, members of the team observed the discussion, following strict rules to ensure that they did not disrupt or otherwise influence proceedings. It was salutary for curators to listen to people who were often well-educated but who were unable to distinguish Baroque from Rococo. When it came to the prototyping phase participation by members of the Project Team was essential in order to be able to gather all the data required. By the final phase of prototyping, with some training in interviewing and observation techniques from the consultant, Paulette McManus, team members were able to carry out all aspects of the evaluation: data collection, analysis and reporting.

The testing of the computer interactives provided an opportunity to consult Museum staff outside the Project Team. Testing sessions were set up in the temporary gallery *Best of British* in the same way as for the public and colleagues were invited to come along and try out the interactives. This was done partly as a way of winning the hearts and minds of those who were resistant to the whole notion of computers in a museum of art and design. It allowed us to show them what the programs looked like, as well as demonstrating that their input was valued. Interestingly, their response was generally very similar to that of visitors, although with the added benefit that they would point out content errors that visitors did not notice.

The post-opening evaluation enabled us to evaluate the success of the galleries and to probe further into issues of relevance to future gallery projects. This final summative phase illustrated the relative strengths and weaknesses of different evaluation methodologies. Quantitative surveys based on structured questionnaires are often preferred by those with little experience of evaluation, because they regard hard numbers as somehow more trustworthy and objective than the 'subjective' data from focus groups and other qualitative methods. However, although the quantitative survey of the new galleries provided some interesting and very positive data, it also raised a number of questions that could only be answered by subsequent studies using qualitative techniques. A quantitative survey is broad-brush and will show trends and generalisations – it answers questions of 'what?' and 'how many?' well. By contrast, qualitative studies get under the skin of the visitor experience and will be more likely to answer the 'how?' and 'why?' questions. We undertook these with a full awareness that the interpretation of surveys is, itself, a subjective process.

Summary of key findings from the evaluation

Front-end research

At the start of the project we commissioned a baseline study of the old British Art and Design Galleries based on structured interviews with 252 visitors as well as a smaller sample of booked groups who filled in questionnaires. A number of the findings from this research had a substantial impact on the development of the project. Many visitors (46%) had no idea what the galleries were called and only 42% realized that they were in galleries dealing with British art and design.[3] Very few visitors had intended to visit the galleries – 73% had no firm intention of doing so and had ended up there by chance.[4]

In the earliest stages of the project the Concept Team had considered a thematic rather than chronological organisation for the galleries. This was rejected and the baseline study fortuitously showed that chronology was a very important conceptual tool for visitors.[5] Other results from the baseline study were shocking, for example the discovery that after 11 minutes 50% of visitors had left the lower level of the old galleries (a substantial 1700 square metres of space); the corresponding figure for the upper level was 8 minutes.[6] Another key finding that spurred the development of the interpretation was the low average rating given to learning in the old galleries – 4.1 out of 10.[7]

In the baseline survey we also asked visitors about various types of interpretation that we were considering for the new galleries. They were quite traditional in their assessment, perhaps because they could not see concrete examples of what we had in mind. In particular, the majority were not in favour of touch objects, videos or computer interactives, all of which have proved extremely popular in the new galleries.[8] This serves to highlight the fact that research findings need to be interpreted with care. Visitors are most reliable when talking about what they are doing at that moment, fairly reliable when discussing past actions, and least reliable when assessing a hypothetical scenario.

Formative research The next step was to undertake further investigation into visitors' response to our plans for the British Galleries. In order to achieve this we carried out an evaluation of the V&A's Silver Galleries.[9] We chose the Silver Galleries because they have a Discovery Area with many types of interpretation that were proposed for the British Galleries, though ours would be different in character. We wanted in-depth feedback as well as to discover underlying trends, so we commissioned three focus groups with six or seven people in each, as well as a survey of 238 people, which provided useful triangulation (where answers to the same questions are gleaned from two or more different methods, making the findings more robust). Surveys, because they are relatively superficial, tend to engender a complimentary 'halo' effect when they concern an august institution like the V&A. By contrast, focus groups allow respondents time to discuss issues in depth and offer a licence to be critical. Each type of evaluation therefore provides quite different results. By using both techniques in the same study we obtained an overall picture somewhere in the middle of these two extremes, which was probably more accurate.[10]

The most significant finding for the development of the galleries was that when visitors could see what we meant by computer interactives and touch objects they were much more positive about them than in the baseline survey. This was the one area where there was a real difference in response depending on whether people had visited the Discovery Area and seen the interactives or not. In the Silver Gallery survey 71% of those who had visited the Discovery Area agreed with the statement 'It would be really good if you could touch some of the objects' compared to 61% who hadn't. The same figures for computer-based exhibits were 70% in favour amongst those who had been to the Discovery Area versus 58% for those who hadn't.[11] The research in the Silver Galleries confirmed our suspicion that interactives and Discovery Areas appeal to all types of visitor, adult and child alike. It was also found that family visitors particularly liked the safety of a defined space where they could keep an eye on their children.[12]

The study highlighted the difficulties visitors had in relating the content of the Discovery Area interactives to the displays in the gallery. This strengthened our resolve to include objects in the Discovery Areas, and, wherever possible, to have interactives in the galleries right next to the object or display they relate to.[13]

Other findings concerned the physical layout of the space in the Silver Discovery Area, which was felt to be too small for the number of exhibits. In the British Galleries Discovery Areas the central cases that obstructed circulation in the Silver Gallery have been avoided. The study also highlighted the need for more than one person at a time to be able to use interpretive devices, and multiple screens for computer interactives, all of which has been incorporated into the British Galleries design wherever possible.[14] It was found that visitors did not see the Discovery Area as an alternative to the main gallery but rather as a complement to it. The total time spent visiting the Silver Gallery was estimated at 12 minutes for those who did not go into the Discovery Area and at just over 20 minutes for those who did.[15]

In the next phase of formative evaluation we tested ideas for display and interpretation in the British Galleries. Focus groups with all of the target audiences for the galleries were held, as well as two groups of non-visitors: heritage-goers and keen home decorators. The non-visitors turned out to be not so different from the visitors in most of their views.[16] In general people were happy for the Museum to define the themes for the galleries. However, it seemed that Style was understood differently to the other three themes (What Was New?, Fashionable Living, Who Led Taste?). Style in art and design poses particular difficulties for many visitors. In the focus groups it emerged that,

people can be huffy and sensitive about being ignorant of style details. Other people pooh-pooh the idea as being too pretentious to bother with. [But] almost everyone who can conceive of visiting the V&A wants to learn a bit about style … [to] leave with a little package of knowledge, which advances them in this fraught area.[17]

The focus groups showed us that visitors differ in the amount of contextual information they need in order to be able to engage with museum objects. The most significant split in the focus groups was between generalists who were history-aware and specialists who were object-aware. Generalists usually need a historical context before they can deal with objects, which means that the Style theme is especially difficult for them.[18]

It was discovered that television was a big influence on visitors' understanding of history, with popular period dramas and the Blackadder comedy series being frequently cited. The Victorian era (1837–1901) is the most accessible to visitors. The Stuart period (1603–1714) is better known than the Tudors (1485–1603), and Georgian/Regency (1714–1837) is the least familiar of all. Architecture and costume were the most useful visual references in terms of helping visitors place the historical period. Overseas visitors in particular had very little grasp of British history, a significant factor given that around half the V&A's visitors are from abroad, and one that led us to avoid the use of dynastic terms in favour of simple dates wherever possible.[19]

The focus groups revealed some gaps in our plans for display and interpretation. The themes of rich and poor were of great interest to visitors and needed to be addressed. Visitors were also fascinated by the creative process.[20] Objects associated with people from humble backgrounds are rare in a museum of high design like the V&A, particularly in the earlier period. It was however possible, by highlighting the makers of objects through labels and other interpretation, to include more 'ordinary' people in the stories told in the galleries.

Prototyping

The final part of the formative phase of visitor evaluation consisted of the testing of prototypes, for which there was a budget of £15,000.[21] This included evaluation of every series of interpretive devices, all the main computer interactives and various issues to do with labels, panels and other gallery text. A total of 44 separate prototyping studies were conducted (including those on computer interactives), all of which are available on the V&A website (see bibliography). A selection of the findings are outlined below, though all were crucial for the further development of the text and interpretation.

In relation to the instructional text for interpretive devices, perhaps the most fundamental finding was that we needed to use diagrams or images wherever possible to ensure that visitors understood instructions. Concise and attractive explanatory graphics are attended to closely by visitors. Text accompanying the diagrams needs to be kept short. A prototype tapestry weaving activity demonstrated this very clearly: not one of 24 visitors attended to the extremely detailed instructions before starting to weave, or while they were weaving. As one visitor put it, 'they're too complex – like an essay on how to boil a potato'.[22]

Titles for activities needed to be carefully considered, for example a drawing activity entitled 'Draw an Acanthus Leaf' was off-putting because it put visitors in a situation where they felt their drawing ability would be judged. 'Try an eighteenth-century Drawing Book' was much less threatening, and visitors undertook their drawings more quickly and less anxiously. This title also elicited more insightful, empathetic comments about the careful, time-consuming work of eighteenth-century craftspeople.[23]

The testing of a prototype *Object in Focus* video showing a nineteenth-century washstand in use provided findings that crucially informed the development of the other gallery videos. Half of the visitors often lost their place in the video as they hunted on the washstand for the details featured in the film.[24] This was due to showing the details in close-up without making it clear where they were on the object. When the final videos were produced a wide shot was always included before a close-up to try to alleviate this problem. The pace of the subtitles was also slowed down so that visitors would concentrate on the object and so that foreign visitors with knowledge of English could understand them better. When viewed by Museum staff away from the gallery, some found the pacing too slow, which demonstrated the importance of testing under gallery conditions.

A fundamental aim of all the interpretation was to help visitors engage with the objects. Testing showed that without an accompanying video, visitors looked at the washstand for an average of 18.4 seconds, compared to the average of one minute and eight seconds they spent looking at the prototype video and object together (the video was around two-and-a-half minutes long). This suggested that visitors will engage with an object for significantly longer if it is accompanied by an interpretive device like a video. Only 5 out of 23 allowed enough time to see the whole video. This confirmed to us that such videos must be short.

The Project Team spent a great deal of time considering the individual object labels and more general panel text, and set up a working group to develop guidelines for writers. One area where visitors' input was needed was the organisation of caption or 'tombstone' text (designer, maker, date, material), especially the order of the information and how much should come before the prose commentary on the object. Four formats for four objects in different media were tested: a chair, a ceramic group of figures, a metal chalice and a sculpted bust of Charles II. Around 25 people tested the labels for each object. The four formats were as follows:

A. 1. Commentary (larger font size)
   2. Date and museum details
   3. Acquisition details

B. 1. Date and materials
   2. Museum details
   3. Commentary (larger font size)
   4. Acquisition details

C. 1. Museum details in prose (larger font size)
   2. Commentary (larger font size)
   3. Acquisition details

D. 1. Museum details, including date
   2. Commentary (larger font size)
   3. Acquisition details

Dates are very important to visitors, and the format that visitors liked most picked out the date as a separate piece of information immediately after the title, followed by the materials used. Visitors preferred the information to be visually separated into 'chunks'. One fifth of visitors liked to pass straight into the commentary after the title. In the event it was decided to combine the two most popular formats.[25] Our chosen order was:

Title
Date
Commentary
Materials
Other production information (e.g. maker, where it was made)
Acquisition details
Museum number

This works well for the British Galleries, which are primarily decorative arts, but is less suitable for fine art galleries. In the Paintings Gallery (opened autumn 2003) the artist has been given before the commentary.

One technique for writing and laying out text that we were keen to try was Ekarving, a system pioneered at the Swedish Postal Museum by Margareta Ekarv.[26] Ekarv was a specialist in writing easy-to-read books for adults with literacy problems. She applied a similar approach to gallery text on the basis that reading in a gallery setting is more difficult than reading a book because the reader is standing up and there are many distractions. The text should therefore be correspondingly simpler. Her key rules are simple sentence structures, everyday language and breaking the lines at natural pauses so that each line deals with a separate concept. The latter produces text that often has quite varied line lengths, sometimes looking like poetry.

Initially three different subject panels in both Ekarved and non-Ekarved form were tested, but this proved rather inconclusive. It was then decided to carry out further testing on full-size mock-ups of the most extreme of the Ekarved layouts and the standard layout of the same text.

Non-Ekarved text panel	*Ekarved text panel*
Chinoiserie	**Chinoiserie**
Chinoiserie was a form of decoration inspired by Chinese materials and design. It was most fashionable between 1745 and 1765.	Chinoisere was a form of decoration inspired by Chinese materials and design. It was most fashionable between 1745 and 1765.
Chinese goods had been imported into Britain since the 17th century. People admired them for their rare materials and curious motifs, that conjured up a fantasy world.	Chinese goods had been imported into Britain since the 17th century. People admired them for their rare materials and curious motifs, that conjured up a fantasy world.
British designers and craftsmen also imitated Chinese furniture, lacquer and porcelain. They often combined Chinese figures and landscapes, with the forms and motifs of the Rococo style.	British designers and craftsmen also imitated Chinese furniture, lacquer and porcelain. They often combined Chinese figures and landscapes, with the forms and motifs of the Rococo style.
Chinoiserie was mainly used in interiors for bedrooms and small dressing rooms. In architecture it was used chiefly for small garden buildings.	Chinoiserie was mainly used in interiors for bedrooms and small dressing rooms. In architecture it was used chiefly for small garden buildings.

The overall sample was very highly educated, which is typical of V&A visitors. What is interesting is that those who preferred Ekarving were even more highly educated than those who didn't. They were also more likely to have English as their second language – 28% of English speakers preferred Ekarving as opposed to 42% of non-native-English speakers. They were also more likely to rate themselves as fast readers, which suggests that the Ekarving layout helps skim-reading.[27] It was decided on the basis of testing and because of the greater demands it imposed upon writers not to use the Ekarved layout, although other aspects of Ekarving were adopted, such as the use of the active voice, straightforward language and simple sentence structures.

There is always a tension between interpretation and aesthetics in any gallery project. In this area, like many other aspects of the project, we wanted visitor input and tested the use of italics and text layout. However, it was felt that we should rely on the designers for guidance on the fundamentals of font size and positioning of labels. In retrospect, this was a mistake, as we had to make expensive post-opening adjustments to a number of the object labels due to complaints about poor legibility.

When it came to testing the computer interactives, the first job was to persuade the software company that it would be beneficial to test with real visitors. The company had initially devised a system of paper 'profiles' of different types of visitor against which they planned to rate the programmes, together with various technical tests. The scores for all the individual tests would be combined to produce an overall pass or fail for the interactive. We felt strongly that, although technical testing was clearly important, it was vital to test the interactives with visitors in a gallery setting, and we therefore insisted that public testing was carried out. Luckily the schedule allowed this. Overall the visitor feedback was extremely helpful in terms of both general content and navigation.

To take just one example, the object database, British Galleries Online, changed substantially as a result of public testing. Navigation proved a real difficulty in the first version, in particular the route back to the home page. The design of the home page itself was also completely revised after the first round of testing in order to make it more inviting and more informative about the content of the programme. Left to right 'swishing' transitions between screens looked sophisticated but were not liked by visitors, some of whom were made to feel queasy by them.[28] When the content for the database was being planned, the initial, very ambitious idea was to provide different information about individual objects depending on how they were accessed, for example whether you had reached the object information screen by following a 'People' or a 'Place' route. However, the option of 'alternative routes' was not noticed by most visitors and not particularly appreciated by those that did. That, combined with the logistical difficulties of actually getting all the text written and installed in the program, led us to abandon the idea.[29]

Summative research Six months after the British Galleries opened, a survey that replicated the original baseline study of the old galleries was conducted, with additional questions on specific aspects of the new galleries, including the interpretation (see appendix 9). Visitors were extremely positive about the new galleries, with a vast improvement against the baseline in most areas. For example, the average score given to the galleries for learning had shot up from 4.1 to 8 out of 10; 64% felt that children would get a lot out of the displays compared to 19% previously; 75% knew what the galleries were called compared to 54% in the baseline. People were now deliberately choosing to visit the British Galleries – 95% claimed to have made a conscious decision to do so, compared with 27% in the baseline. Time spent in the new galleries was much greater – the notorious baseline figure of 11 minutes, after which 50% of visitors had left the lower level, had improved to 37 minutes, with the corresponding figure for the upper level standing at 45 minutes.[30]

The interpretive devices, Study Areas, Discovery Areas and Film Rooms proved popular with visitors.[31] Six out of ten visitors used one of the dedicated areas, while a similar proportion (64%) had used at least one interpretive device, either there or in the main galleries. Amongst visitors who used the interpretive devices and Discovery Areas, around 90% felt that it both enhanced their appreciation of the objects as well as improving their knowledge of the subject matter.[32]

The usage by visitors of different types of interpretive devices was as follows:

Videos – 41%
Handling activities – 33%
Lift the flap – 32%
Computer interactives – 26%
Text-based activities such as facsimiles and visitor response – 20%
Audio programmes (many not fully installed at time of testing) – 14%[33]

There are roughly equal numbers of device in each category so they were reasonably comparable.

The interpretation was spontaneously mentioned by 19% of visitors as contributing to their learning in the galleries.[34] Only 1% of visitors felt that the interpretation was a hindrance or distraction.[35]

A number of issues thrown up by the survey required further investigation. One finding that caused concern was that, despite all the interactives and Discovery Areas, fewer children appeared to be visiting the new galleries than the old galleries. The percentage of children fell from 26% in the baseline survey to 5% in the post-opening one.[36] However, as the former was conducted during school holidays and the latter during term time, we commissioned a demographic survey in May 2003. The percentage of child visitors went up to 10%, though this was still substantially less than in the baseline survey. The explanation for this probably lies with (a) the introduction of free admission in November 2001, which led to a dramatic increase in individual adult visitors, and (b) the lack of promotion of the galleries as child friendly, within and outside the Museum.

Another area of the survey where more information was needed was visitors' awareness of the four themes of the galleries. Style was mentioned by 5% of visitors when asked how they thought the displays were organised but none of the other themes were mentioned at all.[37] This was addressed by a subsequent qualitative study, which found that around half of the sample of 35 visitors had become aware of some of the themes during their visit. They often did not use the exact wording from the panels ('the themes are *The development of life styles* and *How luxury developed*') and sometimes picked up the themes visually rather than from text.[38]

The subsequent in-depth study of the interactives revealed more information about patterns of use as well as critical success and failure factors.[39] Adults on their own or in pairs were the most likely to use interactives, while unaccompanied children were the least likely to (based on

1000 observations and 100 interviews). Adults tended to use interactives as individuals, while families gravitated towards activities that allowed joint participation. Families also favoured interpretive devices that gave some sort of tangible output, such as the printout from the 'Design a coat of arms' activity.

Visitor behaviour in museums was categorised in the study as browsing, searching or researching. These three types were defined as follows:

Browsers – Casual, incidental or non-specialist interest visitors motivated by leisure, aesthetic, family, social, informal educational or self-improvement drivers.
Searchers – Intentional visitors, focused and self-motivated, exploring and pursuing a developing formal or informal interest or hobby.
Researchers – Intentional visitors driven by academic, professional or strong personal interest.

The evaluation found that the interactives in the British Galleries have the potential to move people on from being browsers to being searchers.

Individual interactives were assessed according to depth of engagement and how that engagement was facilitated (unaided, using reference material or helped by a member of staff or another visitor). This produced an overall success rating for each. Not surprisingly, different types of interactive showed different types of engagement. For example, 88% of visitors used the *Design a Coat of Arms* computer program in a way that was characterised as either discovery (learning something as a result of the interaction) or immersion (longer engagement, making links, discussing discoveries). The majority were able to use the program intuitively without reference to instructions or a person before starting.[40] By contrast, the *Scaling Up* drawing activity appealed to a much smaller group of visitors with 70% engaging in a manner defined as exploration (touching but not learning) or orientation (looking but not touching). Nonetheless, for 20% this proved an immersive activity that they could do intuitively.[41] As the researchers point out: 'with so many interactives, it is not reasonable to expect that all visitors will interact successfully with all interactives. They will browse at some and engage more closely with others, depending on their level of motivation and interest and the dynamics within their party.'[42]

Practical design and ease of use emerged as particularly critical in relation to the success or failure of interpretive devices. Successful devices:
- are obvious to visitors in terms of the position in the gallery;
- have an easy relation to the object;
- are in eye-line with the object;
- allow collective usage;
- facilitate behaviour modelling;
- are in a familiar format.[43]

Conclusion   At the outset of the British Galleries Project the Concept Team decided that one way in which the new galleries would be different to the old galleries was that they would be visitor-focused. Evaluation and visitor research was key to achieving this goal. Without consulting visitors and listening carefully to their views, the British Galleries would be more inward-facing and less engaging. Many simple mistakes were avoided through prototyping, and by carrying out surveys at the start and end of the process we were able to show in concrete terms how the new galleries were used differently. The resultant body of research is an important resource for future projects both at the V&A and in other museums.

Notes   1. Selwood, Sara, for the Policy Studies Institute, *Survey of Visitor Research at the V&A 1986–1996* (1998), unpublished report.

2. All the British Galleries visitor research can be found on the V&A website at http://www.vam.ac.uk/bg_visitor_research (consulted 27 August 2003).

3. Creative Research (1997ii), *Audience Research for the British Galleries: Quantitative Research Findings*, vol.2, p. 106, hereafter as Creative Research (1997ii).

4. Creative Research (1997i), *Audience Research for the British Galleries: Quantitative Research Findings*, vol.1, p. 87, hereafter as Creative Research (1997i).

5. Creative Research (1997ii), p. 113.

6. Creative Research (1997i), pp. 81–84, 87.

7. Creative Research (1997ii), p. 141.

8. Creative Research (1997ii), pp. 161–62.

9. Phase 1 of the Silver Galleries opened in 1996.

10. Creative Research (1998i), *Audience Research for the British Galleries: Silver Gallery Discovery Area. Part 1: Introduction, Summary of Findings and Recommendations*, pp. 6–7, hereafter as Creative Research (1998i Silver).

11. Creative Research (1998ii), *Audience Research for the British Galleries: Silver Gallery Discovery Area. Part 2: Main Findings of Quantitative Research*, p. 66, hereafter as Creative Research (1998ii Silver).

12. Creative Research (1998i Silver) pp. 7, 11 (appeal of interactives to all types of visitor); p. 12 (family visitors).

13. Creative Research (1998i Silver), pp. 17–18.

14. Creative Research (1998i Silver), p. 12 (physical layout); p. 19 (multi-user activities).

15. Creative Research (1998ii Silver), p. 40.

16. Fisher, Susie, *et al.*, *The British Galleries Project at the V&A: Are People in Tune with New Plans for the Interpretation? Qualitative Research with Visitors and Non-visitors* (1998), pp. 32–35, hereafter as Fisher (1998).

17. Fisher (1998), p. 44 (themes); pp. 48, 62 (style in art and design).

18. Fisher (1998), pp. 11–13.

19. Fisher (1998), p. 40 (familiarity with Stuart period); pp. 41–43 (architecture and costume); p. 28 (overseas visitors).

20. Fisher (1998) pp. 7, 37.

21. This did not include the computer interactives where a sequential phased development is usual, with testing at one or two key stages for which we used work in progress (see pp. 154–5).

22. McManus, Paulette (1999i), *Miscellaneous Activity: Tapestry Weaving: Prototyping Research Report 21*, p. 2.

23. McManus, Paulette (1999ii), *Draw an Acanthus Leaf: Prototyping Research Report 3*, p. 3.

24. McManus, Paulette (1999iii), *Object in Focus Video: William Burges' Washstand: Prototyping Research Report 2*, p. 3.

25. McManus, Paulette (1999iv), *Order of Information in Object Labels: Prototyping Report 7*, p. 9.

26. Ekarv, Margareta, 'Combating Redundancy: Writing Texts for Exhibitions', in Hooper-Greenhill, E. (ed.), *The Educational Role of the Museum* (Routledge, 1994). Ekarved text has been employed at a number of museums and galleries in the UK, most recently in Manchester Art Gallery, which reopened in 2002, following major redevelopment work.

27. McManus, Paulette (1999v), *Ekarved Text Layout: Prototyping Research Report 5*, pp. 5–6.

28. McManus, Paulette (2000), *ICT Prototyping Phase 6 Evaluation: British Galleries Online*, pp. 5, 7.

29. Brod, Nick, and Hinton, Morna (2000), *ICT Prototyping Phase 8 Evaluation: British Galleries Online*, p. 4.

30. Creative Research (2002ii), *Summative Evaluation of the British Galleries: Report of Research Findings*, p. 40 (average learning score); p. 62 (appeal to children); p. 39 (name recognition); p. 73 (deliberate choice to visit); p. 72 (time spent in the galleries), hereafter as Creative Research (2002ii).

31. However, another study that combined both qualitative and quantitative methodologies provided the surprising finding of low level of usage – at least on a single Saturday afternoon – of the Study Rooms (Morris, Hargreaves, McIntyre, *Engaging or Distracting? Visitor Responses to Interactives in the V&A British Galleries* [2003], p. 27, hereafter as Morris, Hargreaves, McIntyre). This finding has not been borne out by observation, and further investigation may explore the use of these areas more closely.

32. Creative Research (2002ii), pp. 50–55.

33. Creative Research (2002ii), p. 53.

34. Creative Research (2002ii), p. 41

35. Creative Research (2002ii), pp. 52, 54. An apparent contradiction was the finding that 17% of visitors agreed with the statement 'my pleasure at seeing the wonderful objects was spoiled by all the interactive exhibits' (Creative Research [2002ii], p. 67). When such contradictions arose, we sought clarity through further investigation, which suggested a lower figure, 6%, most of

whom were very focused visitors with clear, pre-set agendas, while some were actually expressing hypothetical concerns rather than reporting their own experience (Morris, Hargreaves, McIntyre, pp. 8, 15).

36. Creative Research (2002ii), p. 19.
37. Creative Research (2002ii), p. 37.
38. McManus, Paulette, *A Qualitative Account of Visitor Experiences in the Displays, Film Rooms and Study Areas of the British Galleries at the V&A* (2003), p. 13.
39. Morris, Hargreaves, McIntyre, p. 5.
40. Ibid, p. 10.
41. Ibid, p. 11.
42. Ibid, p. 11.
43. Ibid, p. 12.

Chapter 12   Visiting the British Galleries – A Personal View

Giovanni Pinna

The relationship that a visitor has with a museum exhibition is an extremely personal thing. A number of years ago Duncan Cameron proposed two alternative types of museum, the Temple and the Forum, by which he meant a museum as a place of veneration or worship as opposed to a museum as a place of exchange and interaction.[1] He maintained that, whilst debate with the public was possible in the latter, the former excluded this possibility. In reality this classification is too rigid, as all those who visit a museum have the intrinsic desire to create their own dialogue with the contents, be they presented in a religiously solemn form or offered as elements for discussion. Furthermore, unlike others, I am convinced that a traditional museum is never an open forum (i.e. prepared to abdicate its internal culture), and I believe that the aim and will of all museums is to communicate their own interpretation of history, art, science or technology.[2] Nevertheless, a visit to a museum, even the quickest and most superficial, is always a dialectic process. What is exhibited – objects, ideas, stories – is the result of selection and interpretation made by those in charge of the exhibition and thus represents the culture of the museum. During a visit to a museum, this internal culture interacts with the visitors' culture. The result is that what the museum transmits is often understood, or reinterpreted, in a manner different from that intended by the transmitters, and differently from person to person.

I was engrossed by the British Galleries, which portrayed for me the history of British design, industrial production, commercial relations and architecture, which, as a palaeontologist, I knew nothing about; my knowledge being limited to the Crystal Palace built for the Universal Exhibition of 1851, and the dinosaurs created under the supervision of Richard Owen which were displayed there when the palace was transferred to Sydenham in 1854.[3] In the British Galleries I felt enveloped by the museum's desire to communicate its culture to me and, as a former museum director, I tried to understand, on a strictly professional level, which elements made my visit so pleasurable and stimulating.

A temporary or permanent museum exhibition can be analysed from many different points of view: it is possible to consider separately or jointly such matters as the subject of the exhibition, the way in which it is dealt with, the quality of the exhibits, the meanings attributed to the individual objects or to groups of objects, the quality of the information and iconographic systems, the overall style of the design and so on. However, I have chosen a point of view which goes beyond the elements I have listed – content, style, quality – and which has led me to look for the general philosophy behind the exhibition and to understand the motivation, the driving force in the museum's internal culture, the aims which led to the realisation of the exhibition and what type of relationship with the public the museum has chosen when communicating the contents of the exhibition. By relationship with the public I do not mean the choice of this or that style of communication, but where this relationship comes on a scale of values that goes from total submission of the visitor to the authority of the museum to a jovial conversation between the museum and the public, via dull, scholastic education, historical narration, the telling of tales or, finally, to the playful interaction between museum and public. I have also tried to place the galleries in relation to exhibition design in UK museums.

Not all permanent exhibitions in museums are the product of a philosophy which is in tune with the scientific and cultural tradition of the museum and its historical mission. This is only the case for those that have been planned within the museum and, consequently, express the nature of the museum. A complex museum, like the V&A, is a unity of collections and intellects which interact to create what I call the museum's culture. This is a highly dynamic force, which is specific to each institution, which makes every museum different from all others and which is transmitted through all the means of communication that it uses, first and foremost through the permanent displays. In any given museum the permanent displays are the result of its internal culture and are also the vehicle through which this culture affects society, contributing to the creation of the cultural heritage.

The creation of cultural heritage and its communication to society are the cornerstones of a museum's action. Indeed, if we consider that each object comprises two parts – its physical aspect (shape, colour, dimensions, material, etc.) and its meaning (which derives from the historical events it has experienced, the interpretation given to it, the relationship formed with those who come into contact with it, the capacity to link the present to the past, etc.) – it becomes clear that, in treating objects and their meanings in a selective fashion, the museum is not only a conserver, but above all a creator of cultural heritage. Each action the museum performs – collection, conservation, documentation, scientific study, communication – is in fact selective and, therefore, from a Darwinian point of view, creative. At this point, then, we can say that the creation of cultural heritage and its communication to society are the cornerstones of a museum's activity.

However, for the exhibition to reflect the museum's internal culture, and contribute, therefore, to the creation of heritage and the communication of its meaning, it must meet two requirements: it must be thought out and planned by the museum's academic and curatorial staff and it must be realised in close intellectual collaboration between the curators and the designers.[4] Any display or exhibition that is not designed and realised on the basis of these two premises has no tie with the museum, does not contribute to the process of creating heritage or to the process of spreading culture, the aims of which are society's cultural growth and awareness of historical and social identity.

In a book on theoretical museology published a few years ago, drawing on a text by André Malraux, the sociologist Kevin Hetherington, wrote:

the museum is a spatial relation that is principally involved in a process of ordering that takes place in or around certain sites or buildings…museums as spatial relations are not just involved in ordering and classifying cultural works and artifacts, they are also expressions of the ordering of the social.[5]

It seems clear to me that this definition of a museum closely parallels my idea of the museum as an elaborator of culture and a producer of heritage, and, coming to the subject of this essay, I am convinced that at the heart of the new British Galleries is a creative process developed within the V&A, in the long and successful Anglo-American museological tradition. However, my observation is not original; Christopher Wilk and Sarah Medlam have pointed out that the British Galleries are the result of research into the history of design and deep reflection on the objects by the museum's staff.[6] The British Galleries are then the result of the process of intellectual ordering and classification within the museum which Hetherington and Malraux consider the basis for defining the museum's cultural action. The British Galleries are also the result of the organisation of the Victoria and Albert Museum, which has made possible both the intellectual co-ordination of this research, and the creation of a cultural relationship between the curators who research and interpret the objects, and the designers who shape them into the galleries.[7]

From a museological point of view, these have been the most important elements in determining the new galleries at the V&A, as they have influenced both the contents and the exhibition design; they have guided the choice of exhibits, the relationship between objects, their arrangement, the information systems and what I would call the display route.[8]

If, excluding political constraints, there is a single reason for programming a permanent display, and that reason is society's intrinsic need to create and know its own cultural heritage – a need in which the museum acts as mediator – there are, nontheless many ways for its practical realisation.[9] Personally, I believe that a museum can choose between three different types of exhibition to communicate its culture – between three communication philosophies, each of which has a different way of interpreting and using the exhibits and a different attitude towards the visitors and their individual culture. I call these three types of exhibition the museology of wonder, rational museology and dogmatic museology.

The museology of wonder is based on the interpretation of the objects in the essentially aesthetic light of an idealistic philosophy. It tends to transport the visitor outside the realm of reality and immerse him in an aesthetically ideal universe. Such museology, the main instrument of which is seduction and the immersion of the visitor in a foreign or marvellous environment, pervades many art museums and almost all picture galleries (but also many archaeological museums) and has ancient roots. It can be traced back to cabinets of curiosity, to the *Kunst und Wunderkammern* where collections of a mixture of *artificialia* and *naturalia* were exhibited with the aim of amazing the visitors and immersing them in an unreal microcosm.[10]

Rational museology, on the other hand, does not consider the aesthetic value of the objects but interprets them instead as sources of symbolic meanings. It uses what Greenblatt calls 'resonance',[11] which makes the exhibits capable of relating the past to the present, of linking different worlds and thus of evoking events and situations.[12] Conceived for a more profoundly social use of museums, rational museology does not reveal axiomatic truths, but tries to convince the public of its theories through the use of arguments which are hard to refute. It also tries to subjugate the public with an elegant and unusually refined ambiance. This museology is typical of many modern archaeological museums and, of course, history museums.

Finally, dogmatic museology has the same desire to interpret the objects as rational museology, but with one major difference: it provides direct, axiomatic information, the truth of which is guaranteed by the intrinsic authoritativeness of the museum. Dogmatic museology does not try to convince; it clearly places the museum over and above the individual culture of the visitors. It uses communicative systems which aim to subjugate the public. It imposes its intellectual superiority, for example, by maintaining a highly specialist level of commentary, supplying an overdose of technical data or using scientific terms which are unknown to most people. Sometimes it attacks the public with methods typical of aggressive advertising – direct slogans, shocking colours and images. Typical above all of scientific museums, this museology has its roots in the principles of positivist philosophy.

It is of course difficult to demarcate the boundaries between the three exhibition philosophies, as a display or exhibition can be partly rational, partly dogmatic and partly wondrous. Furthermore, political manipulation of museums can use all three exhibition types, cutting through the boundaries between them. However, I consider this classification useful for understanding what culture a museum has developed internally and which philosophy is at the heart of its culture.

Wilk and Medlam have written that in the V&A's 1951 display of British design, 'the aim had been to present a series of "masterpieces", each set against neutral colours and plain backgrounds in the belief that they would "speak for themselves". The values were those of the world and the emphasis was firmly on the aesthetic.'[13] At that time the display was a clear example of the museology of wonder. Today the same objects are displayed in the new British Galleries in a totally different light. The aesthetics of the individual object and its artistic importance have given way to a consideration of its social and historical interpretation. The exhibits are not displayed in the new galleries so that each of them interacts individually with the public on an aesthetic level, arousing admiration for the shape, delicacy or complexity of the work. Each object is, instead, displayed in a manner that presents it as an element of the economic, social and productive history of the nation, a starting point for reconstructing the customs of British society from the sixteenth century to the end of the Victorian period, during which time Britain moved from being a net importer of luxury goods to being the 'workshop of the world'.

The museology of wonder has, then, given way to a museology which tells a story reconstructed in libraries, curators' offices and the Museum's storerooms, a story which is, of course, interpreted, and therefore partial, but which is the result of the Museum's culture, a culture which has modified the interpretation of the collections and the individual objects, and has shifted the emphasis from the aesthetic to the social, cultural and historical.

The stories told in the galleries of a museum are always conditioned by two elements: by the nature of the collections and by the interpretation of history. Since history is always interpreted on the basis of physical objects, be they artifacts or documents, the collections are the element which determines the scope of the story. Just as a museum of rural traditions, whose collections consist of agricultural tools, cannot fail to illustrate the rural life of the lower classes, so the destiny of the V&A's collections, which are the result of a selection of high-quality objects, is to tell the story of aristocratic, cultural and economic élites. This is just what has happened: in the sinuous historical and chronological display designed by Casson Mann the story of four centuries of British design and production unfolds, but only in relation to the influences these had on the customs of Britain's nobility, the gentry and in the latter parts of the gallery, the bourgeoisie. Of course this elitist story has its social limits, but it also has a clear educational and, if you like, political aim. In this the V&A has not denied its origins, its historical tradition and the mission it was assigned when it was founded.

So then, has the British Galleries an 'economic' mission, as a display of national pride and identity? Yes, but with style! Nothing in the British Galleries is exalted. There are no heroes, but there emerge groups of people and actions that contributed to the freedom and power of the nation, and also to a civilised life. No object is displayed as a single work of art either. Each element is put into context through its relationship with other exhibits, places or trends. They are all part of a display process which aims, first and foremost, to relate and interpret rather than to be artistic. Handel's statue relates to the fashion of public gardens in London, Canova's *Three Graces* introduces the idea of collectors and collecting in the Neo-classical period, while the paintings by Turner, Roberts, Redgrave and Constable, the labels for which do not over-emphasise the artists' names, are displayed as they were bought in 1857, as works by contemporary artists purchased as models for the students in the National Gallery of British Art in South Kensington.[14]

The public is prompted to discover, by following the repeated rhythm of the themes used in the galleries – *Style, Who Led Taste?, Fashionable Living, What Was New?* – by following the panels which introduce each section, by reading the texts, by using the touch screens in order to go into the subjects in depth, and by trying to do the quizzes provided on some of the showcases. The abundance of information, the sheer size of the exhibition and the thousands of exhibits on display, all invite the public to return to the Museum many times. From this point of view it is a traditional museum which I like very much, going totally against the tendency in many European museums to give in to the demands of mass tourism. While in Berlin a gallery is being built which will cross all of the Museum Insel, so that tourists who are in a hurry can see just the principal masterpieces of the city's museums, the V&A is proposing an exhibition which must be looked at, read and commented on, which does not appear didactic and which, above all, avoids spectacle, apart from that caused by the sheer beauty of the exhibits.[15] This shows a decision to distance itself from an exhibition style which was fashionable in the 1980s and 1990s, and which, in England, was adopted by important museums such as the National Maritime Museum, the Natural History Museum and the Science Museum. These adopted an aggressive style which uses the communication methods of the advertising world, the visual impact of the setting and the colourful aggressiveness of Pop Art, which strikes and stuns the spectator, simplifies concepts and treats all visitors like children and in which, in my opinion, lies the seed of cultural globalisation.

The British Galleries have been built to seduce the visitor with the beauty of the individual exhibits, each clearly the result of careful choice, but also with the exhibition's organisation and design, and with attention to detail. A new printing font has been devised for the information panels. Casson Mann have divided up the available space, creating a series of more intimate rooms, in which the visitor does not run the risk of getting lost or losing the thread. The colours, bold, but soft enough not to overwhelm the exhibits, also determine the spaces and the sequence of the story. This unfolds in a succession of showcases and display panels in which objects are mixed regardless of typologies, the only guide being the sense of the story. Classification by type has been abandoned in favour of the story; just as in reality no object is truly isolated, each is shown in relation to other objects.

I regard this as a major museological revolution, perhaps equal only to the one natural history museums were obliged to undergo after the Darwinian revolution which swept away the fixedness of the organic world and its schematic organisation, to make way for a dynamic inter-taxonomic vision of the world. In the British Galleries there is no giving in to the monumentalism or sensationalism popular with many great Continental museums which are constantly trying to attract an increasingly large public and in which, more often than not, one feels immersed in a world which is totally alien to daily life. In the British Galleries the public is invited to feel at home, it is not bombarded with continuous stimuli, it can photograph the exhibits which are monitored discreetly, and it is free to use all the information facilities devised by the Museum, without feeling guilty if it chooses not to.

Seduced by the refinement of the exhibits, the delicate balance achieved in presenting them and by the delicacy of communication, the visitors become in some way captive to the galleries. This is the Museum's subtle stratagem to impose its own interpretation of history and society, without accepting discussion from the outside world. It is true that in the British Galleries visitors are encouraged to question their sensations, to express an opinion about the exhibition, to participate in various ways, through electronic discussion pages, with writing and drawing activities, with manual activities, by wearing period costumes or answering the quizzes proposed here and there around the galleries. However, it is always the Museum which guides the games and sets the rules; the public can move intellectually, but always within the limits imposed by the Museum.

From this point of view, as far as the British Galleries are concerned, the V&A is not a Temple, neither is it a Forum, but the new exhibition is a good example of what I call rational museology.

Notes

1. Cameron, D.F., 'The Museum, a Temple or the Forum', *Curator* (1971), vol.XIV, no.1, pp. 11–24.

2. '… now, few serious museums would see themselves as anything but fora.' Augustus Casely-Hayford, 'A Way of Being: Some Reflections on the Sainsbury African Galleries', *Journal of Museum Ethnography* (March 2002), no.14, pp. 113–28.

3. Colbert, E.H., *The Great Dinosaur Hunters and Their Discoveries* (New York, 1984).

4. Curators in the sense described in *Manual of Museum Management*, by Gail Dexter Lord and Barry Lord (Walnut Creek, 1997).

5. See Hetherington, K., 'The Utopics of Social Ordering – Stonehenge as a Museum without Walls', in Macdonald S., and Fyfe, G. (eds), *Theorizing Museums* (Oxford, 1996), pp. 153–76, which draws on Malraux, A., *The Museums Without Walls: The Voices of Silence* (London, 1954), pp. 13, 128.

6. Wilk, C., and Medlam, S., 'Quatre siècles d'art britannique au Victoria and Albert Museum', *L'Estampille* (February 2002), pp. 40–47, hereafter as Wilk and Medlam.

7. The co-ordination of the various intellectual components is a fundamental process in the internal dynamics of the museum, as it is at the heart of the creation of the unitary culture. The unitary culture, in turn, determines the success or failure of the exhibitions, and therefore the validity of the museum's communication process.

8. By display route (*percorso espositivo*) I mean the realisation, in a series of successive displays, of the museum's cultural content (i.e. the organisation of an idea and its practical realisation in the museum space). The organisation of the display route underpins the whole exhibition, linking its topics in a logical sequence, thus creating the cultural message (see also Binni, L., and Pinna, G., *Museo, storia e funzioni di una macchina culturale dal cinquecento a oggi* [Milan, 1980], p. 112).

9. For an analysis of the relationship between politics and museums, see Pinna, G., 'El control político de los museos', *Experimenta* (2001), 36, pp. 111–14.

10. Flinden, P., *Possessing Nature: Museums, Collections, and Scientific Culture in Early Modern Italy* (Berkeley, 1994).

11. 'The power that the exhibit has to go beyond its own formal boundaries and assume a wider dimension, evoking in those who look at it the complex and dynamic cultural forces from which it emerged and of which the observer can consider it to be a representative sample.' Stephen Greenblatt, quoted in Karp, I., and Lavine, S.D., *Exhibiting Cultures: The Poetics and Politics of Museum Display* (Washington, 1991).

12. Pomian, C., *Collectionneurs, amateurs et curieux* (Paris, 1987).

13. Wilk and Medlam, p. 42.

14. These labels indicate the subject of the painting first, then the date, the explanation of the painting and finally the artist's name (see pp. 211–12).

15. Poor Nefertiti, twice removed from her own story! First she was taken from Tell el Amarna, her natural environment, and then from the archaeological context of the German missions, exhibited as a coherent whole in the Egyptian Museum in Charlottenbourg.

Conclusion

Christopher Wilk

The British Galleries opened on 20 November 2001, as scheduled.[1] They also opened to a chorus of positive press that went well beyond our expectations. The galleries were described as 'brilliantly intelligent', 'superbly designed', 'a triumph of curatorial ingenuity'.[2] The V&A received more press, and more positive press, than it had ever received for a single project. In the first months after the galleries were open, attendance increased four-fold.[3]

At the very beginning of the project, we had argued that the redisplay of these galleries would 'fundamentally affect the visitor's perception of the whole Museum' (see appendix 1). In 1996 that belief required a leap of faith; by November 2001 it seemed somewhat of an understatement. The British Galleries were credited with reviving the institution. Newspaper and academic press referred to the 'How the V&A came back from the brink' or that 'the V&A is now back on course'.[4] While such statements were welcome in terms of the public image of the Museum as a vital and successful institution, they gave little credit to the quality of gallery projects completed before the British Galleries and to that of the scholarly output of the Museum before 2001. The success of the British Galleries was founded on the work of Museum staff throughout the 1990s, not just in what appeared, as if a magic wand was waved, in 2001.

Indeed, it became easy to forget that controversy surrounded the project from its inception, both within the Museum and in the wider heritage sector in the UK. This was owing to the close scrutiny of the project by sections of the media and by individuals who took a keen interest in the project, many of them part of Britain's cultural establishment, and also to the forthright educational aims of the project which attracted attention because they were a departure from business as usual in the national art museum and gallery sector. From the beginning, this approach specified that the galleries would address the needs of different audiences in different ways, and that new forms of gallery interpretation, including new technology, would be seen next to objects in the galleries. Such choices were based upon a questioning of some of the most cherished premises of traditional museology and it must be said that within some sectors of the British arts world and among some in the press, this was seen during the planning stages of the galleries to be deeply threatening, even dangerous.[5] With the opening of the galleries such responses largely evaporated.

The fact that so many groups and individuals in Britain consider themselves to be stakeholders in a large national museum, that its activities are the subject of widespread discussion and that this attracts considerable press attention was, and remains, deeply gratifying as well as, at times, frustrating. Naturally, the wide range of differing opinions expressed can never be fully satisfied, but the vigour of debate can be immensely useful and stimulating and stands very much in contrast to the lack of such debate, outside of narrow museum circles, in many other countries.

Throughout the period of the design and construction of the galleries, we had turned back to our original ideas as expressed in the Development document, both as a means of checking progress and as a reminder of our original aspirations. The opening of the galleries and a subsequent period during which we could observe the public in the galleries provided us with another and perhaps more crucial opportunity to do so.

We were very pleased that most of what we had set out to accomplish was achieved – at least from our perspective – though we were frustrated by our lack of success in several specific areas (some of which have already been highlighted in previous chapters). We had hoped to provide the means by which non-English speakers could have access to gallery text through some form of audio technology. However, because the Museum did not have a building-wide audio tour of any kind – which would have provided pick-up and deposit points at the Museum's two public entrances – it proved impractical and was too expensive to have one solely for the British Galleries, which have more than a dozen points of entry. Having discovered, however, that a majority of foreign visitors to the Museum had English as a second language, we made every effort to provide video captions that were intelligible enough and which stayed on the screen long enough for non-native speakers, and we edited gallery text in the hope that it would be similarly understood.[6]

Gallery lighting, which in many parts of the gallery worked spectacularly well, especially in terms of lighting objects from different angles and at different intensities, was insufficient in certain parts of the galleries. At the point of interface between graphic and lighting design, as well as that between selection of objects and graphics, we clearly made certain mistakes which left us with some labels that are either too small or very hard to read. Some of our more cherished ideas – including the use of torches integrated into case fronts – were little used by visitors. In all of these examples, steps continue to be taken to rectify or improve the situation.

These and other inadequacies, however distressing for the team, who, naturally, tended to notice them far more than the visiting public, could not take away from the tremendous impact of the gallery on the public and on museum colleagues. And it could not diminish the ways in which the British Galleries, already by the time of opening and much more so after, were changing practice within the V&A. That the educational and interpretive elements of a gallery had to be considered from the very start, and that educators had to be involved from the beginning became standard practice. The notion of integrating interpretation has been widely accepted. The process of undertaking large, inter-departmental galleries, at least up to the time of writing, has followed that established by the British Galleries in terms of having at its core a framework document through which anyone interested could follow the ideas of the team.

As the galleries age, various elements may begin to seem very much of their time. That is a natural occurrence in museums. Changes will also inevitably be made, including the display of new objects, the insertion of entirely new displays and the replacement of interpretive elements. Through the years visitors will respond differently to galleries. Ultimately it is those responses which will decide their success or failure.

Notes

1. The project also came in just under budget. For details see chapter 5, pp. 63–4.

2. Anna Somers Cocks, 'If Architecture is the Mother of the Arts then This is the Whole Family', *Art Newspaper* (Nov. 2001), p. 11; Richard Morrison, 'If You've Got It, Flaunt It', *The Times* (16 Nov. 2001), pp. 2–3; and Richard Dorment, 'The Great British Variety Show', *Daily Telegraph* (21 November 2001), p. 20.

3. Free admission was introduced at the V&A to coincide with the opening, as it was at the end of the year by all national museums that had formerly charged (this had been an election pledge of the Labour party). While all these museums doubled their attendance, the V&A's rose far more dramatically, owing to British Galleries publicity.

4. *The Sunday Times* (18 November 2001), Culture Section, cover, and Editorial ('Overlapping Narratives: The V&A's British Galleries'), *Burlington Magazine*, vol.CXLIII, no.1184 (Nov. 2001), p. 669.

5. Joanna Pitman, 'Smile! You're Being Done Up', *The Times* (Arts Supplement, 22 July 1998, p. 23), wrote that 'the museum world is deeply divided over ... the approach ... The worry is that the galleries will be turned into a glorified theme park.' See also John Whitley, 'The V&A Team', *Daily Telegraph Magazine* (17 May 1998), p. 53. Certainly, senior members of the team had to address what seemed to be irrational fears on the part of some that the V&A was discarding

its birthright rather than addressing key problems in its displays. See also Anthony Burton, *Vision and Accident: The Story of the Victoria and Albert Museum* (London, 1999), pp. 247–48.

6. Creative Research (1997i), Audience Research for the British Galleries: Quantitative Research Findings, vol.1, pp. 27–28 and Creative Research (2002ii), Summative Evaluation of the British Galleries: Report of Research Findings, pp. 25–26.

1. Tudor gallery (58) showing the
Haynes Grange panelling sunk
into the raised gallery floor. Photo
by Derry Moore.

2. Room from Bromley-by-Bow,
1606 (gallery 58).

3. Elizabethan gallery (57)
showing the Great Bed of Ware.

4. Discovery Area (gallery 57).

5. Tudor gallery (58) showing
Achieving Splendour.

6. Tudor gallery (58) showing
Achieving Splendour.

7. Stuart gallery (56) showing **Margaret Laton's Jacket and Portrait.** *Photo by Derry Moore.*

8. Stuart gallery (56c) showing **Britain and the Indies.** *Photo by Derry Moore.*

9. Stuart gallery (56) showing **New Technical Skills.**

10. Visitor using fibre optic torch to view miniatures in the Stuart gallery (56).

11. Visitor opening drawer in the Stuart gallery (56).

12. *Stuart gallery (54) showing State Bed from Melville House, Fife, about 1700.*

13. *Stuart gallery (54) showing Stoke Edith Hanging, 1710-20.*

14. Room from Henrietta Street, London, 1732, as displayed in the British Art and Design Galleries, 1994.

15. Room from Henrietta Street, London, 1732, reinstalled 2001 (gallery 54). Photo by Derry Moore.

16. *Georgian galleries (53 and 54) showing* Rococo and Palladianism. *Photo by Derry Moore.*

17. *Georgian galleries (53 and 54) showing Roubiliac's statue of Handel, 1738. Photo by Derry Moore.*

18. Georgian gallery (52b) showing **Taking Tea,** *with video screen to right.*

19. Georgian gallery (52) showing **Portraiture** *and* **Chinoiserie.**

20. Study Area (gallery 121) with Cornelia Parker's Breathless, 2001, brass band instruments suspended on wires.

21. Film Room showing laser-cut 'linenfold' panelling.

22. Study Area (gallery 55).

23. The Music Room from Norfolk House, London, 1756, as displayed in the British Art and Design Galleries before 1995.

24. Norfolk House Music Room, reinstalled 2001. Photo by Derry Moore.

23

24

25. Georgian gallery (118) showing Neo-classicism. *Photo by Derry Moore.*

26. Georgian gallery (118) showing Robert Adam and his Rivals.

27. *Georgian gallery (118a) showing* **Entrepreneurs: Chippendale** *and* **Mr and Mrs Garrick, a Fashionable Couple.**

28. *Georgian gallery (118a) showing* **Expansion of the Export Trade.**

*29. Georgian gallery (119)
showing Canova's* **Three Graces,**
1814-17. Photo by Derry Moore.

*30. Regency gallery (120).
Sculpture of* **Bashaw,** *1832-4
with, beyond,* **Elegant Pursuits**
and **Being British.**

29

30

31. Regency gallery (120) showing **Medieval Revivals** *and* **Marketing Art and Design.**

32. Room from Lee Priory, Kent, 1794 (gallery 120). Photo by Derry Moore.

33. Victorian gallery (122) showing Gothic Revival, *including* Object in Focus *video screen next to William Burges washstand, and date set into floor.*

34. Victorian gallery (122c) showing Technological Innovations.

35. Victorian gallery (122)
showing **The Great Exhibition,
1851.**

36. Discovery Area (gallery 122b).

*37. Victorian gallery (122)
showing* **Classical and
Renaissance Revival.** *Photo by
Derry Moore.*

*38. Victorian gallery (123)
showing the model for the Albert
Memorial. Photo by Dennis
Gilbert/View.*

*39. Room from The Grove,
Harborne, Birmingham, 1878
(gallery 125). Photo by Derry
Moore.*

*40. Victorian gallery (125)
showing **Influence of Japan**.
Photo by Derry Moore.*

41. Victorian gallery (125)
showing **William Morris.**

42. Victorian gallery (125)
showing **Arts and Crafts** *and*
The Scottish School.

43. Gallery 56 in 1994.   *44. Gallery 56 (Stuart gallery) in 2003.*

45. Store adjacent to gallery 118, 1996.

46. The same space (gallery 118a) 2003.

45

46

47. *Sketch for* **Protecting Possessions** *(gallery 56), by Dinah Casson, spring 2000.*

48. *Full-size paper templates for trial layout of* **Protecting Possessions,** *spring 2001.*

49. *CAD drawing of* **Protecting Possessions,** *showing changes made after templating exercise, May 2001.*

50. *Stuart gallery (56) showing* **Protecting Possessions.** *February 2003.*

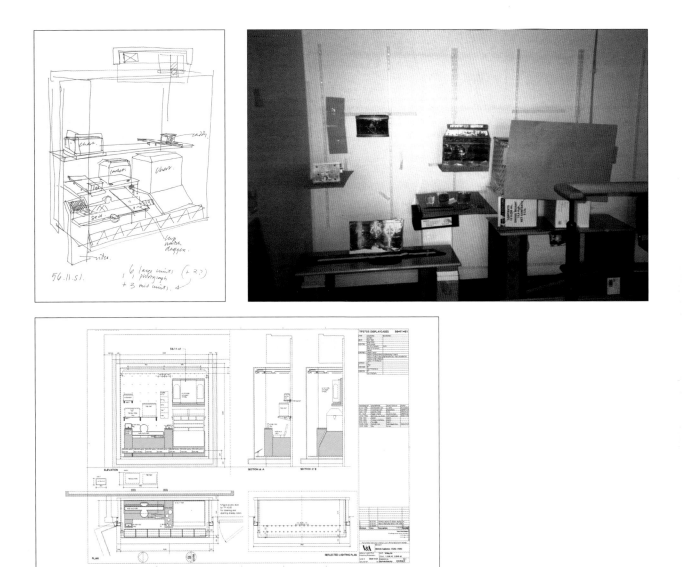

51. *Watercolour sketch for* **The Grand Tour** *and* **Neo-Classicism,** *by Dinah Casson, spring 2000.*

52. *Photograph inside scale model showing Georgian gallery (118).*

53. *CAD drawing of Georgian gallery (118), showing* **The Grand Tour,** *1999.*

54. *Georgian gallery (118) from the doorway showing* **The Grand Tour** *and* **Neo-classicism.**

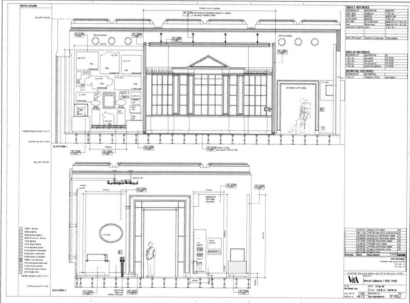

55. Watercolour sketch for Tudor gallery (58) showing early version of The Court of Henry VIII, by Dinah Casson, spring 2000.

56. Watercolour sketch for Discovery Area (gallery 52), by Dinah Casson, spring 2000.

57. Watercolour sketch for Georgian gallery (118) showing **Entrepreneurs: Wedgwood** *and* **Boulton,** *by Dinah Casson, spring 2000.*

58. Watercolour sketch for Study Area (gallery 55), by Dinah Casson, spring 2000.

59. Watercolour sketch for Victorian gallery (122) showing **The Great Exhibition,** *by Dinah Casson, spring 2000.*

60. Visitors using **Wear a Ruff** *activity in the Discovery Area (gallery 57), spring 2002.*

61. Visitors using **Construct a three-legged armchair** *activity in the Discovery Area (gallery 58), spring 2002.*

62. Visitor using **Handling Collection** *in Stuart gallery (56).*

63. Model of Chiswick House in Georgian gallery (54), autumn 2001.

60

61

62

63

64. Visitor listening to **Talking about Art** *audio featuring sculpture of the dog Bashaw in the Regency gallery (120).*

65. Visitor using a **Style Guide** *in Victorian gallery (122), spring 2004.*

66. Visitors using computer interactives in the Study Area (55), spring 2002.

67. Visitor using **Write a Mini-Saga** *activity in Discovery Area (57), 2000.*

66

64

67

65

68. *Tudor gallery (58). The walls are painted a strong ochre yellow. Against these, the objects in* **Renaissance** *are shown against red polished plaster. The colour is continued in the case with a background of powder-coated metal matched in colour to the plaster.*

69. *Elizabethan panelling in the Spenser Room at Canons Ashby. Its painted decoration gave us a visual source for the ochres and reds so often listed in contemporary documents. Country Life Picture Library.*

70. Georgian gallery (118). The Grand Tour, *including plaster casts purchased by the architect Decimus Burton, some possibly from the collection bought in Italy by Robert Adam. Photo by Derry Moore.*

71. J. Zoffany, *Charles Townley and his Friends, 1781-3. Townley Hall Art Gallery and Museum, Burnley, Lancashire. Bridgeman Art Library.*

72. Victorian gallery (122). **French Style,** *showing the striking contrast between a strong yellow and an equally strong red, here given depth with a stippled finish.*

73. *The idea for this striking contrast was taken from a colour scheme for the Octagon Drawing Room at Raby Castle, Co. Durham, that survives from the 1840s. Country Life Picture Library.*

74. *Temporary* **Best of British** *gallery, 1999*

75. *Temporary* **Best of British** *gallery, 1999.*

76. *Temporary* **Best of British** *gallery, showing trial for gallery colour schemes, 1999.*

77. *Temporary* **Best of British** *gallery, showing prototype* **Spot the Difference** *activity, 1999.*

Appendices

Appendix 1
Development of the British Galleries
May 1996

Christopher Wilk, Sarah Medlam and Gail Durbin

Introduction These galleries cover two floors of the Museum on the south and west fronts. Their re-display will significantly affect the visitor's perception of the whole Museum and their successful completion will consolidate the work that the Museum has undertaken in recent years on the galleries of Asian cultures and such projects as the Glass and Silver galleries.

Central Idea The galleries will present art and design in Britain from 1500 to 1900, using the V&A's uniquely rich and extensive collections and the Museum's expertise in interpreting them. As the area covered by these galleries is equivalent itself to a moderately-sized museum, there will be variety in interpretation and design, to maintain interest and excitement, and in order to allow us to address the needs of different museum audiences. The galleries must reflect in their own elegance and careful design the high quality of the objects displayed.

We intend to provide experiences by which as many as possible of the Museum's visitors can have a real sense of involvement with the national collection of design and art. The Museum was founded with an overtly educational aim. Though many of our visitors now come to the Museum in their leisure time, learning is no less part of their experience, and the new displays must support their understanding and enjoyment of this great public collection.

Themes Within the chronological arrangement of the galleries a framework of three themes will allow the vast complexity of the subject of design and art in Britain to be approached by as many as possible of our visitors. It is intended that the themes should provide an overall structure and intellectual consistency to the galleries. They are: (1) Style, (2) Taste, (3) Innovation.

Examples of subjects within the themes might be: [Style] the influence of Italy and the Low Countries on the Tudor Court, the historical revivals in the Victorian period; [Taste] the influence of the court in the 17th century and of the private client in the 18th; and [Innovation] the influence of drawing schools in the mid-18th century, and the impact of machinery on mass-production in the 19th century.

It is recognized that no series of themes can be comprehensive but those listed above address some of the key issues raised by the V&A's wide-ranging collection and by consideration of the history of design itself. A separate paper on themes will be produced.

Audiences We have identified the following audiences for this display:
– Independent adult visitors/learners
– Specialists and amateur enthusiasts
– Students in further and higher education
– The local community
– Foreign visitors
– Minority groups
– Schools
– Families

These are not listed in order of priority and membership of the groups will overlap. The list is a long one because of the size of the project; in a smaller gallery we might have chosen one or two target audiences. It seemed that in this project the Museum had an important opportunity to address a wide range of its visitors.

We do not intend to have specific galleries for schools or students, for example, but we plan to select certain areas of the collection which might be of particular interest to specific audiences, and to ensure that the interpretation and display methods used for these areas are chosen with such audiences in mind and will serve their needs. The targeting of particular displays need not preclude their use by other visitors - we aim to be inclusive rather than exclusive.

Each audience will be addressed specifically several times within the run of galleries. Throughout the displays we will pay attention to the different ways visitors learn from museums, so that the traditional dominance of text in displays is varied with opportunities to undertake activities in relation to objects (see below

Interpretive methods'), to listen, or simply to absorb the atmosphere of displays.

The question of audiences and interpretive techniques suitable for those different audiences is a complex one and we recognize that research on this subject must continue as part of the planning of these galleries, and that continuing review of our success in understanding these needs and responding to them will underpin the planning of all future projects in the Museum.

Interpretive Principles The galleries will be arranged chronologically and by theme within that sequence. The team have discussed other options but believe that abandoning chronology would be perverse and would deprive our audiences of an important method of orientating themselves within such a long run of galleries.

Themes will be repeated in slightly different forms, using different subjects, at various points in the galleries.

The displays should make clear the subjective decisions which have been made in the course of planning the displays, eg, in relation to the choice of objects or the appearance of period rooms. We want our approach to be clear to the visitor.

The galleries must be educationally effective. Visitors seek information, explanation or participation to give value to their visit.

These galleries will consciously seek to direct interested visitors to other galleries in the Museum, as well as other sites and institutions where they may follow up specialist interests.

Strategies for dealing with non-English speaking visitors must be developed.

Design Principles The galleries should be visually exciting; some parts should be beautiful, even glamorous. The galleries are sufficiently large to encompass variety in terms of design as well as of interpretation.

Whilst we see variety as central to this scheme, the design must maintain cohesion and continuity. Graphic style will be one of the major devices which will be used to do this.

Axial vistas will be developed to lead the visitors through the galleries, although period rooms will limit these in certain areas.

Though listed building regulations must be adhered to, an over-reverential attitude to the interior architecture of the building is undesirable and would amount to cowardice.

Storage areas adjacent to these galleries will be considered as part of the scheme, to house plant for the galleries and as part of the display areas where appropriate.

Parts of the displays will be evocative and mood-inducing, encouraging an emotional response as well as a strictly intellectual one.

The pace of the galleries should vary.

It should not be assumed that visitors will follow a prescribed route or that they will visit all of these galleries at one time. There are currently many ways to join these galleries from elsewhere in the Museum and there are likely to be more. Every entrance will have orientation devices that will make clear where you are, what the subject of the gallery is and possible routes. Plans will be orientated at each point to take account of the physical viewpoint of the visitor in relationship to the galleries.

With tourist-visitors likely to form a large audience for these galleries, it will be necessary to create the possibility of quick tours, linking highlights of the collection.

Where possible objects will be on open display.

We should explore opportunities to allow objects to be viewed in the round. Objects displayed on open plinths must be at least an arm's length away from visitors

Where possible labels should be next to the object that they describe; if this proves impossible, then numbers (or a similarly effective means) should be used. It should not be assumed that visitors will easily follow schematic layouts of labels related to the physical relationship of objects in a display.

Period rooms will be treated in a variety of ways and where possible visitors will be able to walk through them. We must give them back a sense of architectural integrity which was lost when they were installed as three-sided stage sets.

Designers must consider how change can be effected in the galleries. We wish to create within the run of galleries small changing display/temporary exhibition areas (possibly 2-4), as well as having the ability to change objects, themes or display areas within the permanent exhibitions.

Elements of massed display (for appropriate themes) may be considered as a means to add variety to the galleries.

Space should be allocated for some sort of seminar room or studio space adjacent to these galleries, and for a performance space within the galleries.

No area should be created that excludes people with physical disabilities. Guidelines will be drawn up for the designers covering physical access, the provision of graphics and related concerns.

Since many guided tours and student groups will use these galleries, space will be required in front of some of the displays so groups can discuss the objects.

Care must be taken in the design of audio-visual methods of interpretation that noise does not form a distraction to other visitors in the galleries

All interpretive facilities should be integrated into the gallery design, so that all such techniques are potentially available to all visitors. Planning for the use of e.g. tape, film, slides, should make provision for full upkeep of such facilities once the galleries are opened, including the replacement of such material at appropriate or necessary times in the 25-year life of the galleries

Visitor facilities Seating will be provided throughout the galleries. Some areas will be designed specifically for visitors to rest, away from the displays.

We would like to consider a small café within the run of galleries.

We would like lavatories to be provided in these galleries.

Two new lifts will be installed to provide access to all floors within the Aston Webb building. A new staircase should also be considered.

Interpretive Methods We will be producing an interpretive plan. The following methods will be amongst those suggested as appropriate, some throughout the galleries, some in selected areas:

– graphic panels and object labels

– computer programmes, including databases and access to the Collections Information System, which will be in course of development during the lifetime of this project

– other computer programmes which will encourage the interpretation of the object, including games, quizzes and computer-aided design programmes

– a facility to print out from such programmes, though the facility might be centralised, rather than being available in all galleries

– models, including touch models for the blind and partially sighted, to explain, e.g. architectural concepts

– portable label books or bats with larger print (mainly for partially-sighted visitors)

– printed support material (e.g. catalogues, information sheets, magazines, books, bibliographies)

– audio tours or information about specific displays or for specific audiences

– videos, films and slide presentations

– simple interactive devices in addition to computers

– handling collections

– discovery areas

– staff in the galleries dedicated to interpretation

Appendix 2
Themes for British Art and Design 1500-1900: An Overview.
16 October 1996

John Styles

Issues In order to establish themes, it is necessary to consider the purpose of the British Art and Design galleries. In contrast to the materials and techniques galleries, the art and design galleries aim to provide a general overview or interpretation of design and the decorative arts in the period concerned. A run of galleries conceived in these terms is best thought of as a sequence of objects that articulates a set of general propositions and arguments about the period, in the manner of an interpretative essay or text. It should not take the form of an in-depth investigation of the problems of object-based study, along the lines of a research monograph or an academic dissertation, nor should it be a succession of art and design 'greatest hits', lacking any coherence other than the celebrity of the objects.

That said, it should be borne in mind that the V&A's collections consist of what a variety of people over the last century and a half – consumers, collectors, curators – have considered to be the best in their field. It is important that British Art and Design represent and explore these notions of excellence. In pursuing this objective, one useful device is to consider the period from the point of view of the 'historical anthropologist'. People today do not necessarily understand why objects were considered beautiful (or otherwise) in periods before the twentieth century. The assumptions behind past cultures were very different from our own and require exploration and elaboration in the display.

If we are to fulfil the confidence that users place in the Museum as an institution of international standing, it is important that British Art and Design is informed by innovative, up-to-date approaches to material culture between 1500 and 1900. To do this, careful consideration needs to be given to the context, meaning, and significance (aesthetic and historical) of the objects selected. Relevant issues here include patterns of consumption, contemporary attitudes to material culture, manufacturing techniques and innovations, and aesthetic debates. To facilitate this process of contextualisation without over-reliance on lengthy labels/panels, the displays should juxtapose objects in such a way that visual distinctions above and beyond the stylistic are emphasised. The right objects carefully juxtaposed can articulate differences in the aesthetic and monetary values that were attached to objects, in the techniques employed to manufacture them, and in the social background of those who consumed them. The objects in the V&A have not been assembled as a social history collection , and the number and range of non-élite objects the Museum holds is limited. Nevertheless, where available, non-élite objects can be useful in such juxtapositions, helping, for example, to explain those notions of 'the best' at work in the period in visual terms.

As one of the world's leading museums of design and the decorative arts, the V&A has the intellectual resources and authority to offer a challenging and innovative interpretation of British art and design in the post-medieval era; an interpretation that is multifaceted but coherent, original but accessible. If visitors to the new galleries are to make the most of them, it is essential that a statement is provided of the organising principles that inform them and an explanation offered of why the objects have been chosen.

The core team has decided that the galleries should present a chronological narrative of the history of British art and design between 1500 and 1900. A narrative implies a story. If we embrace the 'interpretative text' analogy outlined above, then the galleries should offer a broad narrative woven from a limited number of themes that run right through the sequence of rooms. After all, this is precisely how general histories and textbooks are written. Although a gallery differs in many ways from a book, these narrative elements remain crucial for constructing an intellectually coherent and historically convincing story, irrespective of whether it is articulated through text or objects.

One inevitable consequence flows from the core team's decision to organise the galleries chronologically. In representing the new galleries to our colleagues and to the world (to sponsors, to government, to critics, to scholars, and to many, although not all, visitors) we shall need to provide a reasonably clear and succinct account of the story we are telling. In many of its details, that overall story will emerge only as the three chronological teams do their work. Nevertheless, it would be foolish to ignore:

(i) that by selecting our three themes, we have already begun to tell a certain kind of story (eg. one that will not simply be a sequence of 'greatest hits'), and that by choosing a chronological approach we are compelled to address certain kinds of questions (eg. what distinguished any period within the sequence from what came before and after? what changed and what remained the same?)

(ii) that each of the three chronological teams will need to consult with the core team on what the themes mean and how their interpretation of the themes relates to the interpretations being developed by the teams dealing with earlier or later periods.

Themes　The three broad themes that the core team has chosen are (i) Style, (ii) Taste and the Consumer, and (iii) Design and Product Innovation. These three can comprehend many of the pivotal issues that have emerged in recent studies (particularly object-based studies) of art and design in the period, without entirely abandoning the style-based approach which was the intellectual foundation of the existing British Art and Design Galleries. They also provide a vehicle for addressing the key questions of geographical and chronological specificity which arise in any 'interpretative text' dealing with art and design in a particular country and at a particular time. What was distinctively British in any particular period during the overall sequence? What distinguished one period from what happened before and after? What changed and what remained the same in the course of a period? How do we use objects to articulate the analytical and didactic problems presented by a period? The themes are intended to serve first and foremost as ways of organising thinking about the galleries. Not every element of each theme will necessarily translate into an individual object or a particular section of the display. Nevertheless, all the issues addressed make a contribution to a coherent understanding of art and design in the period and should inform the broad conception of the sequence as a whole.

The chosen themes are intended to be as broad and accommodating as possible. Nevertheless, their presence does impose certain disciplines on the gallery teams. Most obviously, it requires the teams to think carefully about how individual objects and topics fit into the themes and hence into the broad conceptual sweep of the galleries. It should be recognised that the very existence of a limited number of themes restricts the opportunities to introduce objects and topics into the displays simply for their own sake.

What does the title of each theme mean? I think the best way I can clarify (i) the meaning of the themes, (ii) the relationship between individual topics and themes, and (iii) a sense of the overall story we are telling is to provide a brief sketch of the key narrative elements for each theme that characterise the period 1500 to 1900; in other words an outline of the main overarching developments.

1. Style　The notion of style is, of course, a familiar one to those who work in the Museum as a means of categorising the way objects look. Style is crucially concerned with questions of form and ornamentation. The theme raises difficult problems regarding how much we should use established terms of art (Mannerism, Baroque, Rococo, Arts and Crafts, etc.), and the balance between telling the conventional story (itself not necessarily familiar to many visitors) and subverting it.
The story:
i. The adoption and Anglicisation of classicism in a variety of guises
ii. Increasingly powerful reactions to and against classicism, leading to its being partially discredited in the nineteenth century
iii. A persisting and unresolved tension between the impulse for ever more demanding stylistic authenticity and the functional demands of the world

2. Taste and the Consumer　The most difficult theme to define, but essentially one that embraces two distinct, though related elements – (a) the changing sources of aesthetic authority (ie. who decided what was considered good or appropriate in art and design), and (b) the changing patterns of living from which designed objects derived their utility and much of their meaning.
The story:

i. A shift (always partial, never complete) in the sources of aesthetic authority away from the Court, the Church and the private patron towards 'civil society' – ie. a wider range of people and institutions (which included critics/writers/periodicals, manufacturing and retail businesses, professional designers, and cultural institutions like the Royal Academy, the Schools of Design, or the South Kensington Museum)
ii. A progressive refinement of domestic (but also to some extent public) life and its material culture, embracing:
(a) the spread and progressive reworking of notions of polite behaviour derived from Renaissance courtly culture (this relates closely to Norbert Elias's concept of long-term changes in behaviour which he characterised as the 'Civilising Process')
(b) an accompanying redefinition and elaboration of what constituted comfort
(c) a huge expansion in the sheer diversity of object types

3. Design and Product Innovation

Again innovation is a reasonably familiar notion, embracing the questions of what was new and how was novelty introduced? For the purposes of the British Art and Design Galleries we can think about this theme in two (related) ways – (a) in terms of products, or (b) in terms of the design process
(a) The pattern of product innovation.
The story:
i. The flow of new products from overseas, initially mainly from continental Europe, but increasingly from the extra-European world
ii. The process of import substitution that turned England/Britain from a country that at the start of the sixteenth century imported a large proportion of the high design goods it consumed to one that by the nineteenth century not only produced most of its own, but exported an enormous range of such goods
iii. The growing importance of native inventiveness, culminating in Britain's role as workshop of the world
(b) The pattern of design innovation.
The story:
i. Designs – from the imported printed design image to the specialist design publication
ii. Designers – From the apprenticed craftsperson and the immigrant designer-maker to the trained design professional

Appendix 3
The Story of the British Galleries 1500-1900
April 1997

John Styles

The new British Galleries at the V&A tell the story of an extraordinary transformation in the history of art and design. At the end of the Middle Ages Britain played a peripheral role in the affairs of Europe. The great centres of European art and culture, of wealth and power, lay to the south and to the east. It was places like Venice and Florence, Antwerp and Paris that dominated European art, not London. Britain, after all, was merely an island on the edge of the world as it was then known to Europeans. It was in 1492 that Columbus landed in the Americas; it was in 1498 that Vasco da Gama reached India by sea. Four centuries later, in Queen Victoria's reign, everything had changed. Britain was the workshop of the world. Its queen ruled over a vast empire that spread around the globe. London was rivalled only by Paris as an international centre of art and culture. Everywhere British artists and British designers were admired and copied. The objects they created were used and displayed throughout the world.

In the new galleries, objects from every collection in the Museum develop the story of this long journey which took Britain from the margins of artistic affairs to their very core. This long and sustained development encompassed much more than the traditional fine arts of painting and sculpture. It embraced the visual arts in all their rich diversity, from furniture to fabrics, from prints to porcelain. It may only have been at the end of this transformation, in the nineteenth century, that British art and design achieved universal acclaim, but at every step along the way the British created works of art that were beautiful, original, and influential. Among these are some of the most famous objects in the Museum's collections – the late-sixteenth century Great Bed of Ware (c.1590), the Roubiliac figure of Handel (1759), George Gilbert Scott's model for the Albert Memorial (c.1863) – but the Museum holds a host of other significant objects that are less familiar, and in some cases almost unknown. The new galleries mix the famous with the unexpected, juxtapose the native and the foreign, and intermingle materials and forms – glass with textiles, furniture with dress. Through displays that combine and contrast remarkable objects in original ways, the galleries capture the sheer scale and excitement of the transformation that took place in British art and design between 1500 and 1900.

The point of departure for the development of the new galleries has been the objects in the Museum's collections. Vast as their numbers are, they impose limitations. They represent objects which a variety of people in the past – consumers, collectors, curators – have considered to be the best in their field. Over the past century and a half the Museum has collected Spitalfields silk gowns, not homespun linen aprons; marquetry cabinets, not plain cottage tables; silver tea services, not wooden plates. Consequently, the focus of the new displays is on high design and the decorative arts, reflecting the V&A's collecting policy over most of its history. These galleries should not and cannot present a broad history of Britain, its peoples and their material life, however much the Museum's objects are implicated in that wider history. Nevertheless, if the galleries strive to present the best work in British art and design across four centuries, that is not to say they have been conceived simply as a sequence of 'greatest hits'. The galleries seek to explain how the range and appearance of objects changed, and to explore why some objects were considered more beautiful than others. To achieve this goal, they necessarily invoke many aspects of a wider British history, including religion and war, empire and industrial revolution.

Like any good story, the account of British art and design offered by the new galleries is constructed around a limited number of narrative themes. The three themes chosen – style, taste and innovation – reflect abiding concerns in art and design scholarship. At the same time they incorporate stimulating new ideas, many of them developed at the V&A, that have transformed our understanding of high design objects over the last twenty years.

The intellectual underpinning of the previous British Art and Design galleries at the Museum was provided by the history of style alone. The new galleries supplement style with other themes, but they continue to demonstrate how the prevailing look of high design objects changed in terms of form and ornament. The story is narrated in new and sometimes unfamiliar ways, laying stress on issues of foreign influence and British response. At its heart is the slow process whereby Classicism, a term which combined the forms and ornament used in the Italian Renaissance with those of ancient Rome and Greece, was adopted in Britain, and slowly became absorbed into British design, to be constantly used and re-interpreted. The triumph of a refined and distinctively British Classicism that is apparent in many Hanoverian objects and buildings eventually provoked a powerful reaction. As a consequence, Classicism was partially rejected in the nineteenth century, as designers and artists experimented with a whole range of stylistic alternatives, ranging from Pugin's revitalised Gothic to the Arts and Crafts style.

Interwoven with the history of style is a history of taste. The story of taste as developed in the new galleries has two distinct but related elements. One is the story of what in the eighteenth century were termed the 'legislators of taste' – the people and institutions that had the power to shape prevailing ideas of what was beautiful and desirable. The centuries from 1500 to 1900 saw a shift (always partial, never complete) in the sources of this aesthetic authority away from the monarch, the Court, the Church and the private patron towards a wider range of people and institutions, including critics, professional designers, manufacturers, retailers, and cultural institutions like museums, design schools and even public exhibitions. The galleries trace this shift through the objects used and promoted by the 'legislators of taste', from the tapestries produced by James I's royal manufactory at Mortlake in the early seventeenth century to the individual and sometimes extraordinary exhibition pieces specially made by firms to be displayed at the international exhibitions of the later nineteenth century.

The other element of the history of taste developed in the new galleries is the story of how high design objects changed the ways the British lived. New forms of religious observance, new ways of eating, new modes of entertainment all required specific kinds of objects, whether they be the English-language Bibles that accompanied the Reformation, the new-fangled knives and forks that appeared on the tables of the fashionable in the seventeenth century, or Francis Hayman's paintings of the 1740s which graced the supper boxes at Vauxhall Gardens. The period covered by the galleries witnessed a progressive refinement of both domestic and public life, with the spread of new and often more demanding standards of behaviour, and an elaboration of ideas of comfort. Almost every manifestation of this growing refinement entailed the use and display of highly decorated objects.

The third theme that runs through the new galleries is that of innovation. Between the sixteenth century and the nineteenth century, objects that were new or unfamiliar cascaded into the possession of British patrons, collectors and consumers in wave after wave of what economists term product innovation. There was a veritable explosion in the variety and range of artefacts available in Britain. The galleries tell the story of this tide of innovation, showing the objects themselves, exploring their origins, and considering the ways new objects and new designs were introduced. The galleries identify those novelties that came from overseas, in the sixteenth century mainly from continental Europe, like Venetian glass and German stoneware, but later increasingly from the extra-European world, with the arrival of Indian printed cottons and Chinese porcelain. They trace the process that turned Britain from a country importing a large proportion of the high design goods it consumed at the start of the sixteenth century to one that by the nineteenth century not only produced most of its own, but itself exported an enormous range of such goods. They emphasise the growth in importance of that native British inventiveness which culminated in Britain's nineteenth-century reputation as the workshop of the world.

In combination, these three themes of style, taste and innovation enable the new galleries to identify the differences between one historical period and another, and between Britain and other parts of the world, without doing an injustice to the abundance and diversity of the objects themselves. It is a narrative that distinguishes what was distinctively British about British art and design, while demonstrating the ways that 'Britishness' was constructed, more often than not, by the creative adaptation of objects and visual ideas that originated elsewhere. It is a narrative that allows the visitor access to a sophisticated understanding of how the look of objects changed, decade by decade, reign by reign. Above all, it is a narrative that captures the grand historical sweep of British art and design in all its richness, from the strivings after magnificence of the Tudors and Stuarts and the mannered gentility of the Hanoverians, to the Victorians' struggle with the opportunities and pitfalls of their new-found material abundance.

The list below shows how each of the displays in the new British Galleries falls under one of the four gallery themes.

Tudor and Stuart Britain, 1500-1714

STYLE
Renaissance, 1500-1600
Jacobean, 1600-1625
Restoration, 1660-1685
Baroque, 1685-1725

WHO LED TASTE?
The Court of Henry VIII, 1509-1547
The Church, 1500-1660
The Court of Elizabeth I, 1558-1603
The Court, 1603-1649
The Nobility, 1660-1720

FASHIONABLE LIVING
Achieving Splendour, 1500-1600
The Bromley-by-Bow Room
Birth, Marriage and Death, 1500-1700
Heraldry, 1500-1600
The Great Bed of Ware
The Dacre Beasts
Dressing for Magnificence, 1600-1630
Imported Luxuries, 1600-1660
The Civil War Years, 1639-60
Protecting Possessions, 1600-1700
Textiles in the Home, 1600-1700
Britain and the Indies, 1660-1720
James II's Wedding Suit
Propaganda and Commemoration, 1660-1714

WHAT WAS NEW?
Skills from Europe, 1500-1600
The Book, 1500-1600
Sheldon Tapestries, 1570-1625
New Forms of Furniture, 1650-1700
Marquetry, 1650-1700
New Technical Skills, 1660-1710
Printed Sources of Design, 1600-1710
Developments in Ceramics, 1600-1710
The Upholsterer as Interior Designer, 1660-1710

Hanoverian Britain, 1714-1837

STYLE:
Palladianism, 1715-1760
Henrietta Street Room
Rococo, 1730-1760
Chinoiserie, 1750-1765
The Badminton Bed
Neo-Classicism, 1760 -1790
Regency Classicism, 1800-1830
Chinese and Indian Styles, 1800-1830
Medieval Revivals, 1780-1830
Lee Priory Room

WHO LED TASTE?
Aristocratic Patrons: the Norfolk House Music Room
Robert Adam and his Rivals, 1770-1790
Entrepreneurs: Wedgwood, Boulton, Chippendale

Horace Walpole, the Collector
Thomas Hope

FASHIONABLE LIVING
Public Entertainments, 1730-1760
Taking Tea, 1710-1760
Spitalfields Silk, 1710-1770
Portraiture
The Grand Tour
Eating and Drinking, 1760-1830
Mr and Mrs Garrick, a Fashionable Couple
The Expanding Export Trade, 1760-1830
The Private Sculpture Gallery, 1780-1830
Being British
Elegant Pursuits
Marketing Art and Design
William Beckford, the Collector

WHAT WAS NEW?
Developments in the Ceramics Industry, 1720-1765
Developments in the Metal Trades, 1740-1840
The Textile Printing Industry, 1760-1840

Victorian Britain, 1837-1901

STYLE:
Gothic Revival, 1830-1880
French Style, 1835-1880
Classical and Renaissance Revival, 1850-1915
Aestheticism, 1870-1900
The Influence of Japan, 1850-1900
Influences of Other Cultures, 1840-1900: India, the Islamic world, China
Room from the Grove, Harborne
Arts and Crafts, 1860-1910
The Scottish School, 1885-1915

WHO LED TASTE?
The Church, 1840-1900
The Great Exhibition, 1851
International Exhibition Pieces
Henry Cole and the Founders of the V&A
The National Gallery of British Art at South Kensington
Advertising Posters
William Morris

FASHIONABLE LIVING
Celebration and Commemoration
Antique Collecting
The Expanding Wardrobe
Eating and Drinking, 1870-1910
Birth, Marriage and Death, 1850-1900
Decorating the Home, 1870-1910

WHAT WAS NEW?
Technological Innovations, 1850-1900
Photography
The Book in the Age of Mass Production
Protecting New Designs
The Freelance Designer: Christopher Dresser
Training for Designers

Target Audiences for the British Galleries
1996
Gail Durbin

Audience	Characteristics	Implications for gallery content and design
Independent Learners Covers a wide range of people, including the casual visitor	Self-directed learning is: - managed as far as is possible by the learner - draws on the learner's own experiences, cultural background and interests - is problem-centred - is motivated by internal incentives and curiosity.	We need to review normal museum practice, which: - is expert-directed and creates dependence on the expert - takes no account of differences in prior knowledge and experience of the visitors - designs displays that take no account of interest that is for a practical purpose related to the rest of their lives.
	Learners see their fields of interest as unending intellectual voyages, not restricted by museum subject boundaries.	We cannot say 'We are not a social history museum' or 'We are not a fine art museum', because to the learner we are whatever he/she chooses to make us.
	Learners may look for breadth as well as depth in the additional information provided.	We need a choice of routes through the information, including leading learners to ideas and information elsewhere inside and outside the institution.
		We may need study areas.
		We need staff in the galleries with an understanding of learning needs and of how to access further information.
	Learners see themselves as part of a larger learning community, where independent learning does not mean isolation. Word of mouth and networks form an important source for these people.	We could develop the concept of a notice board (virtual or actual) for the sharing of information and ideas stimulated by the displays.
Families	Families arrive in groups of 2–6 people. Children are generally in the 0–13 age range, with older ones preferring to go off on their own. Accompanying adults may be grandparents rather than parents. At the Science Museum typically a family group is 1:1.	We need to include objects and interpretative methods that appeal to children.
		We need to design galleries to allow access for pushchairs.
		We need to present some displays at a very low level. We could include items that can be discovered by opening doors or peering through small spaces. Low-level technology and low-cost interactives do not necessarily mean low-level learning.
	Families value the opportunity for social interaction and for active participation and appreciate being in comfortable surroundings. They want to spend leisure time together on a worthwhile pursuit. Adults articulate a need for children to be occupied all the time.	We need displays that encourage conversation between adult and child.
	The parking, café and shop will be as important as displays in contributing to a good family experience.	We need to ensure that promotional literature on the galleries stresses all the ancillary facilities.

Audience	Characteristics	Implications for gallery content and design
	Children from early years learn principally through direct experience, physical action and play.	We need displays that encourage activity and participation.
	The needs of the child to explore a new place takes precedence over any chance to indulge a sustained interest of the part of the adults. The child generally drives the visit, going from one object that attracts him/her to another in a random manner. The adult uses the displays and labels to ask and answer questions.	We should use simple text that allows adults to scan text quickly for information and ideas to be assimilated rapidly for use in conversation. We need to include labels that ask questions.
	Adults like being provided with ideas and suggestions for activities or discussion with their children. If adults do not know the answers, they are liable to make them up.	We should avoid labels that contain isolated facts about individual objects and seek instead to encourage visitors to respond to displays, to find relationships between objects and to create their own meanings, related to their own lives and experiences.
	Complex, overarching conceptual structures are likely to be missed.	
	Different activities sometimes require different behaviours.	We should consider which activities should be integrated with the displays and which should be separated.
Foreign visitors There is a lack of research in this area.	Look for a pleasurable and entertaining activity and share some of characteristics of independent learners.	
	Want to see examples of British culture	
	May want to go round quickly and want some guidance on key items.	We should find a way of offering a rapid tour of the highlights.
	May have sore feet and be tired from seeing too many sights.	We should provide seating.
	May have a limited grasp of English.	Every message should as far as possible be presented through the objects.
		We should ensure that text is simple with one idea in each sentence and no complex clauses or obscure vocabulary.
	May have little knowledge of British history and will be unable to name monarchs or periods in history.	We should avoid terms such as Hanoverian or Victorian.
	May have an entirely different educational and cultural background, which could lead them to draw unintended conclusions from the display. May be offended by some ideas/items.	We need to consult and look for cultural differences that may lead to misunderstandings and adapt plans as necessary.

Audience	Characteristics	Implications for gallery content and design
Local community	Want to make repeat visits.	We need to include elements that encourage repeat visits; these could be temporary exhibits or changing elements built into permanent displays.
	May make short visits.	We should provide ways of focusing on single objects or groups of objects.
	May make visits with family or guests. If guests, then much of their energy on visit may be devoted to maintaining social relations and little to the displays.	We should think about designing the space to encourage the social elements of visits.
	Want to see items close up, and from every angle.	We should consider display techniques or the use of video.
	Want to handle objects.	Any handling of material in the gallery is likely to be inadequate for these purposes. We should offer this service away from the gallery.
		We could relate service to open storage.
	Want to see masterpieces.	
	Want to see many variants of the same object.	We should consider typological displays of some objects. We could refer visitors to the Materials and Techniques Galleries.
	Do not need general background information, but need specific information about individual objects.	We could provide access to the computer database of collections.
Minority communities	Visitors from Hong Kong, the Indian subcontinent and the Caribbean will be the most significant groups.	We should consider grouping objects from, or designs influenced by, China and India rather than scattering them throughout the galleries, in order to make more impact and to facilitate guided tours.
	May not speak English as their first language.	We need to ensure that text is simple, with one idea in each sentence and no complex clauses or obscure vocabulary.
		Meanings should as far as possible be presented through the objects themselves.
	May not share the cultural assumptions of the majority population.	There is a risk that that the gallery is seen as too Eurocentric. Consultation is needed in this area.
Further/higher education	Arrive in groups but may not stay together.	We need to provide space for groups, guided tours, sitting and talking.
		We need space for drawing.
	Curriculum-led (art colleges, theatre studies course, vocational courses, design history, social history, English literature). The boundary between FE and HE is no longer so rigid, and numbers from FE are significantly larger than from HE.	We need to research courses.

Audience	Characteristics	Implications for gallery content and design
	But the range of ability levels is now very great in a period of mass higher education, so that those following highly academic courses a smaller proportion than previously. Some 16-year-olds in FE may not be very literate.	We need to provide information at a variety of levels and easy access to other resources such as databases, catalogues etc. Some of this will need to be in great depth and some will need to be wide-ranging.
	Stress on coursework rather than exams leads to requests for access to objects other than those exhibited in cases.	This may be better dealt with in study rooms and stores.
	Tutors (other than those in design history) often lack an understanding of the role of objects in teaching.	We need to make explicit what can be understood from objects.
Schools 5 million school visits a year to museums nationally	Arrive in groups of 30 or more.	We need to ensure there are appropriate spaces in the relevant galleries for work and for social gathering.
	School groups are the most democratic groups in museums because they represent all sectors of the community.	
	Schools choose carefully where to go, matching museum provision with their own needs.	
	Driven by the National Curriculum in England and Wales and the National Curriculum for Northern Ireland (up to 16), and the 5–14 National Guidelines in Scotland. Public examinations drive work from 16–18.	
	Increasing stress on coursework rather than simply exams reinforces the need for resources such as museums and objects.	We need to offer help in studying objects.
	The curriculum requires both the acquisition of knowledge and an understanding of the nature of the subject discipline.	We need to place emphasis on objects as sources of historical understanding.
	National Curriculum topics of particular interest to schools in the British Galleries are: *History* The Tudors; The Victorians (History Key Stage 2 [7–11 years]) The Galleries were not used much for the Civil War (Key Stage 3 [11–14 years]) as there are other more relevant museums elsewhere.	It is important that: - the Tudor and Victorian galleries include objects and ideas that relate to the curriculum and that are accessible to people from age 8 years upwards. - we include points about using objects as evidence; what can and cannot be learned from them; about bias in collections, or in the interpretation of objects or collections by museums. Because of group sizes, it is better if some of the key objects and displays are spread out in a gallery.

Audience	Characteristics	Implications for gallery content and design
	Art Many pupils aged 7–16 are brought to the V&A to look at the art and design of other cultures as well as the influence of art from our own past.	It is important that relationships between Britain and the rest of the world are made explicit and that objects from other countries are displayed in the gallery for comparative purposes. We should avoid simply pointing people in the direction of other galleries and hoping they will: a) get there; and b) retain key images in their minds.
	Technology Pupils aged 7–16 use the museum to look at a wide range of ways in which design problems have been solved.	We need to relate design problems to design methodology.

Appendix 6
Interpretive devices
1999
Gail Durbin

Interpretation is the means by which we will encourage a response from our visitors and the development of understanding, interest and enjoyment. We aim to be inclusive rather than exclusive. During the planning of this project we will constantly check the balance of our interpretative ideas to make sure that we are dealing with the needs of all our audiences and the variety of their learning styles. We accept that not every display will appeal to every visitor but we intend that whatever a visitor's learning style and reason for visiting, they will find something in most galleries that relates to their needs and interests.

Explanation of repeating interpretative ideas

Some methods of interpretation will be used more than once throughout the galleries. We would generally expect the interpretative device to be placed near the objects concerned as an integrated part of the display but some of the more messy activities have been grouped together and put in Discovery Areas specifically designed for families and experiential learners.

The numbers in round brackets after the subheads indicate the total number of such devices that were originally budgeted for throughout the whole run of British Galleries but exclude those devices to be found in the Discovery Areas. The numbers in square brackets give the totals as installed including those in the Discovery Areas.

Screen-based interpretation (42)

Short Gallery AV titles (6) **[6]**
These AVs will be short and shown in the galleries rather than in AV theatres.

The subjects will be:
The Melville Bed
Vauxhall Gardens
Taking tea - using animated silhouettes, to explain the ritual, equipment and etiquette of tea drinking in the eighteenth century
The Adam Interior
The building of the Crystal Palace - a computer animated film showing the building of the Crystal Palace. Very short and simple including the fact that the hoarding timber was used for the floors.
Queen Victoria's Diamond Jubilee - archive film

Object in focus videos (15) **[8]**
These short videos will show visitors what can be learnt from a single object by close observation. They will be used for objects with significant features that can only be seen through close observation or by opening, turning or working the object. They will show evidence of faking or of original colours only visible in obscure spots. They will be shown on a small screen next to the object being featured, thus creating a sense of intimacy or even the feel of an animated label. In most cases there will be a soundtrack and the same restrictions will apply here as are listed under 'Music'. The videos will last no more than three minutes. They will be appropriate for independent visitors, families and foreign visitors and will appeal to imaginative and experiential learners.

How was it made video (15) **[6]**
A sub-set of the above focusing on the way things were made.

Major AVs (6) **[3]**
The purpose of these AVs will be to cover very large topics which pull the subject matter of the galleries together in an entertaining and accessible manner. They will cover a broad chronological sweep and will cut across the collections in a different way to the subjects in the framework document. These AVs will use a wide range of multimedia techniques including virtual reality to put their message across. They will be shown in the AV areas where people can sit down comfortably to watch.

The subjects will be:
The Tudor Court
A day at the Great Exhibition
Houses and gardens (to include architecture)
Britain and the expanding empire
The story of the galleries (exact title to be decided)
Dining

Gallery computer interactives (15) [22]

Wherever interactives are used there should be seating for at least two people. In some cases it may be appropriate to have a large monitor above. We should not expect people to stand. Where there is sound this should not be audible round the galleries. The totals in square brackets in this section refer to the number of programs, not the number of terminals. Different versions of the Style terminal are counted as separate programmes.

Object Database
The object database will be located in the Study Areas. The engine for this database will be the Collections Information System (CIS). This is a detailed object database which has been developed for all collections management and cataloguing functions. Information on all objects in the British Galleries will be available.

However, rather than present the full database to inexperienced users, an easier front-end will be developed. This will provide a step-by-step guide to gathering information at the user's preferred pace and will allow the visitor to approach individual objects through subject areas. The database will be largely driven by images. This model of an intermediate database which can link directly into CIS records will also be used in other galleries and study rooms across the Museum.

Registration Marks [1]
This interactive will show visitors that it is possible to date a design through a registration mark and will introduce them to the additional information that is obtainable about individual objects from the Public Record Office. The program will be on a terminal in the galleries but a slightly different version will also be made available on the V&A website. Through the website people will be able to date their own objects from home and have a hot link to the PRO's own website.

The display 'Understanding Objects' will show how manufacturers began to protect themselves from plagiarism in the nineteenth century through the registration of designs. Next to the terminal some objects with registration marks will be placed on open display. Further objects will be in a case with their marks visible. Visitors will be invited to choose one of the objects and then either enter the registration number or work their way round a diamond mark inserting the appropriate numbers and letters. They will then be given the design registration date of the object and the option to see any further related material lodged at the PRO, such as drawings or fabric samples, as well as details of designers or manufacturers. As an alternative visitors can enter the registration details of an object that belongs to them (many people bring such objects to the Museum for dating). In this case, instead of showing them what the PRO holds about their object, we will show them the type of material held there and tell them how to set about further research at the PRO.

Style Terminals [9 different versions]
Audience research shows that many visitors have very little understanding of style but are keen to acquire the knowledge. Styles are shown and described within the galleries but it is not possible to explain the basics of that style every time a style term is used. The style terminals will act as a reference point so that visitors understand that they can turn to them for a simple description of a style supported by visual examples. People will be shown what motifs and other details to look for to identify a style and examples will be given of the style in room settings. Examples of

links with other styles will be given. Visitors who want to test their ability to identify styles will be able to opt for a quiz.

Nine terminals will be placed round the galleries in Style subjects, and on each terminal the styles near the terminal will be offered as the first choice to explore. Those who navigate to deeper levels of the programme will be able to access other styles seen further away in other galleries. The programme will also be available in the Study Areas where any style can be selected.

Explore Terminals [2]

Using touch screen technology visitors will be able to explore not only the pictorial content of paintings but also the cultural context in which they were produced. *The More Family* painting in the Tudor gallery lends itself particularly well to this approach. Visitors will be able to touch features in the painting that interest them, and will be given close-up views and further information or pictures of other related objects in the collection. Why does More's father wear a red robe? What books do his daughters clutch? What is the significance of the clock or the double-S chain round More's neck? The answers will help visitors to understand more about the life of a wealthy courtier and scholar in Tudor times. The painting was based on an earlier drawing by Holbein and the technology will allow us to fade one picture into the other showing the people who were added to the second version. Who's who in the painting *The Opening of the Great Exhibition* by Selous will also be explored in this way.

Design terminals [8]

While the terminals described above will be a means of providing visitors with further information, the Design terminals will encourage learning by asking visitors to apply what they have learnt in the gallery to solving a design problem.

'*Design an eighteenth-century landscape*' asks people to create an eighteenth-century style print of a natural landscape that they have modified to make it more picturesque. Visitors place features such as a lake, a path, a temple, groups of trees and flower beds and are given the ability to scale them to create perspective. They will be provided with the criteria which people used in the late eighteenth century to judge a picturesque landscape. There will be an option to print out their design. Another terminal will invite visitors to '*Design a Spitalfields silk pattern*'. They will be able to choose a motif, a colourway and the way of repeating the pattern (half-drop, mirror image, rotation, etc.). Once completed, apart from viewing it on screen, they will have the option to print out the design as a colouring sheet for children or as a squared embroidery or knitting pattern.

The design activities for the Discovery Areas will be linked. Visitors will be able to:
- design a coat of arms using authentic heraldic terms and print it out with an automatically generated heraldic description;
- create a monogram from their own initials;
- create a Victorian hand bill;
- generate a family tree, either their own or the royal family's (there will be three versions of this, one for each Discovery Area).

The novel feature of this linked design will be that information entered in one Discovery Area will then be made available in another Discovery Area. The Museum will also be able to use the technology to track movement between Discovery Areas and choices that people make about the computer programs.

Visitor Response Terminal [1 program; 2 terminals planned]

The intention of the Visitor Response Terminal is to create more of a dialogue between the Museum and its visitors as well as between visitor and visitor. At various points round the gallery paper and pencils will be provided next to relevant objects to enable visitors to share their thoughts about a specific display through words or drawing. (For example, in 'Objects of Commemoration' we ask visitors to talk about any object they own that reminds them of a particular event). We will edit responses and display them in a ring binder. Using the Internet, however, it will be possible to embark on broader and faster dialogue. A 'guest critic' will be invited in to start a new thread to the debate each month. One month an art historian may be asked to review a theme shown in the galleries, another month a design history lecturer may critique the galleries. Subsequent threads might be led by a primary teacher talking about ways of using the galleries to support the National Curriculum or a collector of Wedgwood talking about their interest in those objects. The debates will be moderated and as time passes the number of threads that visitors can tap in will increase.

The terminals will be in the Study Areas. All guest critics will have their photograph and a short biography included next to their contribution. Subsequent contributors will have the option of identifying themselves and having their own photograph taken and included. We will make these discussions available on the V&A Website.

Audio Programmes (30)

Talking about design audio programmes **[11]**
These audio programmes, delivered by a device next to the object(s) rather than through a device carried by the visitor, will give visitors the subjective views of named individuals about the design of a specific object or group of objects. There will be two types of audio programme:

a) historical writing by designers, critics, makers and owners about specific objects or groups of objects on display. These will, where possible, refer to observable features of the object(s).

b) present-day comments by designers, artists or craftspeople about the way the objects have influenced their own work, or comments by critics or curators with a stimulating viewpoint. The comments will generally be spoken by the individuals concerned.
Both types of programme will last up to 90 seconds. This approach will be directed to specialists and independent learners and will appeal to imaginative and common-sense learners.

Telling tales **[10]**
At certain points in the displays storytelling will be used to explain the objects. Normally this method will be used to illuminate objects decorated with scenes from classical and biblical stories that are no longer familiar to us; but it may also be used in other circumstances when there is a good story behind an object or an important figure. Preference will be given to stories that help visitors look at the objects. Any other story will have to be completely gripping to hold the visitor's attention. These audio programmes will be delivered by a device next to the object(s) rather than through a device carried by the visitor. The programmes will be of interest to families, foreign visitors and independent learners and we will make a special effort to ensure that the stories are appealing to children. They will appeal to imaginative and experiential learners.

Music **[8]**
Occasionally it will be possible, for those who wish, to listen to appropriate music or sounds to create a period atmosphere. We do not intend to provide ambient sound. We wish to use a wand, telephone handsets, or whatever technology is available, to direct the sound to specific individuals. A list of the pieces included in the compilation will be available and where songs are included the words will be made available. Care will be taken to provide an authentic sound. This approach will be aimed at all audience types and will appeal to all types of learners.

Hands-on interpretation (6)

Dressing up **[5]**
Dressing up activities give children an opportunity to experience what it was like to wear dress from the periods covered by the British Galleries. The replica dress and accessories will be as accurate as possible, balanced with the need for garments to be

sturdy and practical. We are planning to offer a a Tudor armour gauntlet, a Tudor or early Stuart ruff, Regency cravats, an eighteenth-century hoop petticoat, a Victorian corset and crinoline, and a Victorian waistcoat.

Drawing activities [4]

Some drawing activities will be placed throughout the galleries. Preference will be given to the type of drawing that would have been practised at the time as part of design education. Appropriate instructions or replica period equipment will be supplied. These activities will be aimed at independent learners, families and HE/FE groups and will appeal to experiential and common-sense learners.

Touch plates [5]

Raised drawings will be produced for architectural models and large architectural features, such as an eighteenth bookcase, for visitors with visual impairments. Architecture is particularly difficult for people with visual impairments to understand by sight alone.

Handling collections (6) [8]

Small handing collections will be included in the displays for people to use independently. These collections will be used especially in the What was New? sections where examples of newly produced materials will be appropriate. Handling objects will not be fragile and will not normally be valuable and in many cases fragments, such as pottery sherds will be used. We may prototype this activity to see what level of security is required. These collections will be aimed at independent learners, families, schools, HE/FE and foreign visitors and will appeal to common-sense and experiential learners. They will be particularly useful for visitors with visual impairments and in all cases they will be given a Braille label.

Touch objects [11]

A single object will be chosen to illustrate many of the Style subjects for people with visual impairments. Style has been chosen as the focus of this series because of our Themes it is the one that is the most visual and difficult for people with poor or no sight. The touch objects may be larger than the objects in the handling collections and they will always be fixed down. They will have a Braille label and a large print label if possible.

Magnetic board activities [1]

This device allows simple matching activities and games suitable for families and others.

Observation-based interpretation (15)

Facsimiles (6) [10]

Occasionally, facsimiles (of a pattern book, trade catalogue or newspaper, etc.) will be placed in galleries for visitors to leaf through. This will be done where the book is intrinsically interesting and relevant to the objects on display. This series includes providing commercially available facsimiles where relevant, as well as producing our own.

A sub-set of this series will be a few pages extracted as examples.

Gallery books (9) [6]

These one-off books invite visitors to form an opinion about an issue raised by a display. They will be designed as 4-8 page, laminated, large-format books with hard covers, that will be left in the relevant gallery next to comfortable seating, for visitors to leaf through . They will generally ask a provocative question or present a problem for the visitor to consider. Answers and opinions will be arrived at by reference both to the objects on display and the contents of the book. Questions will relate to one or more subjects but will not require the visitor to walk through more than one gallery and preferably the visitor will be able to see all the relevant material from a seated position. The contents of the book might include more questions, contemporary quotations or illustrations, opinions from curators, conservators and others, cartoons and any other material that has a bearing on the question. It is not intended that the visitor record their conclusions. If the contents of the book can be used in isolation from the objects then the book will have failed. The gallery books will be most appropriate for the independent learner and will appeal most to analytical and common-sense learners.

Lift the label activities [7]

This type of device will be used where the visitor is asked a question to which there is a specific answer that should not be revealed until the visitor has had time to look and think. We might ask what common phrase an object has given rise to or we might ask them to puzzle out the meaning of a riddle on an object. The answer will be under he label.

Spot the difference activities [6]

Objects will be grouped to demonstrate particular differences (e.g. surfaces imitating others, European copies of Asian products) and visitors will be invited to decide which objects fall into which categories. This form of interpretation is essentially an enhanced labelling device beside displays of comparable objects.

Mystery object displays [3]

These displays present unusual objects and ask visitors to try to puzzle out their function. We would like the design of these displays to further the element of mystery and for solutions to be presented in an intriguing way. They will be appropriate for families (some might be placed very low, at child's eye level) and will appeal to analytical and common-sense learners.

Visitor response [6] At points in the gallery we will encourage visitors to respond to particular displays through writing and drawing. The questions will be of an open ended and simple nature, e.g next to Objects of commemoration we will ask people to share with other visitors information about any object they possess that reminds them of a particular person, event or period. We will provide paper and pencil and a slot through which the response will be posted. We will edit responses, type them up, laminate them and put them in a binder. The binder will be displayed where the question was originally asked, for other visitors to read and enjoy.

Miscellaneous [16] The miscellaneous category includes the following interpretative devices:
- Classical orders (matching activity)
- Make a rubbing of Adam patterns
- Assembling a chair
- Replica zograpscope
- The Great Exhibition Maze Game
- Make a rubbing of Victorian coinage
- Stereoscope (replica)
- Build a table
- Mutoscope (replica)
- The Lamb and Flag chair (*son et lumière*)
- Examining a piece of Victorian carcase furniture
- Demonstration/Opinions/Examination area
- Ceramics under UV light
- Books of identification marks
- The Minton Snake Vase flip book
- Laying the table flip book
- Build the Crystal Palace (construction)
- Stuart style motifs (rubbing)
- Assembling a three-legged armchair
- Tapestry (weaving)
- Making plaited cords

Audio guide	We are not planning an audio guide as an integral part of the gallery interpretation (although this is something that might be produced for the Museum later).
Text/Graphics	A summary and hierarchy of graphic provision (wall panels, labels) will be produced along with guidelines for writing and editing.
Period Room Interpretation	For each room we will provide the following information. – map showing location of house – image of house – plan showing location of room – ground plan of room (if needed in addition to above) – original function of room – model? – decisions made by the V&A about the current display
Orientation	Orientation will cover physical and intellectual orientation. Orientation will occur at all entrances to the galleries and will be identical in all cases with the following exceptions: - plans of the galleries will be orientated so that they relate to current position of the visitor reading the plan - information about nearby galleries or sequence of galleries will change as appropriate.

1. *Physical orientation*
Each orientation point will have:
- a plan showing the layout of the galleries (showing all subjects) on the relevant floor
- the position of the current viewer 'You are here'
- what you will find if you go one way, what you will find if you go another
- the plan should also show Discovery Areas, seating if possible, the exit, the short route[?], toilets, lifts [what else?]
- something to indicate that the display is on two floors

2. *Intellectual orientation*
At all points there will be a standard means of explaining:
- the purpose of the galleries
- their division into three themes and the division of the themes into subjects
- what graphic devices we have chosen to indicate the different themes throughout the galleries
- how the chronological development works

Format
We may add:
- photographs to show people what they will see

Could be a panel or a 'pod' but should be low tech. To make it obvious it needs to be free-standing or outside the entrance. It should not be on the wall round to the side of the entrance where it will be missed

Dedicated spaces	Some, but not all, of these have all been indicated within the body of the Framework document. This is a summary:

Discovery areas
These areas will contain participatory activities aimed at families and independent learners, which will particularly appeal to common-sense and experiential learners. These areas may also contain small displays. We have grouped here many of the ac-

tivities such as making things or dressing up that will create mess and are better separated from the main run of the galleries, but the space should be designed in such a way that it encourages everyone to come in and take part. Noise will have to be contained within these spaces without the use of doors. It should be possible for small family groups to sit down and do things together. In the body of the Framework Document we have indicated the kinds of activities that will occur in each of these areas.

Performance areas
In these areas we will run occasional small concerts or theatrical performances related to the displays, during museum opening hours. They will be used largely for independent learners and families but will occasionally be used for school and college groups. Performances will appeal to imaginative and experiential learners. We would like to accommodate up to 40 people. The Norfolk House Music Room will be used on the lower floor and the AV space on the upper floor will double as a performance space. Since these events will be only occasional and will disrupt the galleries for only a short time these spaces can be shared with other activities. Unless the area normally has fixed seating we will also need a lockable store for seating.

AV areas
Formal AV areas will be used for major multimedia presentations (as opposed to shorter AVs which will be incorporated within the displays). On both floors they will be positioned in the areas most used by groups and will accommodate no less than 35 seated people. Noise should not spill into the displays.

How will visitors know what is on?
- provide slave monitor outside room showing what is running inside
- indicate digitally outside the room that we are currently × minutes through a 12-minute film (we do not wish to indicate this within the space)
- indicate digitally outside and inside the room (on the screen) that the next film will start in 30 seconds or whatever
- indicate digitally outside the room the timetable of films so that if this is changed the timetable changes automatically.

Lighting within the room
- there should be sufficient ambient light within the room for people to find their way to a seat
- we would like the light level to rise for about 60 seconds between each film to encourage people to move on.

Booking
- we have considered the need to close the room so that it can be used for booked groups and we have thought about any signing that might be necessary but have decided that the complications of taking and arranging bookings are disproportionate to the possible benefits. We plan to go ahead without a booking system. We will review this after the space has been in operation for a few months and introduce a low tech solution later if required.

Altering the programme
- we would like it to be possible for a member of the Museum's staff (but not a member of the public) to intervene and change the programme or the order of the programmes or stop the programmes to run a seminar in the space. This should be dealt with digitally and the new timetable to become immediately apparent on the public signage outside the space. Please advise us if this is difficult/costly to achieve.

AV/slides
- Normal mode of presentation will be through video presented digitally. Because it is also intended to use the space for the occasional seminar we will need provision for double screen slide presentation.

Study areas

Study areas will allow independent learners and specialists as well as school and college students to find out more about the collections. There should be one on the lower floor and a smaller version upstairs. They should provide for the following functions:

- computer access via 5-6 monitors to collections information, library catalogue and other sources of information
- centralised access (on monitors mentioned above) to all the databases and interactives that are also scattered round the galleries
- print-out facilities for the computerised databases and other computer interactives together with change machines, smart cards or whatever technology allows people to pay for their print-outs
- collections of about 100 reference books for on-site study
- collections of about 50 video tapes and 50 CD Roms for on-site study (to be watched on monitors mentioned above)
- tables and chairs for study for 10-12 people (preferably not all at a single table)
- informal seating for 10-12 people
- accommodation for staff (not office)
- internal telephone

The following may be in the study areas or may be located elsewhere:
- 40 stools to borrow to use in the galleries for drawing or gallery talks
- store for materials to maintain and replenish interpretative devices throughout the galleries
- lockable store for materials related to performances and teaching activities. It should be able to accommodate the Museum's Activity Cart for families and could double as a changing room for performances.

We need further advice on securing the items in the study areas.

Fashionable living:
Achieving splendour 1500-1600
58.03
This will be a large display

Related displays:
Heraldry, The Court of Henry VIII, Bromley-by-Bow period room

The purpose of this display is to show the luxury goods which were desirable as symbols of status and wealth; and which embodied ideas of the exotic, the rare and the extravagant as means of establishing and reinforcing reputation.

Striking uses of exotic and expensive materials (shell, gold thread), combined with costly imports (porcelains) and representations of personal and family standing (portraits, stained glass arms) stressed the elevated position occupied by aristocrats and the wealthiest merchants. Sumptuary laws controlling the consumption of such goods reinforced their luxury and rarity. The use of these objects in domestic surroundings made comfortable with costly handworked textiles (cushions, hangings), and for occasions, such as feasts and banquets, further emphasises the importance of display and a concern with novelty which corresponds with the acute consciousness of rank in this period. Heraldic devices proclaimed ownership, loyalty and status.

Objects on open display

Leicester armorial tapestry	T320-1977
Possible rotation is T124-1931 (Grotesque tapestry with pride and avarice)	
Lotto carpet, to be shown flat	903-1897
ROTATE with Lotto carpet T348-1920	
Linen-fold panelled armchair with renaissance motifs on upper section of back	W39-1920
Painting: portrait of Commander Honing	176-1880
Stained glass Beaupré panel	C60-1946
Stained glass Beaupré panel	C63-1946
Stained glass Beaupré panel	C65-1946
Stained glass Beaupré panel	C66-1946
Stained glass Beaupré panel	C67-1946
Stained glass Beaupré panel	C69-1946
Stained glass Beaupré panel	C70-1946
Stained glass Beaupré panel	C71-1946
Stained glass Beaupré panel	C72-1946

- Cased objects: 58.03.s2

Miniature: group portrait of *The More Family*,	P15-1973
Fascinating, densely- informative group portrait	

- Cased objects: 58.03.s1

Gilded and painted glass panel with heraldry	C335-1930
Casket (mother of pearl)	M245-1924
Porcelain ewer with gilt mounts	7915-1862
Iznik pot with gilt mounts,	1561-1904
Porcelain mounted bowl	M945-1983

Nautilus cup	M117-1984
Stoke Prior double-bell salt/pepper container	283-1893
Standing bowl, silver gilt	M352-1912
Covered silver cup	LOAN:BERDEN.1:1&2
Small standing silver cup	M247-1924

- Textiles

Embroidered banqueting scene	T125-1913

ROTATE WITH Embroidered cushion cover T21-1923
Embroidered cushion cover T31-1914
And others tbc

Embroidered valance depicting garden pleasures	T137-1991

ROTATE WITH a smaller cushion cover so that it no longer shadows T125-1913
T136-1991 (another two valances from this group are T135 and T138-1991)

Blackwork embroidered smock	T113, 114, 115-1997

ROTATE WITH another to be found

Embroidered long cushion cover	T80-1946

ROTATE WITH T79-1946 cushion cover with hunting scenes

Embroidered hanging (made into a chasuble in 18th century)	T257-1967

- Case: 58.04.S1 (formerly listed with Bromley-by-Bow room)

Bradford table carpet, (on fourth, 'artificial' wall)	T134-1928

ROTATE WITH Gifford table carpet, T151-1930

Interpretative ideas:
Computer interactive: *Explore a Picture: More family Portrait*. The More family portrait (P.15-1973) will be the basis for a touch-screen interactive that allows visitors to explore the details of dress, jewellery, furniture, gardens, architecture, religion, plate, musical instruments, clocks, books, the personalities in the portrait and to read transcriptions of the inscriptions. This will be aimed at schools, families, FE/HE students and independent learners and will appeal to common-sense and experiential learners.

Label images:
None

Objects considered for the display but rejected:
Miniature portrait of Jane Small by Holbein (P40-1934)
White linen damask (Flemish) with portrait of Queen Elizabeth (T215-1963)
Jewellery including pieces from the Cheapside hoard
Rock crystal casting bottle (M78-1910)
Belchamp hall snaphance, pistol and powder flask (M948, 949, 950-1983)
Set of banquetting roundels
Musical instruments
Clock
Silver spoons
Small glass panels from Preston Hall with moral texts (Circ319 to 331-1919)
Picinio sword (M55-1947)
Book: Turbeville *In Commendation of Hawking* (1575)
Man's linen shirt (T326-1982)
Night cap (T55-1947)
Spanish/Italian shoes (singles)
Holbein carpet (T41-1928)

VICTORIAN INTERPRETATIVE IDEAS
DRAFT BRIEF FOR *HANDLING ACTIVITY:*

ID ENCAUSTIC TILES (DJ)

Brief agreed by Concept Team, 14/7/00
Major amendments to content, design and text/graphics, 31/10/00, MH
Note about order of mounting objects + corresponding amendments to text/graphics required, 18/11/00, MH
Handling No. added 5/12/00 DJ
New handling No. added 5/12/00 DJ
Further amendments to Format, Design and Text/graphics, 8/12/00, MH
Display requirements amended, 14/12/00, MH
Object names amended, 13/2/01, MH
References to raised lettering deleted, 26/2/01, MH

Aim The purpose of this activity is to allow the visitor to touch and see the changes in shape of an encaustic tile as it goes through the various production stages. This will help the visitor to understand how the tiles were manufactured.

Audience This handling collection is aimed at all audiences and will be especially useful for visitors with sight impairments. It will appeal particularly to experimental learners and also to common-sense learners.

Format The collection will consist of samples showing the stages of making an encaustic tile, together with tools and two 19th-century encaustic tiles. There will be accompanying text.

Content There are four elements to this activity:
1. Mould and tools: plaster mould surrounded by a wooden former, which will be cased, i.e. will not be handled (23.3 cm L × 23.3 cm W × 7.6 cm D approx) (NCOL. 22-2000); mawl (mallet) (20 cm L × 5 cm dia, head 10cm) (NCOL. 17-2000); scraper (NCOL. 22-2000) 10.1 cm L X 4.4 cm W × 0.05 cm H.
2. Three sample tiles: tile removed from the mould (15 cm L × 7.5 W × 2.75 cm D approx) (NCOL 16:1 – 2000); tile with slip added (15 cm L × 7.5 cm W × 2.75 cm D approx) (NCOL. 14:1 – 2000); finished tile (15 cm L × 7.5 W × 2.75 cm D approx) (NCOL. 14:1 – 2000).
3. Two original encaustic tiles from the Palace of Westminster C. 1:1&2-1985. (15.3 cm L × 15.3 cm W × 2.5 cm D). These tiles will show the inlay partly worn, linking the method of production demonstrated using the half tiles with an original tile.
4. Instructions for doing the activity including diagrams.

Design The handling collection will be located in the *Gothic Revival* display, next to the displayed section of the tiled floor from the Palace of Westminster (C1: To 81-1985). Space is limited for this display, therefore replica half tiles will be used. They will be made as a whole tile but cut vertically in half. Attention will given to safety and security of the objects. However, we also need to be able to allow people to feel the weight of the replica half tiles. The replica half tiles will be have to fired to make them more robust. The tile samples and Palace of Westminster will all be fixed down. The tools will be tethered. The plaster mould will be mounted on the wall with protective casing. The case for the mould should be scratch proof. The various tools, samples and original tiles need to be mounted in the sequence that they come into the process of making encaustic tiles. The order is set in the text document.
   The design of the display mount will indicate that they are handling objects. The surface that the objects are mounted on should offer a contrast in colour to the objects. The handling collection should be at a height where it is accessible to adults,

children and wheelchair users. Standing adults may have to reach their hands downwards to touch the samples but should not have to bend over.

There should be a hand symbol to indicate that this is handling activity. This should be a standard colour for all handling and touch activities. It should be raised and in a material that is not cold to touch. It should be large enough for each digit to be clearly distinguishable (the prototype is a bit small).

The main label text will be in regular type next to each sample. Braille text will be on a pull-out board next to each sample. The boards could feature the same colour as the hand symbol to make them easy to locate.

Text/Graphics required	a) 'Please touch' unit containing: Title of activity in Braille and in regular type 'Please touch' in regular type raised hand symbol – **N.B. Not included in Graphics Tender** b) Graphic panel setting out the stages of the process together with the name and Museum number under each object – regular type in whatever size is agreed for interpretative devices. c) Braille information on a separate sheet or each object. This will be slightly different to the text for sighted visitors.
Drawings to be commissioned	4 single line drawings
Photography to be used on panels and labels	None

Appendix 9
Summative Evaluation of the British Galleries
Overview of Findings
Creative Research, 2002

1.1 Summative Evaluation of the British Galleries
Overview of Findings Introduction
The new British Galleries were opened to the public in November 2001 following complete refurbishment and redisplay. They represent a flagship for future presentation and interpretation in the V & A incorporating as they do a variety of more interactive interpretation methods in addition to the more conventional text panels and object labels.

To help in the development of the Galleries, a baseline survey of visitors to the old Galleries was carried out in December 1996 - January 1997. Six months after opening, an evaluation of the new Galleries was undertaken. This overview provides the key findings of this evaluation, with comparisons between the two surveys where relevant.

1.2 Demographics
The profile of visitors to the new Galleries was broadly similar to the old Galleries. There were similar proportions of men and women, a heavy weighting towards those in social grades ABC1 and high levels of educational attainment. The ethnic mix was also consistent; predominantly white and English speaking (as a first or second language).

The main difference in the profiles was the incidence in the current sample of more older visitors over 55 (29% as compared to 15% in the baseline survey) and fewer younger visitors under 24 (12% as compared to 21% in the baseline survey). In particular, there was a marked absence of children visiting the new Galleries, which is possibly a result of the timing of the research.[1] This is something that requires further investigation.

1.3 Comparison between the Old and New British Galleries
1.3.1 Appreciation of the Galleries' Content and Organisation
75% knew the galleries were called the British Galleries. In the baseline survey, 54% suggested a name or theme for the Galleries and 78% of these thought they dealt with things British or English. (42% of the total baseline sample thought the Galleries dealt with things British or English.) The figures are not directly comparable however since the old Galleries were not signposted 'British Galleries' but rather simply 'Britain' plus dates for the period covered.

61% were aware that there was an intended start and end point to the galleries compared to half that number in the baseline study (29%).

73% could suggest a theme or a way in which the galleries were arranged; in most cases, this was chronologically. The 73% who suggested a chronological or other ordering in the new Galleries compares with 42% of visitors to the old. In addition, more than half of the sample at that time did not know there was a particular organisation to the Galleries. This compares to 27% with respect to the new Galleries. This suggests that the new Galleries are far more successful at conveying the fact that the material is presented chronologically.

Overall, this represents an improvement compared to the baseline survey, although the proportions of visitors that explicitly referred to the four themes of style, taste, fashionable living and what was new was, perhaps, not as large as the Museum might have wished for (5% mentioned style, there were no other direct mentions of the other themes).

1.3.2 Learning in the British Galleries
The new Galleries were rated significantly better than the old British Galleries in terms of how much people felt they had **learned** from their visit:

- the average rating out of 10 for learning was 8.0, with 67% of the sample giving a rating of 8 or more. This compares **extremely favourably** with the baseline study when we recorded an average score of just 4.1 out of ten (half the current score) with just 19% visitors giving a rating of 8 or more.

- the proportion stating they had learned more from the British Galleries compared to other parts of the Museum rose from just 9% in the baseline study to 36% here.

Moreover, respondents identified a great diversity of topics about which they felt they had discovered something new while in the Galleries.

One in five (19%) commented without prompting that the methods of interpretation deployed within the Galleries had contributed to them learning something.

1.3.3 Interest in the British Galleries
There can be no doubt that visitors also found the new British Galleries considerably more **interesting** than the old Galleries:

- the average rating out of 10 for interest was 8.6 with 86% giving a score of 8 or above. This compares to an average rating of 7.1 in the baseline survey with 46% giving a rating of 8 or more.
- the proportion rating the Galleries 'more interesting' than other parts of the Museum was up from 12% to 33%.

Perhaps not surprising, given its scope and size, nearly every visitor could find something of particular interest to themselves in the Galleries. When asked what they found particularly interesting the range of answers was very diverse, suggesting that no matter what your taste or interest, you can find something in the Galleries.

1.3.4 General Attitudes
As part of the baseline study, we asked visitors to indicate the degree to which they agreed or disagreed with a range of statements about the Galleries. These statements were developed from the findings of an initial qualitative evaluation of the old Galleries. We recorded some significant increases in the number of positive responses

- the single biggest change in terms of this set of statements was that while the old Galleries were felt to have very little to offer children (only 19% agreed in the baseline survey that children would get a lot out of the Galleries), the new Galleries were seen to offer younger visitors a great deal more (64% agreed that children will get a lot out of a visit).
- other large shifts in opinion were recorded about the style of presentation – definitely not old-fashioned (only 11% agreed that it was old-fashioned compared with 46% in the baseline study), the fact that the Galleries are just like a museum should be (93% agreed compared with 53%), it is warm and welcoming (89% agreed compared with 64%), the historical sequence is very clear (79% agreed compared with 53%).
- although 31% agreed that the Galleries were too dark, this was nevertheless an improvement on the 49% that felt this before. Moreover, there was a small increase (from 78% to 84%) who agreed that the light levels were restful.
- similarly, there was a small increase in the proportions **disagreeing** that the Galleries were too cluttered (88% up from 73%).
- finally, there was almost universal agreement this time round that you can see how things used to be (97%) which was an increase of 13% from 84% in the baseline study.

1.3.5 Behaviour in the Galleries
The overall pattern of movement through the Galleries reflected the intended route: 59% of respondents started at the Cromwell Road entrance on Level 2 and 40% left from the Cromwell Road entrance on Level 4. In the baseline survey visitors tended to enter on Level 2 either at the Exhibition Road (36%) or via the Cromwell Road (21%) entrance. Thereafter there was no discernible pattern.

The time visitors estimated that they spent in the Galleries was considerably greater with the new compared to the old. On average, visitors estimated they spent 54 minutes on the lower level, compared with 17 minutes in the old galleries. On average, visitors estimated they spent 62 minutes on the upper level, compared with 14 minutes in the old galleries.

Those that had entered both floors at the time of their interview estimated they had spent, on average, 82 minutes in the Galleries. In the baseline survey we did not have enough respondents who had visited both levels to determine how long they spent in the Galleries altogether.

Three quarters (77%) of the sample claimed to be aware that the Galleries were located on two levels compared to just over half (56%) in the baseline and significantly more visitors had either already visited the other floor or planned to do so (69% compared to 44%).

A staggering 95% indicated that they made a conscious decision to visit the British Galleries, with 40% of all visitors deciding before they came to the Museum. This compares with 27% and 17% respectively for the old Galleries.

These findings all represent considerable improvements compared with the baseline study.

1.4 Response to the New Elements of the Galleries

1.4.1 Use & Appreciation of Interactive Elements

The old British Galleries did not contain any interactive elements (thus, there are no comparative data). The new Galleries represent the V&A's first large-scale attempt to incorporate interactives into its exhibits. The survey therefore included a number of questions to evaluate how visitors received these.

69% of respondents, at some point during their visit, used one or more of the interactive elements including the interactive areas (such as the Discovery and Study Areas) and the individual exhibits (such as the video programmes and the handling activities).

1.4.2 Interactive Areas

57% of visitors stopped and used one or more of the interactive areas (e.g. at least one of the Discovery Areas, Film Rooms and Understanding Objects) and, on average, they stopped and used two different types of area.

In order of popularity, the most used interactive areas were the Discovery Areas (37% of all visitors visited at least one), the Film Rooms (28%), the Study Areas (25%) and Understanding Objects (25%).

Equally importantly, the majority of visitors, irrespective of whether or not they used **any** interactives, felt that these areas enhanced their appreciation of the objects on display (64%) and helped them improve their knowledge of the subject matter (63%). Only 1% of the sample felt these areas actually detracted from their appreciation of the objects on display and less than 1% felt they hindered their efforts to improve their knowledge of the subject matter.

1.4.3 Interactive Exhibits

64% of visitors stopped and used at least one of the different types of interactive exhibits. As there were approximately equal numbers of each type of interactive exhibit, any differences in levels of use probably reflect the fact that some types of interactives were more popular with visitors than others.

On average, 'users' used between two and three different types of exhibit. Most popular were the video programmes (41%), the handling activities including handling collections, touch objects and touch plates (33%) and the 'lift the flap' exhibits including life the label and spot the difference (32%).

The computer interactives were used by over one quarter of the sample (26%), the text-based interactives including facsimiles, questions of design and visitor response by 20% and the audio programmes by 14%. The last figure can be explained in part by the fact that a number of the audio programmes were not working at the time of the research.

Among those using at least one interactive exhibit, 93% felt they enhanced their appreciation of the objects and 89% felt they helped improve their knowledge of the subject.

Across all visitors (including non-users), 71% felt these types of exhibits enhanced their appreciation of the objects on display and 68% said they helped improve their knowledge of the subject. As above, the proportions stating that the presence of these exhibits detracted from their experience was 1% (appreciation of objects) and less than 1% (knowledge of subject matter).

1.4.4 Awareness of Various Facilities

67% were aware of the Gallery Assistants and 21% had spoken to one of them. Of those who had done so, 74% agreed that 'the gallery assistants were well informed and helpful'.

In contrast, levels of awareness of the emailing and printing facilities were low (70% unaware of emailing, 69% unaware of printing) and thus levels of use were also low (12% and 5% respectively).

1.4.5 Attitudes to the Interactive Elements

Visitors were asked to express their level of agreement/disagreement with a number of statements which related to the use of interactive elements.

- 92% agreed 'the methods of display help to make the objects come to life'
- 89% 'enjoyed the variety in displays and interactives'
- 89% 'really enjoyed the combination of objects to look at and activities to carry out'
- 87% felt that 'computer-based interactive exhibits are right for these galleries'
- 87% felt 'it's really good being able to touch some of the objects on display'
- 86% of those seeing a video/film agreed 'the videos/films give you a feel for the historic period'
- 79% agreed 'the interactive exhibits encouraged me to look more closely at the objects'
- only 17% agreed that 'my pleasure at seeing the wonderful objects was spoiled by all the interactive exhibits'.

1.4.6 Labels and Panels

These were generally shown to work well – 92% agreed that 'the labels and panels worked well to explain the topics of the displays' and 91% agreed that 'the labels and panels helped me look more closely at the objects'.

There was some negative response to the size of the typeface of some of the labels with 38% agreeing that this was too small (49% did not think so).

Similarly, just over a quarter of our sample (27%) agreed that the position of some of the labels makes them difficult to read, while 60% disagreed with this statement.

1.5 Overall Assessment

In just about every aspect, the findings set out in this report provide a ringing endorsement for the way the Museum has chosen to re-develop the British Galleries. The visitors in our survey have been extremely positive in their views about what they found in the Galleries and the way it has been presented.

If we were to look to find some criticisms within all the positive news, we would pick out the following observations. The apparent lack of children being attracted to the Galleries; the fact that the Galleries are continuing to appeal to the Museum's traditional audience; the fact that although the Galleries are organised around four main themes (in addition to the chronological arrangement), these themes are not being clearly communicated to visitors; many visitors are unaware of some of the e-mailing and printing facilities available to them; some visitors find some labels difficult to read due to a combination of size of type and location.

Of particular importance is the way visitors have reacted to the inclusion of a variety of interactive elements. Given that fact that this is the Museum's first large-scale attempt to use interactive elements in the galleries, these are extremely significant findings. The interactive elements were widely used and appreciated. Although 30% of our sample chose not to use **any** of the interactive elements, there was nothing to suggest that this group was hostile to the idea - they were simply less enthusiastic. Indeed, there was some evidence to suggest non-users were simply less engaged with the subject matter of the British Galleries. Another possibility is that they were 'passive users', that is, they were happy to stand and watch other visitors interacting with these elements and derived something from doing so.

Overall, the picture is one where the majority of visitors used the interactive areas and exhibits and was favourably disposed towards them. There is no evidence that the minority of visitors that did not use the interactives were hostile to them.

In this respect, the British Galleries provide an extremely successful model for future exhibitions at the V&A. When done well (as in the British Galleries), these methods of display can greatly enhance the visitor's experience.

Overall, from a visitor perspective, the new British Galleries must be considered a great success.

Notes   1. The baseline study was carried out during the Christmas holiday period, December 1996 and January 1997, covering both weekdays and weekends mainly during the school holidays. The current survey was carried out from 6th to 24th May (excluding 17th and 18th May when a conference was taking place). Interviewing took place on weekends and weekdays including one Wednesday evening opening period. Thus, the fieldwork was conducted during the school term.

The British Galleries 1500-1900
were made possible by generous gifts from:

Heritage Lottery Fund
The Clore Duffield Foundation
Mr and Mrs Edwin Davies OBE
Sir Harry Djanogly CBE
The Monument Trust
The Weston Family
The Wolfson Foundation

The John Ellerman Foundation
The Friends of the V&A
The Headley Trust
Parnassus Foundation / Jane and Raphael Bernstein
Märit and Hans Rausing
Paul and Jill Ruddock
The Basil Samuel Charitable Trust

H. Blairman & Sons Ltd
Mr and Mrs Benjamin Bonas
Mr and Mrs Raymond M. Burton
The Clothworkers' Foundation
Nicholas and Judith Goodison
Christoph and Katrin Henkel
Lauchentilly Charitable Foundation
Mrs George Levy
Mallett & Son (Antiques) Ltd
Michael Marks Charitable Trust
The Worshipful Company of Mercers
Old Possum's Practical Trust
Sara Lee Corporation
The Trusthouse Charitable Foundation
Frederick and Kathryn Uhde
Jeremy and Kim White Foundation
Mrs Corinne Whiteley
Mrs Charles Wrightsman
Zochonis Charitable Trust

And many other donors

Appendix II
List of Construction Work Packages

Structural Alterations	Griffith McGee
Services enabling works	CommTech
Internal hoardings	Sykes & Sons
Structural steelwork	CMF Ltd
Plant-room cladding	Mitre Cladding
General builders work	J. Coffey
Dry lining (fit out)	Stevensons of Norwich
Raised Floors	FSG Ltd
Marble works	Stonewest Ltd
Glazed doors	Carlton Benbow
Small metalwork	Benbow Interiors
Specialist joinery, furniture	Kilby & Gayford
Period room frames	Westminster Partitions
Display metalwork	Westminster Guild
Decorations	Peter Burton
Glazed screens	Spectrum Glass
Graphics	Service Visual
Display cases	Goppion
Period rooms	St Blaise
Object reinstallation	Momart
Mechanical installations	Emcorr
Electrical installations	Lowe & Oliver
Specialist lighting	Profile Glass
Lift installation	Guideline Lifts Ltd
Security installation	Leerose
AV installations	SEC Ltd
Enabling works	O'Keefe
Construction Managers	Exterior

Architect	G A Associates
Quantity surveyor	Walfords
Structural engineer	Alan Baxter and Associates
Project management	Bovis (from 2000 Bovis Lend Lease)
Interior designer	Casson Mann
Historic Decoration Consultant	Mlinaric, Henry and Zervudachi
Lift consultant	SVM Partnership
Services engineer	SVM Partnership
Lighting designer	Richard Aldridge
Planning supervisor	Walfords
Construction manager	Exterior
Graphics Consultant	Rose Innes Associates
Disability Consultant	Earnscliffe Davis Associates
IT/AV Consultant	Karen Donoghue
IT/AV Consultant	Momentus New Media
IT/AV Consultant	Oyster
IT/AV Consultant	The Edge
Architectural models	The Network Modelmakers
Audience Research	Creative Research Ltd
Audience Research	The Susie Fisher Group

Breathless 2001
By Cornelia Parker (British, born 1956)

Made in London
Silver- plated brass musical instruments suspended on stainless steel wire.

Breathless takes the form of a hypothetical brass band, a collection of defunct instruments acquired from the dusty back rooms of the British Legion, Salvation Army, Collieries and other establishments.

No longer played, these horns shared the fate of being squashed by the weight of one of our most famous historical monuments, Tower Bridge. The deed was done by one of the giant 22-ton accumulators, part of the bridge's original hydraulic lifting mechanism. _One Victorian institution literally knocked the wind out of another._

The brass band in Britain could be seen as the musical equivalent of the stiff upper lip. Many of the institutions in which they originated have become virtually extinct, but the bands played on. In _Breathless_, the hushed ensemble has been resurrected to become a museum object suspended in limbo. It occupies a no man's land between two floors, a new space formerly filled by ceiling and floor. A vibrant working-class culture has been brought into the British Galleries of the V & A in the guise of a heraldic rose. From above, the work appears as a silvery pool of polished silver-plated instruments sounding out from the floor. From below, the tarnished underbellies of the same, silhouetted against the white ceiling to echo the ornate ceilings preserved in the adjoining galleries.

The piece is an attempt to explore a number contradictions. I wanted to create something that would explore ideas of duality: light/dark, silence/noise, comedy/tragedy, consciousness/unconsciousness, upper class/lower class, north/south, inhaling/exhaling, death/resurrection, black cloud/silver lining.
I see the work as a ghostly last gasp of the British Empire.

Cornelia Parker

(Instruments squashed by Tower Bridge machinery with the kind permission of the Corporation of London.)

Bibliography

Publications by V&A staff

Burton, Anthony, *Vision and Accident: The Story of the Victoria and Albert Museum* (London, 1999)

Carpenter, Tim, and Oakley, Victoria, 'A Concise Approach: Managing Information for the British Galleries Conservation Programme', *V&A Conservation Journal* (Autumn 2001), no. 39, pp. 4–5

Costaras, Nicola, 'The British Galleries Project from a Paintings Conservation Perspective', *V&A Conservation Journal* (Autumn 2001), no. 39, pp. 23–24

Hinton, Morna, 'The Screen Test', *Museum Practice* (Spring 2003), pp. 53–57

Hubbard, Charlotte, 'Too Big For His Boots – The Relocation of the Wellington Monument Model', *V&A Conservation Journal* (Autumn 2001), no. 39, pp. 8–9

Humphrey, Nicholas, 'The New British Galleries at the V&A', *V&A Conservation Journal* (April 1998), no. 27, pp. 4–7

Jackson, Anna and Hinton, Morna, *The V&A Guide to Period Styles: 400 Years of British Art and Design* (London, 2002)

Jordan, Fi, 'Reverse Painting on Glass in the British Galleries', *V&A Conservation Journal* (Autumn 2001), no. 39, p. 6

Leader, Marilyn, 'The Conservation of a Crewelwork Bed Curtain', *V&A Conservation Journal* (Autumn 2001), no. 39, pp. 31–32

Frances Lloyd–Baynes, 'Managing the Unmanageable: Lessons in Content Management from the V&A's British Galleries Project', *Dramaturgy in Museum Communication: The Change of Meaning in Virtual Spaces* (forthcoming, 2004)

Metcalf, Simon, North, Anthony R.E. and Balfour, Derek, 'A Gun–Shield from the Armoury of Henry VIII: Decorative Oddity or Important Discovery?', *V&A Conservation Journal* (Autumn 2001), no. 39, pp. 14–16

Mitchell, Bridget, 'Book Display in the British Galleries', *V&A Conservation Journal* (Autumn 2001), no. 39, p. 7

Murdoch, Tessa, 'Fit for a King: The State Bed from Melville House, Fife', *Apollo* (January 2002), vol. 155, no. 479, pp. 3–9

Parry, Linda, 'Morris's Masterpiece is Unrolled', *Country Life* (20 September 2001), pp. 178–79

– 'Best of British: Textiles and Dress in the British Galleries at the Victoria and Albert Museum', *Hali* (March–April 2003), issue 127, pp. 112–17

Powell, Christine, Mallinson, Fi, and Allen, Zoe, 'An Overview of the Gilded Objects Treated for the British Galleries', *V&A Conservation Journal* (Autumn 2001), no. 39, pp. 10–11

Powell, Christopher, and Wills, Sophy, 'Conservation or Restoration? The Treatment of an 18th Century Clock', *V&A Conservation Journal* (Autumn 2001), no. 39, pp. 21–22

Pretzel, Boris, 'Ephemeral or Permanent? Illuminating the Bullerswood Carpet', *V&A Conservation Journal* (Autumn 2001), no. 39, pp. 29–30

Rivers, Shayne, 'East Meets West: the Althorp Triad', *V&A Conservation Journal* (Autumn 2001), no. 39, pp. 12–13

Snodin, Michael, and Styles, John (eds), *Design and the Decorative Arts: Britain 1500–1900* (London, 2001)

Stevens, Donna, 'The Weld Censer: Making Sense of an Object', *V&A Conservation Journal* (Autumn 2001), no. 39, pp. 28

Styles, John, 'Innovation and Design in Tudor and Stuart Britain', *History Today* (December, 2001), pp. 44–51

– 'A New Gallery at the Victoria and Albert Museum,' *History Workshop Journal* (1995), Issue 40, pp. 239–43

Styles, John, *et al*, 'Treasure Island' [outline of narrative historical themes and the content of the galleries], *V&A Magazine* (September–December 2001), pp. 16–26

Webber, Pauline, 'Chinese Wallpapers in the British Galleries', *V&A Conservation Journal* (Autumn 2001), no. 39, pp. 25–27

Wilk, Christopher, 'The Victoria & Albert Museum at the Grosvenor House Fair', *Apollo* (June 1997), pp. 3–10

– 'V&A modernisation' (Letter), *The Times* (6 August 1998), p. 19

– 'The V&A British Galleries', *History Today* (December 2001), pp. 3–5

– 'Yanking Victoria', *Nest* (Winter 2001–02), pp. 132–51

– 'The British Galleries – Britain 1500–1900', *Christie's Magazine* (January/February 2002), pp. 86–89

Wilk, Christopher, and Medlam, Sarah, 'Quatre siècles d'art britannique au Victoria and Albert Museum', *L'Estampille* (February 2002), pp. 40–47

Winch, Diana, *The British Galleries 1500–1900: A Guide Book* (London, 2001)

Articles published before the opening of the British Galleries

Adamick, Paula, 'Style of the Centuries', *The Scotsman* (30 October 2001), p. 8–9

'An Ace Caff with a Spiral of Gloom Attached', *Evening Standard* (11 August 2000), p. 30

Bailey, Martin, 'V&A Tackles Britain Head–on', *Art Newspaper* (May 1996), no. 59, p. 19

– 'V&A British Galleries Delay', *Art Newspaper* (September 1998), no. 84, p. 11

Binney, Marcus, 'Bedding Down for the Night at the V&A', *The Times* (21 September 2000), p. 24

Borg, Alan, 'Museums, Money and Modernity', *The Times* (6 December 1997), p. 22

Crace, John, 'Playing to the Gallery', *Guardian*, Education (13 November 2001), pp. 2–3

Fay, Stephen, 'Best of British', *House & Garden* (November 2001), pp. 148–53

Gibbons, Fiachra, 'Brassed Off', *Guardian* (20 November 2001), p. 10

Irving, Mark, 'Peeling off the Shrouds in a Shrine to Design', *The Independent on Sunday*, Visual Art Culture (15 April 2001), p. 4

Jury, Louise, 'V&A Gives First Glimpse of Its Hidden Treasures', *The Independent* (5 April 2001), p. 11

Kramer, Miriam, 'Report from Europe', *Antiques Magazine* [US] (November 2001), p. 606

Logay, Anne, 'L'Ouverture des British Galleries: le Musée des Arts Décoratifs du XXIᵉ siècle?' [Interview with Christopher Wilk], *Demeurs et Châteaux* (October–November 2001), no. 128, pp. 26–28

Middleton, Christopher, 'Moving Pictures', *The London Magazine* (November 2001), pp. 32–34

Morrison, Richard, 'If You've Got It Flaunt It', *The Times* (16 November 2001), pp. 2–3

Myerson, Jeremy, 'History in the Remaking', *V&A Magazine* (January–April 1998), pp. 10–12

Niesewand, Nonie, 'Victoriana Gets a Facelift', *The Independent*, Architecture and Arts (23 August 1999), p. 8

'Onward March the Thought Police', Editorial, *Country Life* (11 January 2001), p. 31

Pearman, Hugh, 'Rocks around the Clock', *The Sunday Times*, Culture (26 July 1998), p. 14

Pepinster, Catherine, 'An Ace Chap with a Sharp New Museum Attached', *The Independent on Sunday* (18 November 2001), p. 27

Pitman, Joanna, 'Smile! You're Being Done Up', *The Times* (22 July 1998), p. 33

Reynolds, Nigel, 'Sleeping Giants Awake', *The Daily Telegraph*, Arts and Books (6 October 2001), p. 7

Scarisbrick, Diana, 'A Tudor Treasure Unveiled', *Country Life* (9 August 2001), pp. 84–85

Slavid, Ruth, 'V&A Unveils £31 million British Galleries Update', *Architects' Journal* (12 March 1998), p. 17

Stringer, Robin, '£15m Lottery Cash for V&A's New Galleries', *Evening Standard* (22 July 1998), p. 7

Strong, Roy, 'The V&A Has Become a Monument to Folly', *Evening Standard* (27 June 2000), p. 13

Whitley, John, 'The V&A Team', *The Daily Telegraph*, Magazine (16 May 1998), pp. 50–53

Worsley, Giles, 'Dusty V&A's New Broom', *Daily Telegraph* (7 February 2001), p. 25

Reviews of the British Galleries

Appleyard, Bryan, 'Victory on the Home Front', *Sunday Times*, Culture (18 November 2001), pp. 6–7

Bragg, Melvyn, 'Made in Britain', *high life* (November 2001), pp. 51–54

Coomer, Martin, 'True Colours: Centuries of British Style at the New–look V&A', *Time Out* (28 November 2001), p. 56

Cranfield, Nicholas, 'Plenty to See, if You Don't Mind the Past Tense', *Church Times* (25 January 2002), p. 34

Davies, Maurice, 'Best of British', *Museums Journal* (January 2002), p. 39

Dorment, Richard, 'The Great British Variety Show', *Daily Telegraph* (21 November 2001), p. 20

Dungavell, Ian, 'Comment: Best of British?', *Crafts* (March 2002), pp. 42–45

Fisher, Lucy, and Roecker, Kimberley, 'Design for Living', *Time* (3 December 2001), p. 100

European Museum Forum (ed.), *European Museum of the Year Award: The Candidates 2003* (Gylling, 2003)

Fox, Celina, 'Made in Britain', *House & Garden* (November 2001), pp. 85–86

Freyberg, Annabel, 'The Difference £31m Has Made to the V&A', *Evening Standard* (13 November 2001), pp. 46–47

Godfrey, Tony, 'Re-presenting History', *RA Magazine* (Winter 2001), no. 73, pp. 16

Greer, Bonnie, 'It's Time to Let the Fat Bloke Sing', *Mail on Sunday* (18 November 2001), p. 13

Hall, Michael, 'A Great Museum Finds Its Heart', *Country Life* (22 November 2001), pp. 50–53

Harvey, Keshia, and Izamoje, Chidi, 'Best of British', *Museums Journal* (January 2002), p. 38

Hensher, Philip, 'Best of British', *Mail on Sunday* (25 November 2001), p. 80

Higgins, Charlotte, 'Golden Oldies', *The Guardian*, G2 (19 November 2001), p. 16

Irving, Mark, 'NAFF! or Not?', *The Independent on Sunday* (18 November 2001), p. 7

Joicey, Celia, 'The Brits: Are the V&A's New British Galleries Going to Revive the Museum's Fortunes?', *RSA Journal* (June 2002), pp. 24–25

Julius, Corinne, 'Best Show in Town', *Evening Standard*, Homes and Property (28 November 2001), p. 17

Lambton, Lucinda, 'Centuries of Style', *NACF Quarterly* (Winter 2001), pp. 43–46

Levy, Paul, 'At Tate Britain and the V&A, Welcome Expansions', *The Wall Street Journal*, Leisure and Arts (6 December 2001), p. A19

– 'Britain's Homegrown Art', *The Wall Street Journal Europe* (7 December 2001), p. 33

Llewelyn-Bowen, Laurence, 'A Taste of British Style at the V&A', *Sunday Express* (18 November 2001), p. 73

McEwen, John, 'The British Galleries at the V&A', *Sunday Telegraph*, Review (18 November 2001), p. 26

– 'The World's Most Glamorous Craft Show', *Sunday Telegraph*, Review (25 November 2001), p. 11

Merrick, Jay, 'Pop Goes the Victoria and Albert', *The Independent* (19 November 2001), p. 10

Morris, Jane, 'Style and Substance', *Museum Practice* (2002), Issue 20, vol. 7, no. 2, pp. 18–23

'Overlapping Narratives: The V&A's British Galleries', Editorial, *Burlington Magazine* (November 2001), vol. CXLIII, no. 1184, pp. 667–69

Pavord, Anna, 'A British Feast for the Senses', *The Independent* (1 December 2001), p. 15

Ricketts, Annabel, 'Ingenious Panache' *Spectator* (1 December 2001), p. 62

Sewell, Brian, 'The Dimming Down of Great British Design', *Evening Standard* (14 December 2001), pp. 22–23

Somers Cocks, A, 'If Architecture is the Mother of the Arts, then This is the Whole Family', *Art Newspaper*, no. 119 (November 2001), p. 11

Street-Porter, Janet, 'Janet Street-Porter', *The Independent on Sunday*, LifeEtc (18 November 2001), p. 2

Sudjic, Deyan, 'Is There an Art to Being British?', *The Observer*, Review (4 November 2001), p. 10

Thorncroft, Anthony, 'South Ken's Ideal Home Exhibition', *Financial Times*, Arts (19 November 2001), p. 20

Articles published after the opening of the British Galleries

Champenois, Michèle, 'Un musée sous l'empire du goût anglais', *Le Monde*, Culture (5 January 2002), p. 5

Conran, Terence, *et al*, 'Treasure Island', *The Daily Telegraph*, Arts and Books (24 November 2001), p. 1

Conti, Samantha, 'A History of Britain Through Arts & Crafts', *Women's Wear Daily* (28 December 2001), p. 9

Dorment, Richard, 'The Great Room of Art', *New York Review of Books* (13 June 2002), vol. 49, no. 10, pp. 32–36

Fenton, James, 'Let There Be Light', *Guardian*, Review (1 February 2003), p. 24

Hirst, Christopher, 'Count on Rick to Explain …', *The Independent*, Weekend Review (24 November 2001), p. 4

'Home Truths: The V&A's Magnificent New Galleries Open to the Public', Editorial, *The Times* (21 November 2001), p. 17

Leitch, Luke, 'One's Been Talking to an Argumentative Tree', *Evening Standard* (21 November 2001), p. 6

Morris, Jane, 'Euro visions' [Museum of the Year Award], *Museum Practice* (Summer 2003), p. 12–13

Motion, Andrew, 'Just Looking' [Poem by Poet Laureate], *Evening Standard* (21 November 2001), p. 6

Neill, Heather, 'V&A: Prince Albert Would Have Loved It, and Teachers Will Too', *The Times Higher Educational Supplement* (7 December 2001), p. 19

Riding, Alan, 'The Stodgy Victoria and Albert Spruces Up', *The New York Times* (5 December 2001), pp. E1–E2, and *International Herald Tribune* (8/9 December 2001), p. 6

Symondson, Anthony, 'Relics that Recall the Golden Age of English Catholicism', *The Catholic Herald* (1 February 2002), p. 14

Thibaut, Matthias, 'Die British Galleries im Victoria & Albert Museum: Perlen nationaler Geschmacksgeschichte', *Handelsblatt*, Kunstmarkt (11 January 2002), no. 8, p. 42

Worsley, Giles, 'My Vision for the V&A' [Interview with Mark Jones], *The Daily Telegraph* (21 November 2001), p. 21

Articles and interviews by/about designers and consultants

Aidin, Rose, 'String Up the Band' [on Cornelia Parker], *The Times*, Times 2 (14 November 2001), p. 13

Beyfus, Drusilla, 'Past Master' [on David Mlinaric], *Daily Telegraph Magazine* (10 November 2001), pp. 54–58

'The British Galleries 1500–1900' [on Rose Innes], *Design Annual: The International Annual of Design and Illustration* (Zurich, 2003), pp. 110–11

Buxton, Pamela, 'Grand Designs' [on Rose Innes], *Graphics International* (February 2002), issue 92, pp. 17–18

Casson, Dinah, 'Behind the Scenes at the Museum', *FX* (February 2002), pp. 78–80

Cornforth, John, 'Garden for a Rainy Day' [on the Stoke Edith Hanging], *Country Life* (6 August 2001), pp. 178–79

– 'New Life for Old Friends' [on the period rooms], *Country Life* (15 November 2001), pp. 80–83

Gardner, Carl, 'Making Light Work' [on Richard Aldridge], *Design Week* (26 February 1999), pp. 16–18

Gentle, Nicola, 'A Study of the Late Seventeenth-Century State Bed from Melville House', *Furniture History*, vol. XXXVII (2001), pp. 1–16

Moore, Rowan, 'I'm Keen that People Who Don't Know Who the Kings and Queens Were Have a Really Nice Time' [on Dinah Casson], *Evening Standard* (13 November 2001), pp. 46–47

Myerson, Jeremy, 'The Exhibitionists' [on Casson Mann], *Design Week* (20 August 1999), pp. 11–13

Pes, Javier, 'Boxing Clever' [on Dinah Casson], *Museum Practice Magazine* (Summer 2003), pp. 28–31

Stocks, Christopher, 'Unholy Relics' [on Cornelia Parker], *Modern Painters* (Winter 2001), vol. 14, no. 4, pp. 32–35

Walker, Aidan, 'Object Lessons' [on Dinah Casson and Roger Mann], *Blueprint* (October 2001), pp. 32–35

Reginato, James, 'King David' [on David Mlinaric], *W* (1 March 1998), pp. 398–403, 410

Web–based resources

Nick Brod '*Diving in at the Deep End – The British Galleries at the V&A*', paper given at the Museums and the Web 2002 conference
http://www.archimuse.com/mw2002/papers/brod/brod.html

Gail Durbin '*Interactive learning in the British Galleries 1500–1900*', paper given at the Interactive Learning in Museums of Art and Design Conference, May 17–18 2002
http://www.vam.ac.uk/by_interactive_learning

Gail Durbin '*Using the Web for Participation and Interactivity*', paper given at the Museums and the Web 2003 conference
http://www.archimuse.com/mw2003/papers/durbin/durbin.html

British Galleries Visitor Research Reports available via the V&A website

British Galleries Baseline Study
http://www.vam.ac.uk/bg_baseline_study

British Galleries Formative Studies
http://www.vam.ac.uk/bg_form_studies

British Galleries Prototyping: Computer Interactives
http://www.vam.ac.uk/bg_computer_interactives

British Galleries Prototyping: AV, Low-tech interactives and Text
http://www.vam.ac.uk/bg_lowtech

British Galleries Summative Evaluation
http://www.vam.ac.uk/bg_summative

Brod, Nick and Hinton, Morna (2000), ICT Prototyping Phase 8 Evaluation: British Galleries Online. http://www.vam.ac.uk/bg_ict_prototyping_phase8

Creative Research (1997i), Audience Research for the British Galleries: quantitative research findings, vol. 1. http://www.vam.ac.uk/bg_quantitative1

Creative Research (1997ii), Audience Research for the British Galleries: quantitative research findings, vol. 2. http://www.vam.ac.uk/bg_quantitative2

Creative Research (1998i), Audience Research for the British Galleries: Silver Gallery Discovery Area. Part 1: introduction, summary of findings and recommendations
http://www.vam.ac.uk/bg_silver_galleries1

Creative Research (1998ii), Audience Research for the British Galleries: Silver Gallery Discovery Area. Part 2: Main findings of quantitative research. http://www.vam.ac.uk/bg_silver_galleries2

Creative Research (2002i), Summative Evaluation of the British Galleries: overview of findings. http://www.vam.ac.uk/bg_overview

Creative Research (2002ii), Summative Evaluation of the British Galleries: report of research findings. http://www.vam.ac.uk/bg_full_summative

Fisher, Susie, *et al.* (1998), The British Galleries Project at the V&A: are people in tune with new plans for the interpretation? Qualitative research with visitors and non–visitors. http://www.vam.ac.uk/bg_visitors_nonvisitors

The Market Research Group (2003), Report on British Galleries: repeat demographic survey. http://www.vam.ac.uk/bg_demographic

McManus, Paulette (1999i), Miscellaneous Activity: Tapestry Weaving: prototyping research report 21.
http://www.vam.ac.uk/tapestry_weaving

McManus, Paulette (1999ii), Draw an acanthus leaf: prototyping research report 3.
http://www.vam.ac.uk/acanthus_leaf

McManus, Paulette (1999iii), Object in Focus Video: William Burges' Washstand: Prototyping research report 2.
http://www.vam.ac.uk/burges_washstand

McManus, Paulette (1999iv), Order of Information in Object Labels: prototyping report 7.
http://www.vam.ac.uk/object_labels

McManus, Paulette (1999v), Ekarved text layout: prototyping research report 5.
http://www.vam.ac.uk/ekarving

McManus, Paulette (2000), ICT Prototyping Phase 6 Evaluation: British Galleries Online.
http://www.vam.ac.uk/bg_ict_prototyping_phase6

McManus, Paulette (2003), A Qualitative Account of Visitor Experiences in the Displays, Film Rooms and Study Areas of the British Galleries at the V&A.
http://www.vam.ac.uk/bg_visitors_experiences

Morris, Hargeaves, McIntyre (2003), Engaging or Distracting? Visitor responses to interactives in the V&A British Galleries.
http://www.vam.ac.uk/bg_visitors_responses

Selwood, Sara, for the Policy Studies Institute (1998), Survey of Visitor Research at the V&A 1986–1996 (unpublished report)

Prototyping reports for low-tech devices
http://www.vam.ac.uk/bg_lowtech

Index

Page numbers in *italic* refer to illustrations, roman numerals to colour plates.

Questo quarto volume degli
Annali del Laboratorio museotecnico
è stato finito di stampare a Cittadella,
su carta velata delle Cartiere Magnani, Pescia
da Arti Grafiche Bertoncello,
nel mese di luglio 2004
per

V&A PUBLICATIONS

160 Brompton Road
London SW3 1HW
www.vam.ac.uk

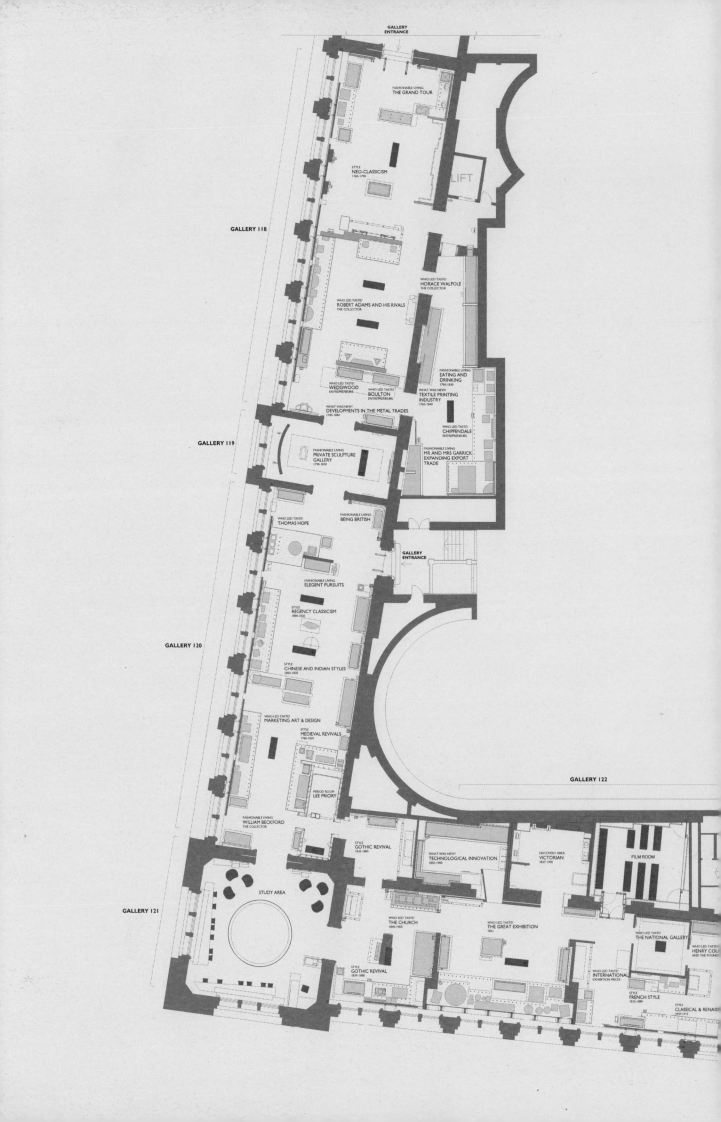

GALLERY
ENTRANCE

FASHIONABLE LIVING
THE GRAND TOUR

STYLE
NEO-CLASSICISM
1760-1790

LIFT

GALLERY 118

WHO LED TASTE?
HORACE WALPOLE
THE COLLECTOR

WHO LED TASTE?
ROBERT ADAMS AND HIS RIVALS
THE COLLECTOR

FASHIONABLE LIVING
EATING AND
DRINKING
1760-1830

WHO LED TASTE?
WEDGWOOD
ENTREPRENEURS

WHO LED TASTE?
BOULTON
ENTREPRENEURS

WHAT WAS NEW!
TEXTILE PRINTING
INDUSTRY
1760-1840

WHAT WAS NEW!
DEVELOPMENTS IN THE METAL TRADES
1760-1840

WHO LED TASTE?
CHIPPENDALE
ENTREPRENEURS

FASHIONABLE LIVING
PRIVATE SCULPTURE
GALLERY
1790-1830

GALLERY 119

FASHIONABLE LIVING
MR AND MRS GARRICK,
EXPANDING EXPORT
TRADE

WHO LED TASTE?
THOMAS HOPE

FASHIONABLE LIVING
BEING BRITISH

GALLERY
ENTRANCE

FASHIONABLE LIVING
ELEGENT PURSUITS

STYLE
REGENCY CLASSICISM
1800-1830

GALLERY 120

STYLE
CHINESE AND INDIAN STYLES
1800-1830

WHO LED TASTE?
MARKETING ART & DESIGN

STYLE
MEDIEVAL REVIVALS
1780-1820

GALLERY 122

PERIOD ROOM
LEE PRIORY

FASHIONABLE LIVING
WILLIAM BECKFORD
THE COLLECTOR

STYLE
GOTHIC REVIVAL
1830-1880

WHAT WAS NEW!
TECHNOLOGICAL INNOVATION
1830-1900

DISCOVERY AREA
VICTORIAN
1837-1900

FILM ROOM

STUDY AREA

GALLERY 121

WHO LED TASTE?
THE CHURCH
1840-1900

WHO LED TASTE?
THE GREAT EXHIBITION
1851

WHO LED TASTE?
THE NATIONAL GALLERY

WHO LED TASTE?
HENRY COL
AND THE FOUND

STYLE
GOTHIC REVIVAL
1830-1880

WHO LED TASTE?
INTERNATIONAL
EXHIBITION PIECES

STYLE
FRENCH STYLE
1835-1880

STYLE
CLASSICAL & RENAIS